I0729558

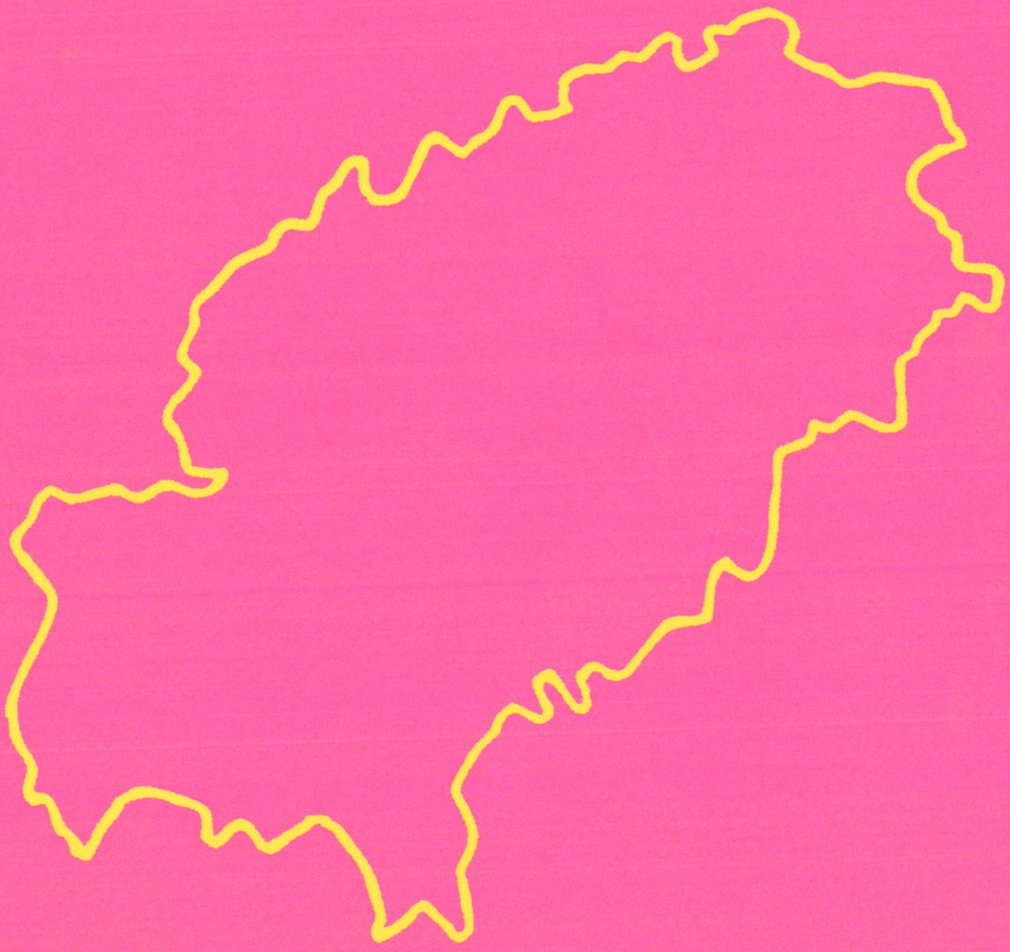

Located in the Mediterranean Sea, in the Balearic Islands archipelago, at 39.0200° N, 1.4821° E, Ibiza is 81 nautical miles from the east coast of Spain and 175 miles north north west of Algiers.

The island covers 221 square miles and began to form as a limestone and sandstone mountain around 60 million years ago, when the African and Eurasian tectonic plates collided. The refilling of the Mediterranean Sea six million years ago created the Island we see today.

First colonised by Phoenician traders from the Levant during the 7th century BC, Ibiza was invaded or ruled in turn by Carthage, the Roman Empire, Vandals, the Byzantine Empire, the Emirate of Cordoba and various sub-kingdoms of Islamic Spain, the King of Norway (briefly) and the Kingdom of Aragon; it became part of Spain in 1715.

Named by the Phoenicians after 'Bes', an Egyptian cult god of household protection, fertility, music, dance, and sexual pleasure.

Neglected by the fascist Franco regime in Madrid, Ibiza became a haven for Spanish counterculture in the late 1940s, attracting colonies of surrealist painters and avant garde artists by the late 1950s, and a population of thousands of 'hippies' by the end of the '60s, including many Americans avoiding conscription in the US. The rise of mass tourism in the 1970s and '80s saw the island become a major holiday destination.

By 1998, with clubs like Pacha, Amnesia, Space and Privilege combining the biggest promotions and DJs from around the world with homegrown nights and talent, plus hundreds of thousands of young tourists arriving every week, Ibiza had become the undisputed epicentre of electronic music and club culture on Planet Earth.

In the mid '00s, the authorities in Ibiza began forcing clubs to close between 6am and 12pm, briefly shutting down Amnesia, Bora Bora and DC10, banning the famous 'club parades' through the streets of Ibiza Town and beginning a years-long period of increased restriction on unlicensed events, open-air daytime music and dancing, and opening hours. The party wasn't over, but it would never be quite the same.

DUNCAN JA DICK

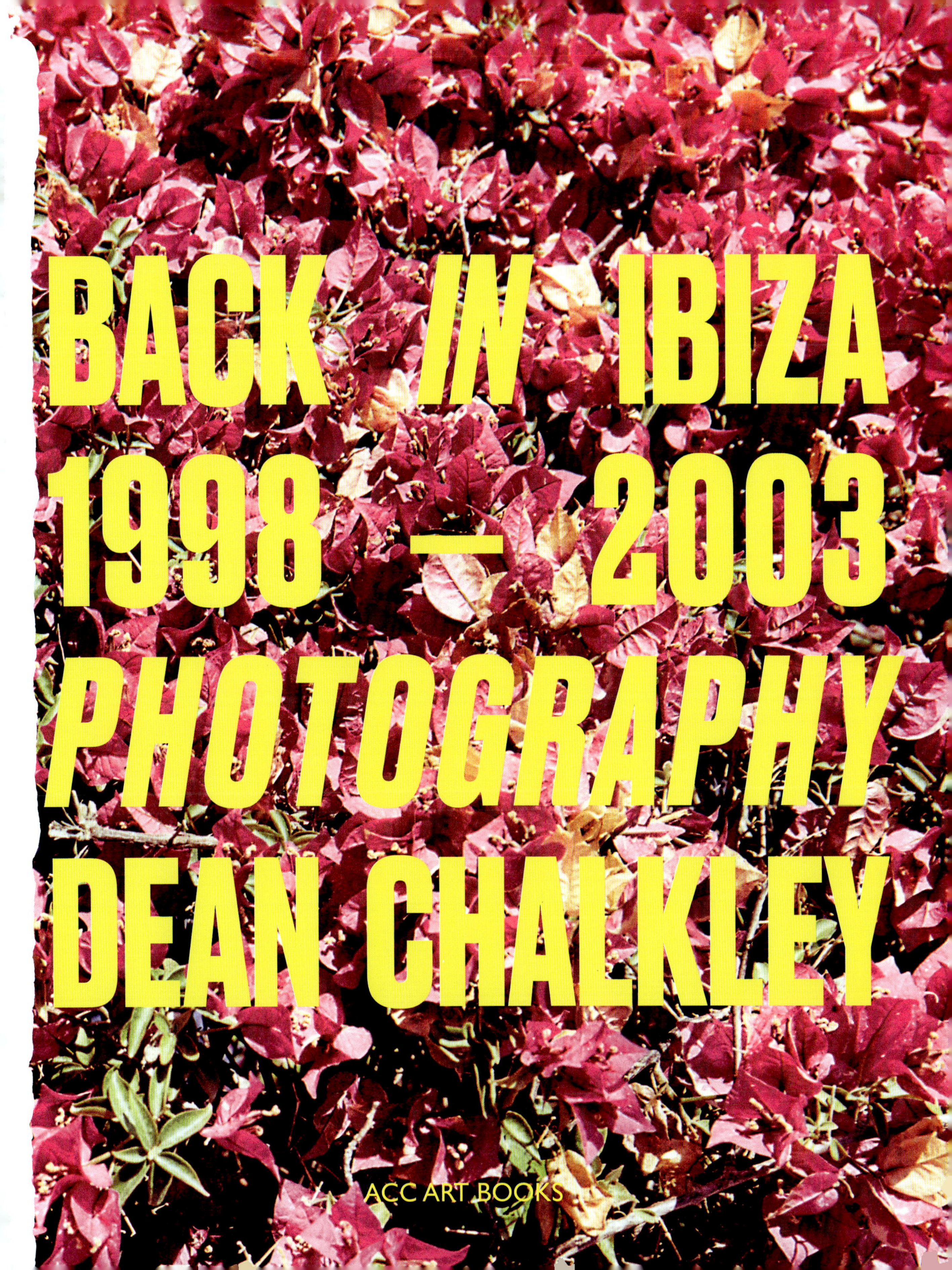
BACK IN IBIZA
1998 — 2003
PHOTOGRAPHY
DEAN CHALKLEY
ACC ART BOOKS

FOREWORD

NEIL STEVENSON
MIXMAG, EDITOR-IN-CHIEF
1998 — 99

Ibiza has had some very different incarnations over the years. There was the Ibiza of the '60s, home to Spanish hippies and gays, fleeing the oppressive Franco regime. There was the Ibiza of the late '80s, the home of 'the Balearic sound' that was discovered by some young Brits-on-holiday called Danny Rampling, Nicky Holloway, Johnny Walker and Paul Oakenfold – who took it home and catalyzed the British dance music scene. Then there's the media-saturated Ibiza of today, dominated by big money, big celebrities, and influencers everywhere creating content against the backdrop of the Mediterranean.

This book is about an Ibiza that came between the Balearic era and today. Ten years after Paul Oakenfold and company had started their Ibiza-inspired clubs in London, the British dance scene had become huge. Ibiza, with its beautiful beaches and huge nightclubs, had become the destination for a summer pilgrimage of clubbers – a dance music Mecca. But despite its popularity, the Ibiza of the late '90s still flew under the radar of mass media coverage. One big reason for this: we were in the pre-smartphone era. Among the huge crowds at Amnesia, Pacha and Privilege, hardly anyone was carrying a camera.

In early summer 1998, I was editor-in-chief of *Mixmag*, the world's biggest dance music magazine. As with all music magazines, we tended to feature the individuals who created the music: in our case, the DJs and producers. Photos of the clubbers themselves were usually confined to the back half of the magazine, among the club listings. It was a sad fact that photos from dancefloors rarely captured the excitement and energy felt by the clubbers themselves. Flash photography could make the dancers look sweaty and scary, and non-flash images were usually dark and blurry.

However, we'd been hearing stories about the glamorous clubs in Ibiza running all night and on into the following day, and wondered if there was a chance to photograph clubbers in a different environment, that included sunshine. At the time, our number-one photographer was Dean Chalkley. We relied on him for our important cover shoots, because of his combination of technical proficiency and imaginative art direction. And photo editor Paola Cimmino had an idea: what if we sent Dean to Ibiza? Could he capture a new kind of clubber imagery?

We reserved four pages for Dean's pictures, just before a big feature on The Chemical Brothers. But then Dean returned from the island with his contact sheets. As we looked at the pictures, we realised that he had produced something we'd never seen before. Instead of the dark blurry smears or flash-lit sweaty ravers, these photographs captured the joy and excitement of the dancefloor. And more than that, they showed the inventiveness and sheer weirdness of the Ibiza scene. Clubs like Manumission were hiring clubbers as workers, and encouraging them to dress up in surreal costumes. This was in turn inspiring the clubbers themselves to dress up more. The original rave scene was dressed down: baggy trousers and t-shirts. What we were seeing here was a mixture of DIY glamour and outright surrealism.

It was clear that we were going to need more than four pages. After a hurried conference with our editorial director, we reimagined the entire issue of the magazine, eventually devoting 30 pages to Dean's photos. What's more, we would send him back to Ibiza repeatedly over the following years to capture more of the extraordinary scenes that were playing out on the island. His photos changed the magazine, and how we portrayed clubbers.

Looking at these images again, more than twenty years later, I'm struck by their unselfconscious joy. Everybody looks lost in the moment, and completely unaware of the camera. Of course, a lot of that is down to Dean's skill and his ability to make the subjects feel comfortable with him. But some of it also illustrates how the world has changed. Cellphone photography and platforms like Instagram and TikTok have taught everyone to be aware of themselves and their image. Everyone, on some level, now thinks of themselves as a brand. Selfie culture teaches us how to compose our features so that we look our best on camera. We are wary of being snapped doing something foolish. In short, everyone is a mini-celebrity, and we carry our image-conscious PR agents around in our heads. Back in Ibiza in the late '90s, by contrast, nobody seemed to care about anything more than losing themselves in the music. There's a delightful innocence there, amid the debauchery. A determination to have the best possible time, without any thought for followers or likes and without any fear of judgement. I'm grateful that Dean was there to capture it. Looking back today at the technicolor exuberance of his Ibiza photos, I only wish I could beam myself back.

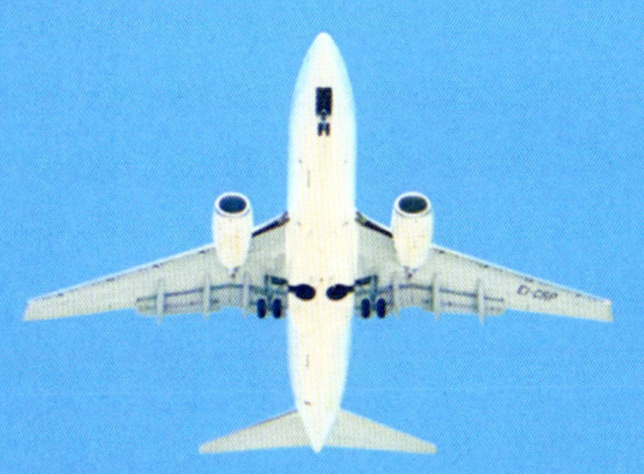

AUTHOR

DEAN CHALKLEY
PHOTOGRAPHER

Since I was a kid, I have been into music. When I was ten years old and living in Southend-on-Sea, my hippie neighbour Chris loaned me all his records before he set off on a pilgrimage to Peru. Listening to the tunes and looking at the record sleeve artwork made me realise the journey that music could take you on. I was hooked. In the early 1980s I got into the mod scene – the music, clothes, scooters and haircuts, embracing a lifestyle and attitude that can exist around music. As I travelled through my teens, going to more and more club nights around Southend, I began hearing and experiencing different music, rare groove, jazz, hip hop and then an exciting new sound called acid house. Towards the end of the '80s, I went to many of the illegal raves that were popping up around the M25. Often only armed with a phone number, my friends and I would turn up in the dead of night at some motorway service station and after a call from the phone box we'd end up following a caterpillar of cars to a field or warehouse containing giant sound systems, strobes, lasers and smoke machines. It felt like something exciting was bubbling up in the UK.

In parallel with these musical developments, I'd been learning about photography. As a teenager, I started taking photographs at car racing events and built my skills at evening classes, then took it further with a part-time A level course, followed by a degree in Blackpool. I'd also started photographing bands, and felt an affinity to people on the periphery of society: extreme body piercers, alternative circus performers and other interesting characters I came across. During my degree, I started working for *Dazed & Confused* magazine, and a couple of years later a contact I had met at *Dazed* joined *Mixmag* and asked if I would do some work for them.

When, in the summer of 1998, I was asked by *Mixmag* to spend ten days in Ibiza, my first thought was, is it going to be any good a decade after the Acid House Balearic explosion? I hadn't yet visited the island, but I'd heard plenty of stories about that early era. But rather than doubting, I thought I should take the opportunity and find out for myself. I shouldn't have worried: what I was about to experience would transcend my wildest expectations.

I was partnered with a journalist who had Ibiza experience, but after a day on the island, he disappeared on some personal rave journey (a not uncommon occurrence in Ibiza) and I was left on my own. This turned out to be a good thing: I was free to explore and follow my curiosity.

I visited the wonderful Manumission parties at Privilege, a giant venue with multiple levels and a DJ booth positioned over a swimming pool. I toured Space, Amnesia, and Pacha, following the clubbers on their journeys as they moved from clubs to after-parties to beaches to sunset bars. I was struck by the incredible joy and liberation I witnessed. Moving freely between people and places, I was overwhelmed by the friendliness and diversity of the crowds, from flamboyant fashionistas, lads and girls on 'big' nights out, to cool clubbers and people on more of a spiritual wavelength. They were all unselfconscious and welcoming. And they all seemed to be having the time of their lives.

I'd decided to shoot mainly with a medium-format Fuji camera. The bigger film size was challenging but also helped me define the look and feel of my work – the camera's fixed lens meant that I had to get in close with my subjects and really engage with them, which I loved. The results were high quality images, with intense colours. At the end of that first trip, when I returned to the *Mixmag* offices with the contact sheets, the editor and art department exploded with excitement. They ended up totally reworking the issue of the magazine to run the images over 30 pages, with almost no editorial, just a few captions. They also asked me if I was willing to go back, and I enthusiastically agreed.

I knew that what I'd witnessed on the island was more than simple hedonism. It felt like a wonderland where people were having genuinely life-changing experiences. Whether they were holiday-makers visiting for a week or two or workers living on the island permanently, people were losing their inhibitions and embarking on a collective search for a good time. And although there were big clubs making money, the experience at that time seemed to belong to the clubbers. I could sense the same spirit that I'd witnessed at those early M25 raves, only in technicolor and on a beautiful island.

Over the next five years, I visited repeatedly - mainly for *Mixmag* - and managed to photograph more and more of the scene. By 2003, things were definitely changing. Music tastes were shifting and celebrity culture was becoming more established. In a few more years, everyone would start carrying a smart phone with a camera and become conscious of themselves as a brand. Ibiza today is very different, but I'm sure many people are still having a fabulous time there. Nothing stays the same, and that's fine. This book stands testament to a time of wonder and alchemy where people gave themselves over to a moment, embracing the reverie, chaos and fun of it all. Putting these pictures together has, for me, been a way to drop right back into that magical time. And I thank you, dear reader, for coming along for the ride…

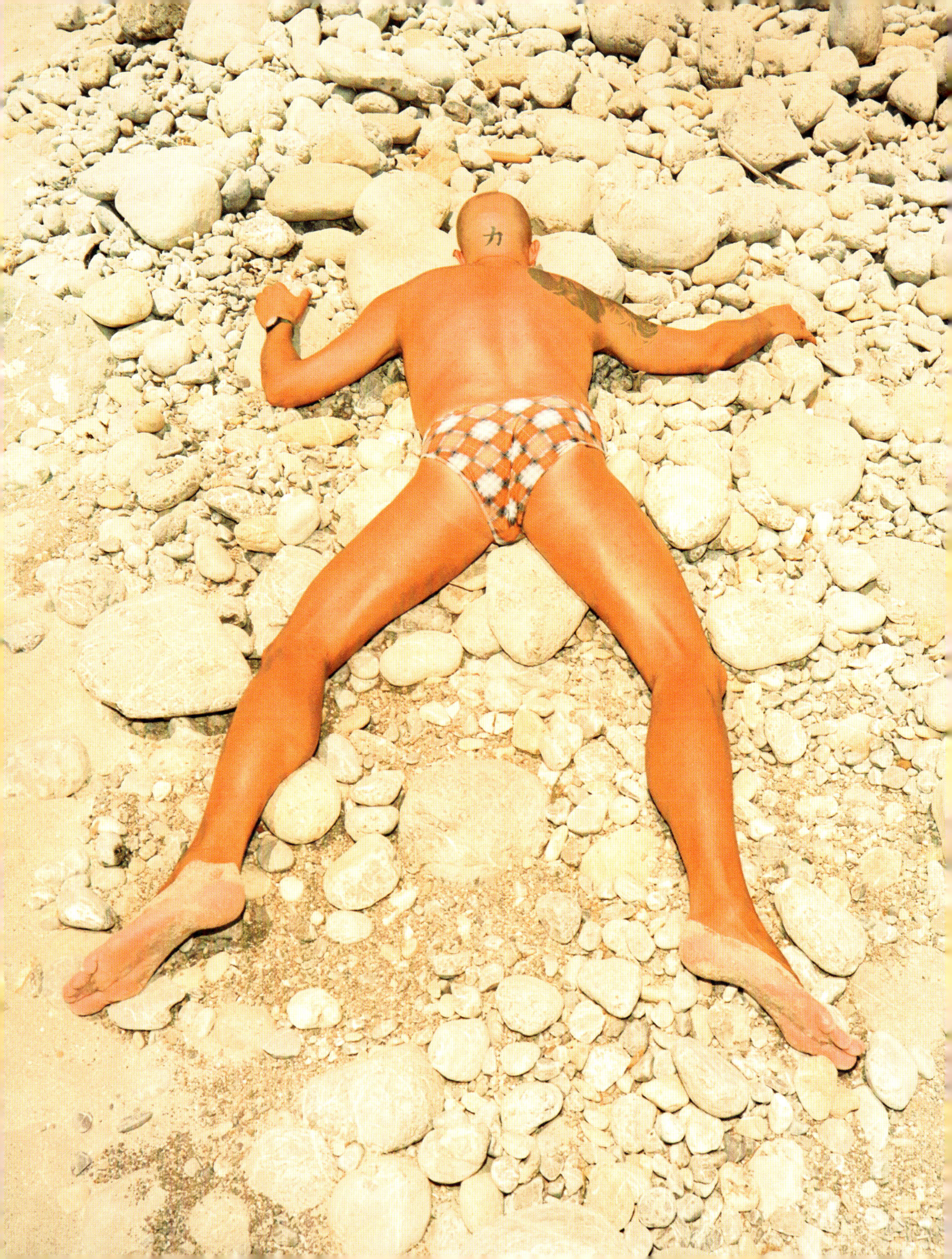

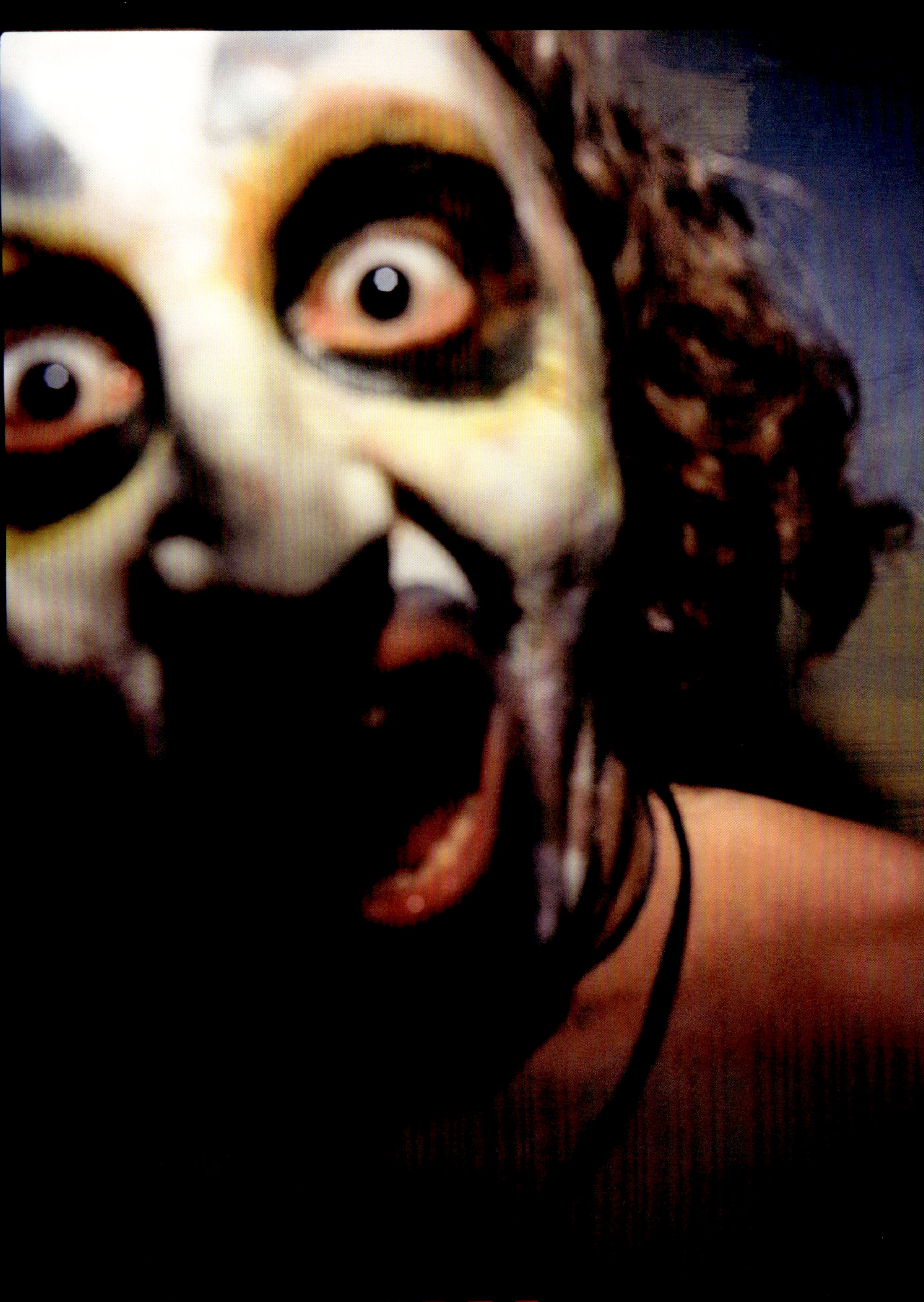

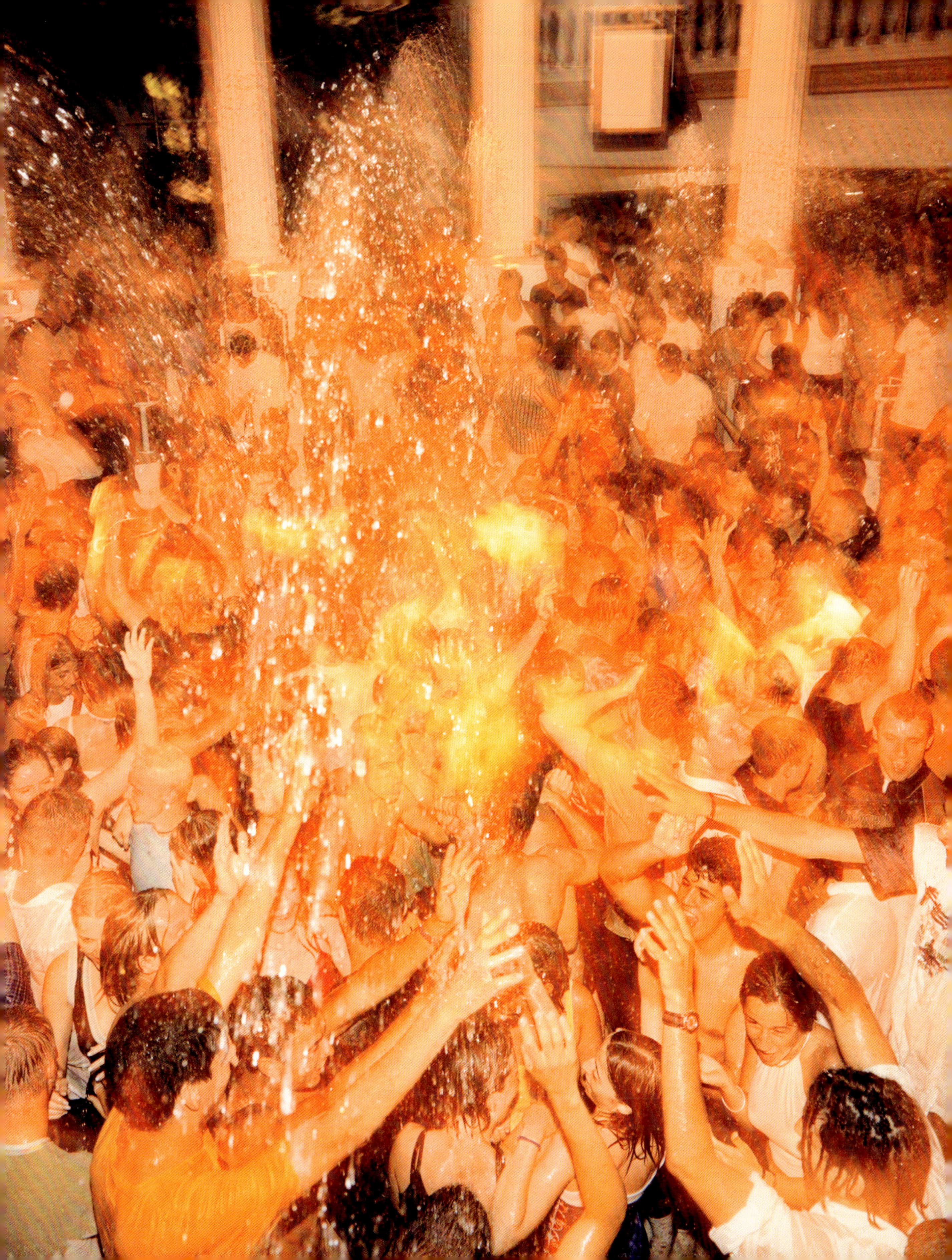

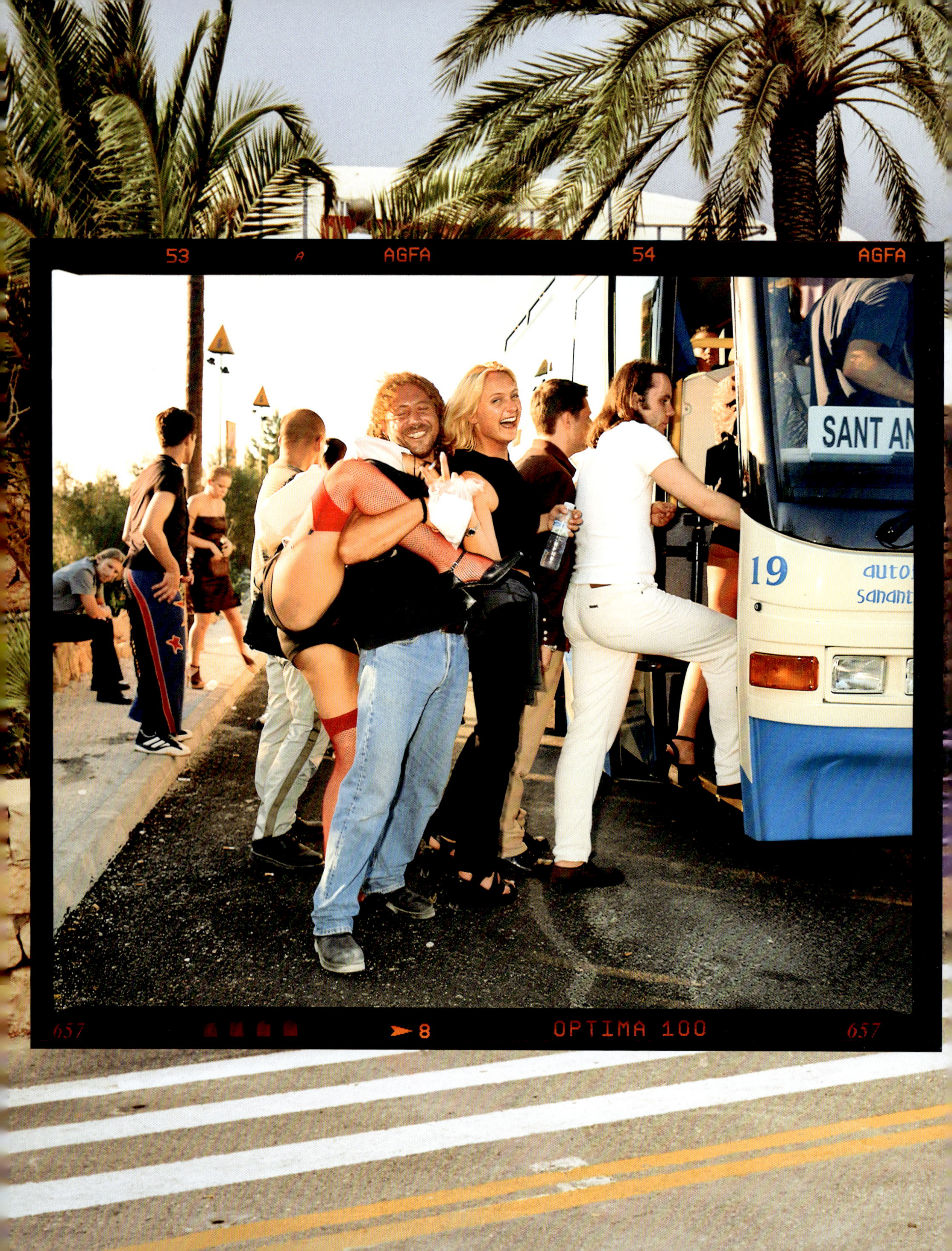

53
A
AGFA
54
AGFA
SANT AN
19
autos
sanant
657
8
OPTIMA 100
657

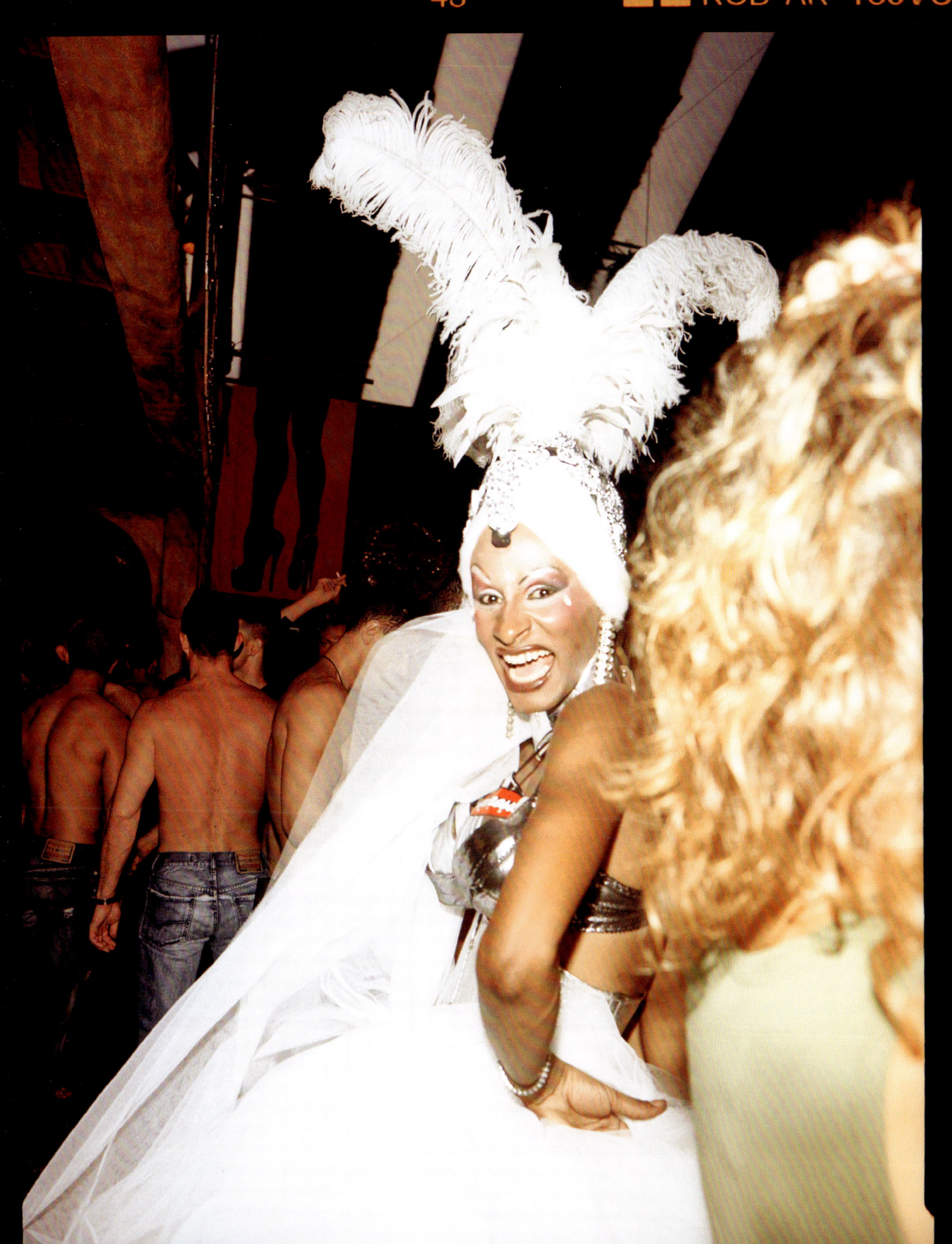

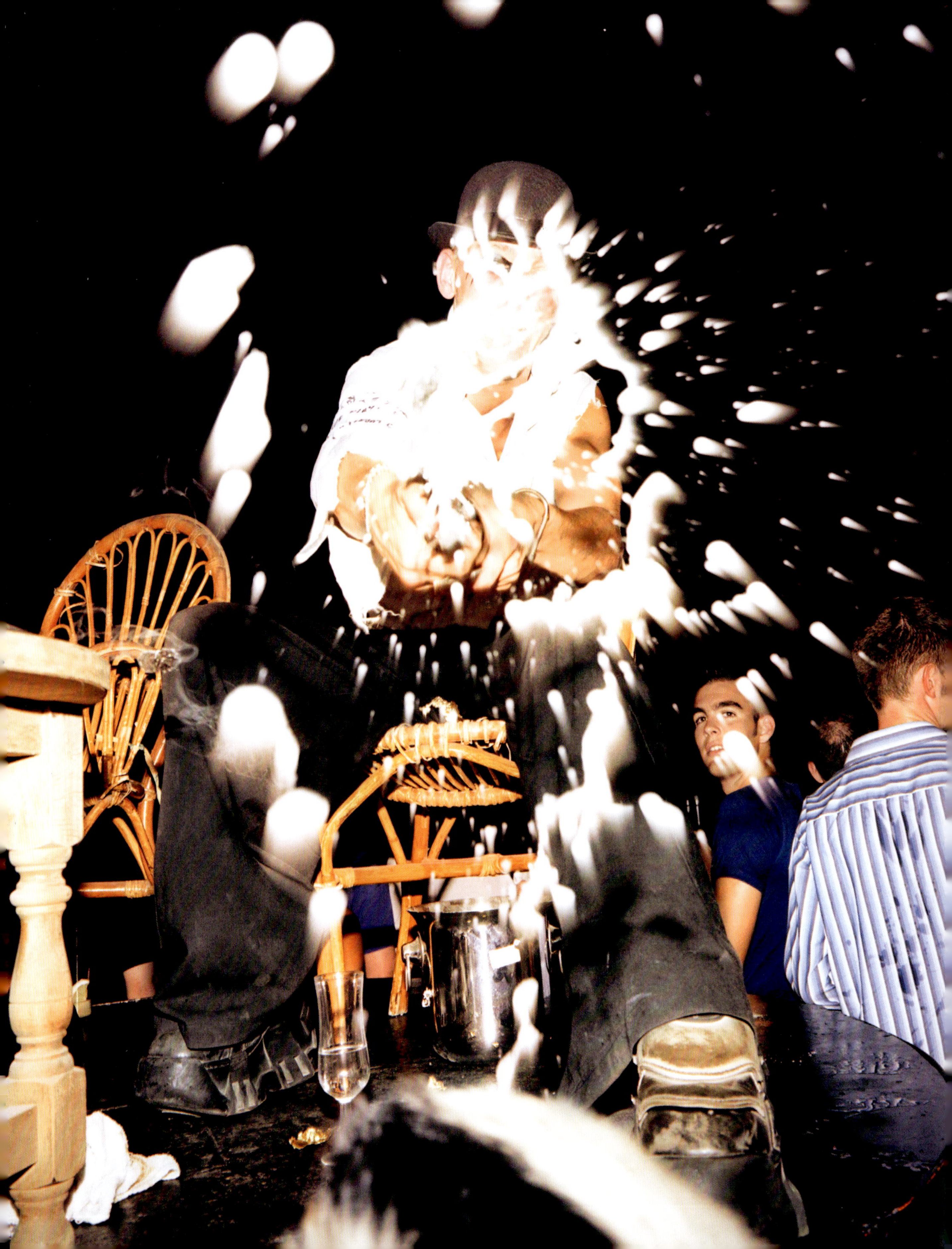

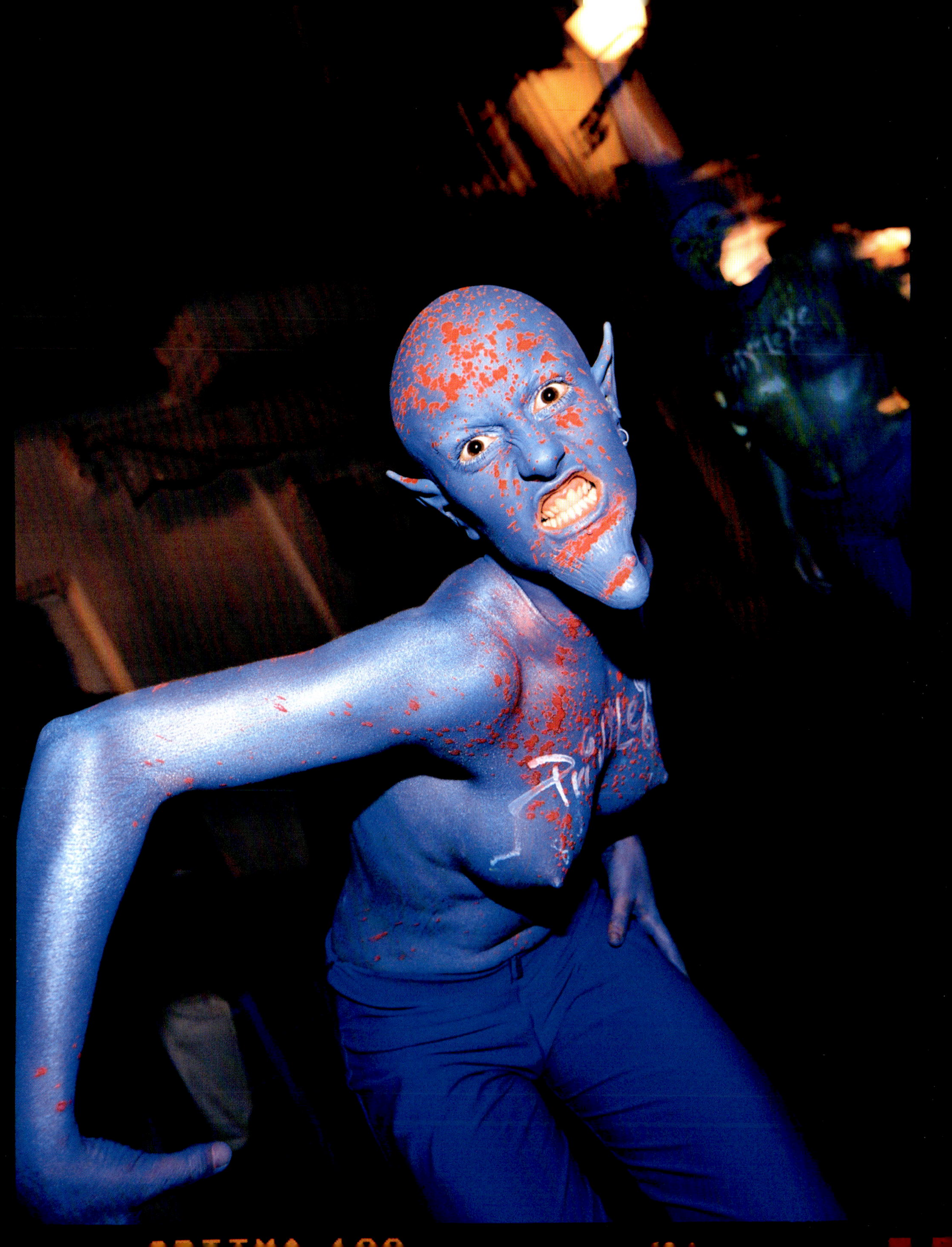

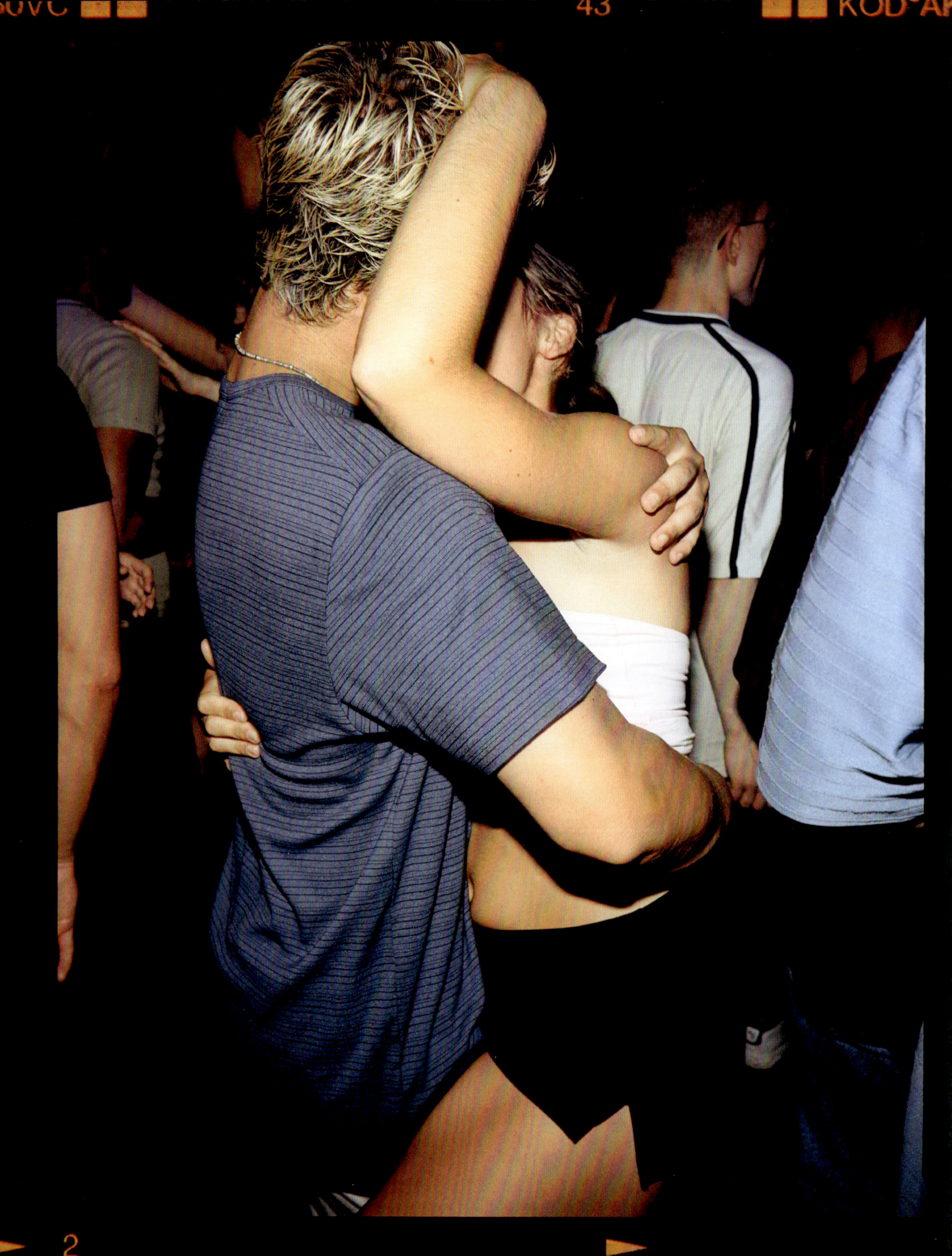

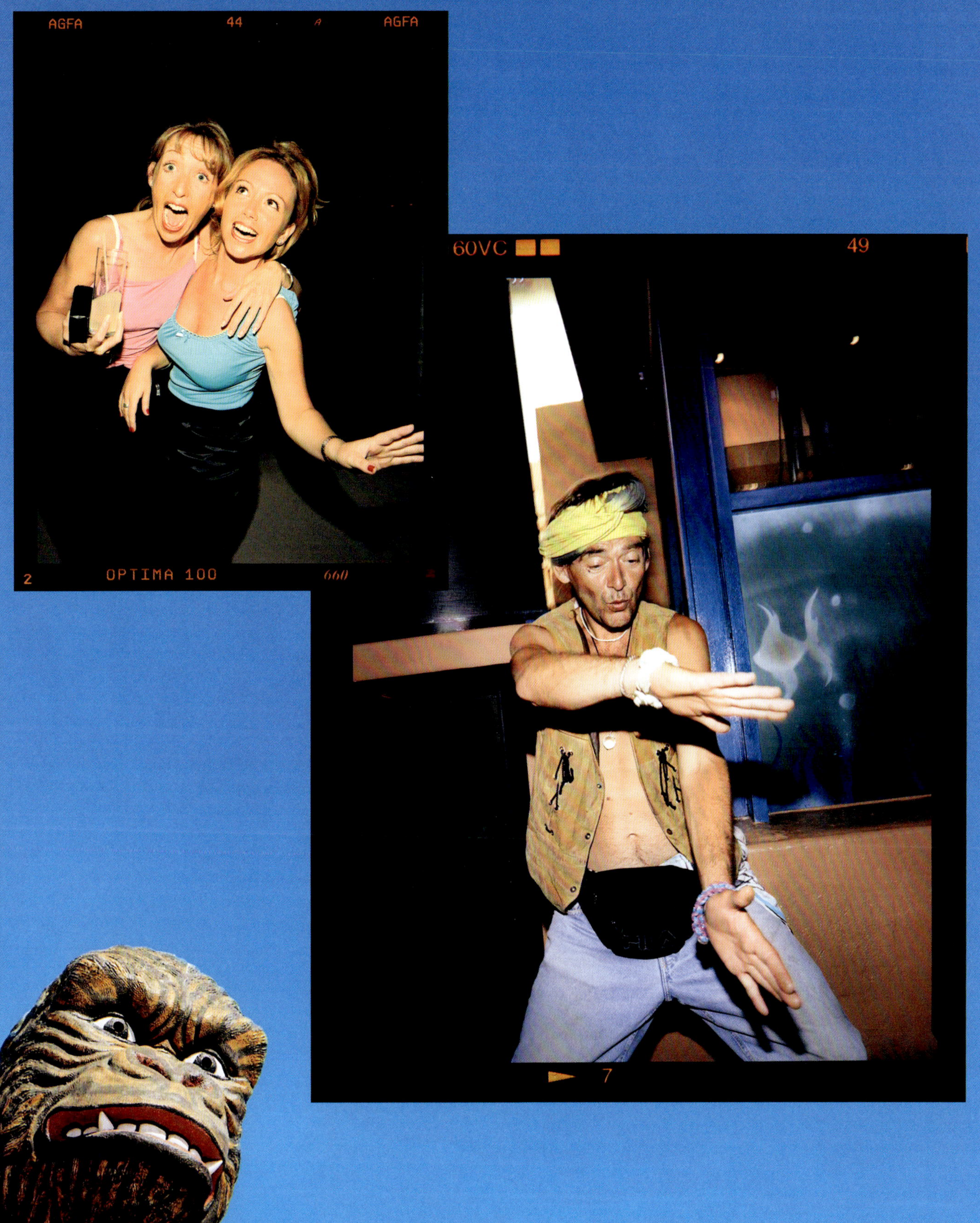
AGFA   44   A   AGFA
OPTIMA 100   660
2
60VC   49
7

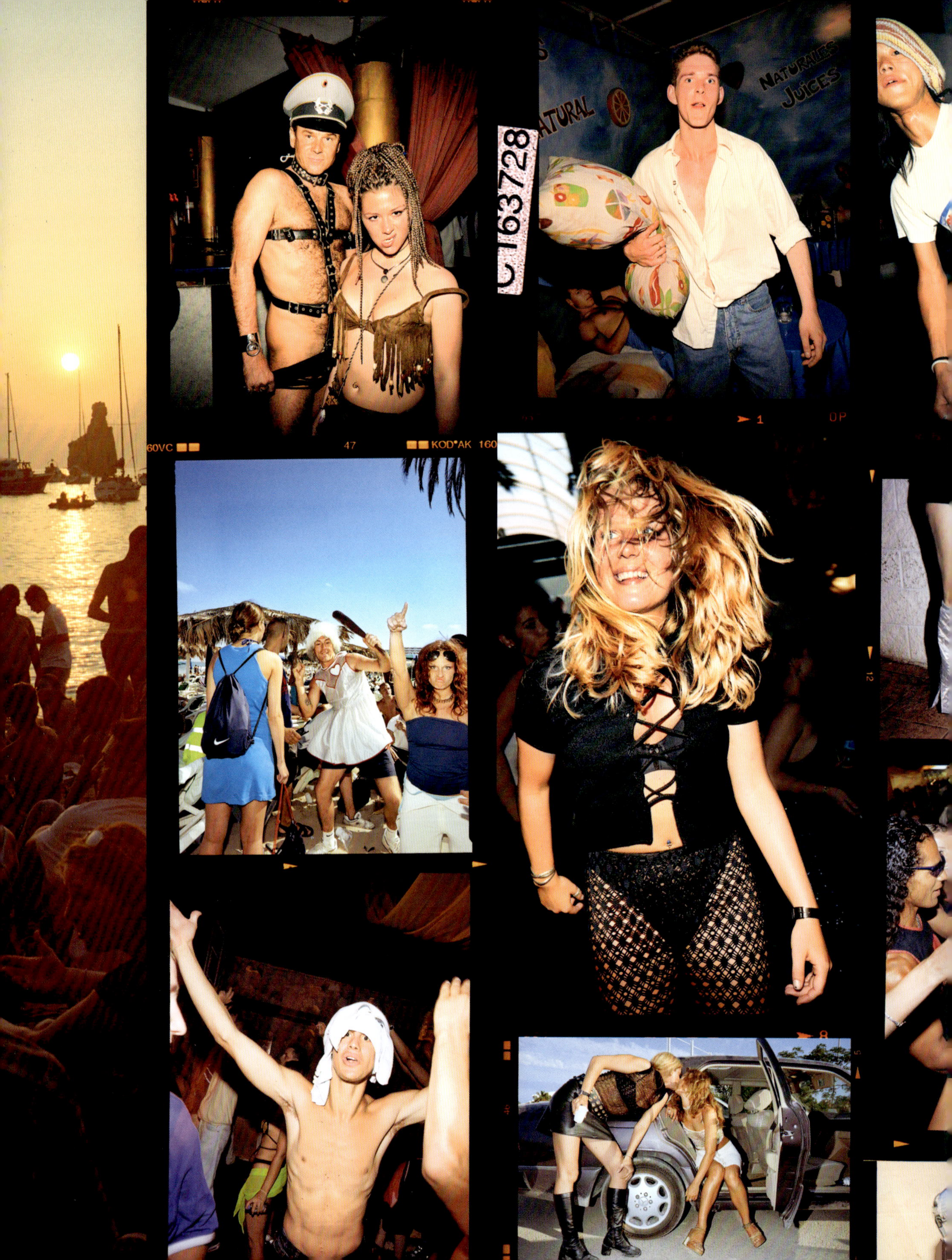

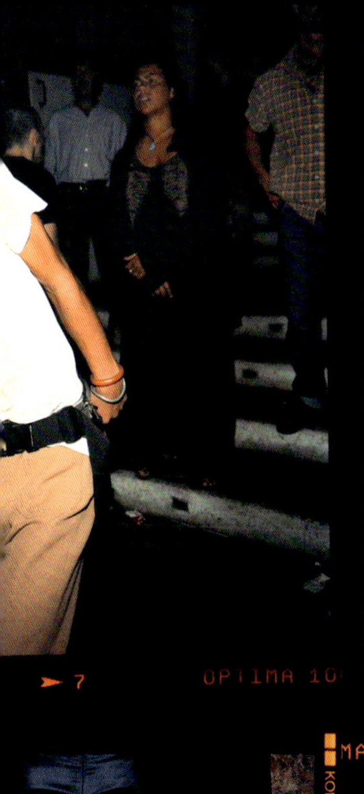
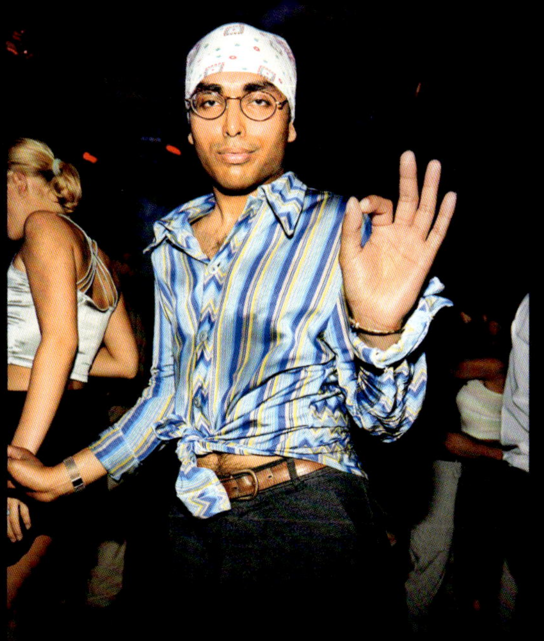
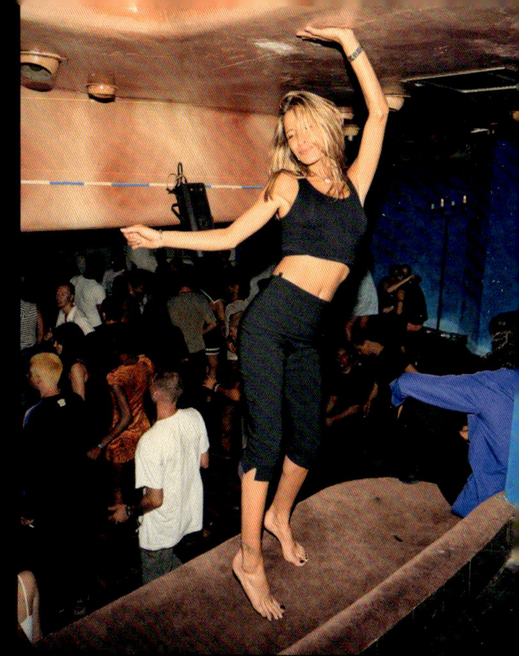
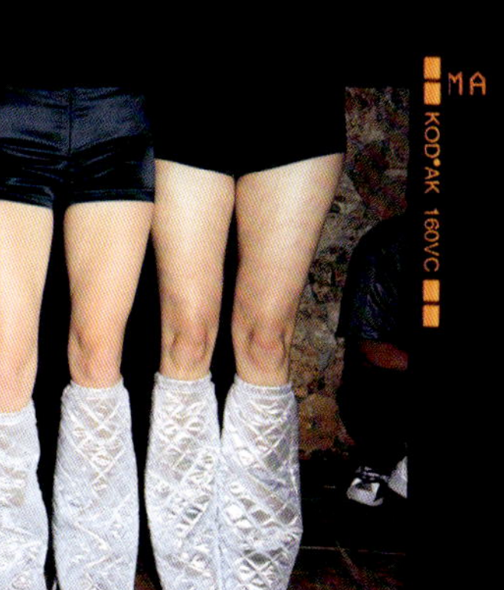
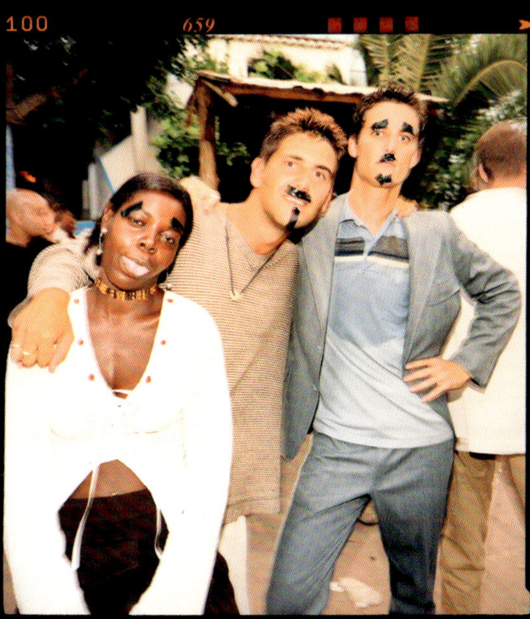
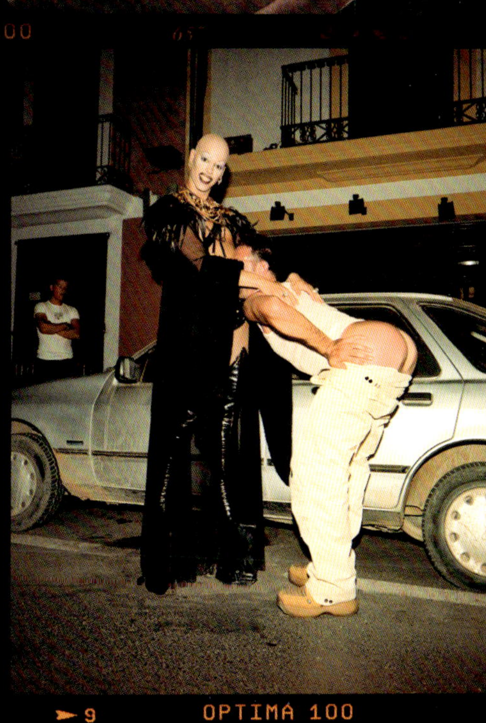
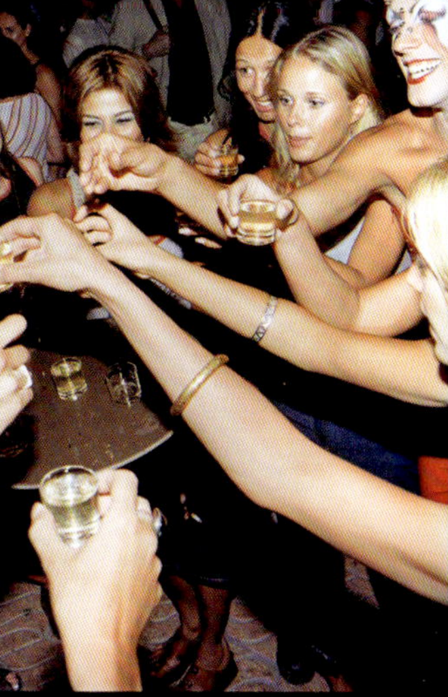
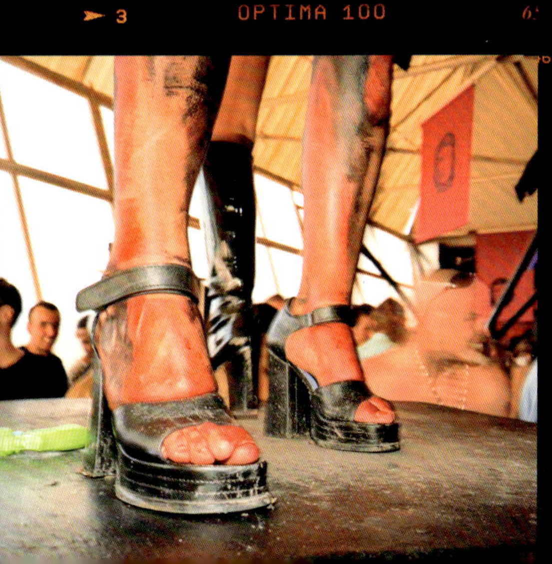
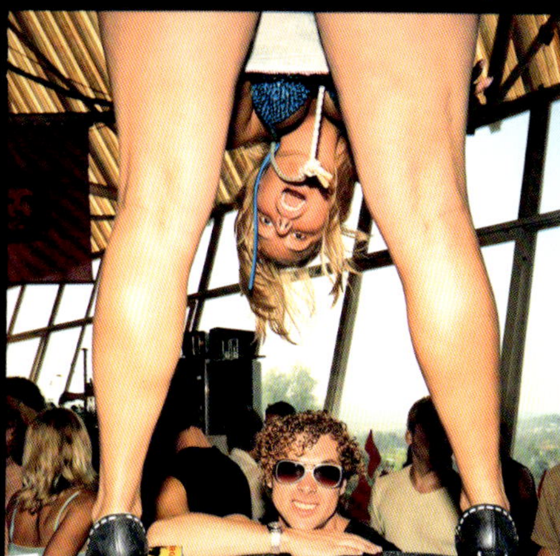
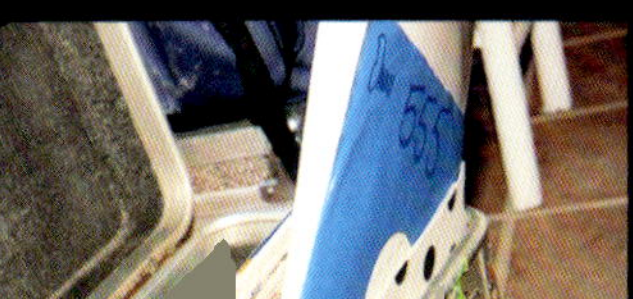

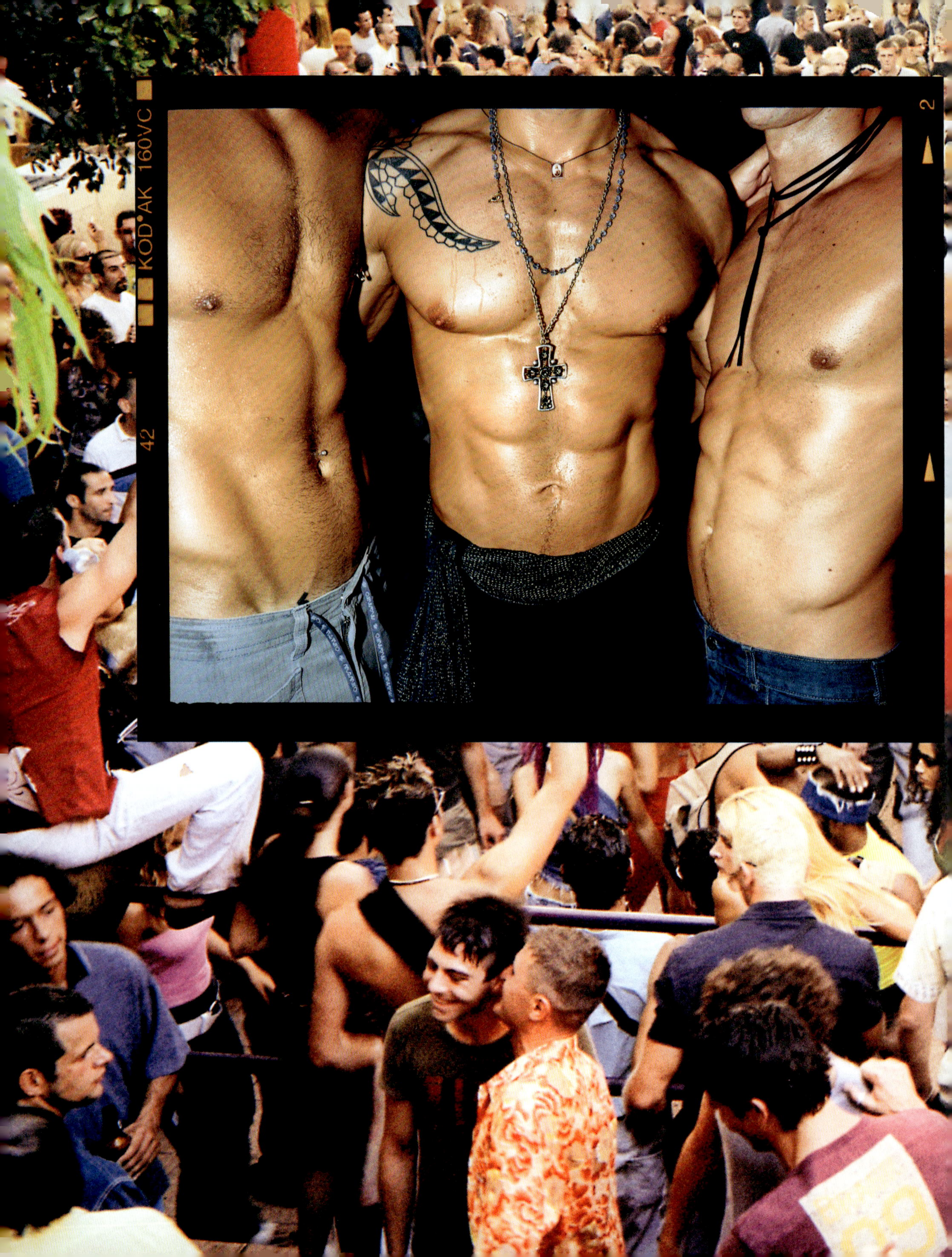
KOD*AK 160VC
42
2

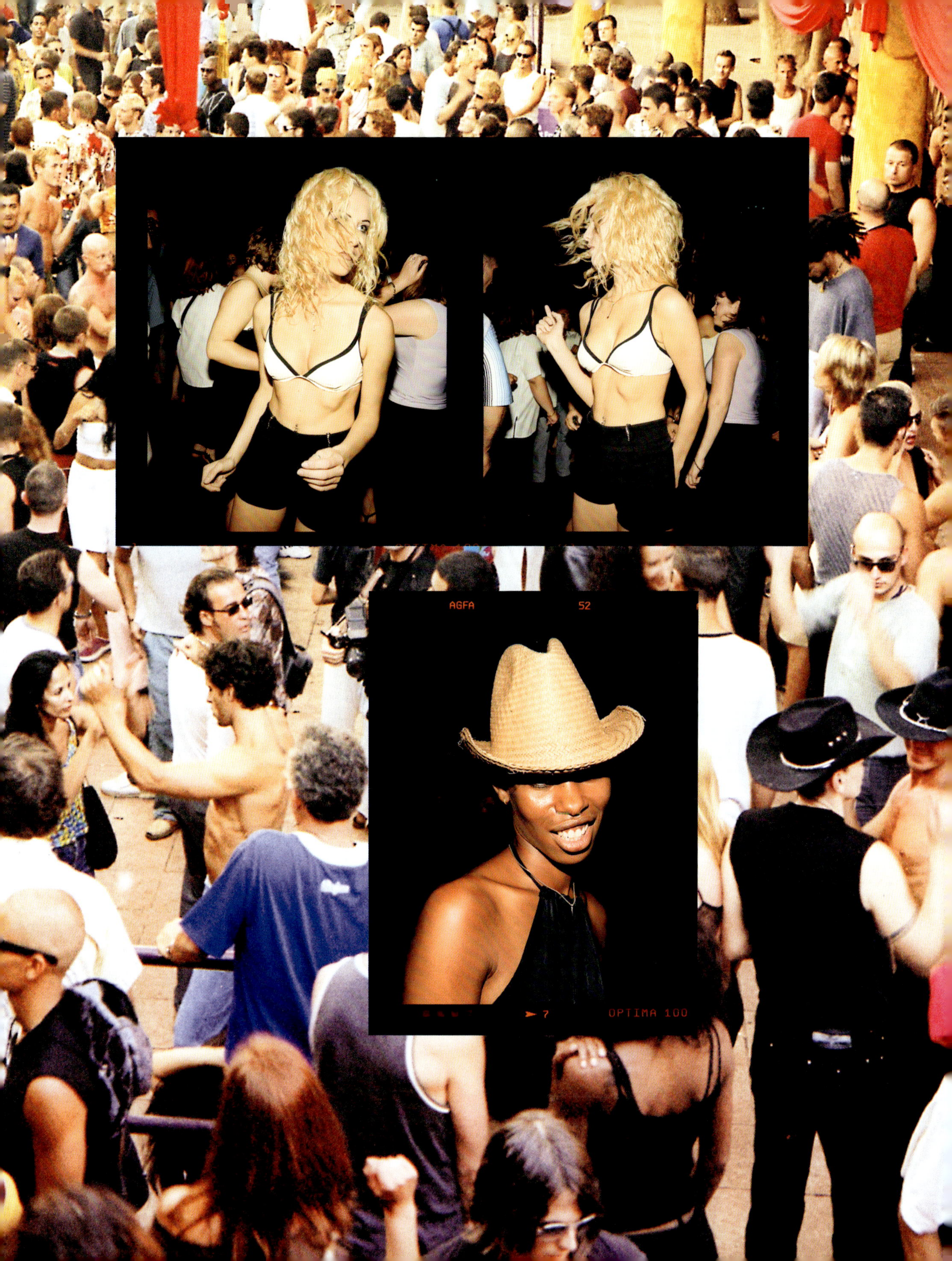

AGFA   52
7   OPTIMA 100

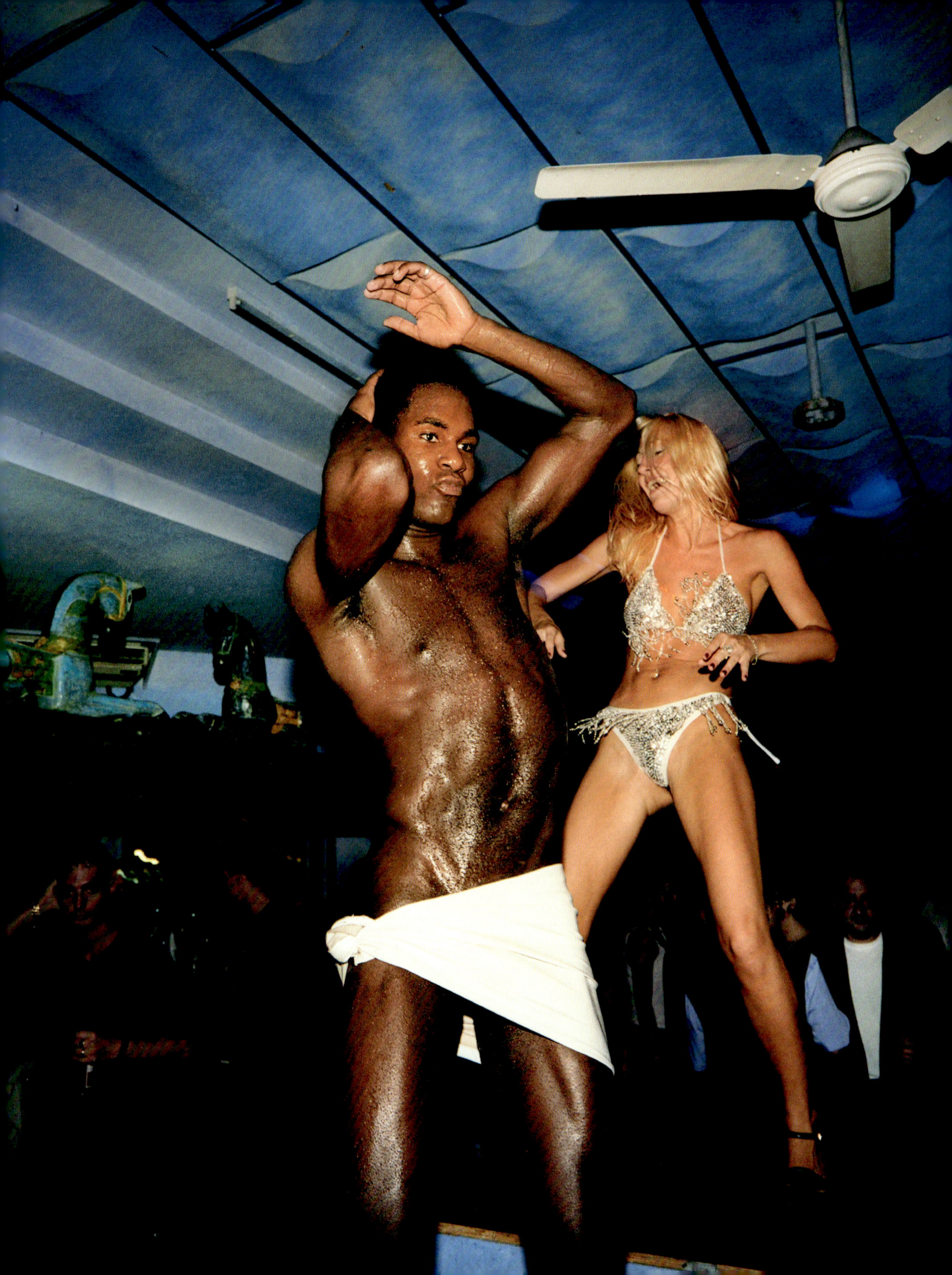

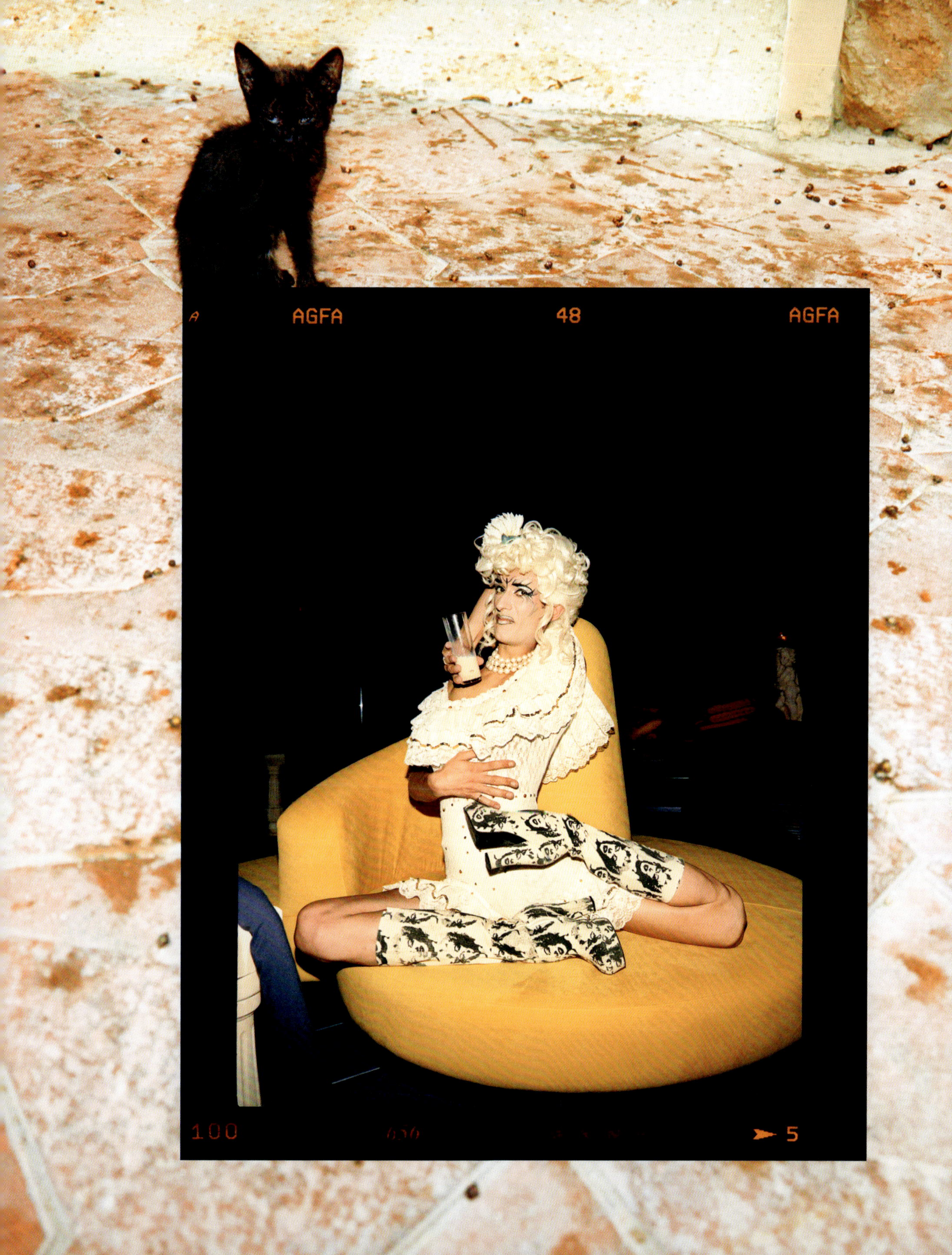
A
AGFA
48
AGFA
100
5

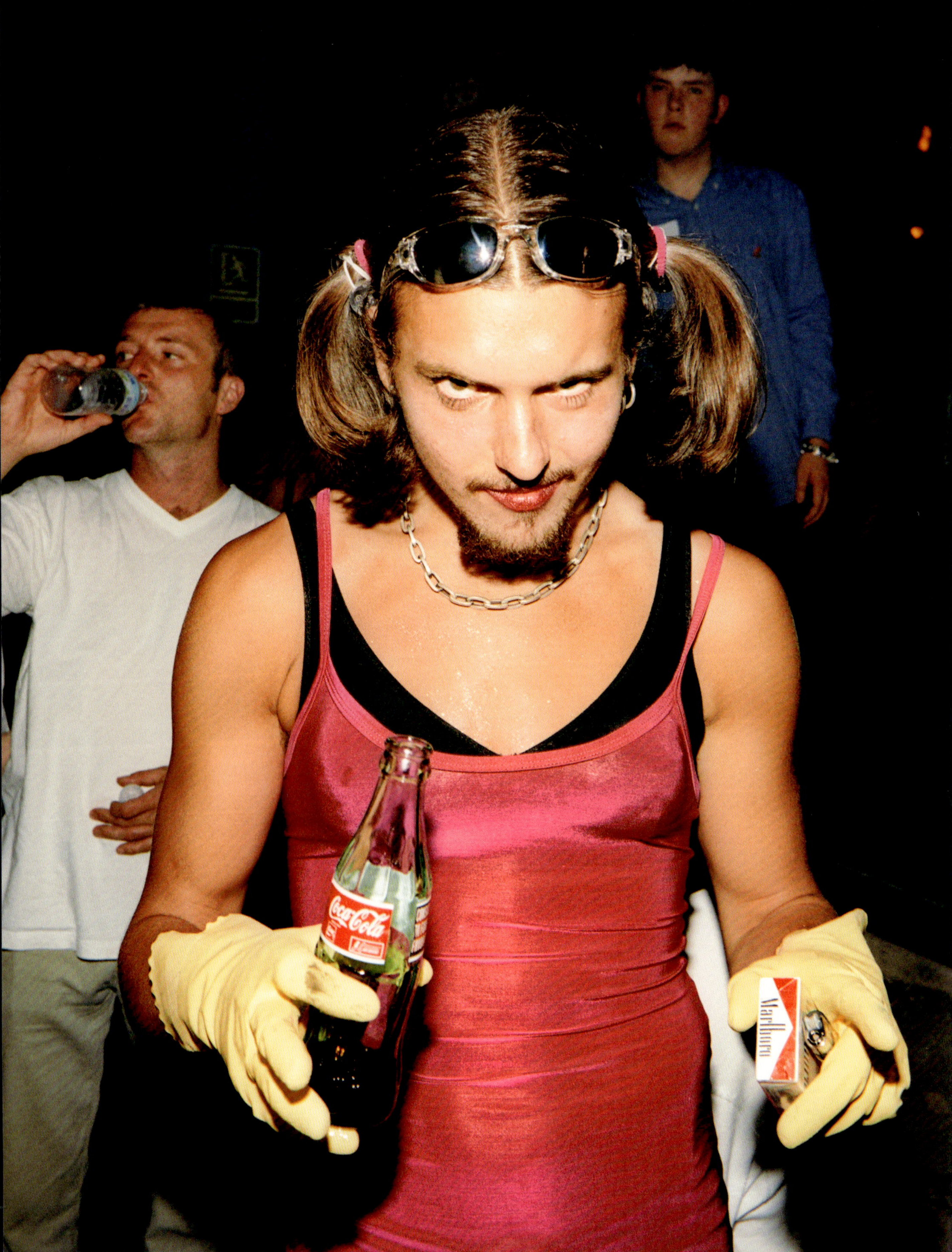

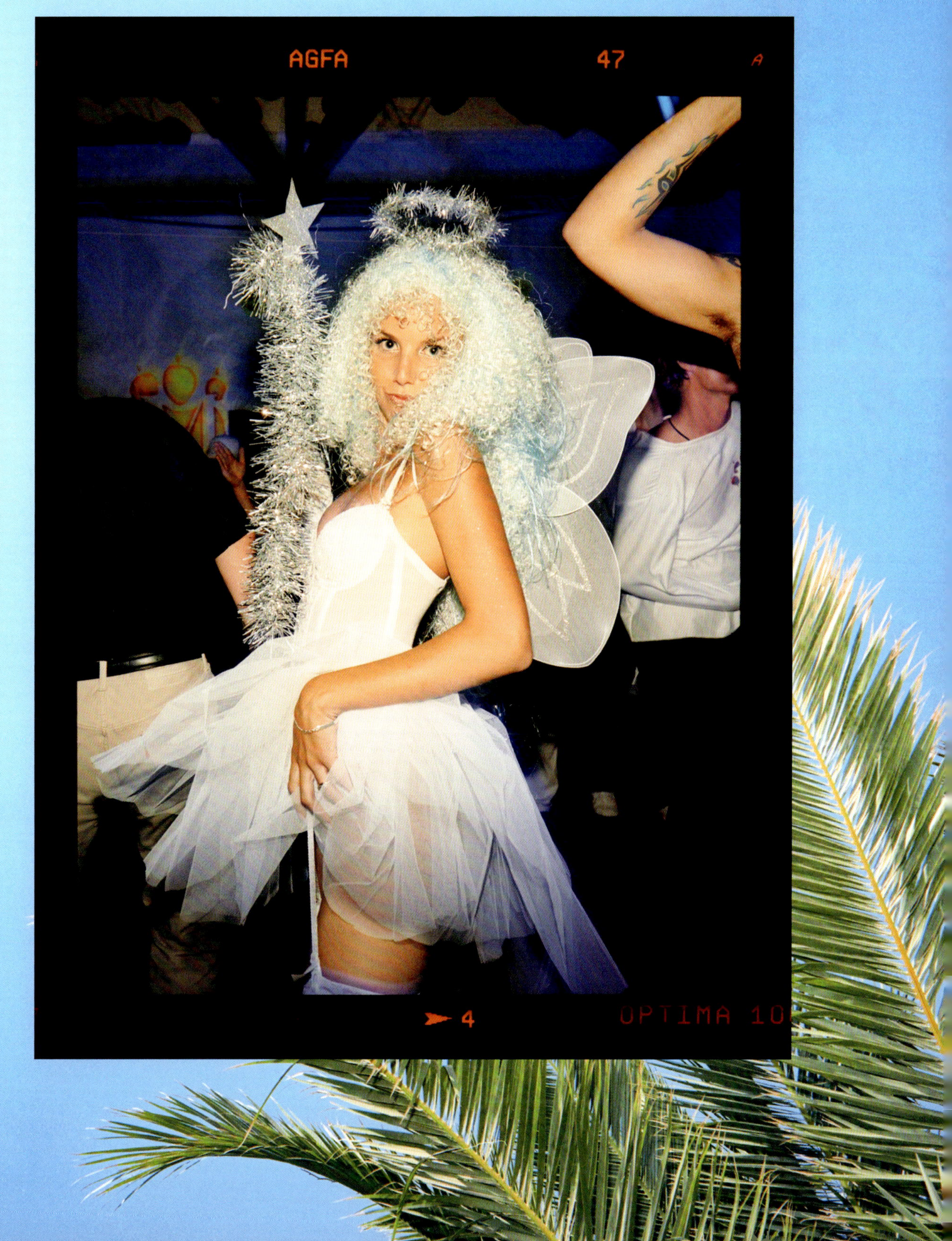

AGFA
47
A
4
OPTIMA 10

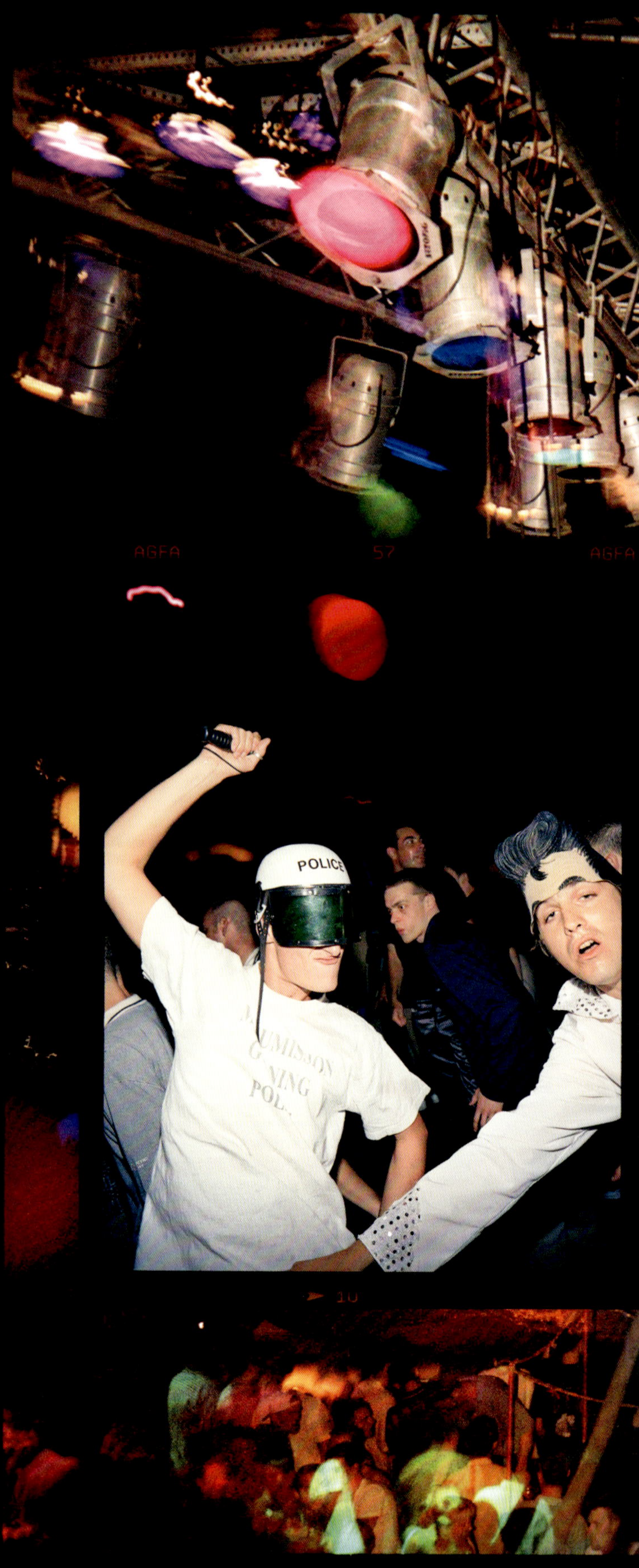

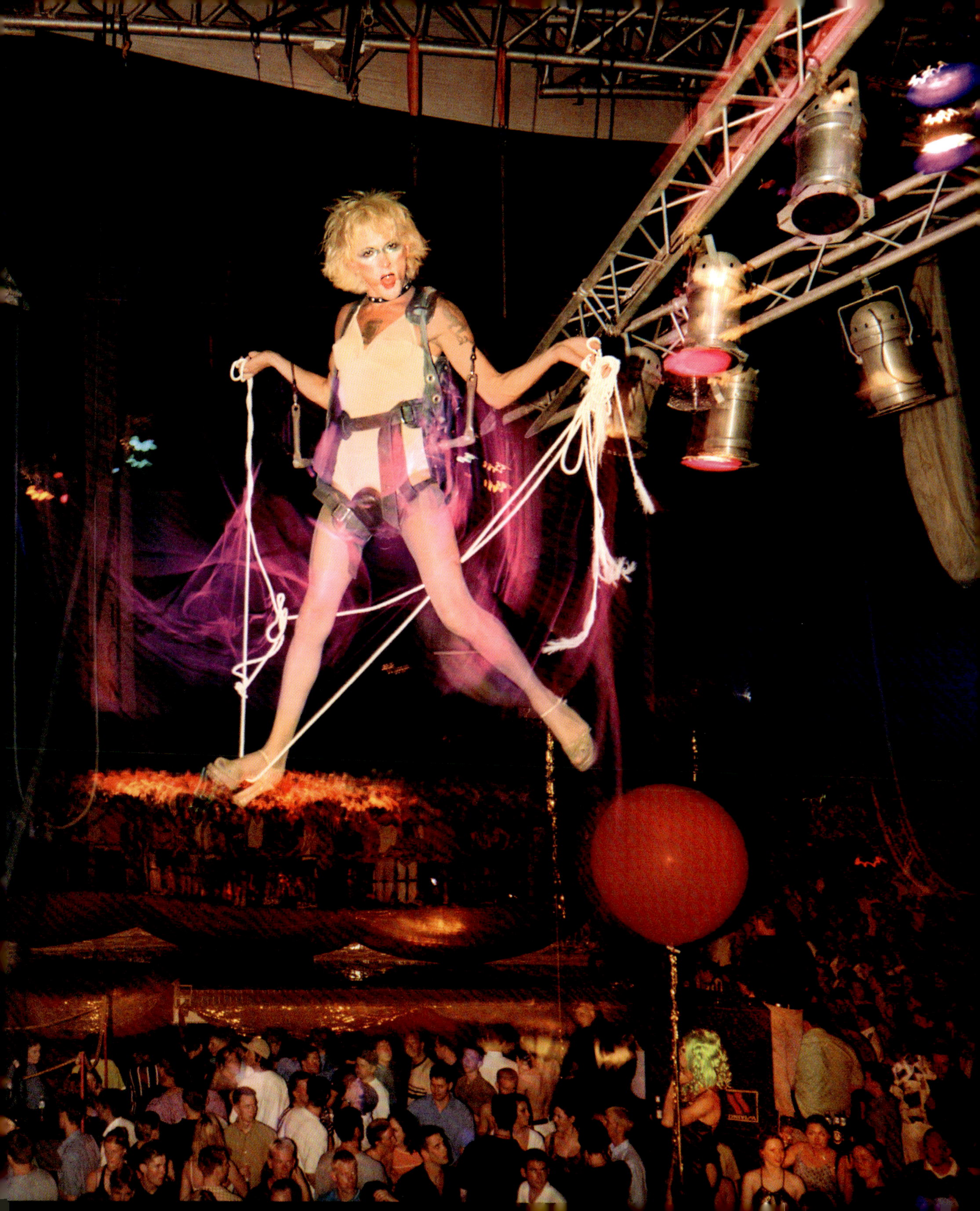

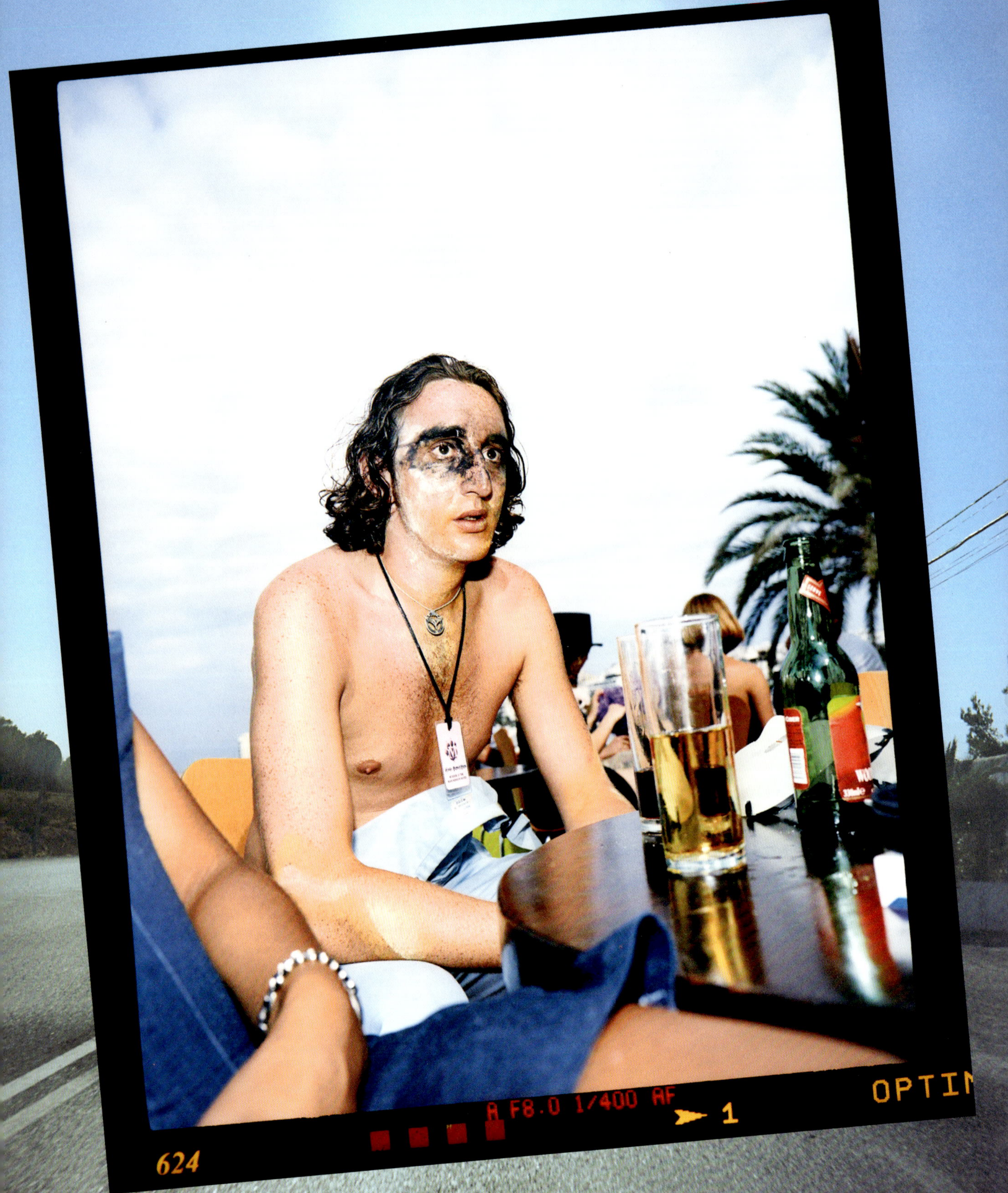
A F8.0 1/400 AF
1
OPTI
624

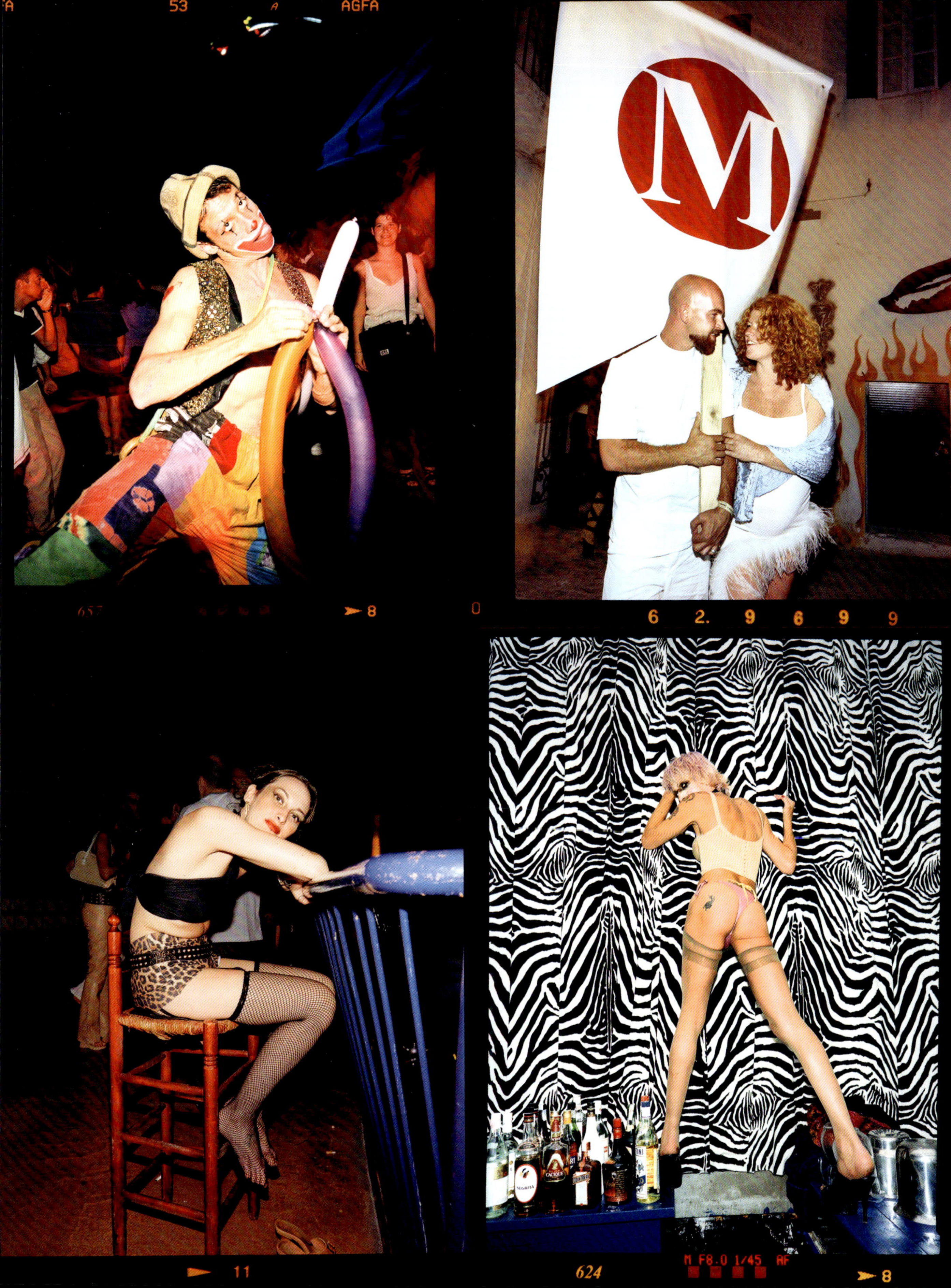

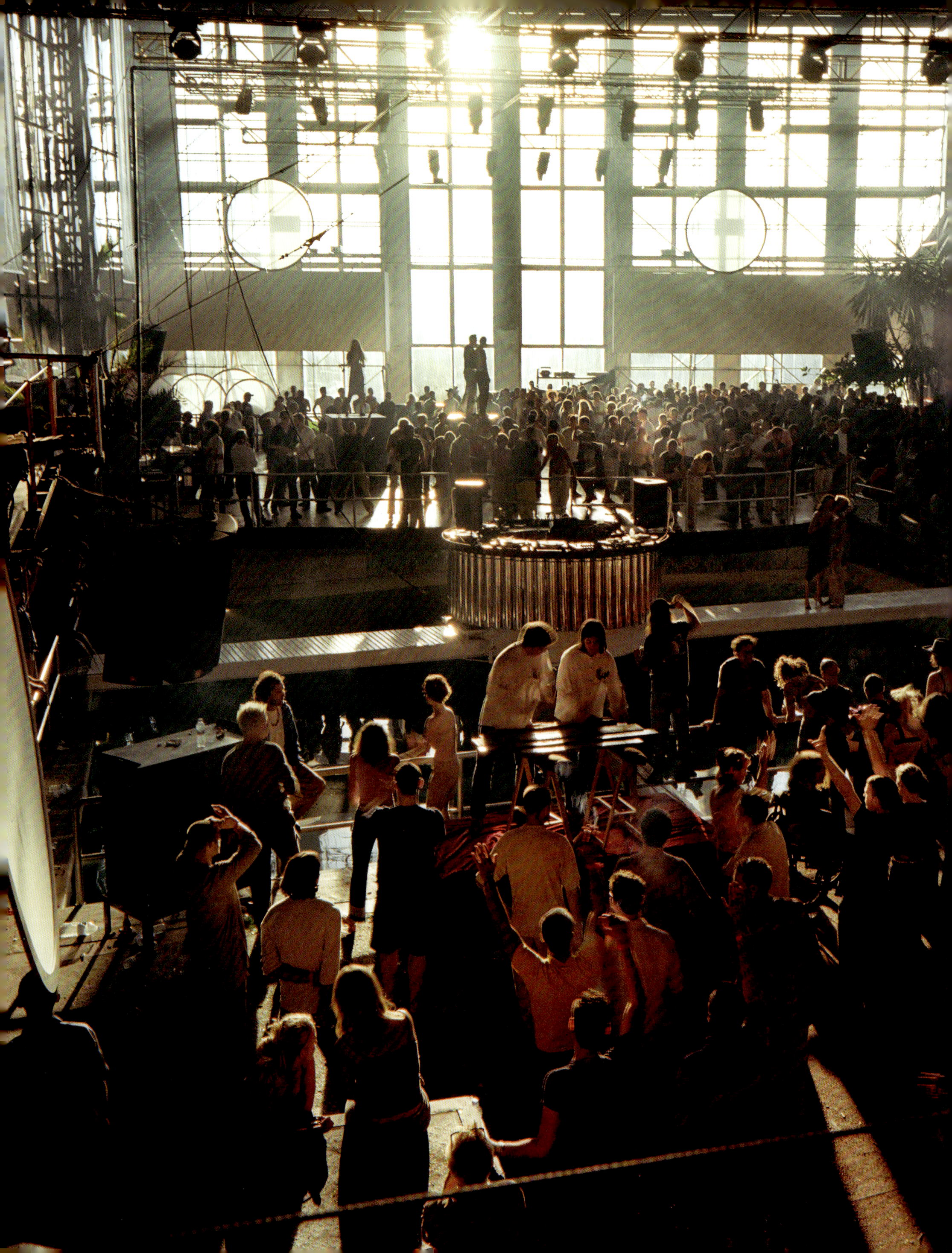

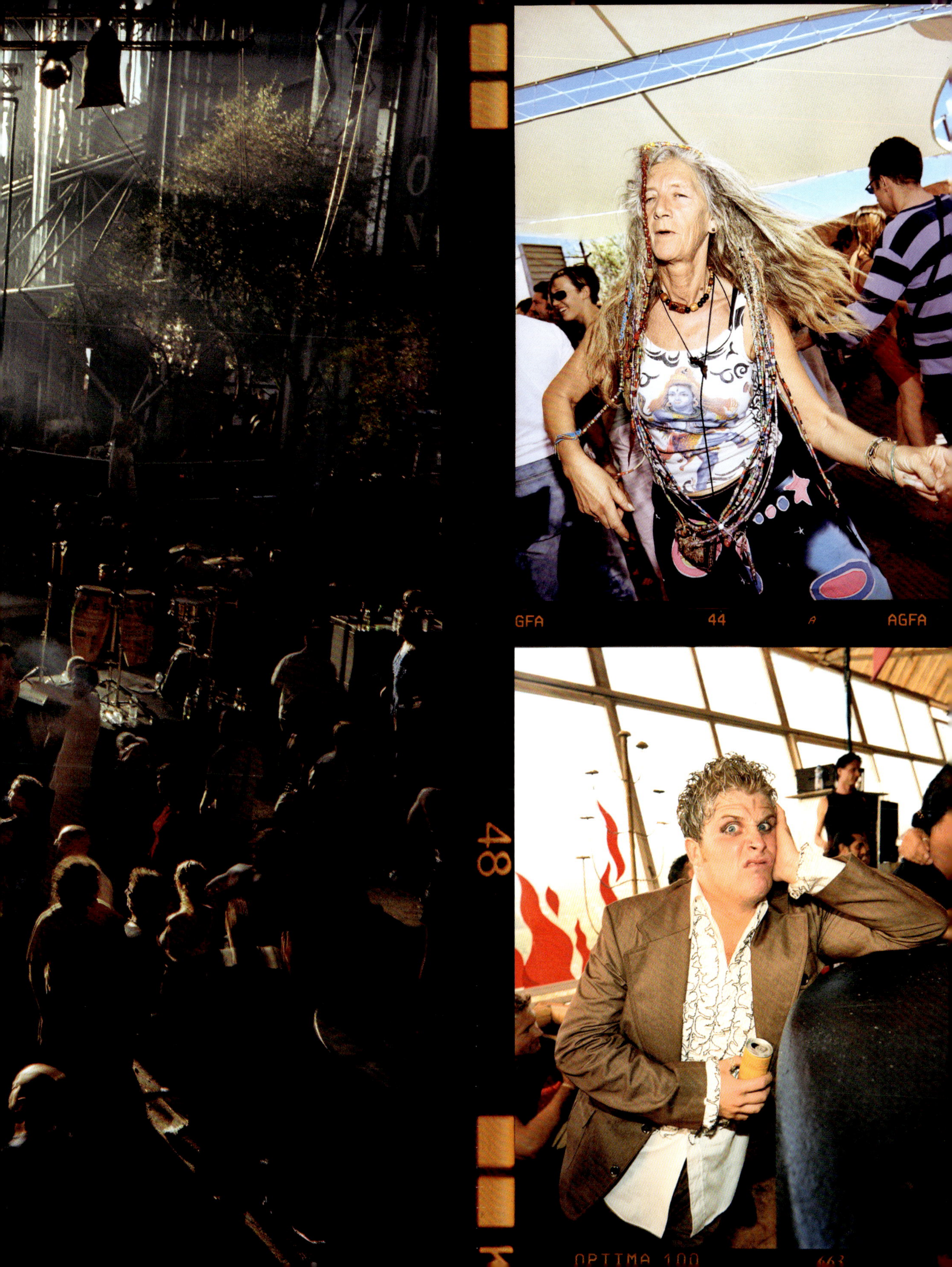

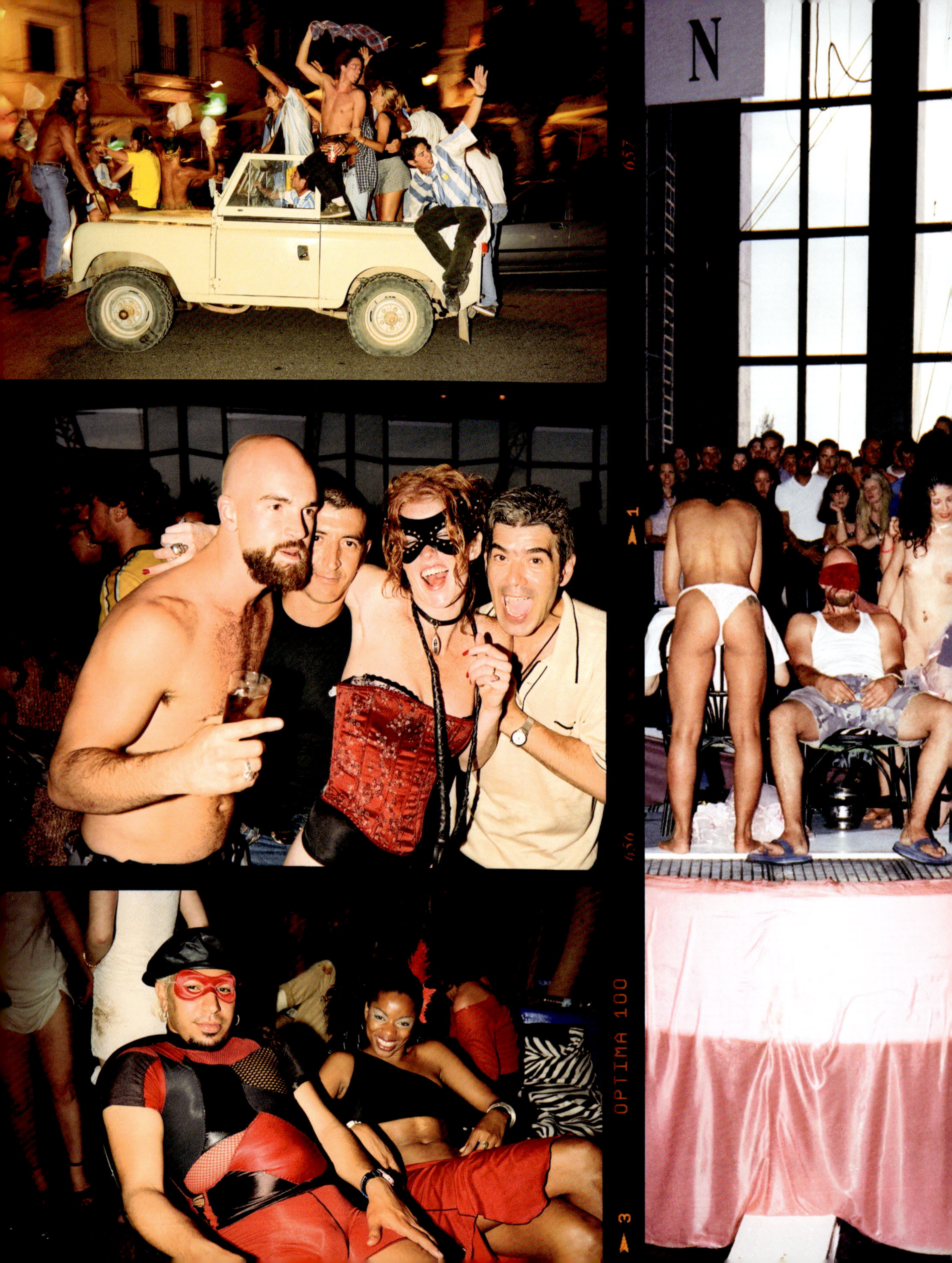

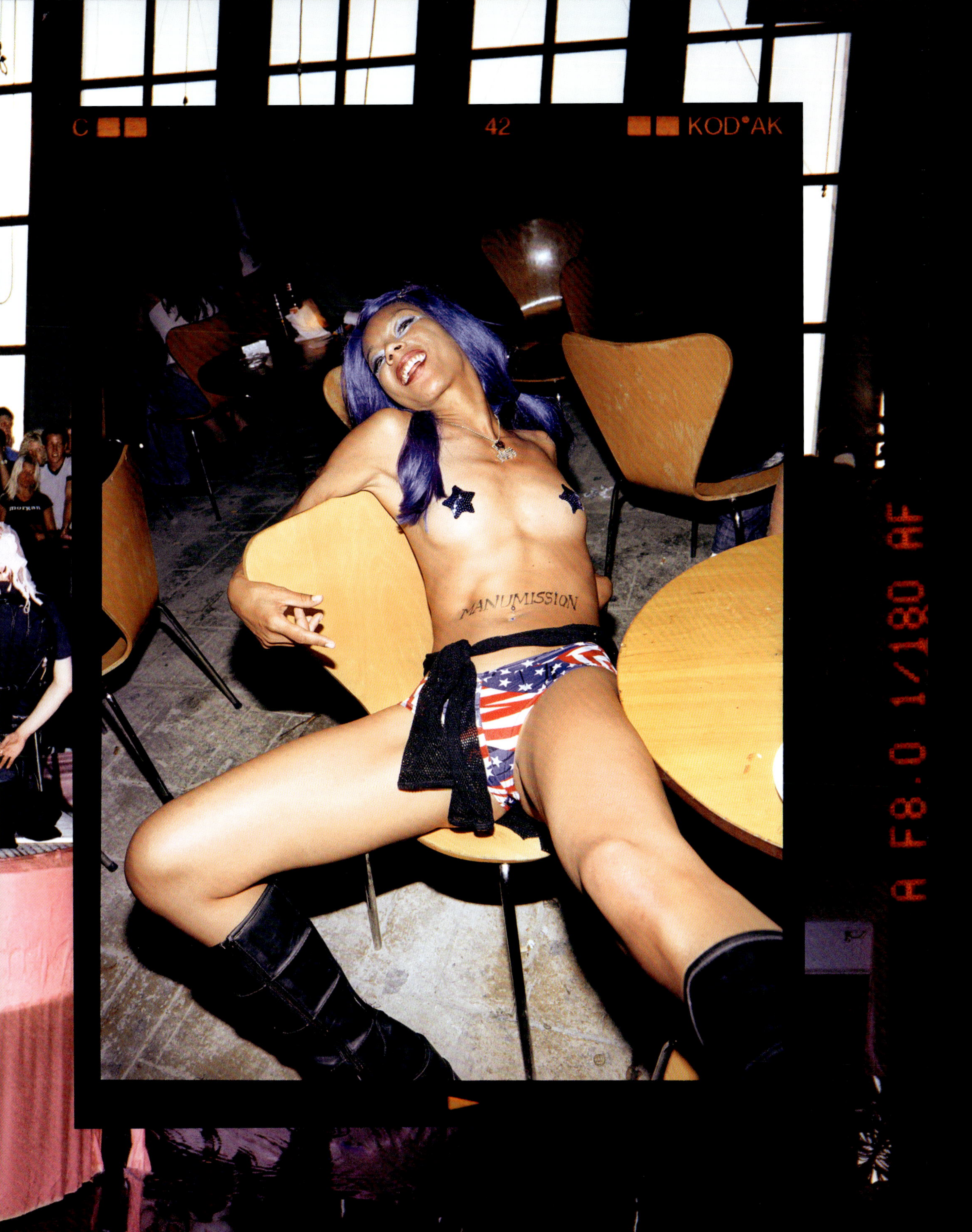

C
42
KOD*AK
A F8.0 1/180 AF
MANUMISSION

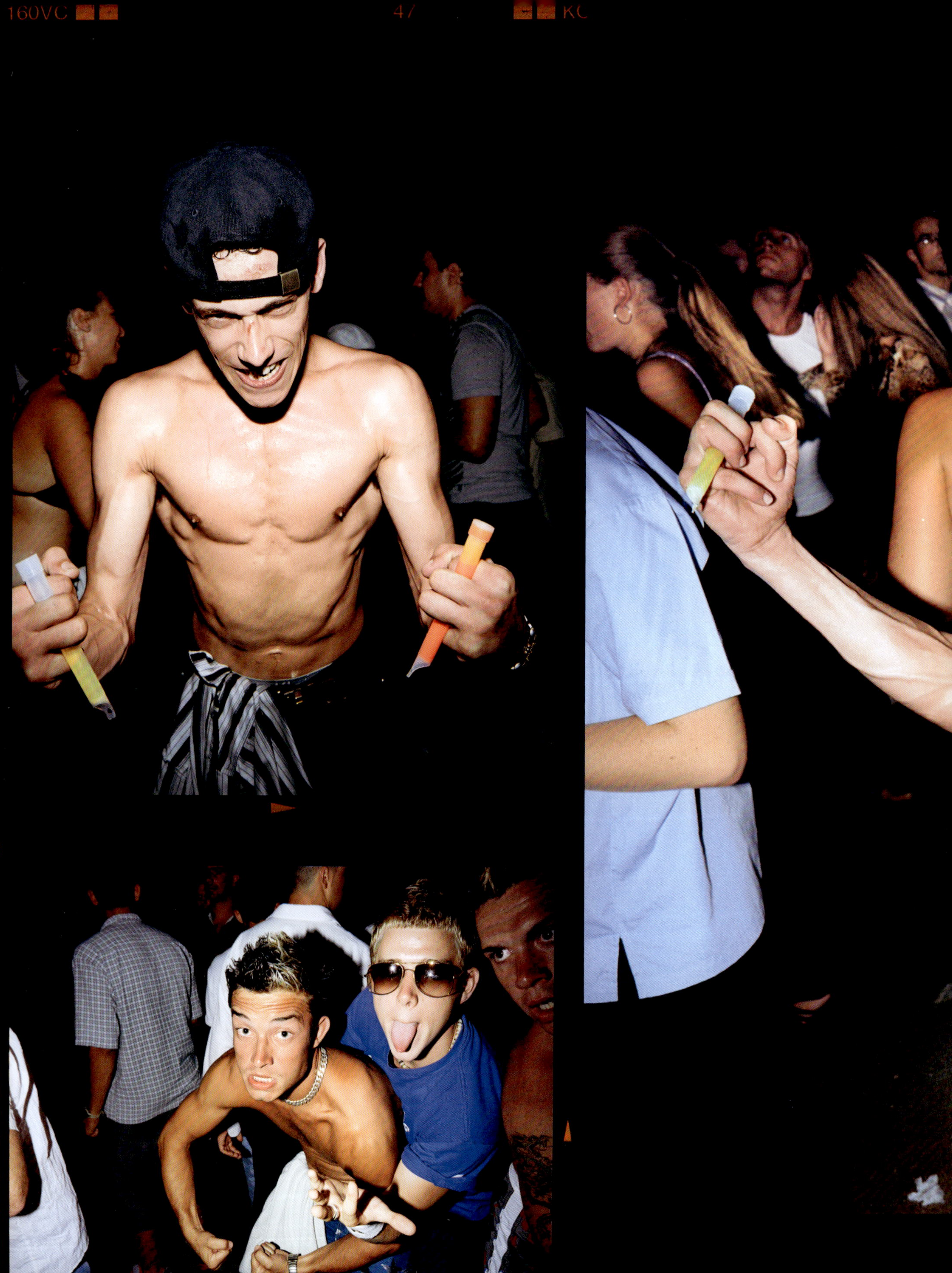

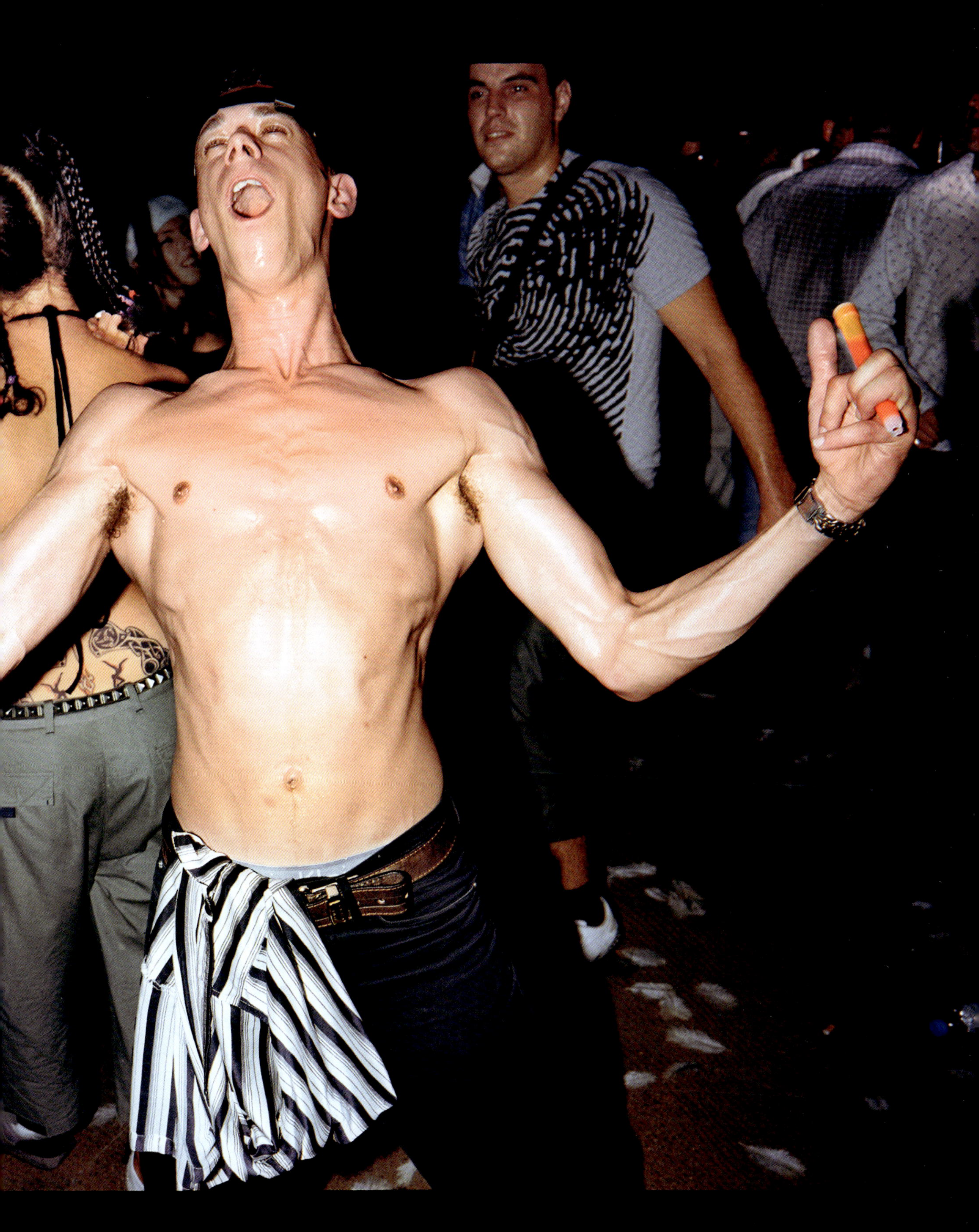

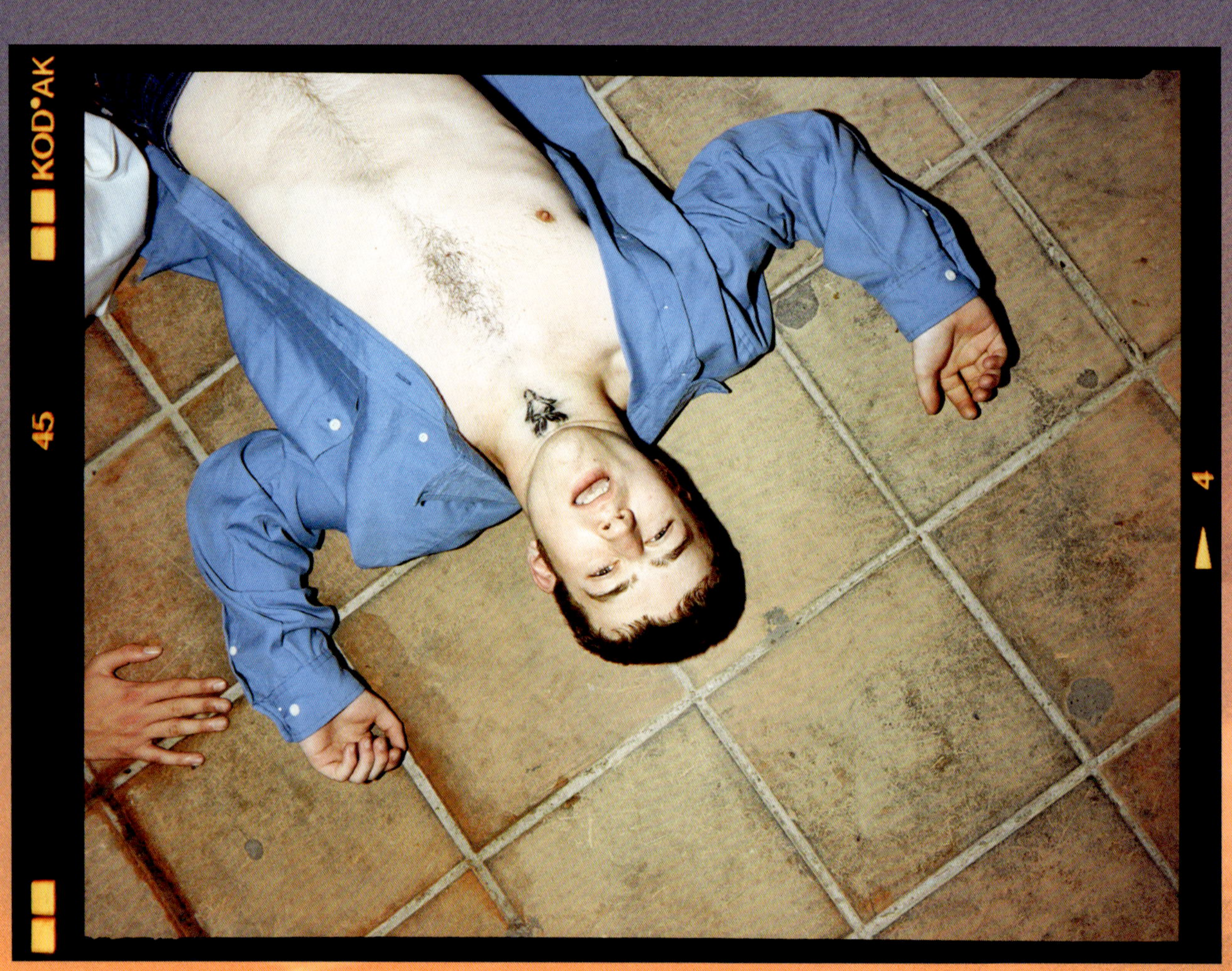
KOD*AK
45
4

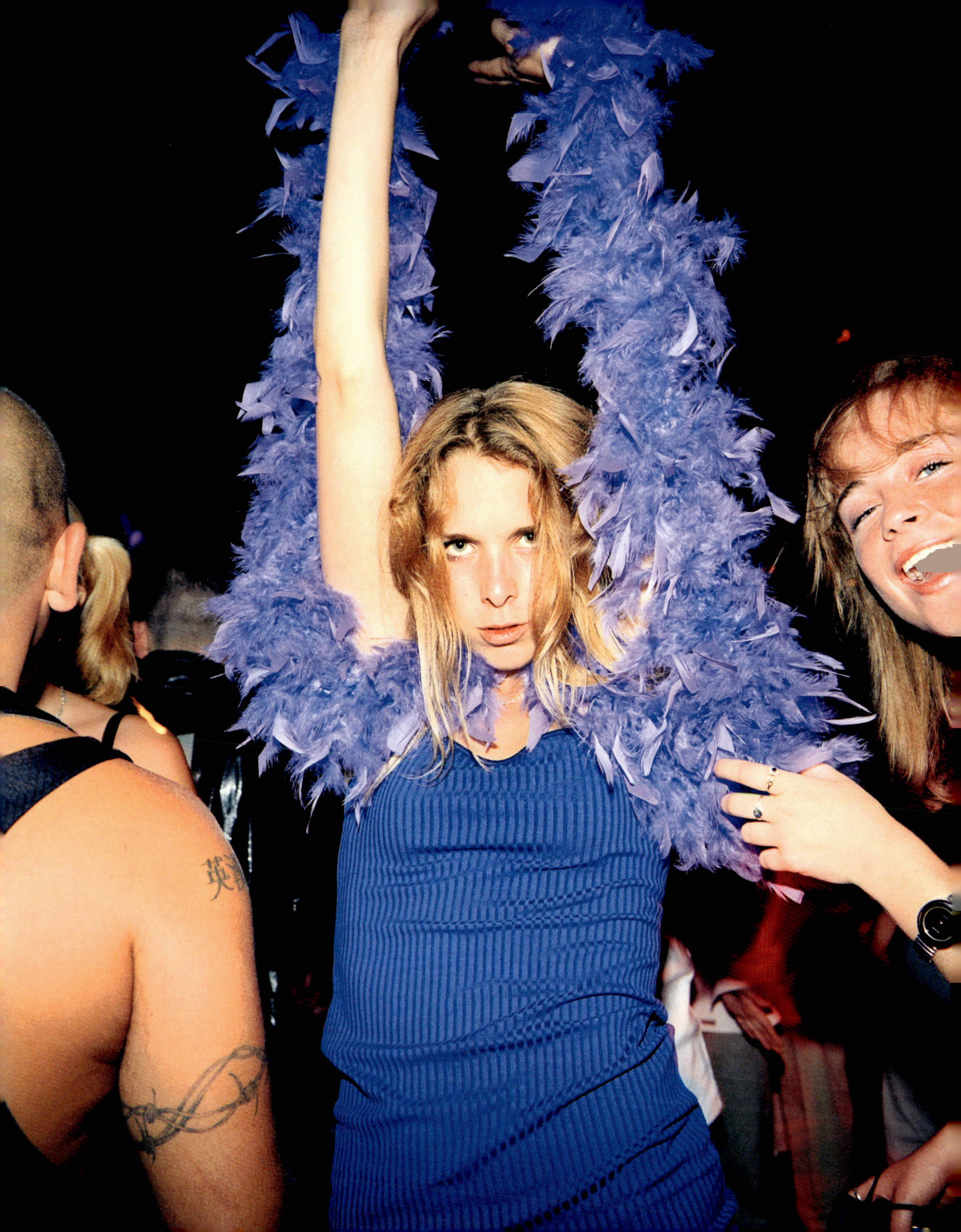

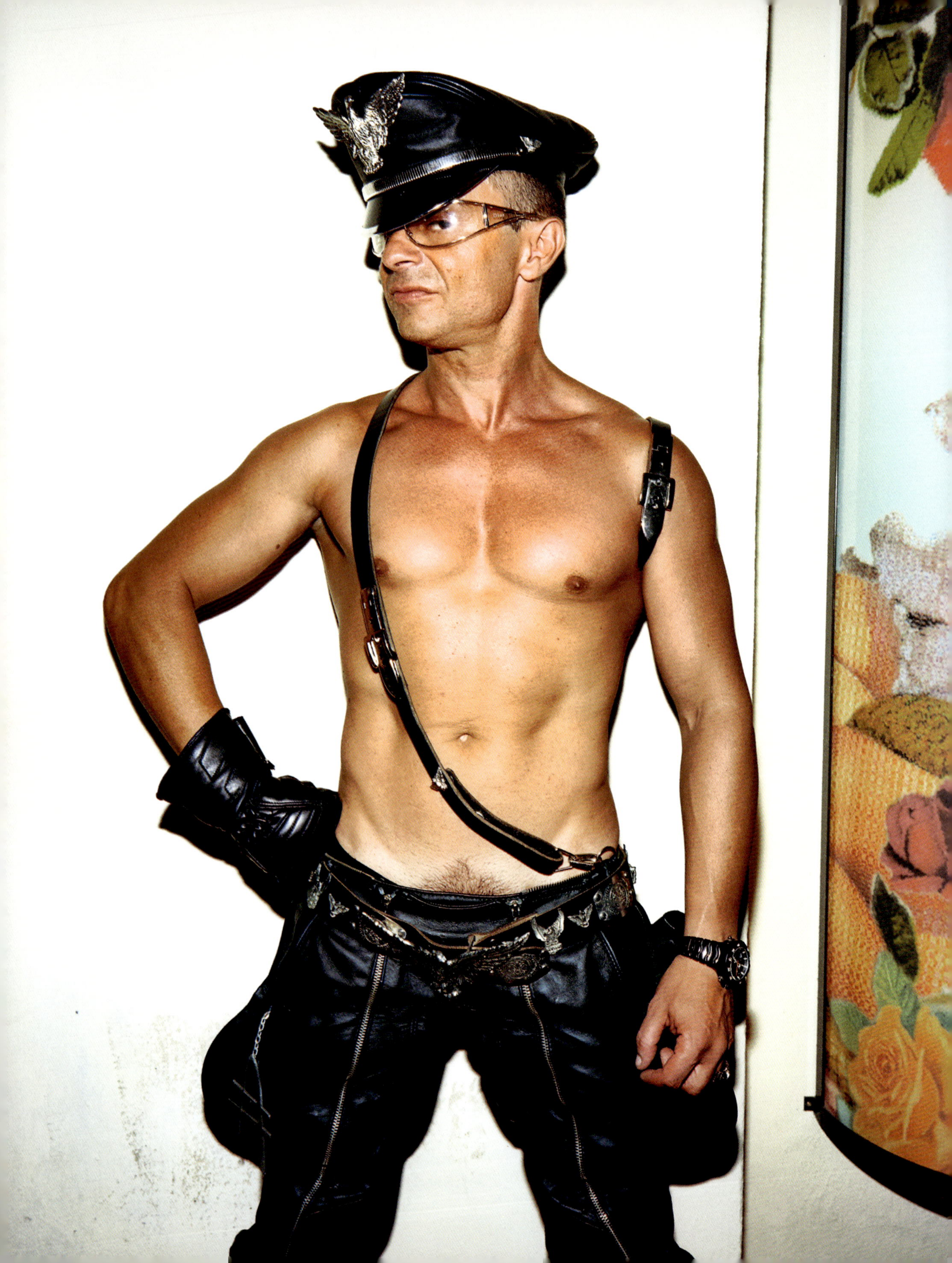

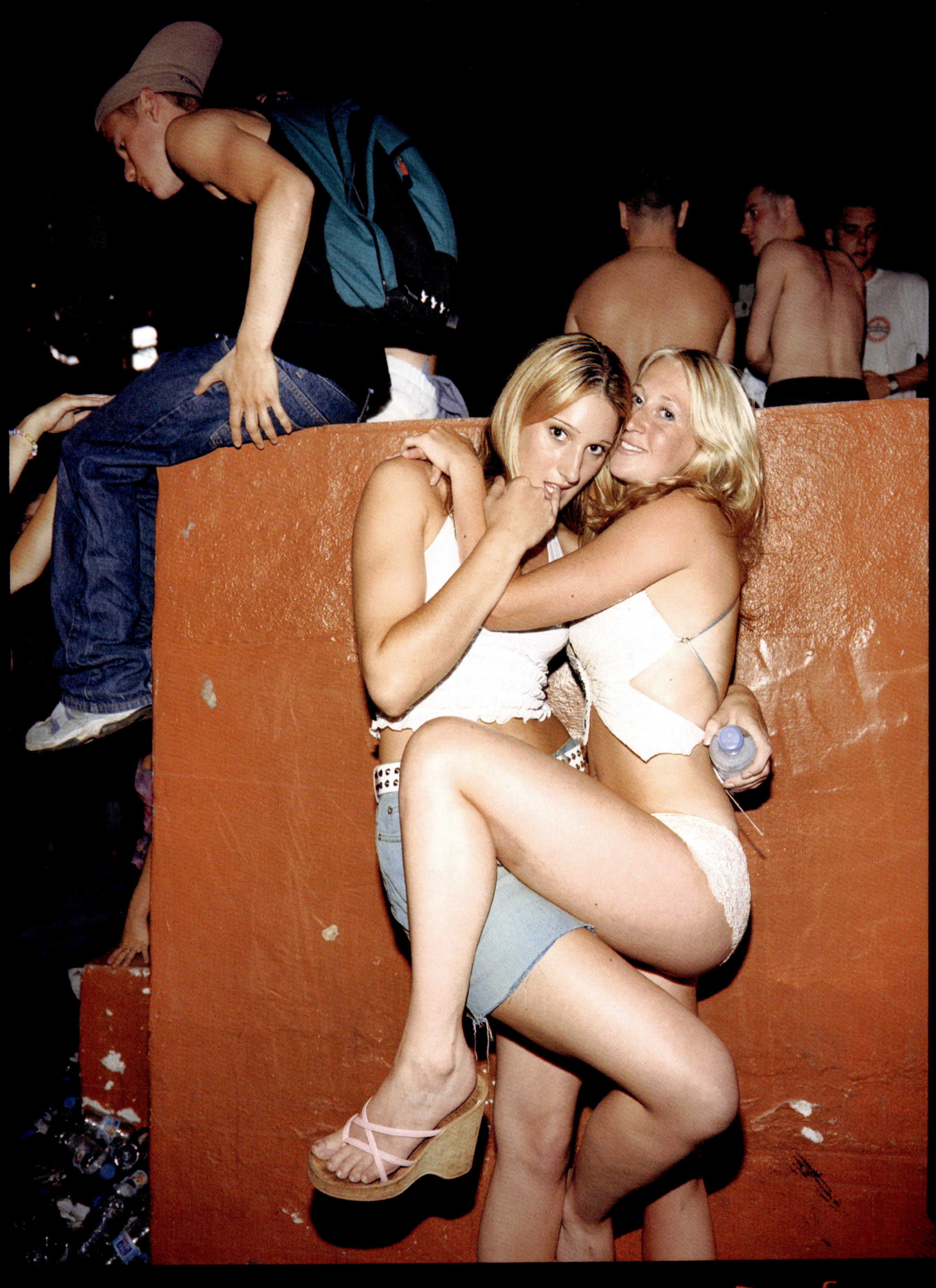

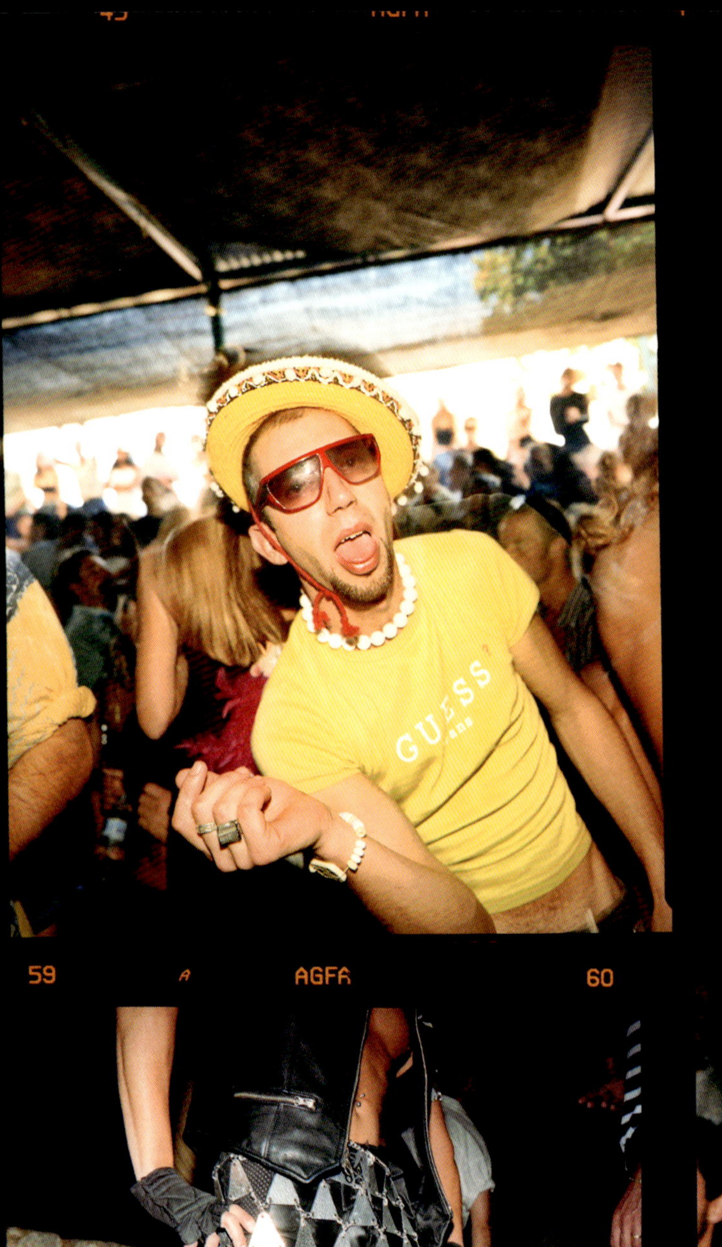
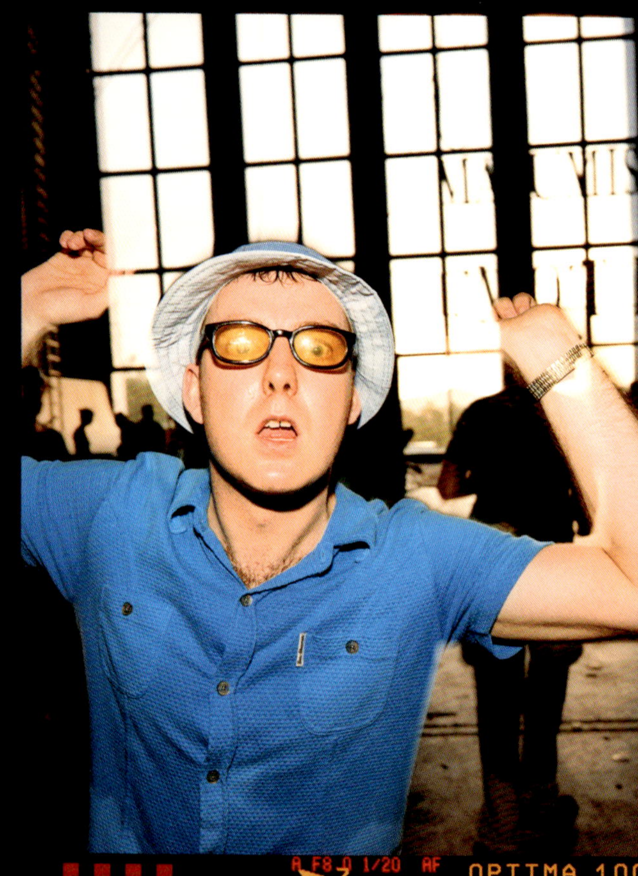
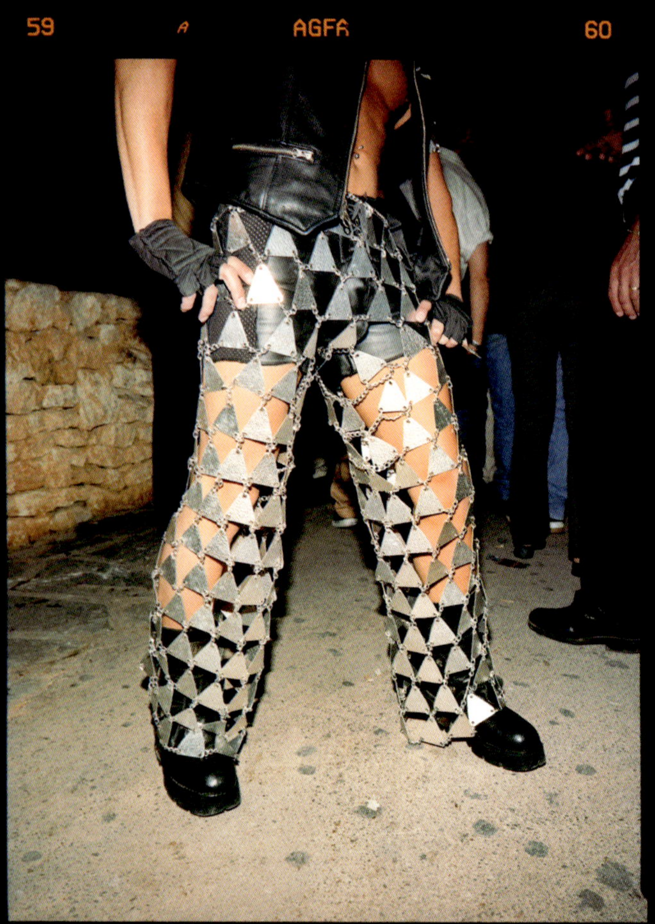
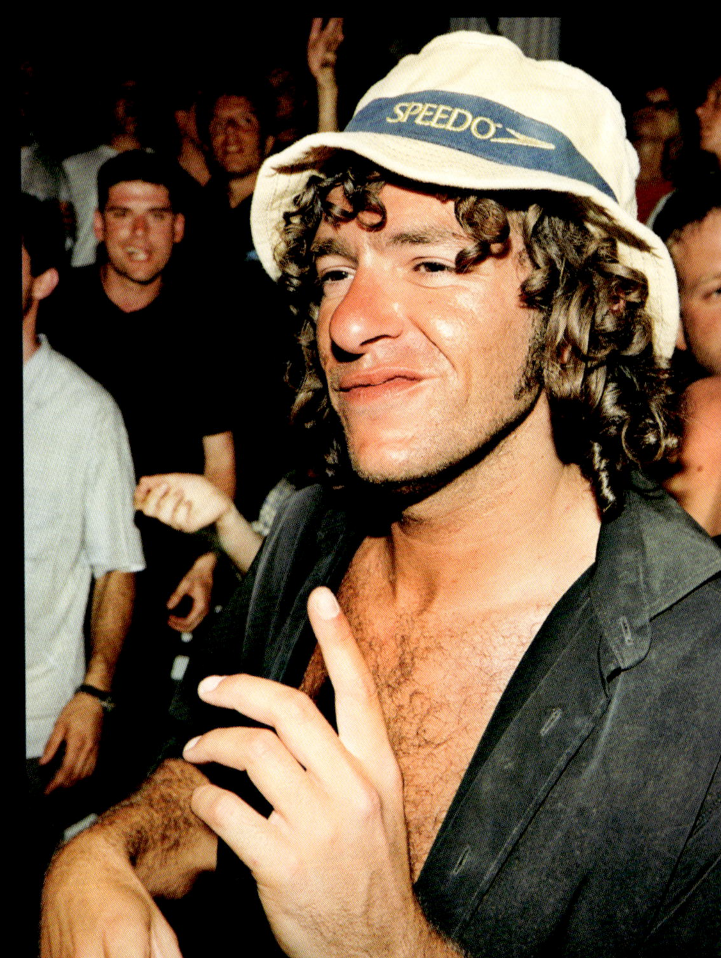

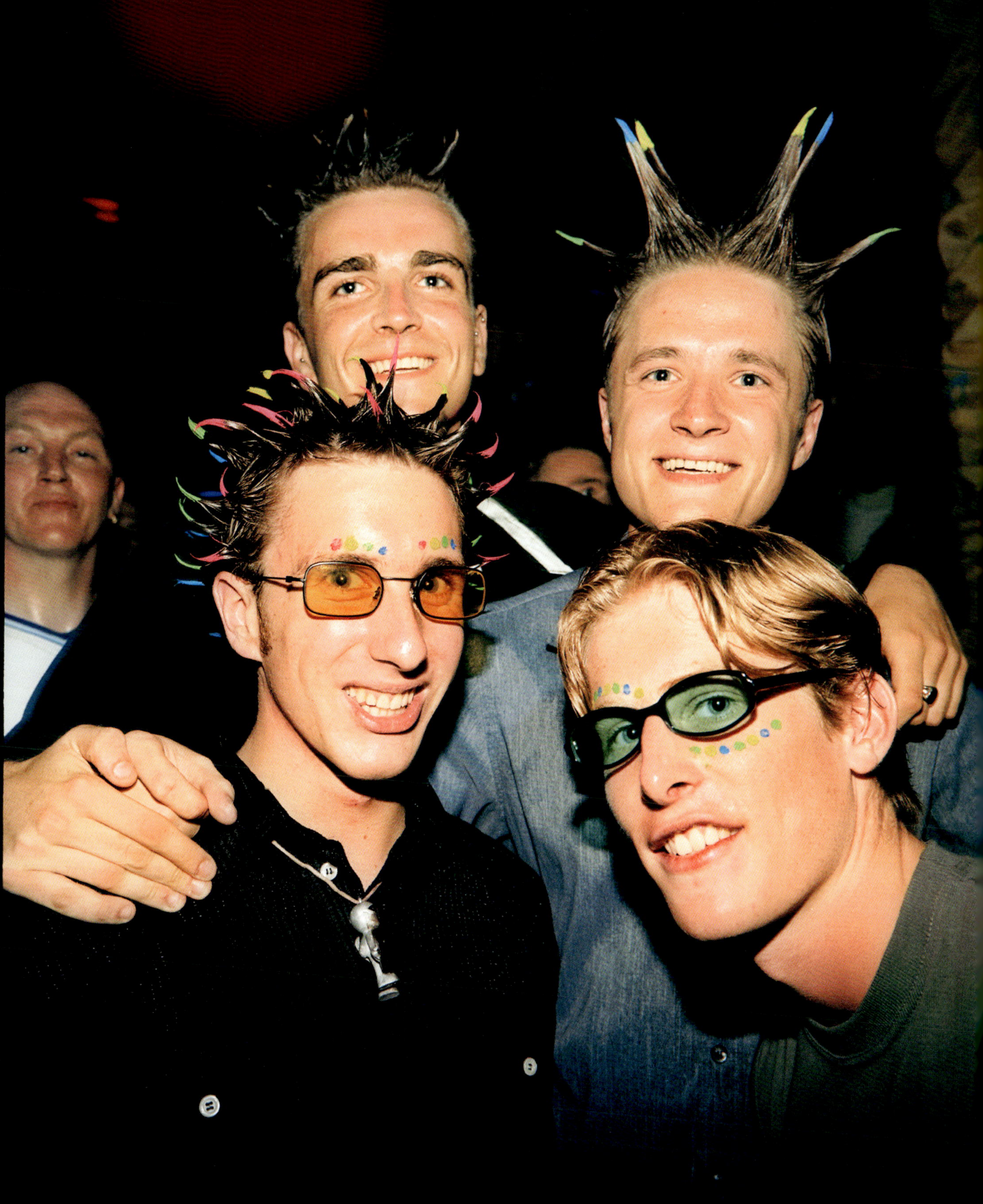

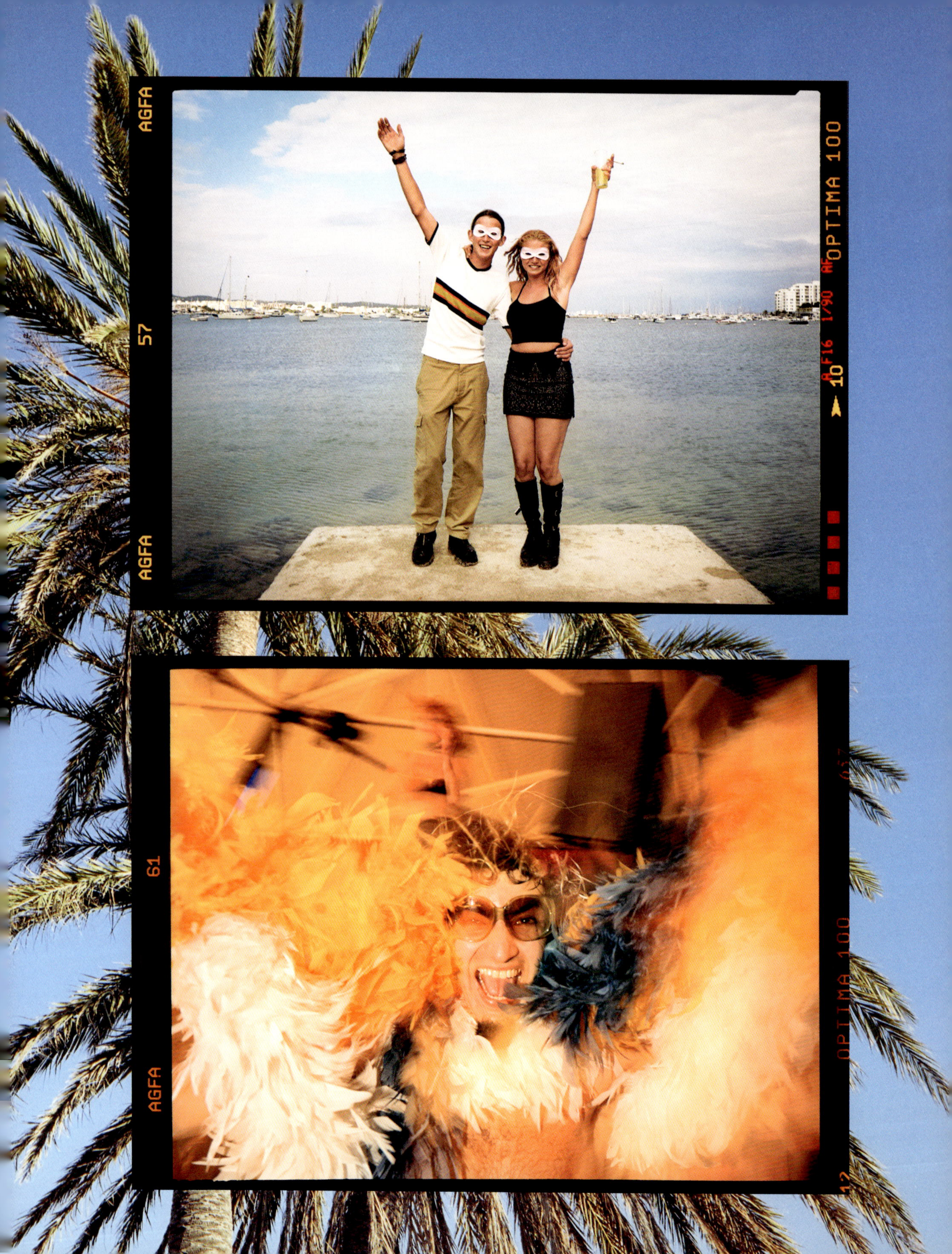

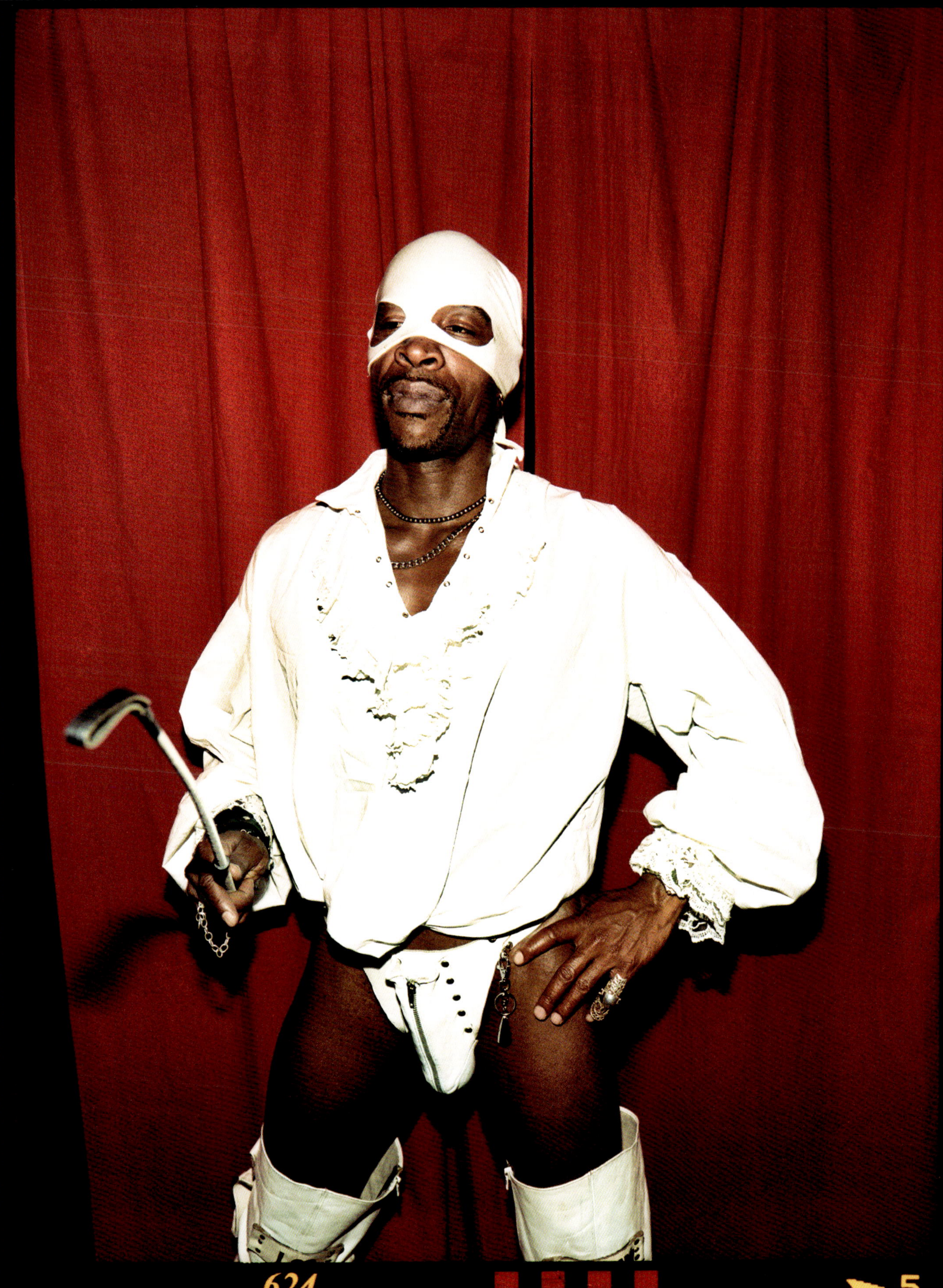
624

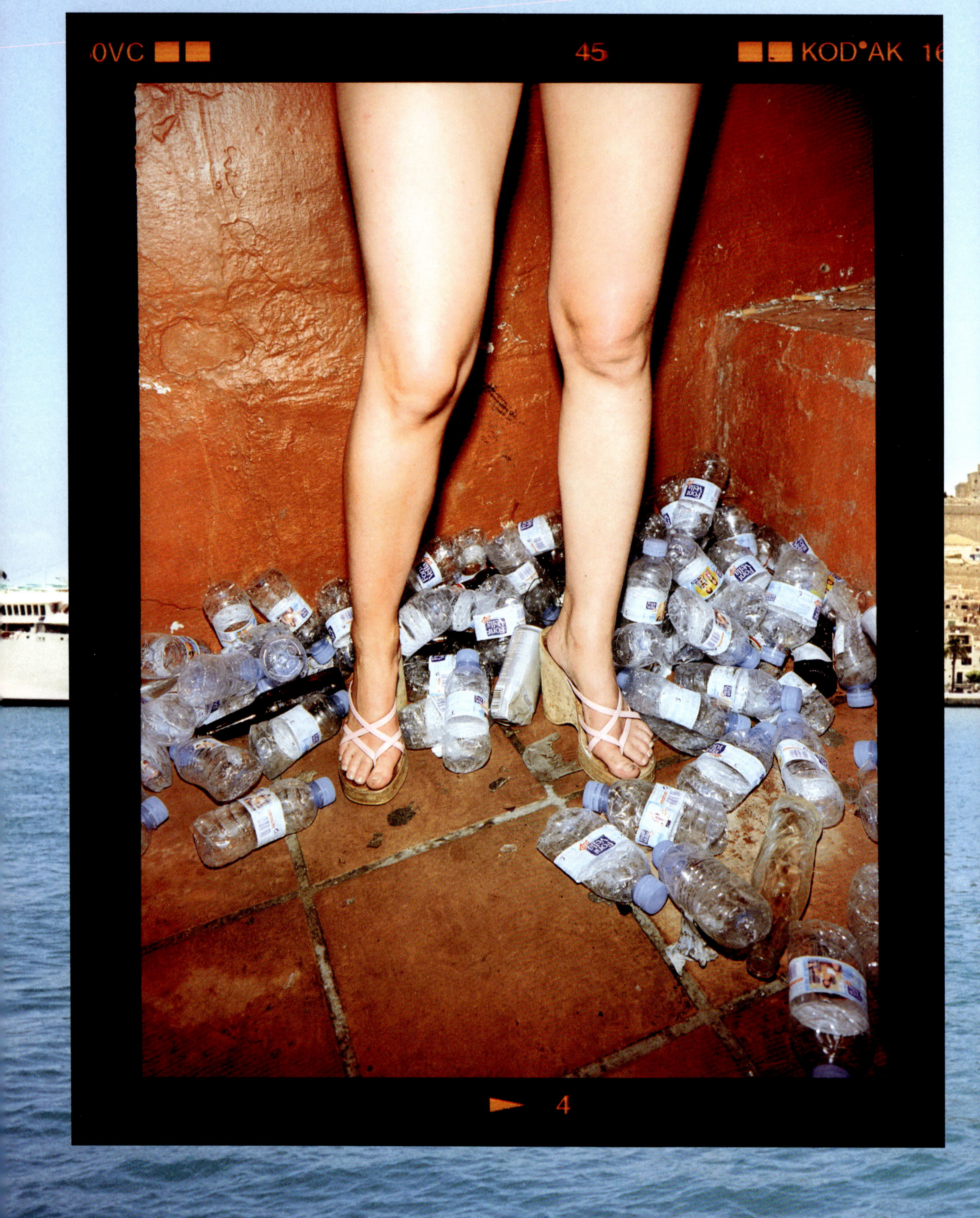

0VC
45
KOD°AK 16
4

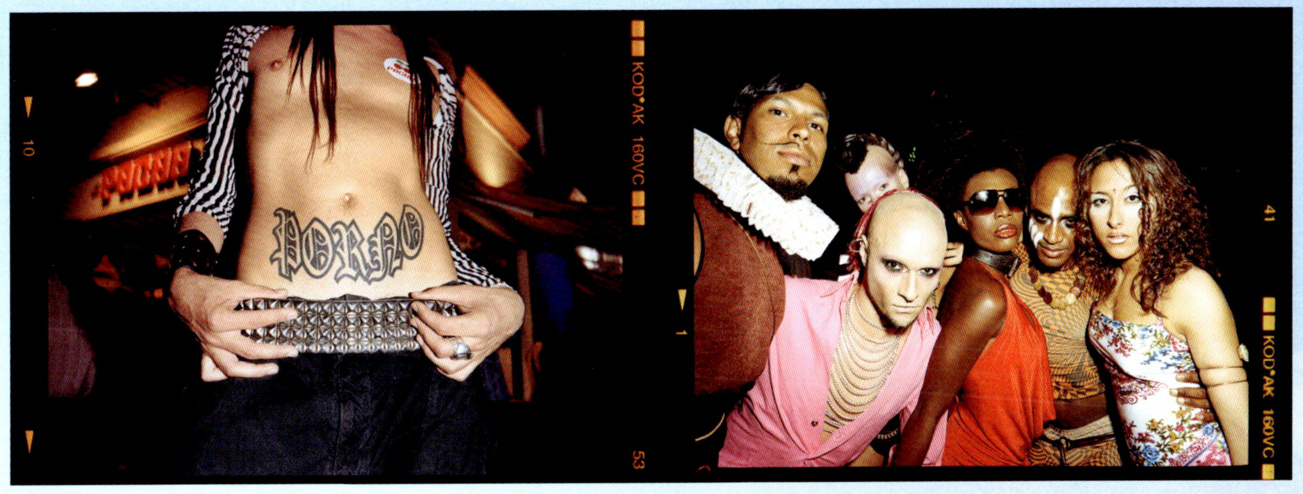

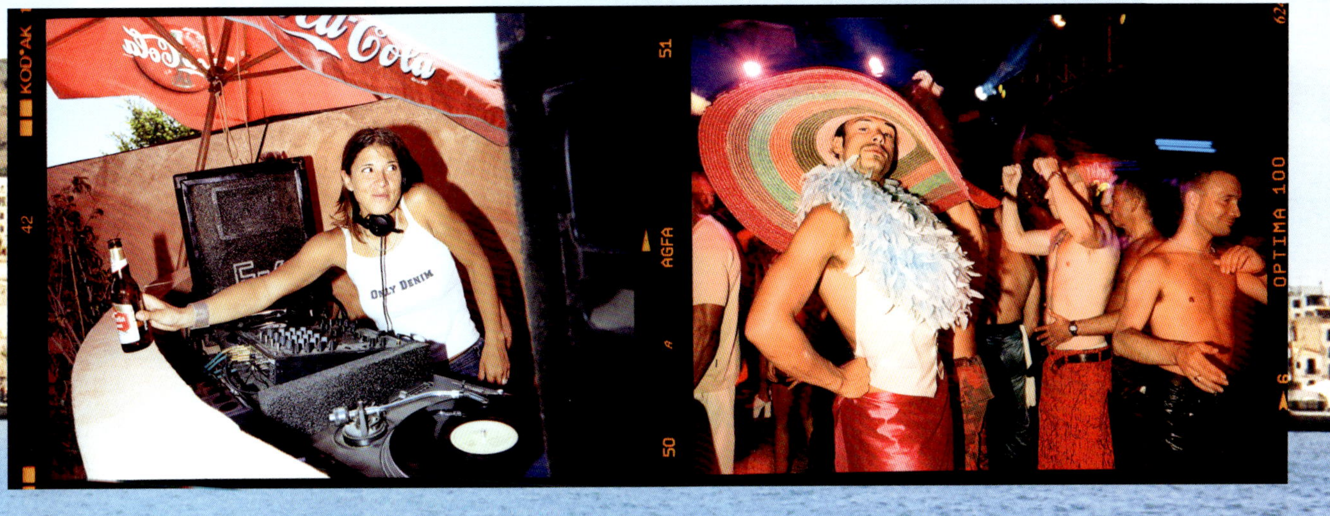

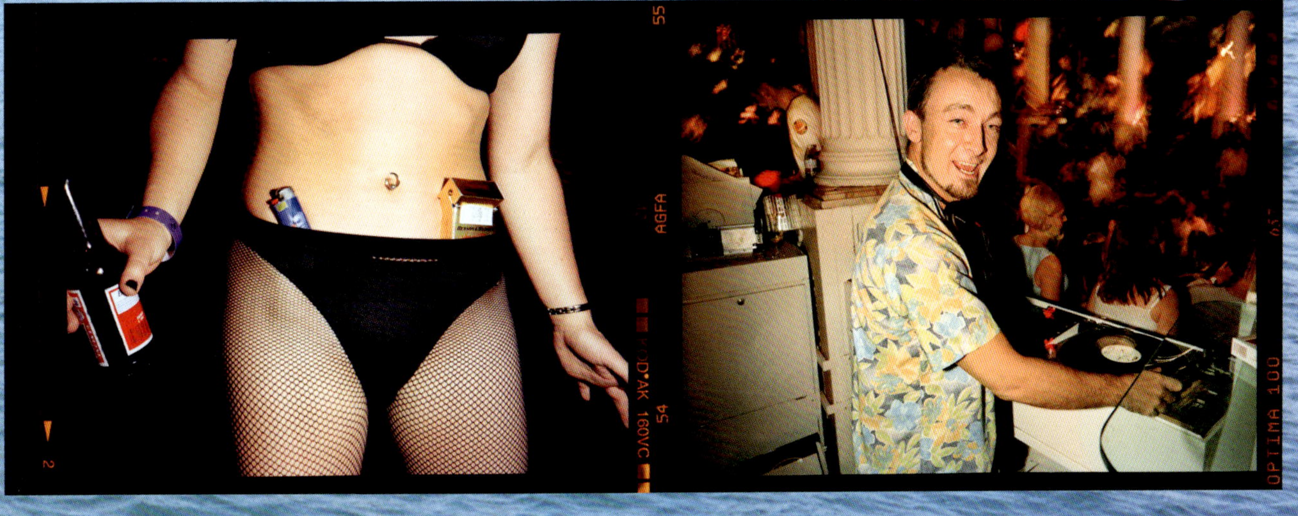

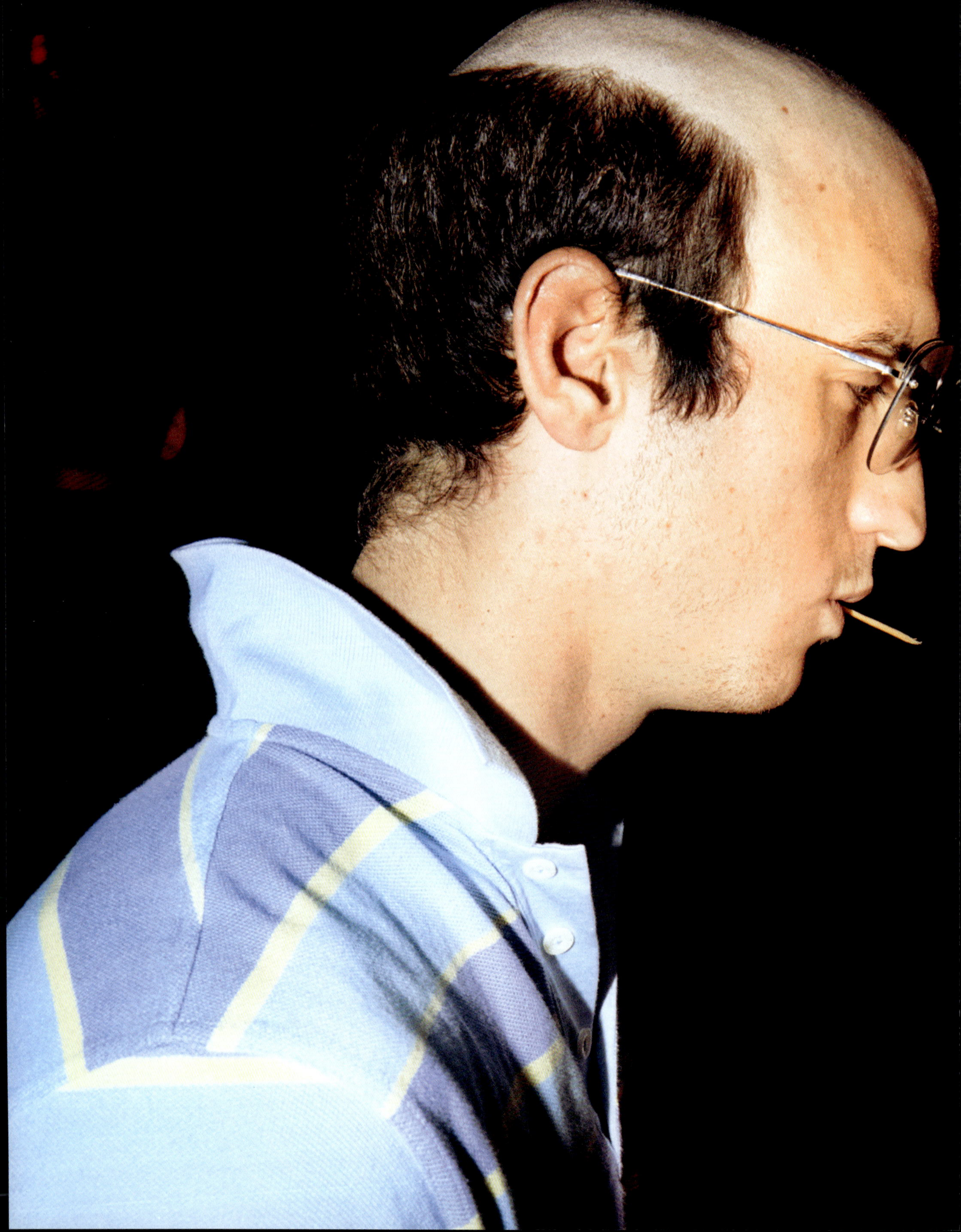

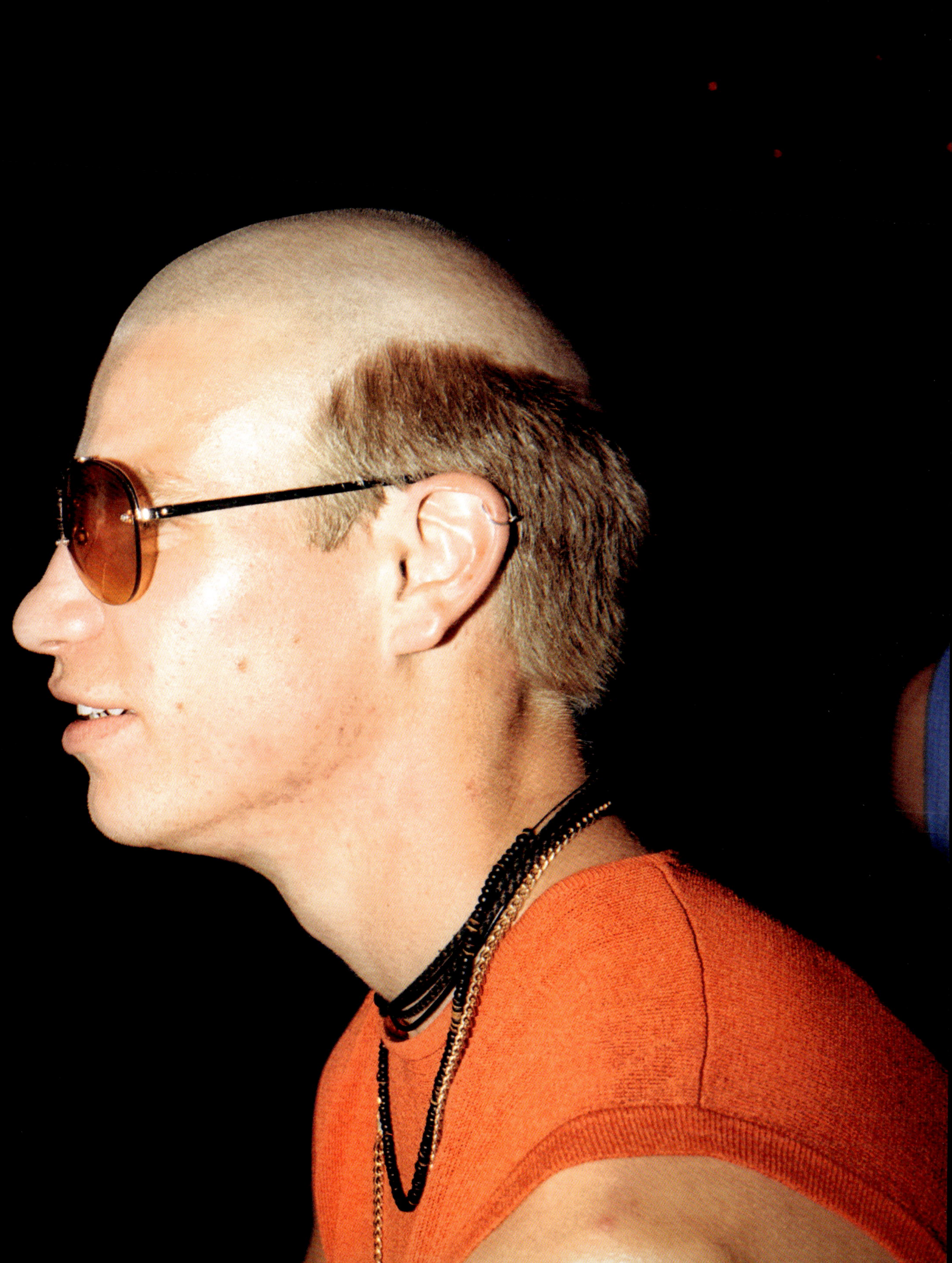

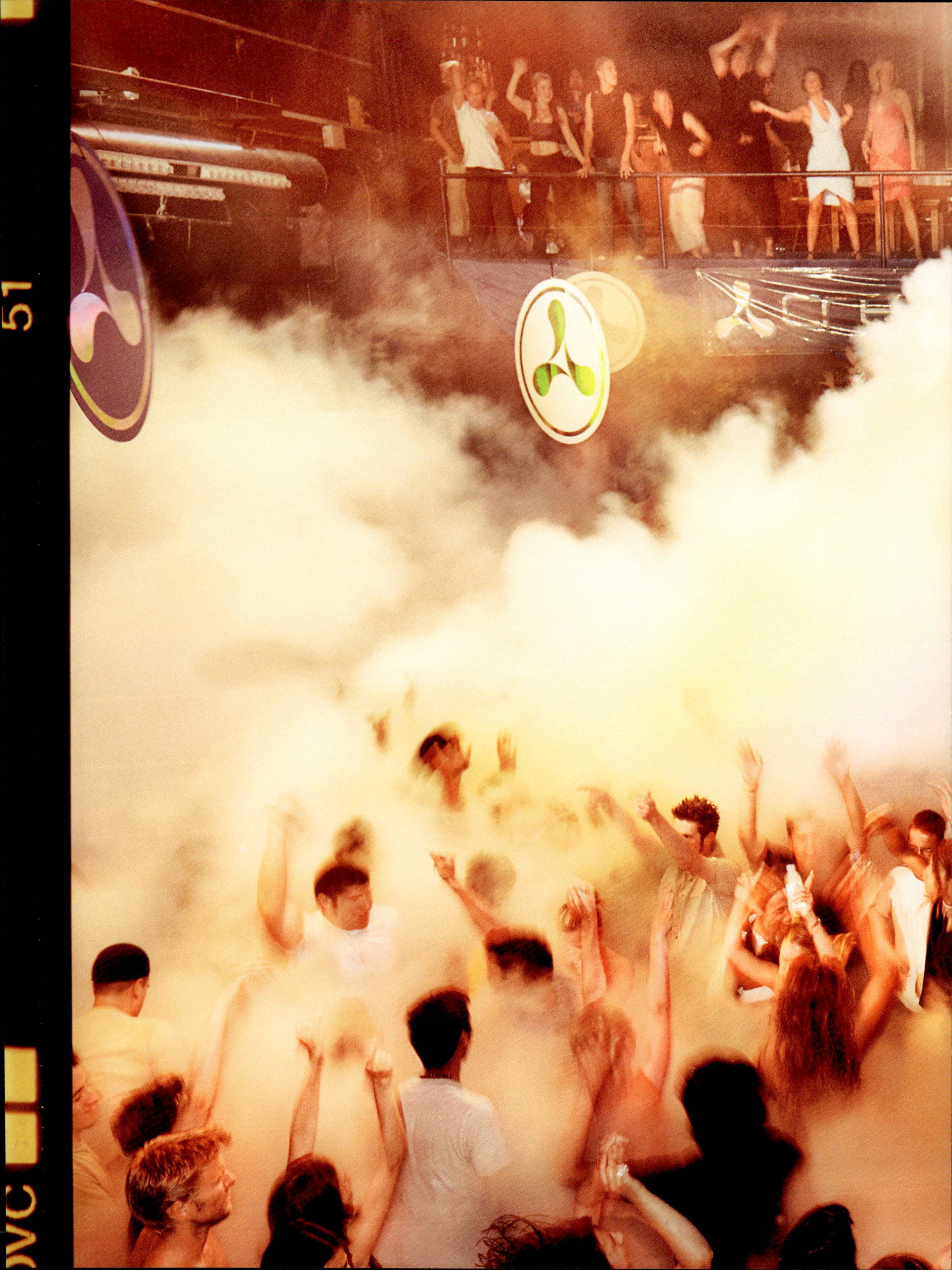

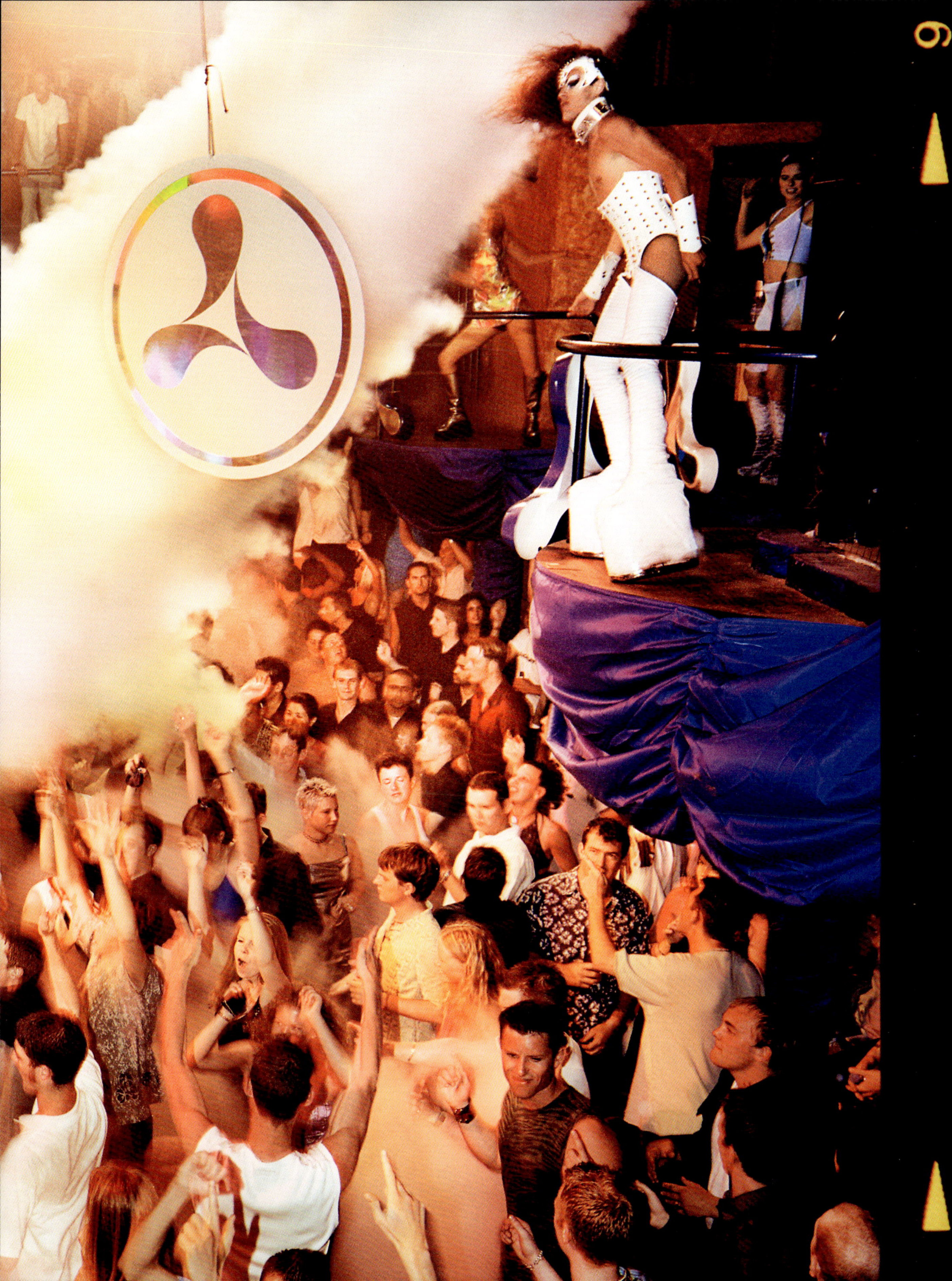

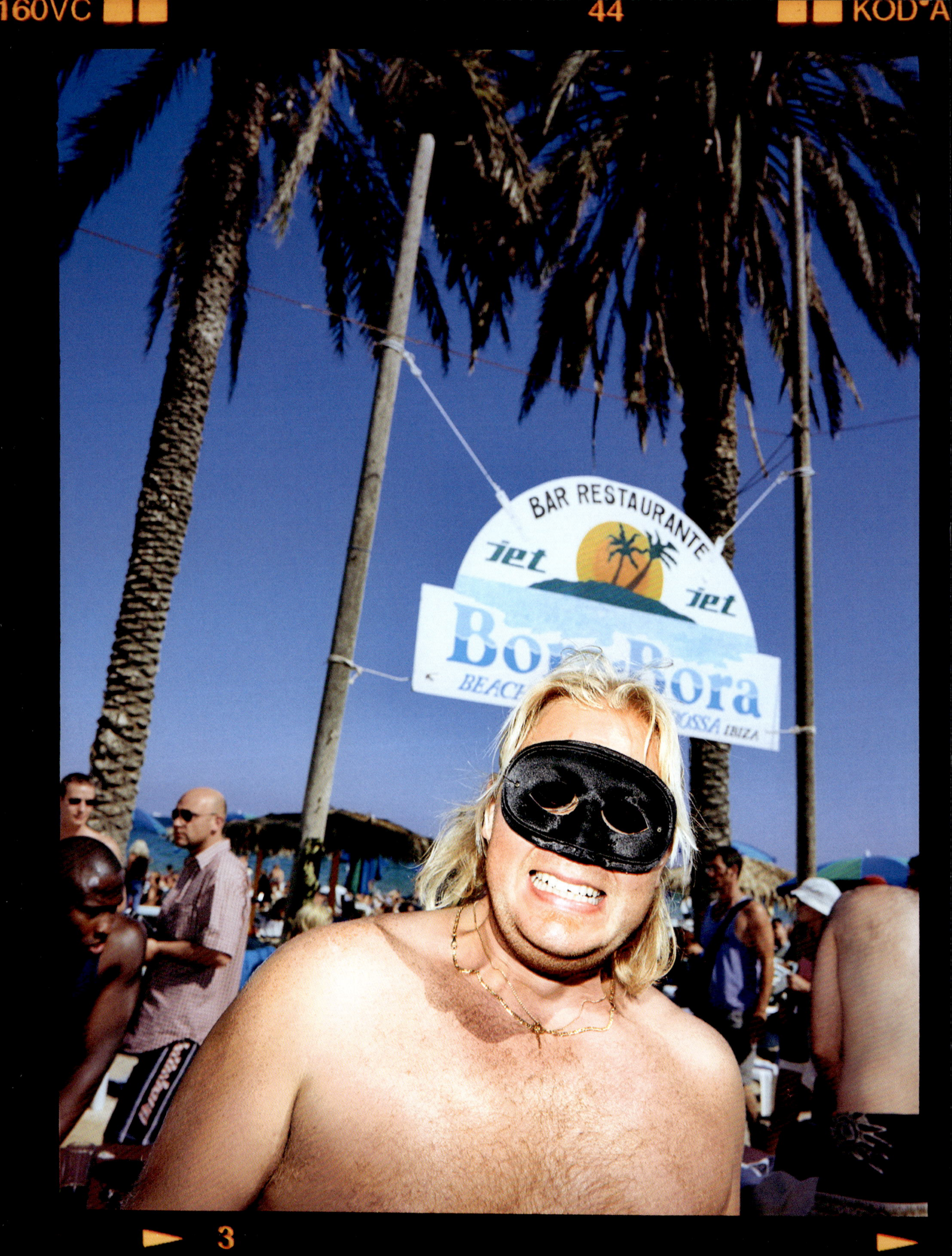

160VC 44 KOD A
BAR RESTAURANTE
jet jet
Bora Bora
BEACH
OSSA IBIZA
3

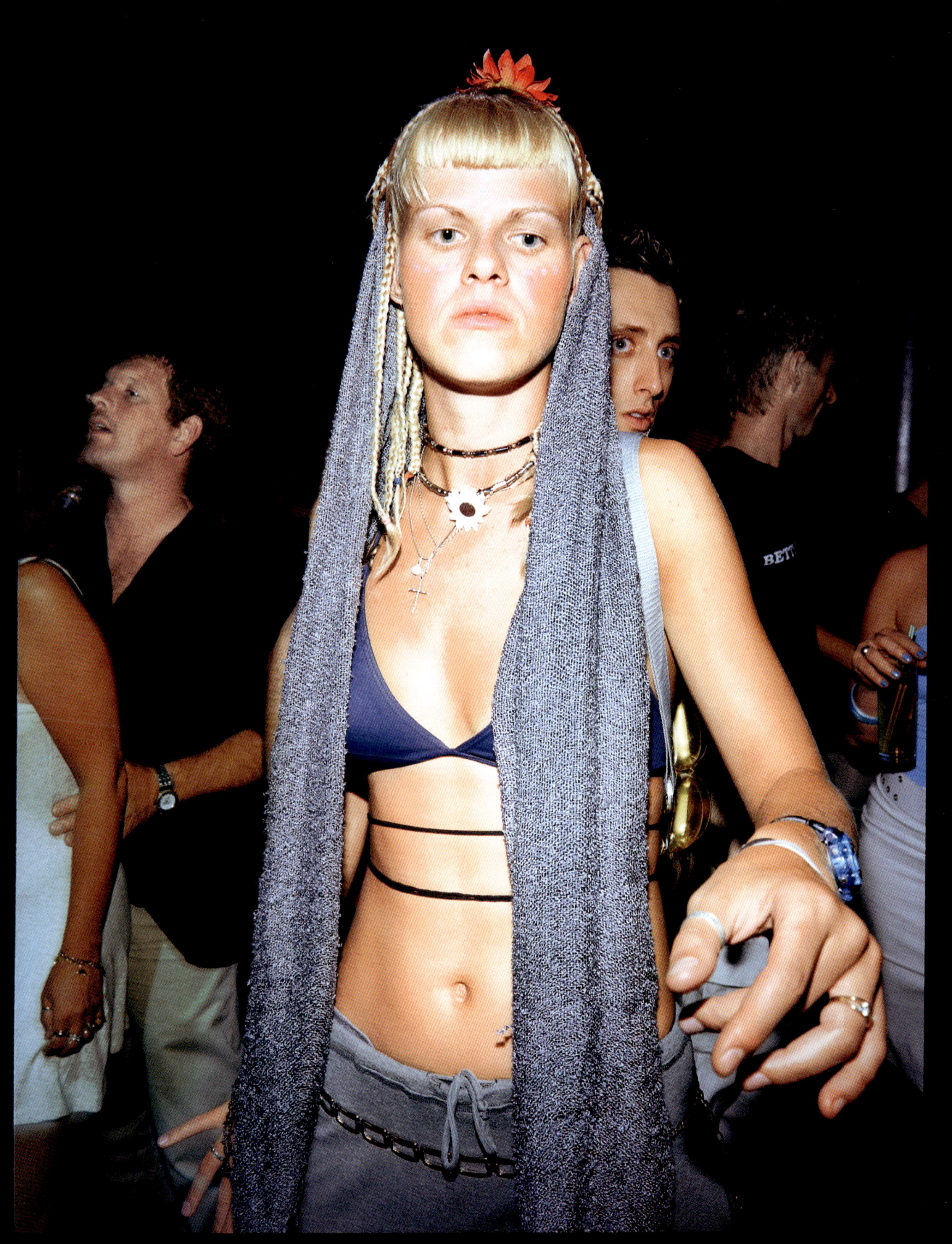
KODAK 160VC
50
8

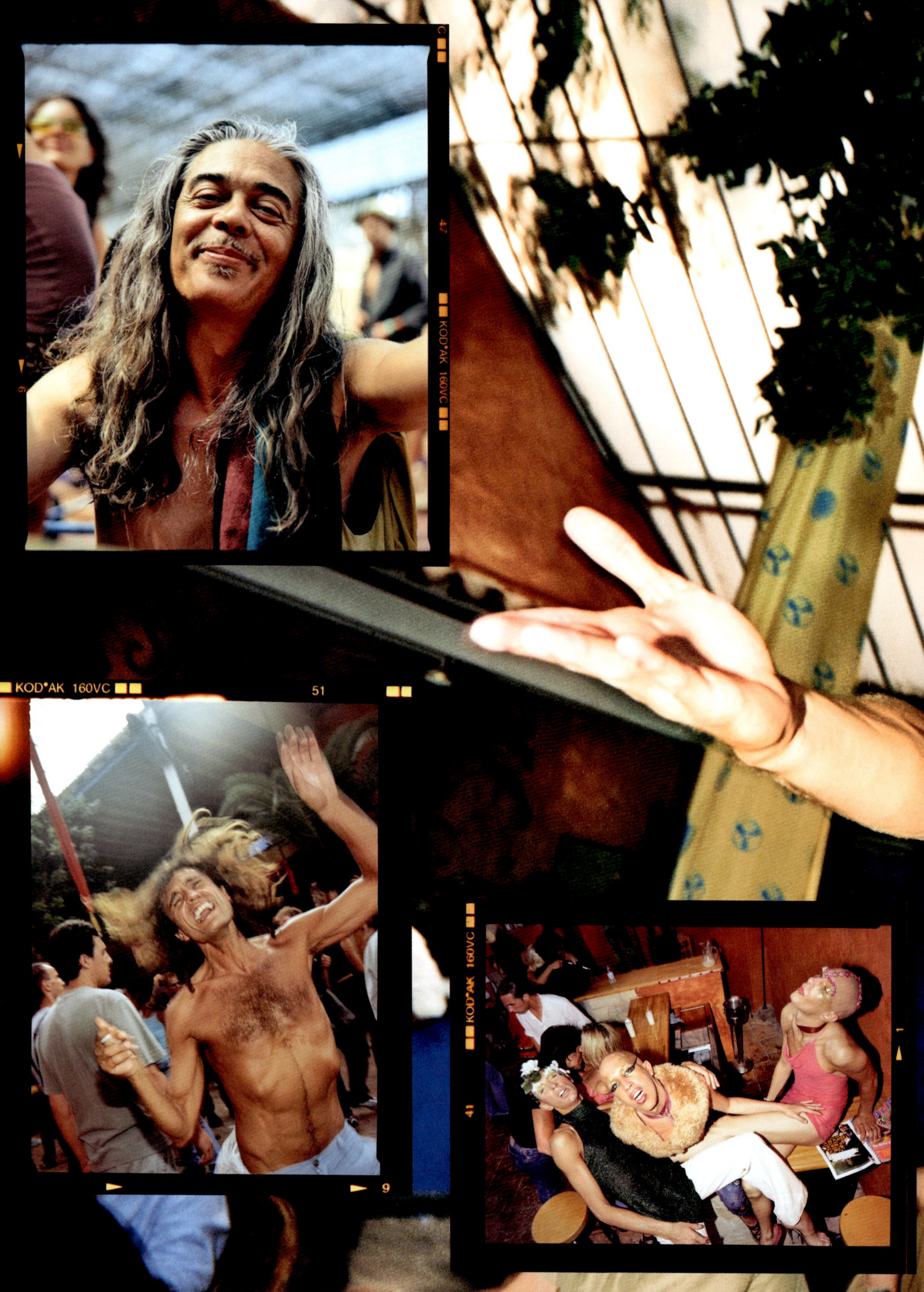

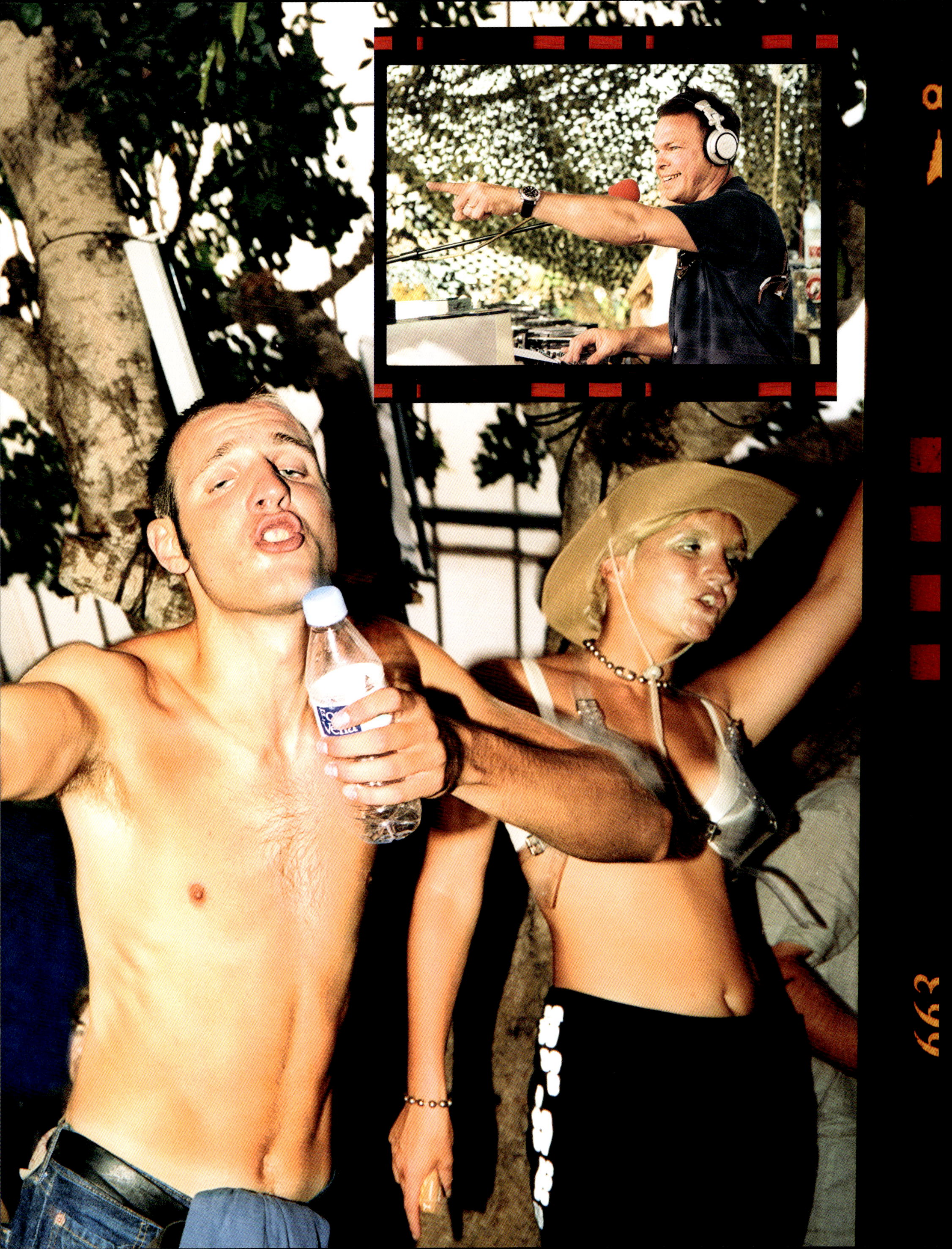

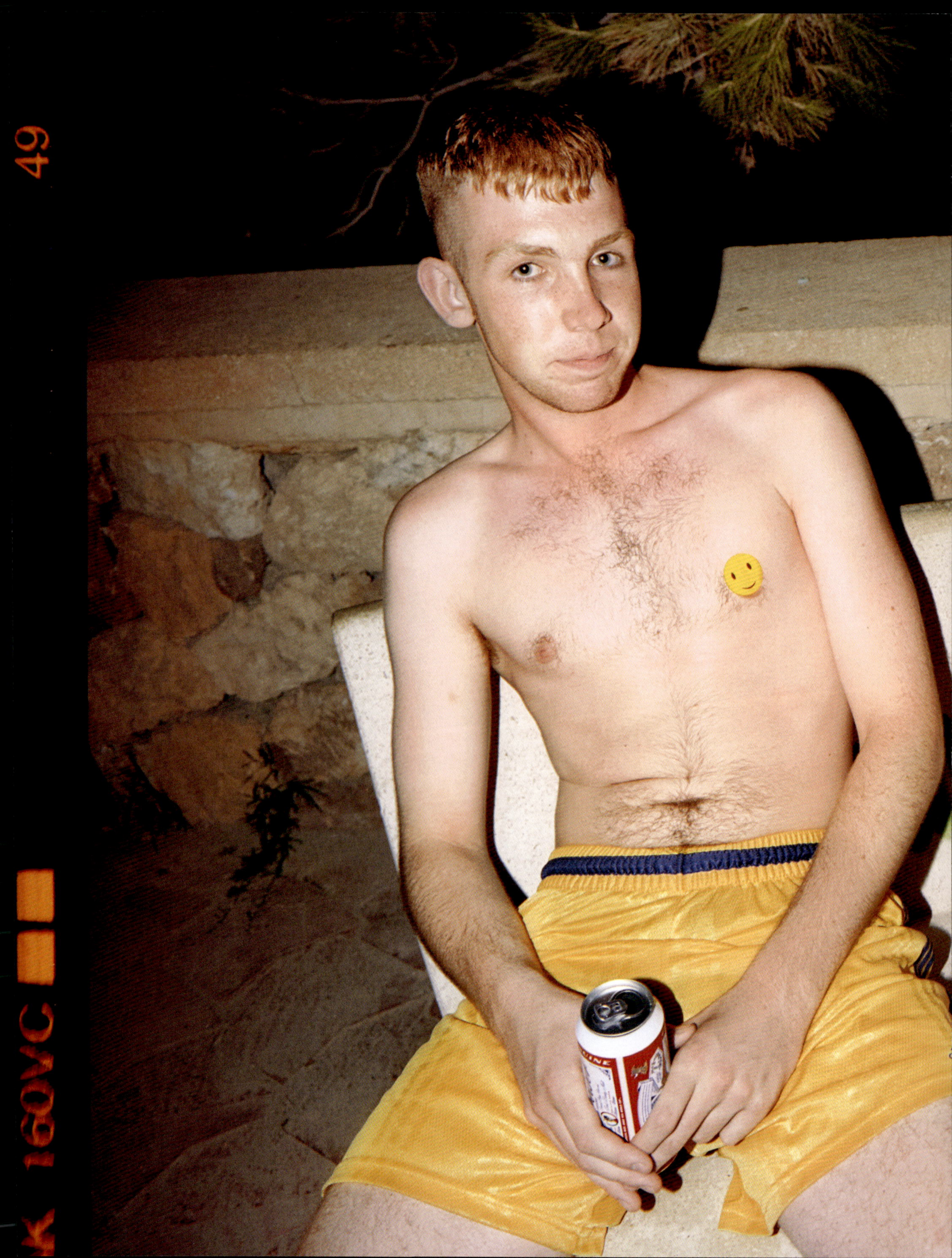

49
K 160VC

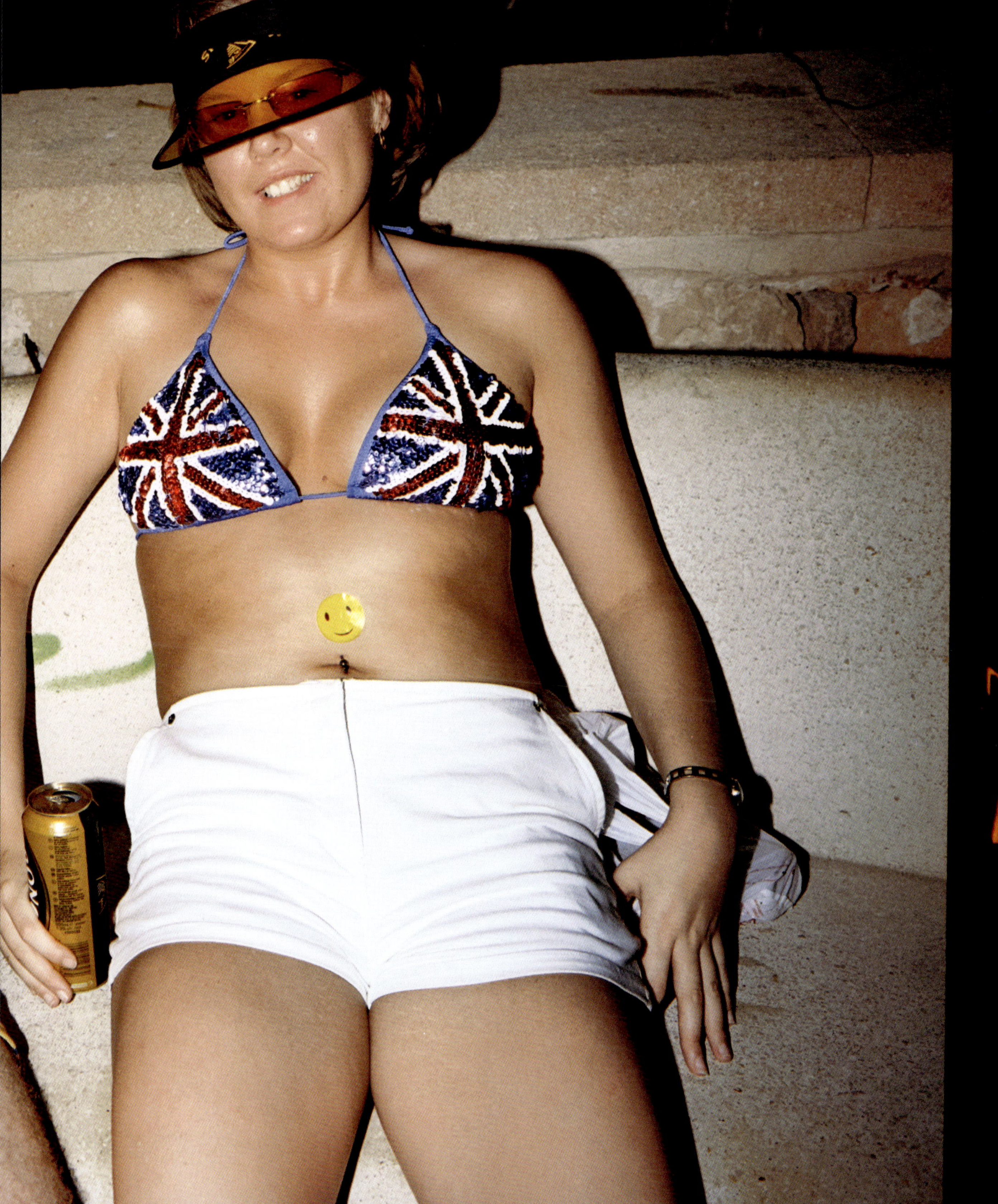

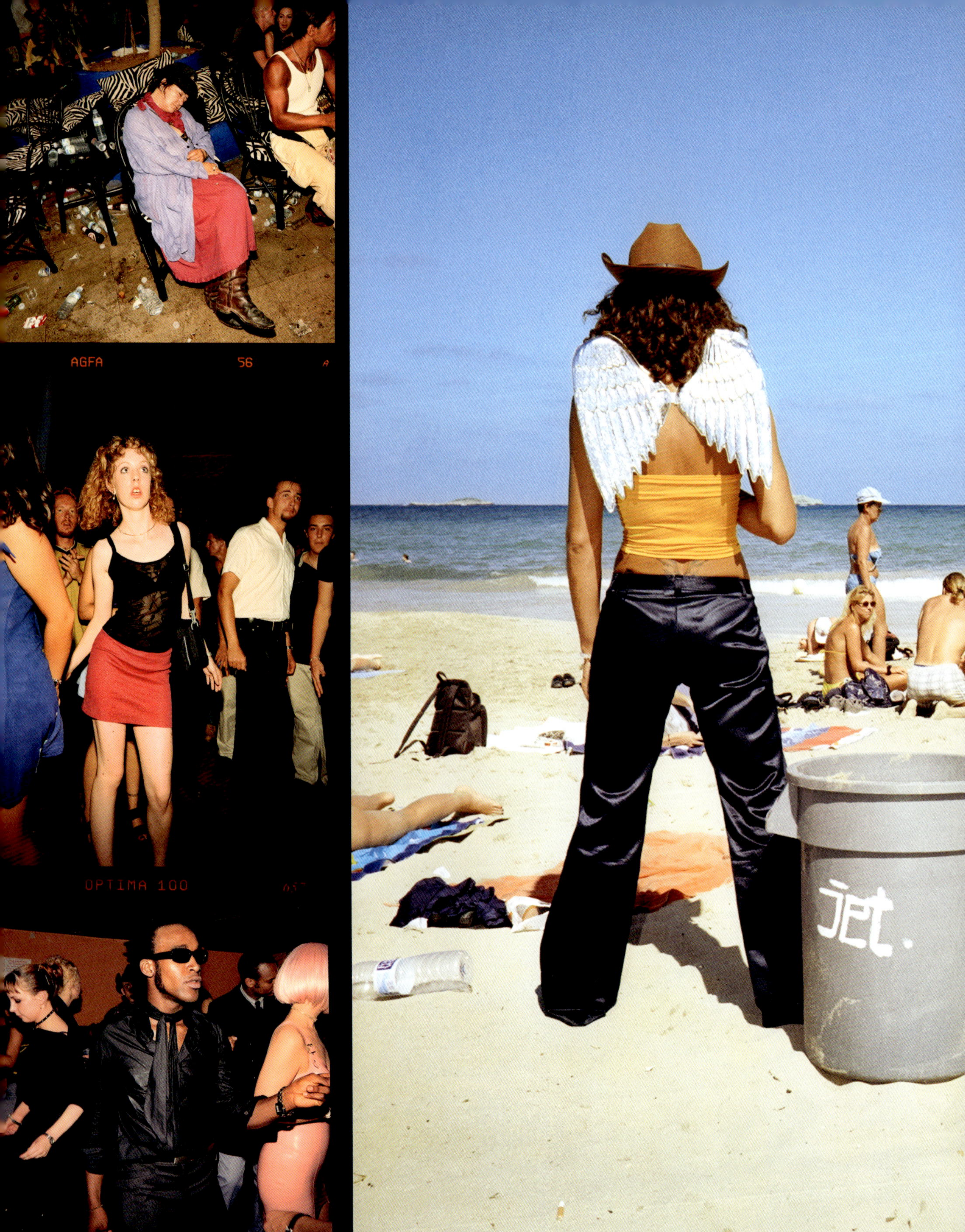
AGFA
56
OPTIMA 100
JET.

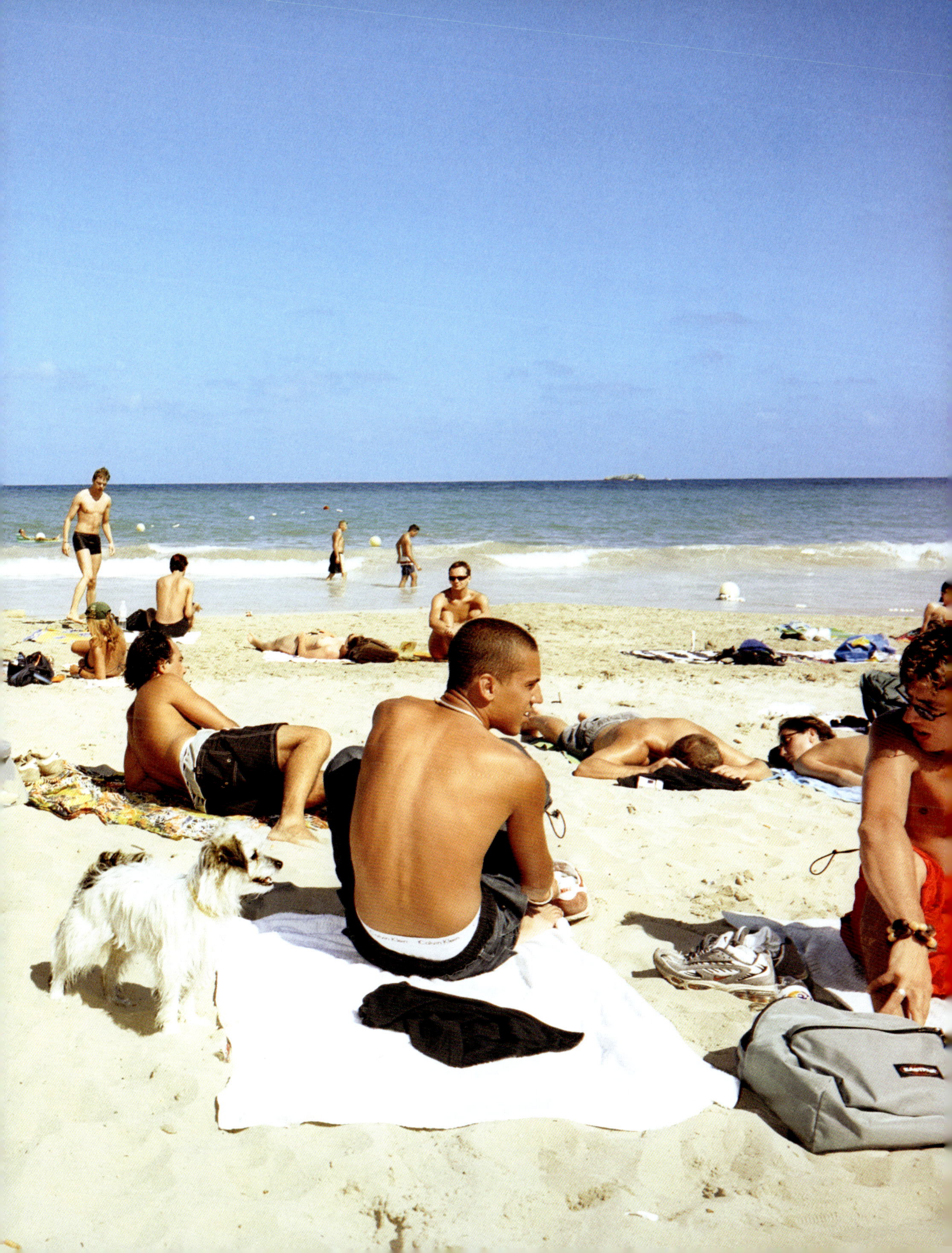

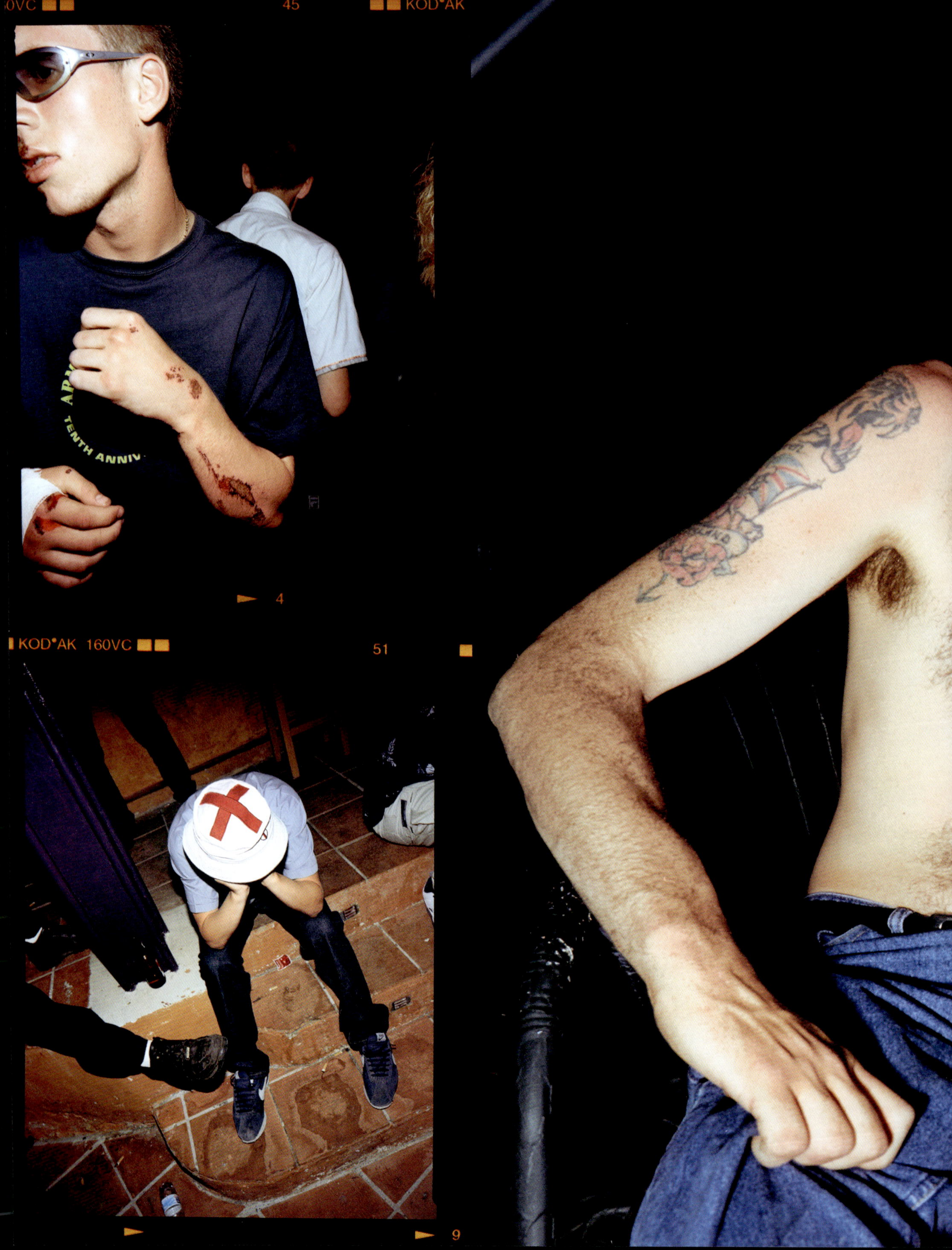

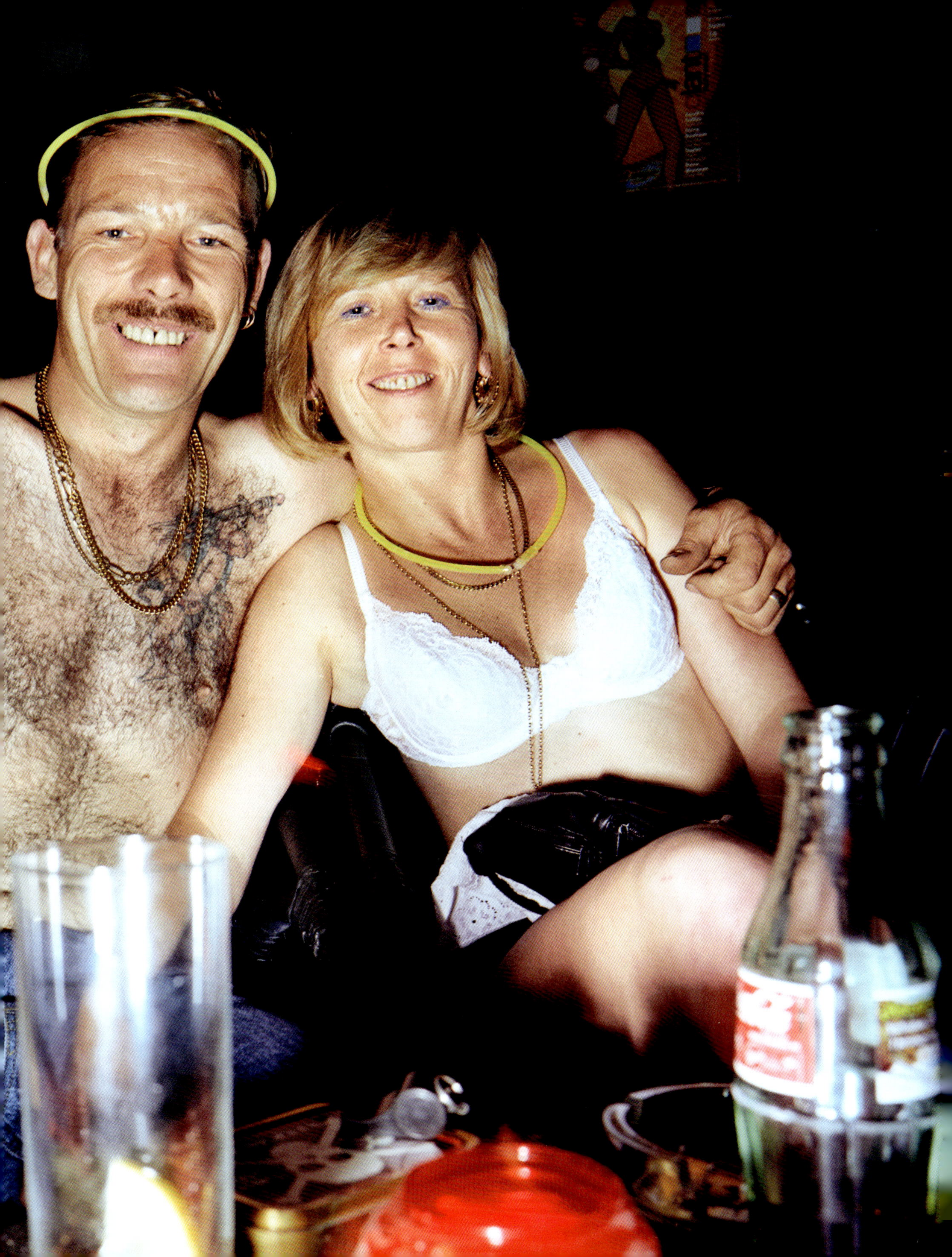

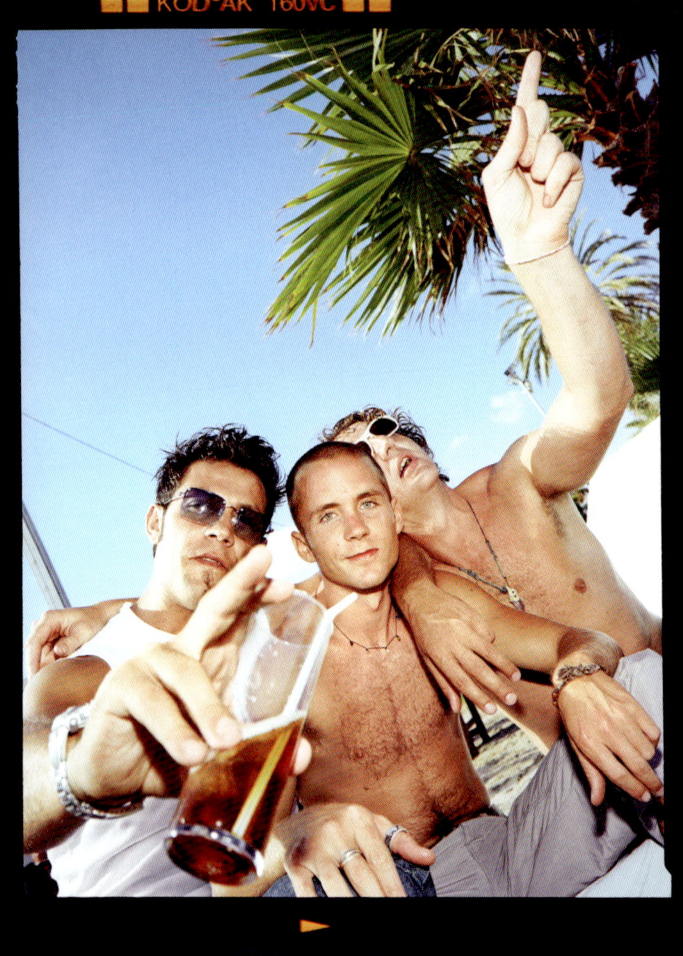
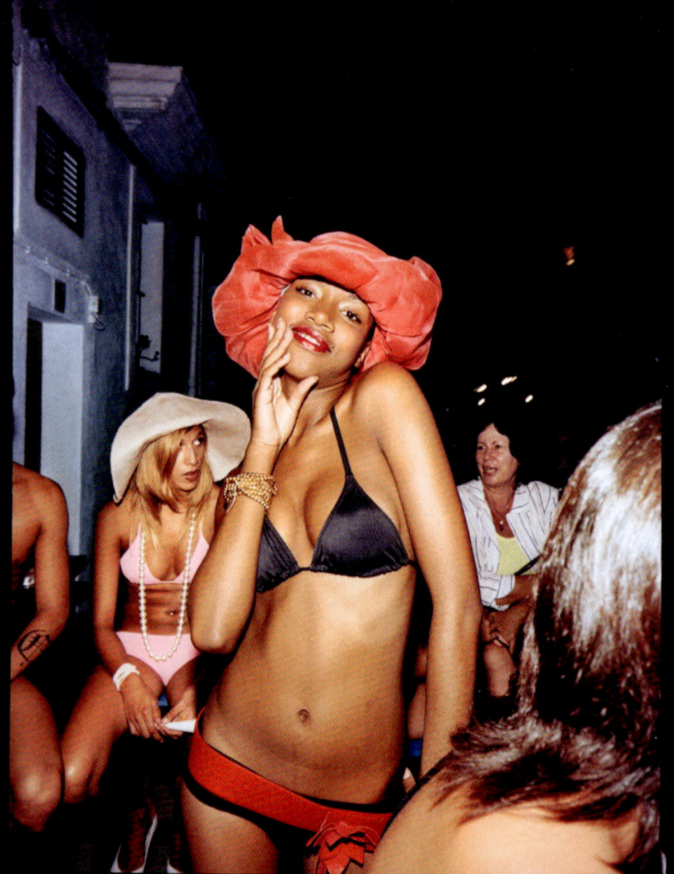
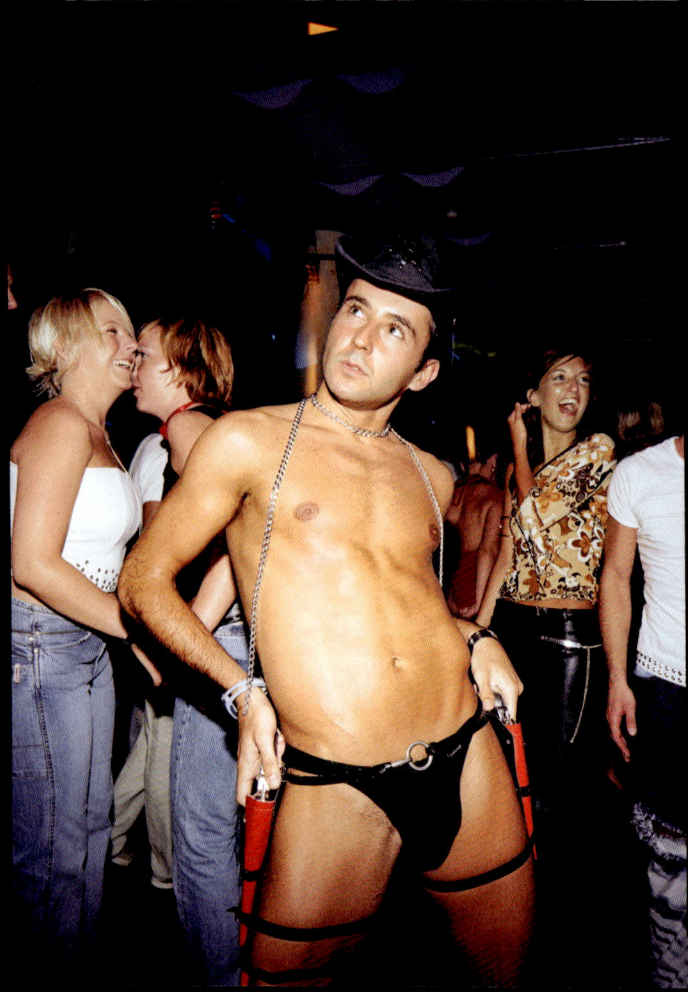
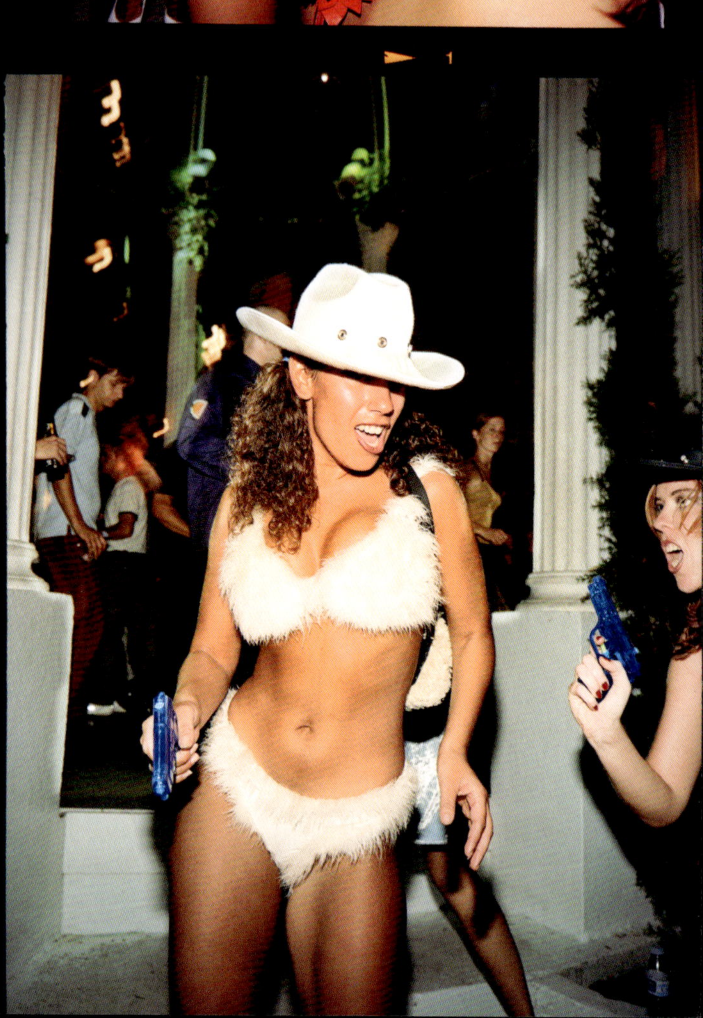

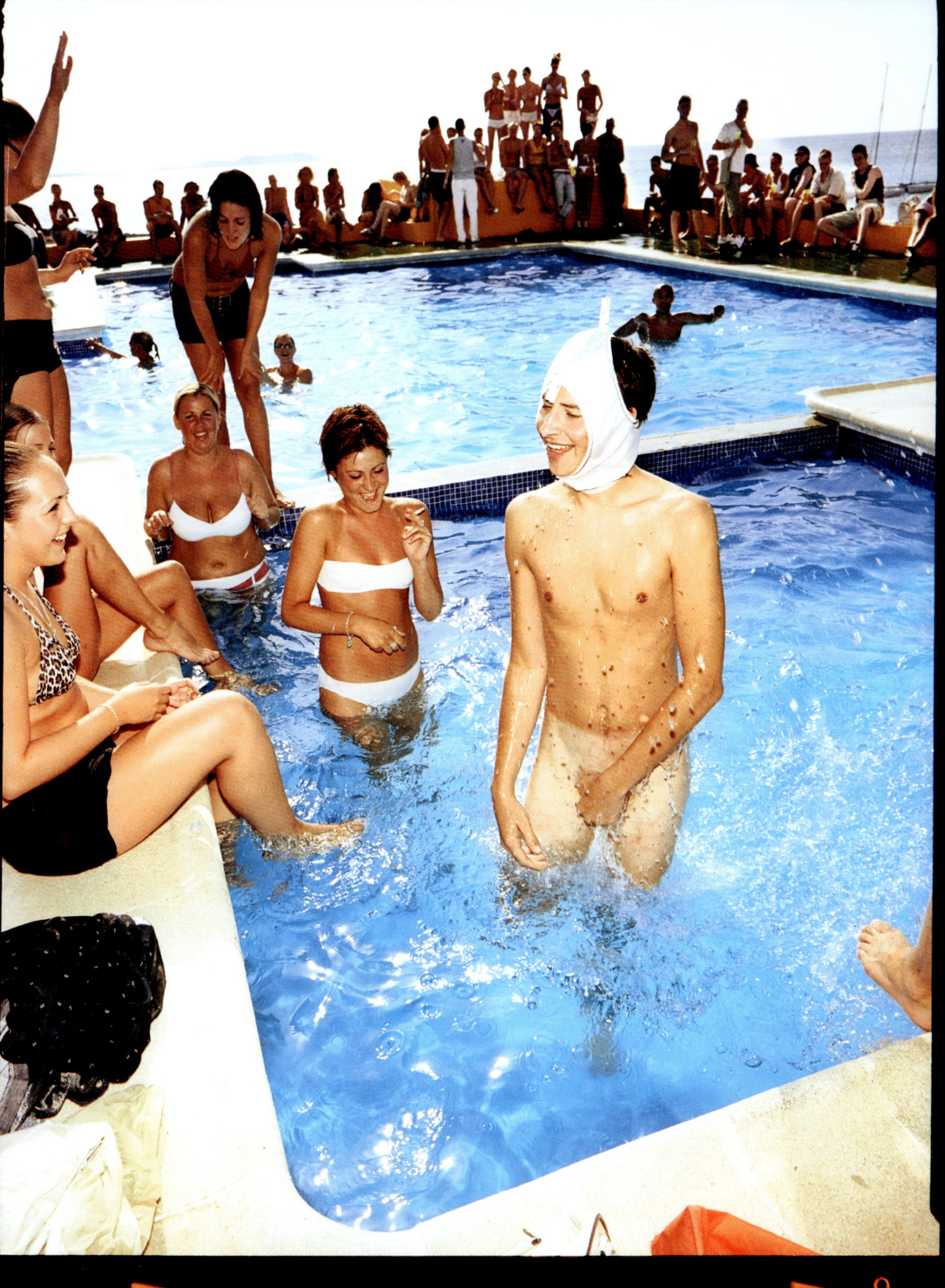

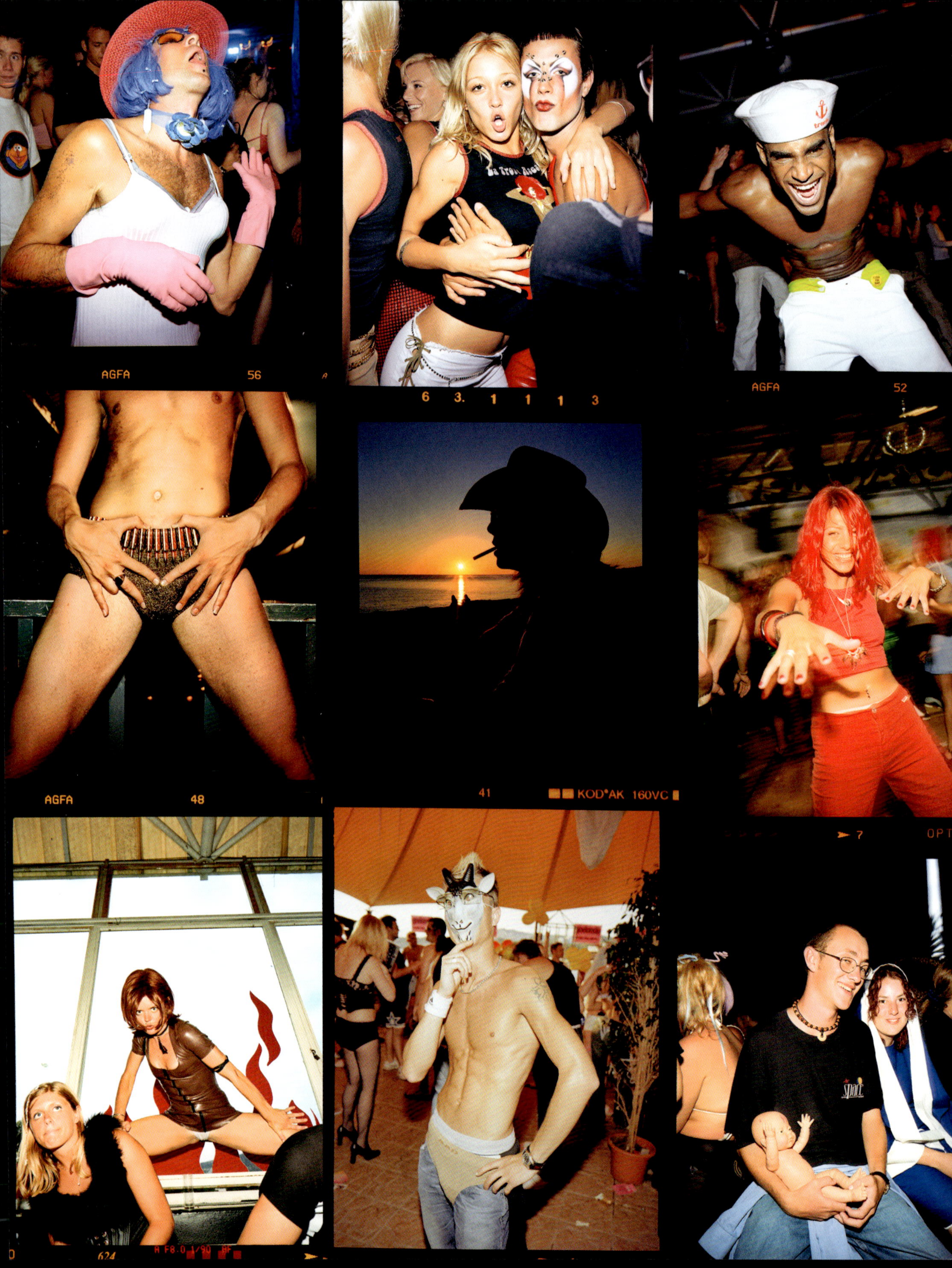

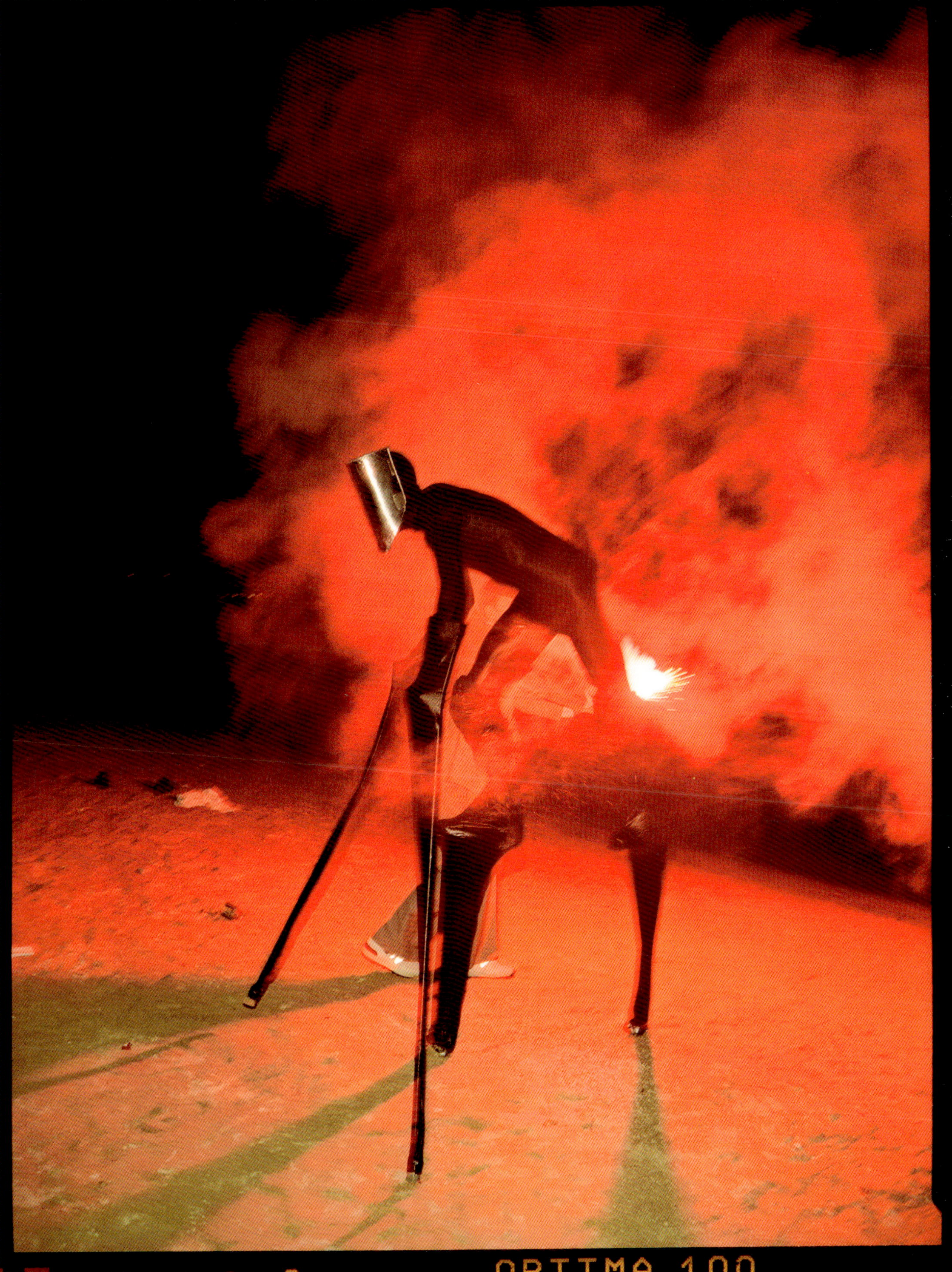

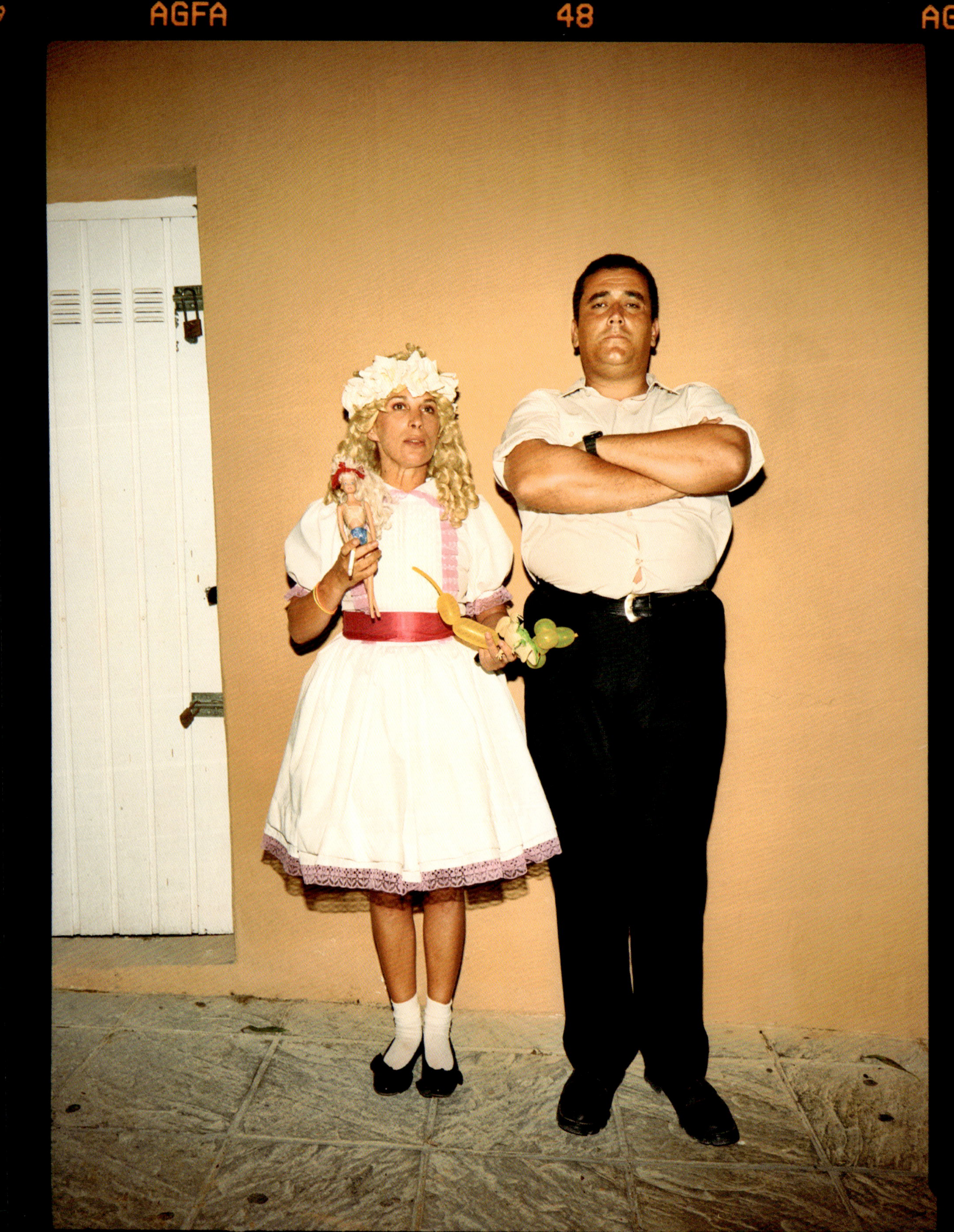
AGFA
48
AGF

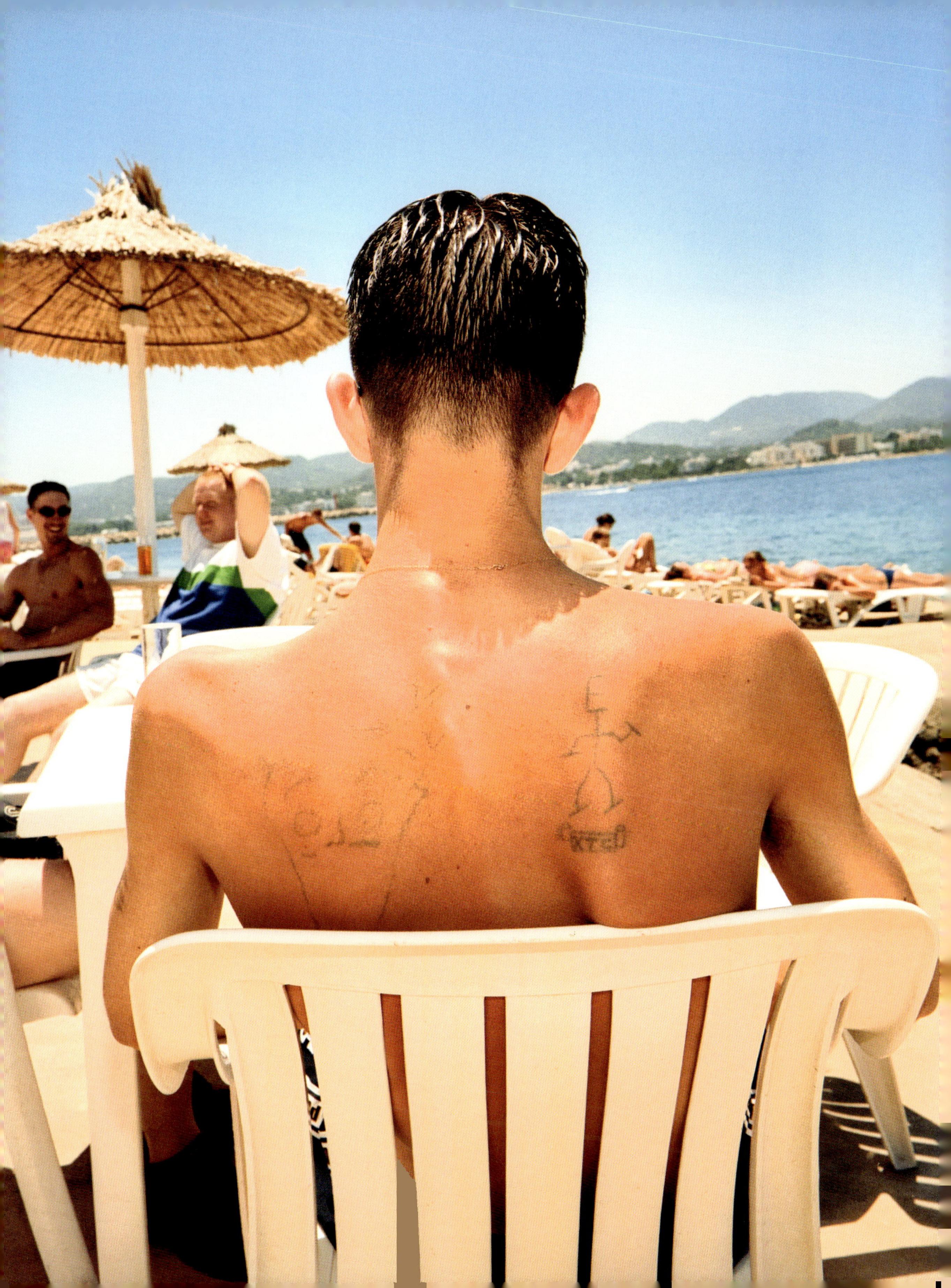

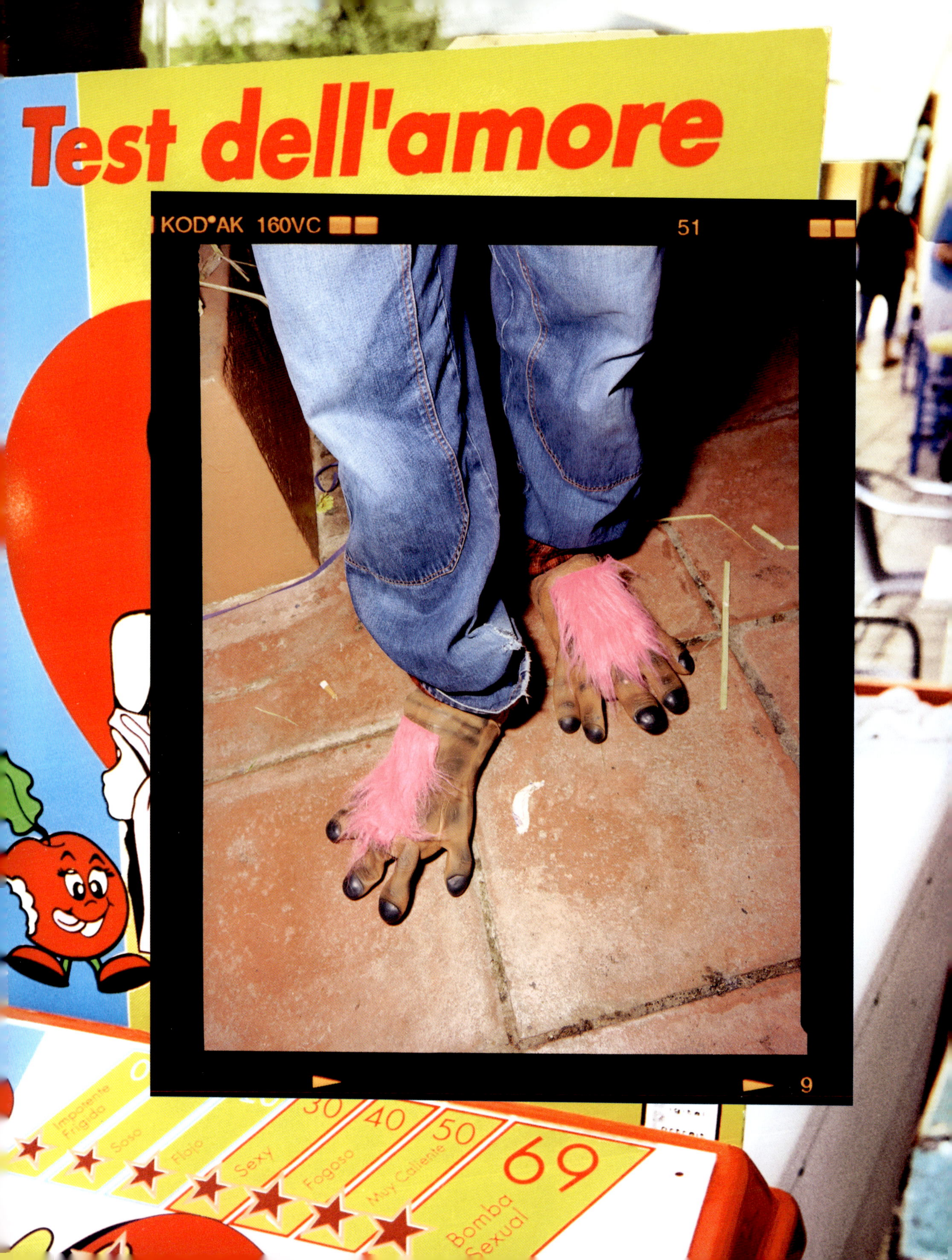
Test dell'amore
KOD*AK 160VC   51
9
Impotente Frigida
Soso
Flojo
Sexy
Fogoso
Muy Caliente
69
Bomba Sexual
30 40 50

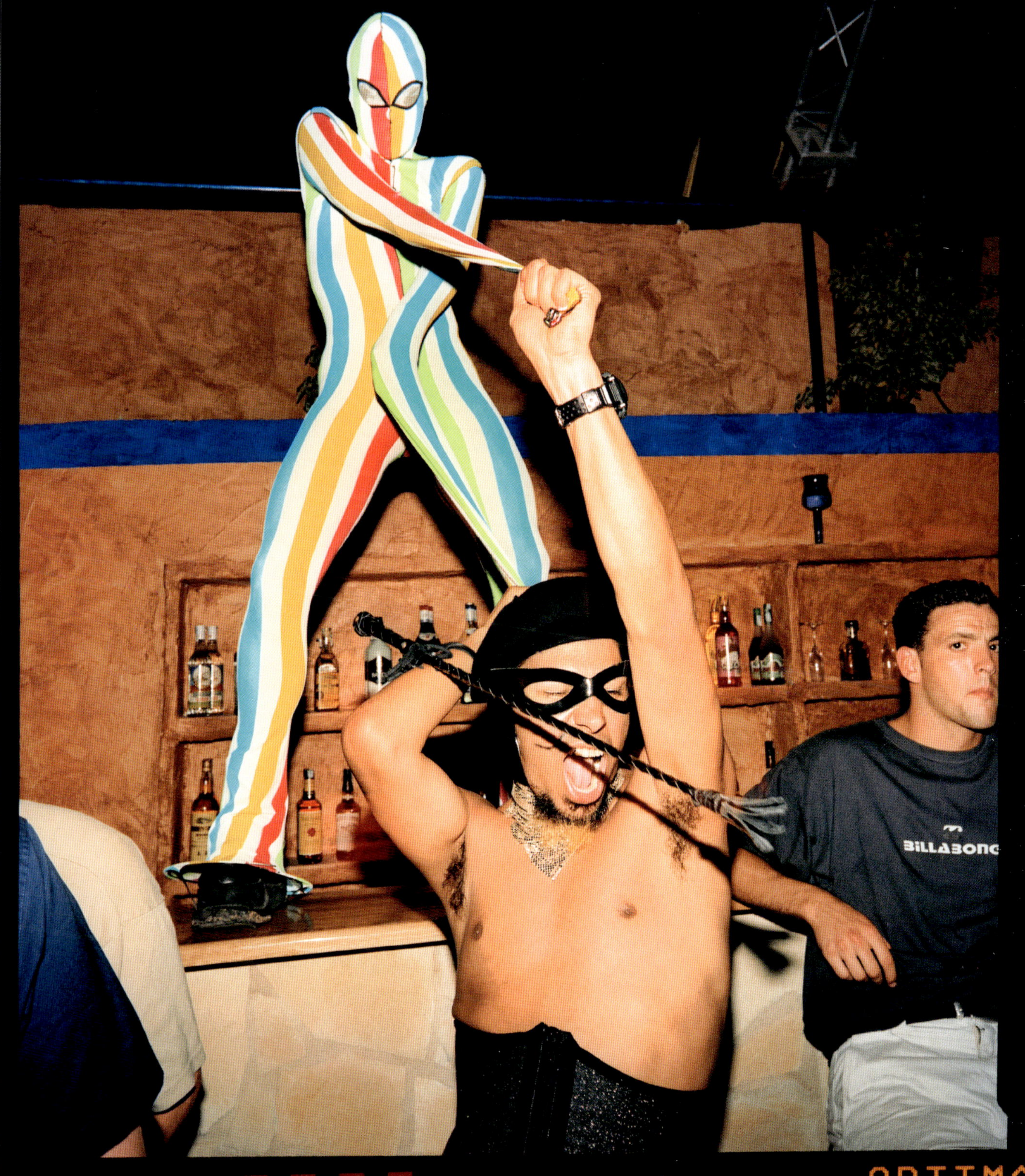
BILLABONG
60
4
OPTIMA

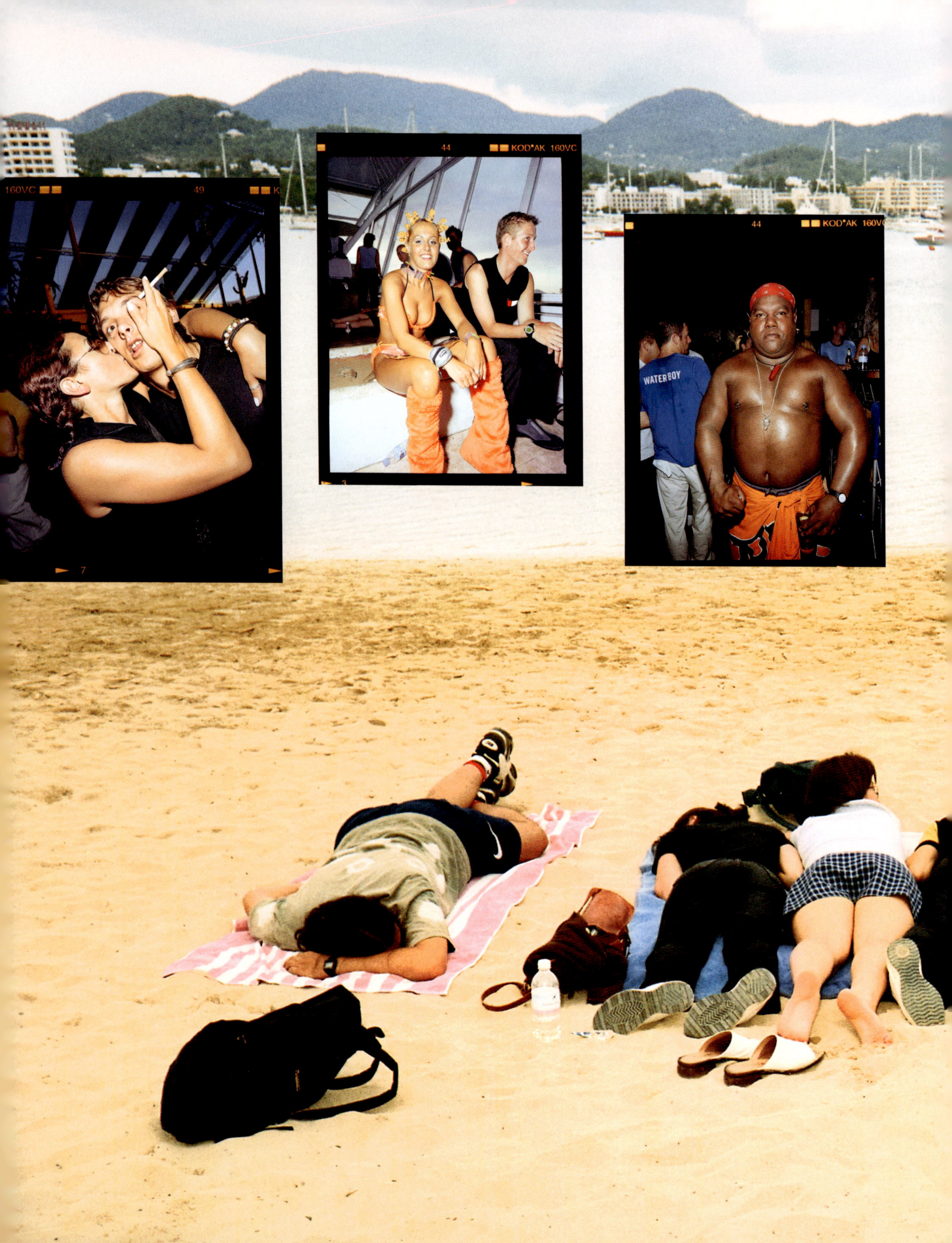

160VC
49
KOD*AK 160VC
44
WATER BOY

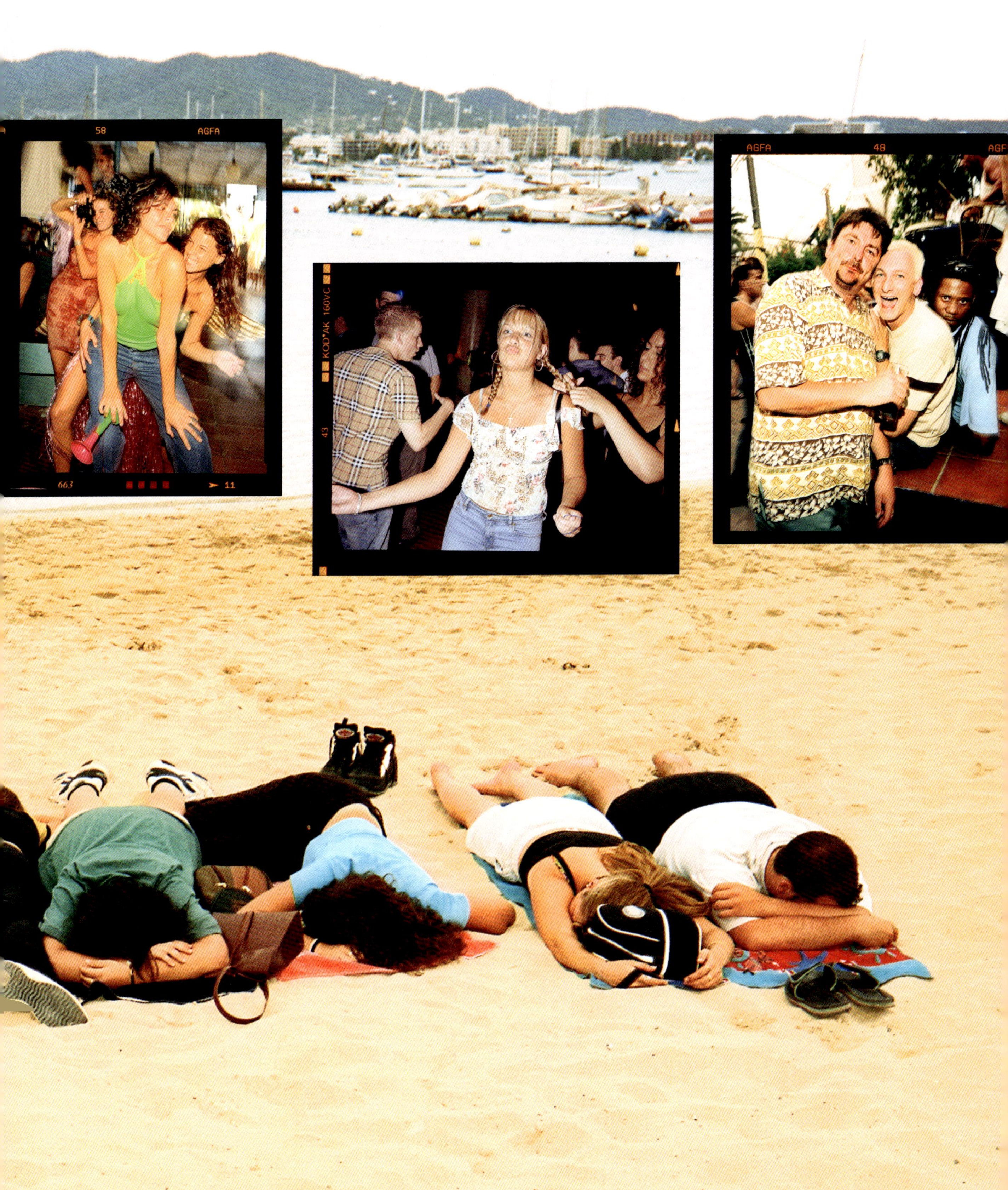

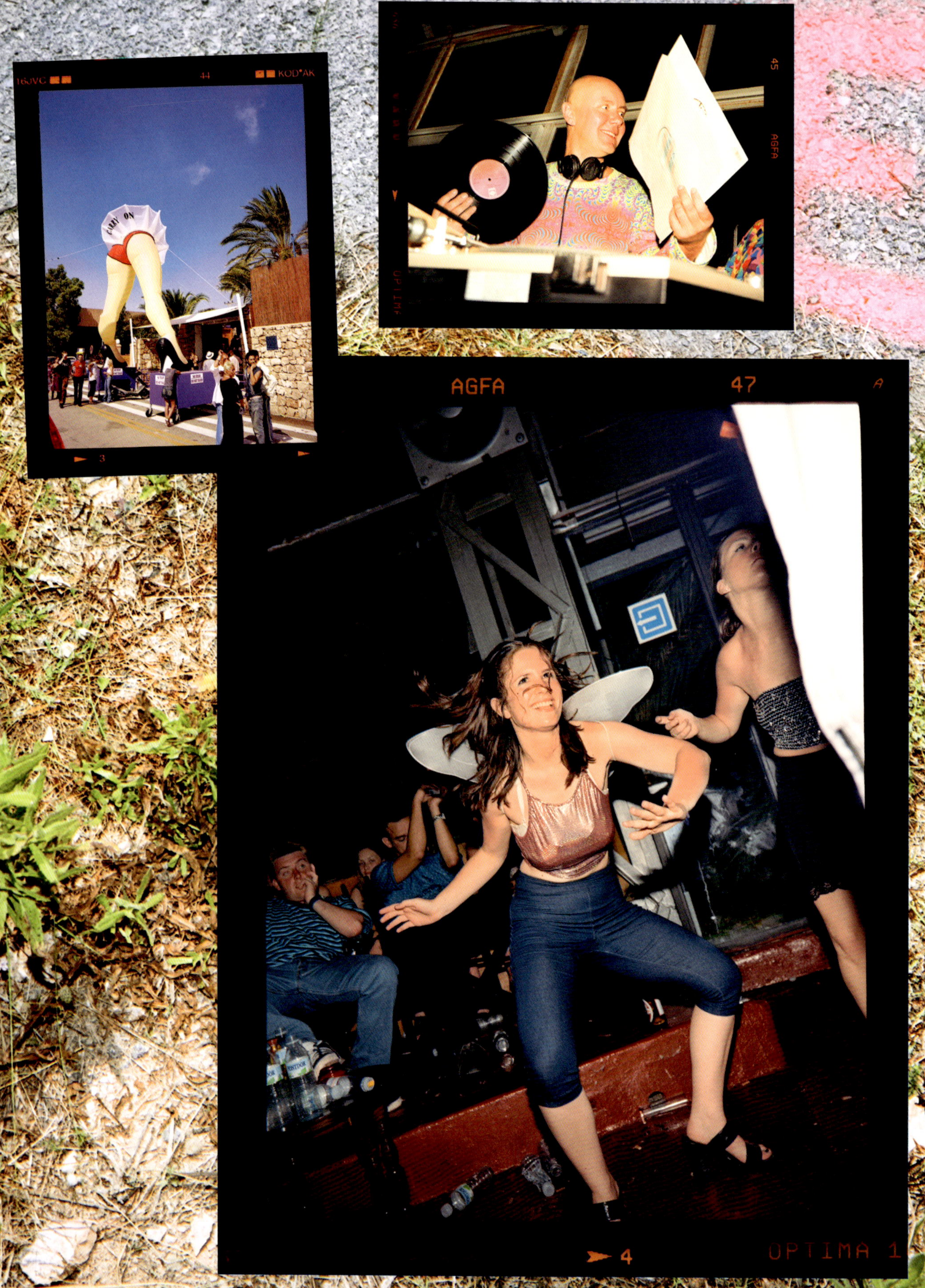

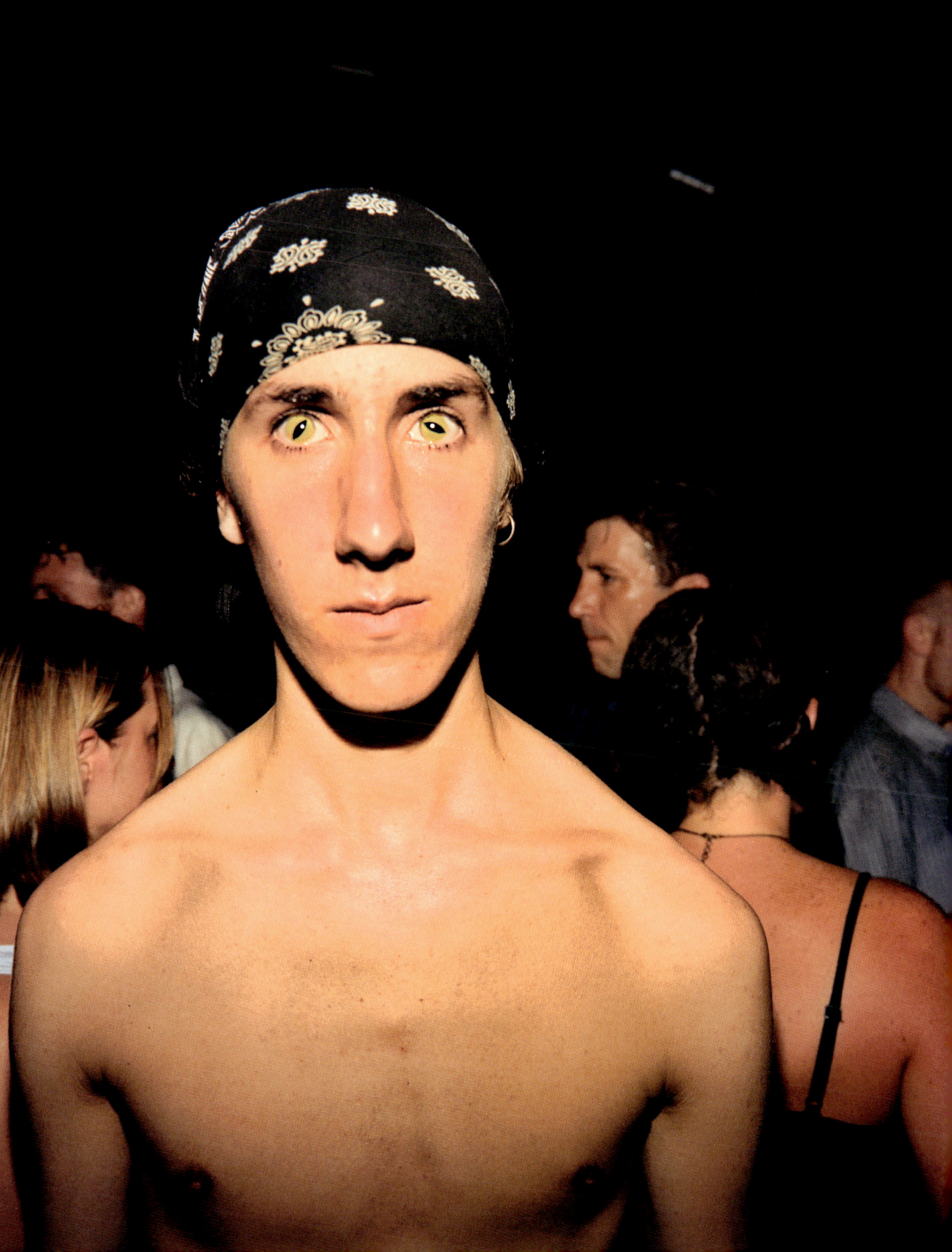

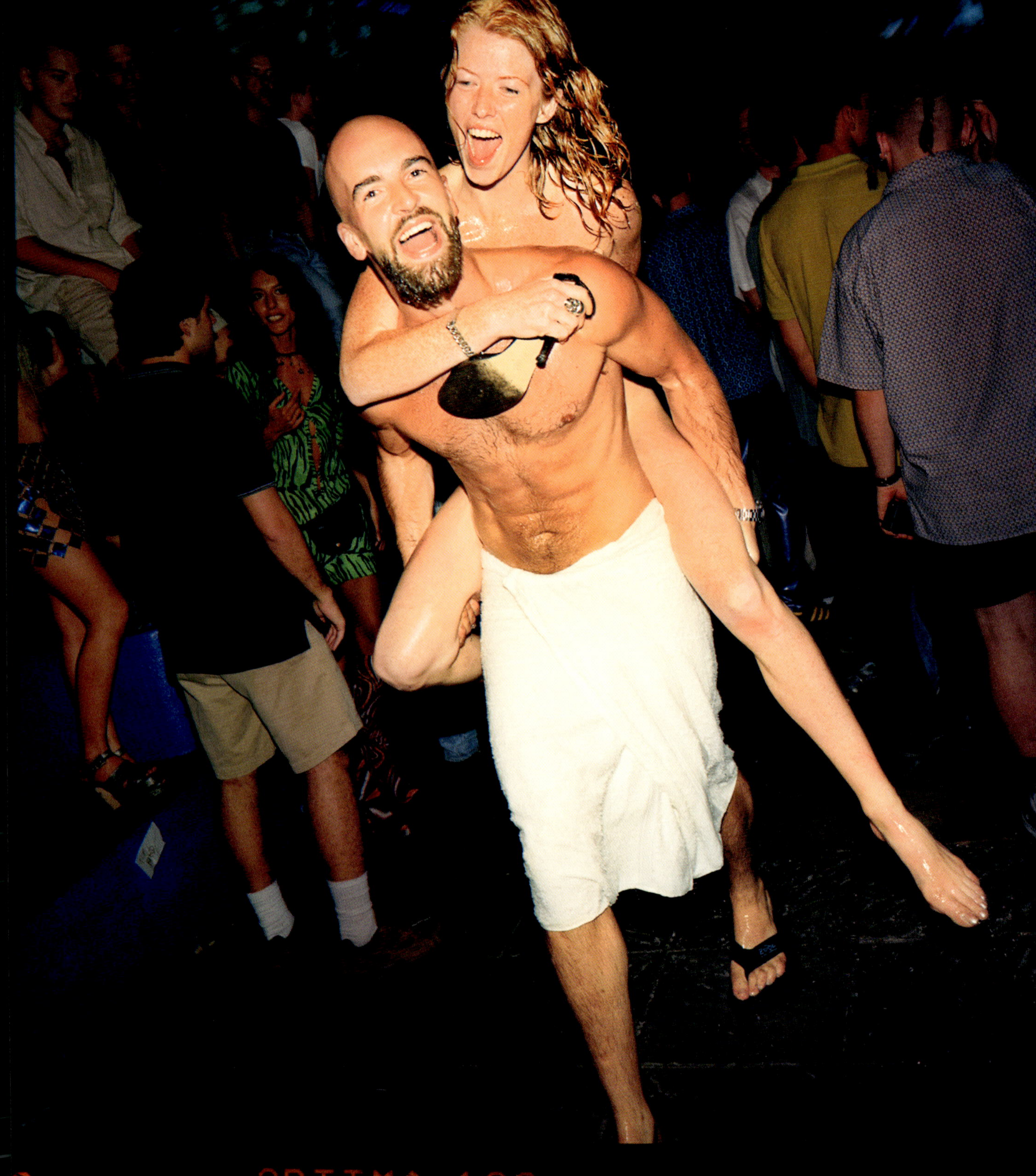
OPTIMA 100

MIKE & CLAIRE MANUMISSION

It was important to us to affect people. Shock them. Inspire them out of whatever reality they came from and just show them that there was another possible way to live, to work, to be.

All of our artistic concepts were autobiographical. There was a love and harmony that flowed through our work and our team – our core collaborators from the photographer to the dancers, acrobats, chorus line and erotic icons to the hand-selected DJs – and that resonated.

Dean Chalkley was there to capture the transition in our art from what might be perceived as wild hedonism with 'Murder at the Manumission Motel' to theatre for the masses. The secret is that it was always an expression, a reaction to the world we saw around us. From anti-violence, to Nostradamus, to fears of cloning. Manumission was our medium. It was about immersive storytelling, creating a world, a night, an ephemeral moment that our audiences would never forget.

VAUGHAN 'AFRI' AFRIKA

Having spent my early years partying in London and New York, nothing prepared me for the lunacy that met me when I first arrived in Ibiza, 1982, on a short holiday. Being a party animal and flamboyant character, I knew directly that this, the Black Sheep Island, was the place for me.

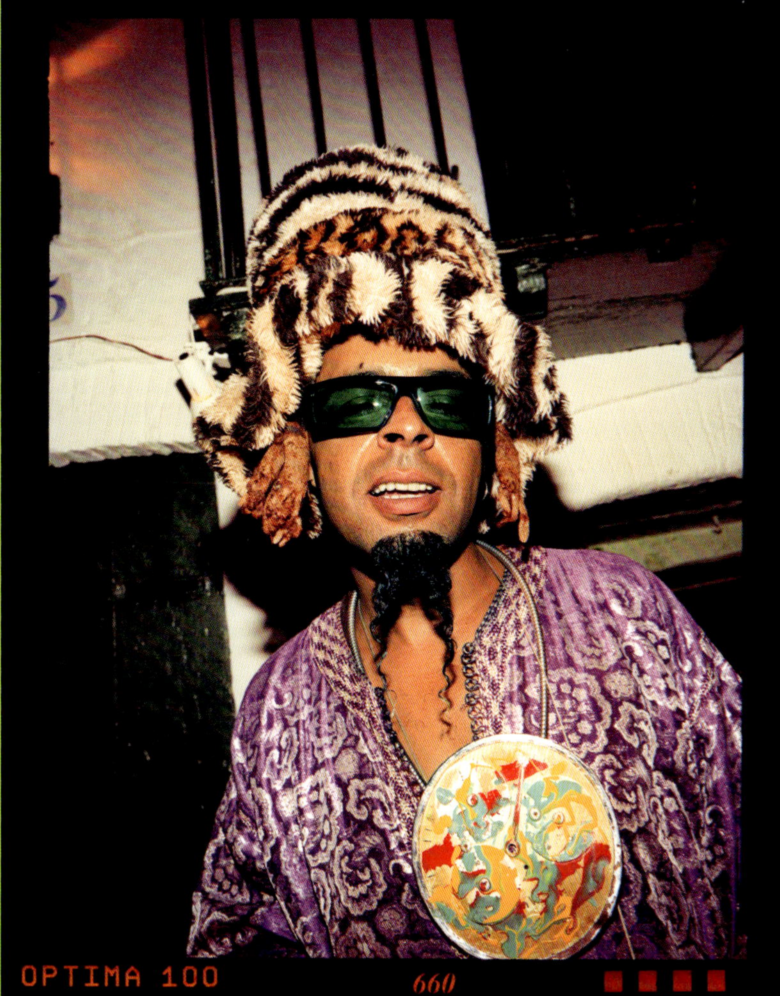

Returning in '83, straight from London, I proceeded to dance on the podiums of Pacha nightclub for the next 12 summers and around the world during the winters. Ibiza had no rules, no controls – you were truly *free to be who you want to be!!!*

Skipping forward to 1998, times were changing but everything was great! Four years earlier, in 1994, I had opened up the iconic Funky Room in Pacha with Nick, my partner from the Rock Bar Ibiza port. Both of these venues were at the forefront of what Ibiza was all about: dance, freedom, music, hedonism, lunacy, fashion, energy, rock & roll, drugs, alcohol, exstacy and LOVE.

Indeed, these times in Ibiza were the best in the world; times when all your celebrities from fashion, music, sports and art could mix and party freely with everyone. Rich, poor, crazy, famous, gay, straight... nothing mattered and nobody cared or judged.

These times were the pinnacle of my beloved island of love. God bless Ibiza and everyone who sailed in her during the 1980s, '90s and early 2000s. Happiness is the key. Big Peace and Love... Yo!

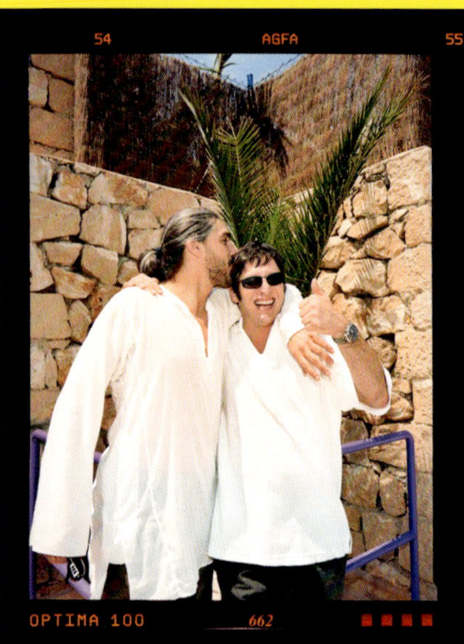

BRANDON BLOCK

I never wanted to be at the coolest party, I wanted to be at the best party!! Ibiza was the best party in the world for years.

Clubland back then was a proper social network and Ibiza has this spiritual energy, right? There's a certain energy there that makes it different. You'd go in those clubs and you'd say 'WOW!! This is an EXPERIENCE!! WHAT A FEELING!!' A proper journey IN music, that's what it was like. So, I didn't have to choose between the coolest party and the best party. Ibiza just happened to be both.

Ibiza has changed because the world has changed and people's attitudes have changed. It was experiential, culturally free. There were no boundaries around anything, no one was judging and you were free to express yourself, people didn't care – it was about having fun. 'Ibiza in the old days was like the best kitchen party you've ever been to, all the time. It was like being in the kitchen with your friends. Literally everyone who arrived was a friend waiting to get involved in the party and that was it... WONDERFUL.

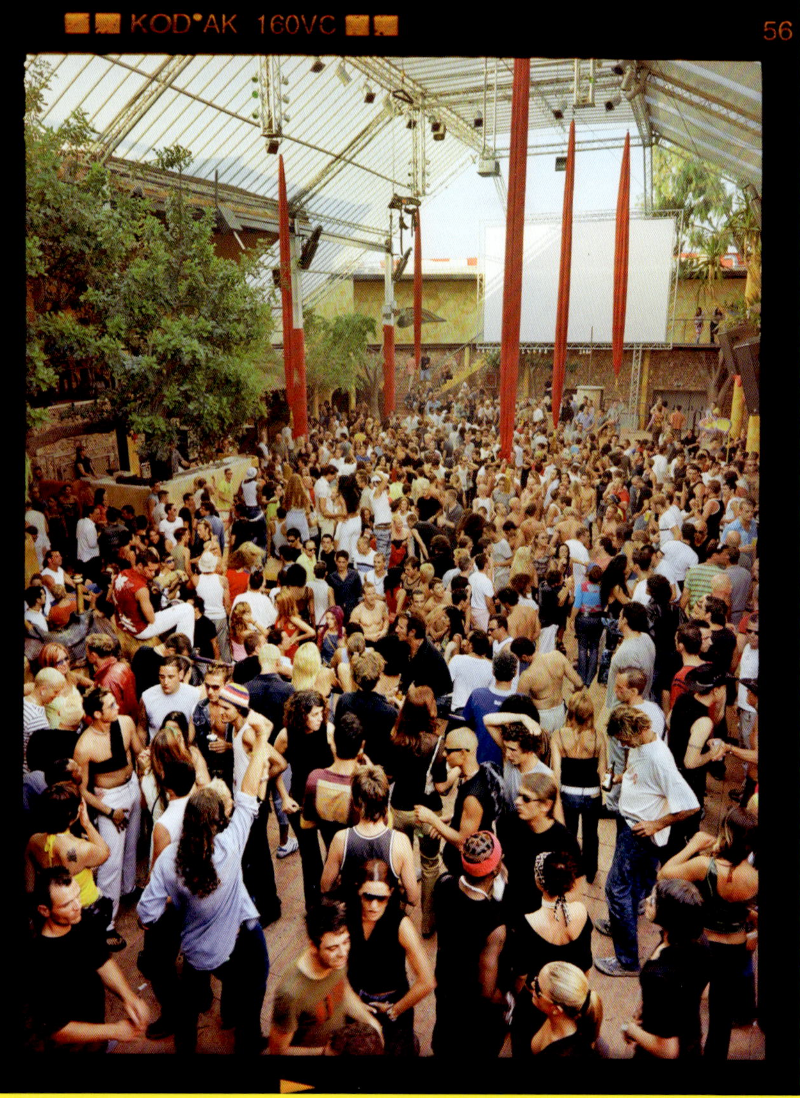

DJ PAULETTE

Ibiza – the dusty home of misfits and superstars, with its precarious roads, dramatic, jaw-dropping landscapes and hedonistic nightlife – was about to kick it up a gear with the help of some superstar DJs and mythical parties like Manumission, Space, Pacha and DC10.

I have fond memories of playing in Amnesia's Garden where I DJ'ed with Norman Jay, Andy Caroll and Phat Phil Cooper – I'm sure it had a tree in the middle? I loved playing in the old Space terrace, whooping with the crowd as we heard the whoosh of the planes taking off and landing overhead. Then there was Hierbas Con Aijello, Lumumba, Jose Padilla and sitting on a wall with all the DJs listening to the intimate Cafe Del Mar experience. And who can forget the original *Essential Selection* broadcasts from Cafe Mambo, chilled artist showcases like Indo and watching the roof open up in Privilege in the early hours.

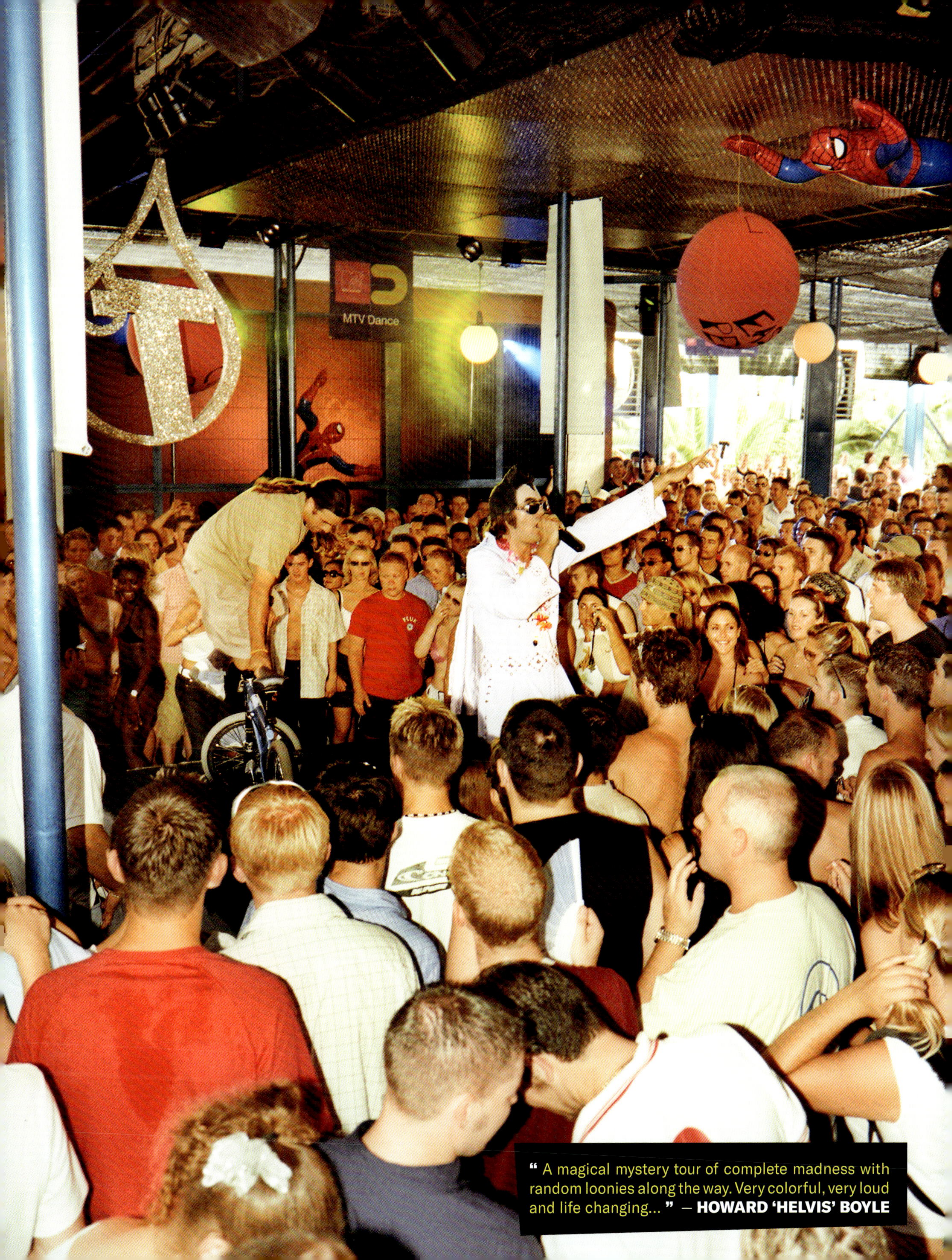

“ A magical mystery tour of complete madness with random loonies along the way. Very colorful, very loud and life changing… ” — HOWARD ‘HELVIS’ BOYLE

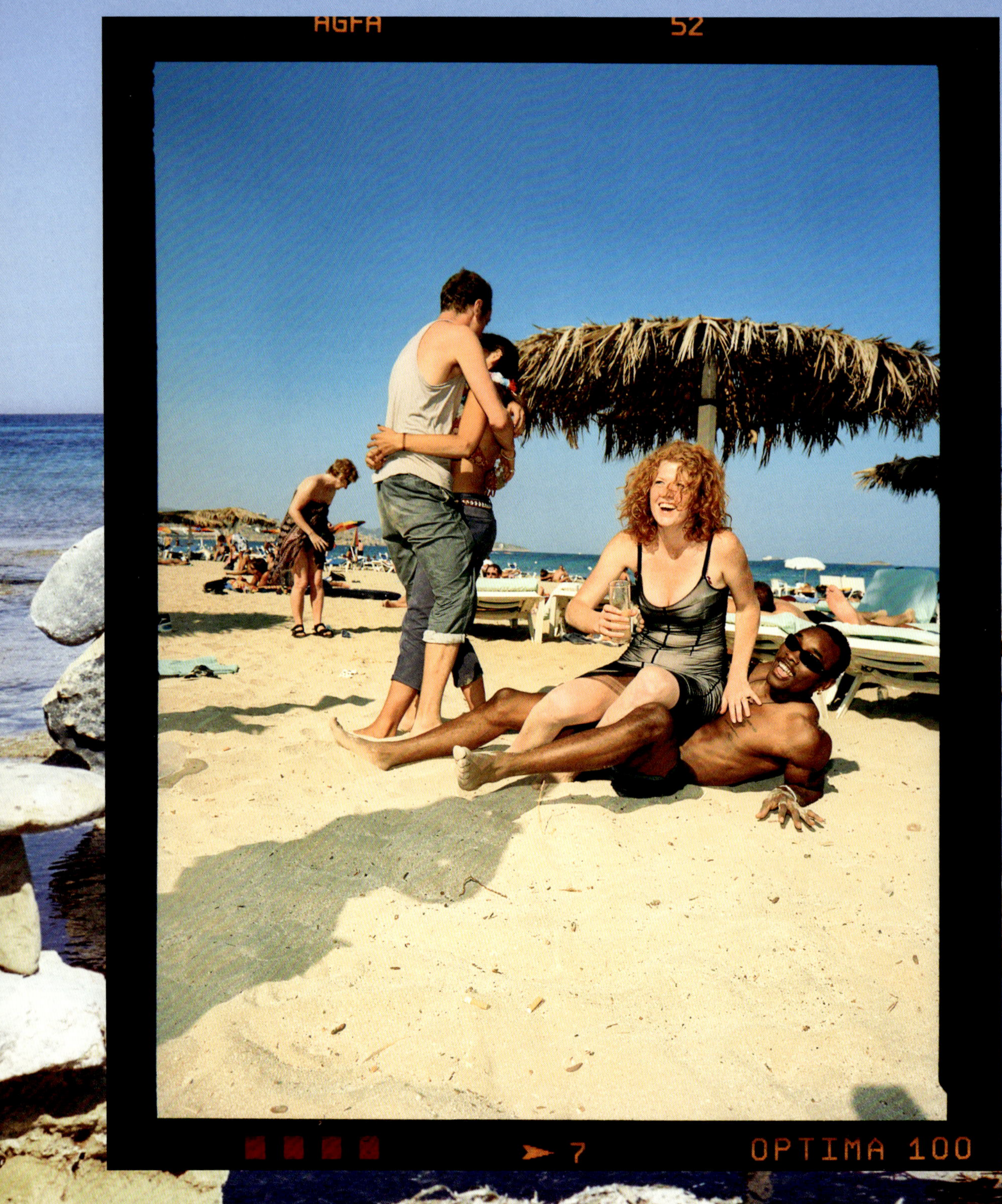

AGFA
52
7
OPTIMA 100

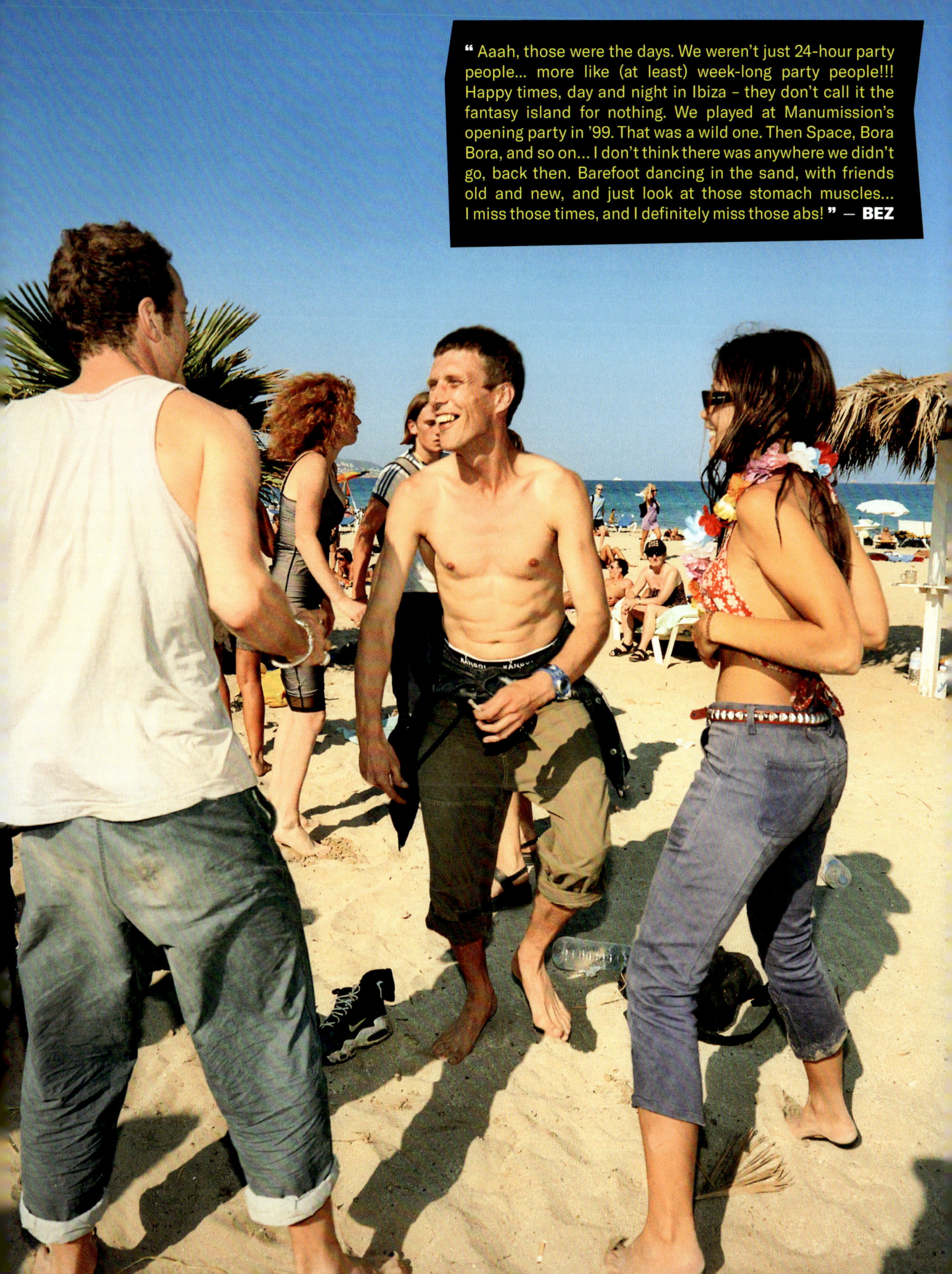

" Aaah, those were the days. We weren't just 24-hour party people... more like (at least) week-long party people!!! Happy times, day and night in Ibiza – they don't call it the fantasy island for nothing. We played at Manumission's opening party in '99. That was a wild one. Then Space, Bora Bora, and so on... I don't think there was anywhere we didn't go, back then. Barefoot dancing in the sand, with friends old and new, and just look at those stomach muscles... I miss those times, and I definitely miss those abs! " — BEZ

DAWN HINDLE

Our Manumission nights were at the height of their fame when Dean was photographing and capturing the spirit and essence of the most hedonistic and surreal party of its generation. Freedom was king and phones hadn't yet taken over; people were really living their nights and experiences, not recording for later. The vibe was ecstatic, the crowd mixed, it wasn't about money, it was about attitude and it was a time when anything could go and it usually did.

People starting their party at 3am, dancing through Privilege till 11am, then rolling into Carry-On at Space and Bora Bora. The heydays of Manumission were more than a trip into the unknown they forged friendships for life and a taste for an intangible energy the regulars would be chasing forever.

COLLEEN 'COSMO' MURPHY

When I moved to London from New York City in 1999, I discovered that dance music was integral to both British culture and individual lives. Although dance music had mainly originated and developed in the USA, it hadn't been embraced by the mainstream in my homeland. Even in cities like New York, house music was still very underground and niche, forever obscured in the shadows by hip hop and R&B. However, because of the acid house revolution and a decades-long obsession with Black American music, the Brits embraced dance music and it was very much overground in

the UK. Even those who were not DJs bought vinyl 12-inches and knew of Larry Heard and Marshall Jefferson. In fact, the month before I moved to London, Louie Vega was my special guest on one of my last community radio shows in New York, *Club 89*, but weeks later in the UK, I heard Masters at Work on BBC Radio One at peak time. The two shores were not just an ocean, but worlds apart.

I was lucky to have experienced dance music at the height of its power in the UK; the time in which Dean Chalkley took these joyous photographs. Both in the UK and in Europe, I witnessed the power of music bringing together people from all walks of life, united by a bassline, a kick drum and a wicked groove. The dance floor almost acted as a spiritual space, a place of musical worship and personal transformation in which the individual ego was superseded by a communal spirit. Chalkley's photographs express the unhinged joy of the individual succumbing to the glory of music along with

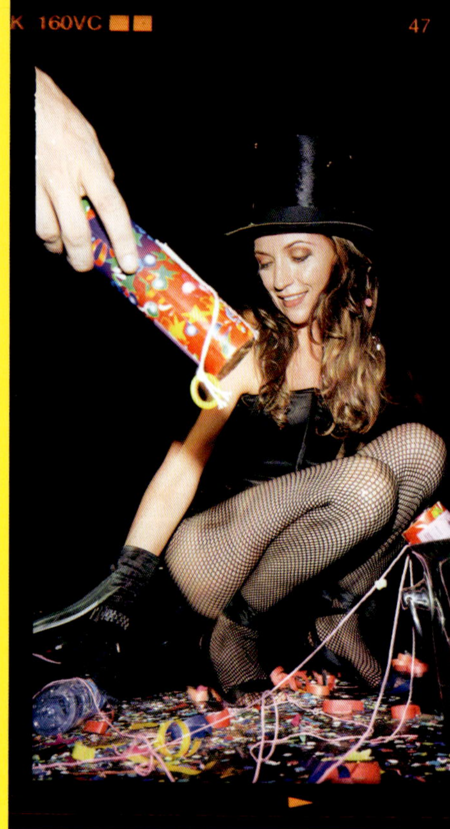

the collective one-ness of the dance floor when everything comes together and is just 'right'. They say a picture can express more than a thousand words, but here they express the overwhelming power of music, which cannot be put into words.

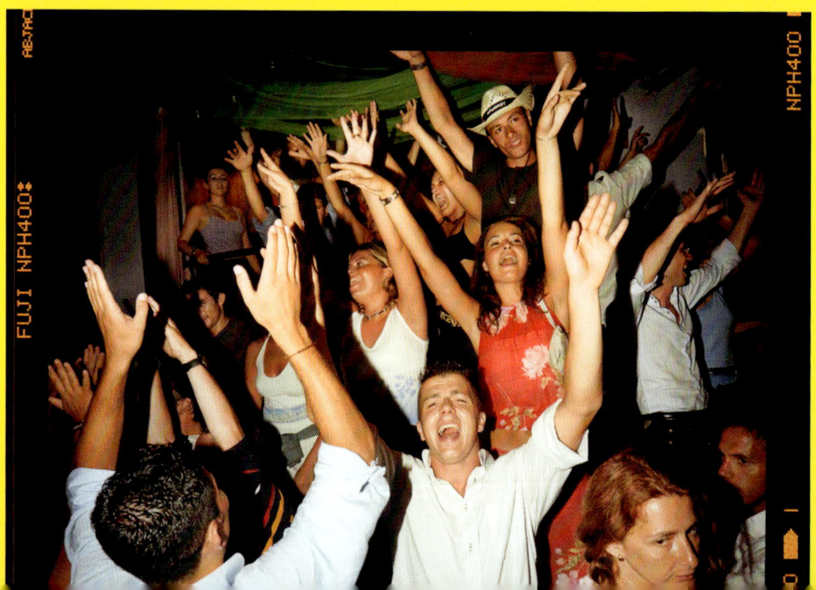

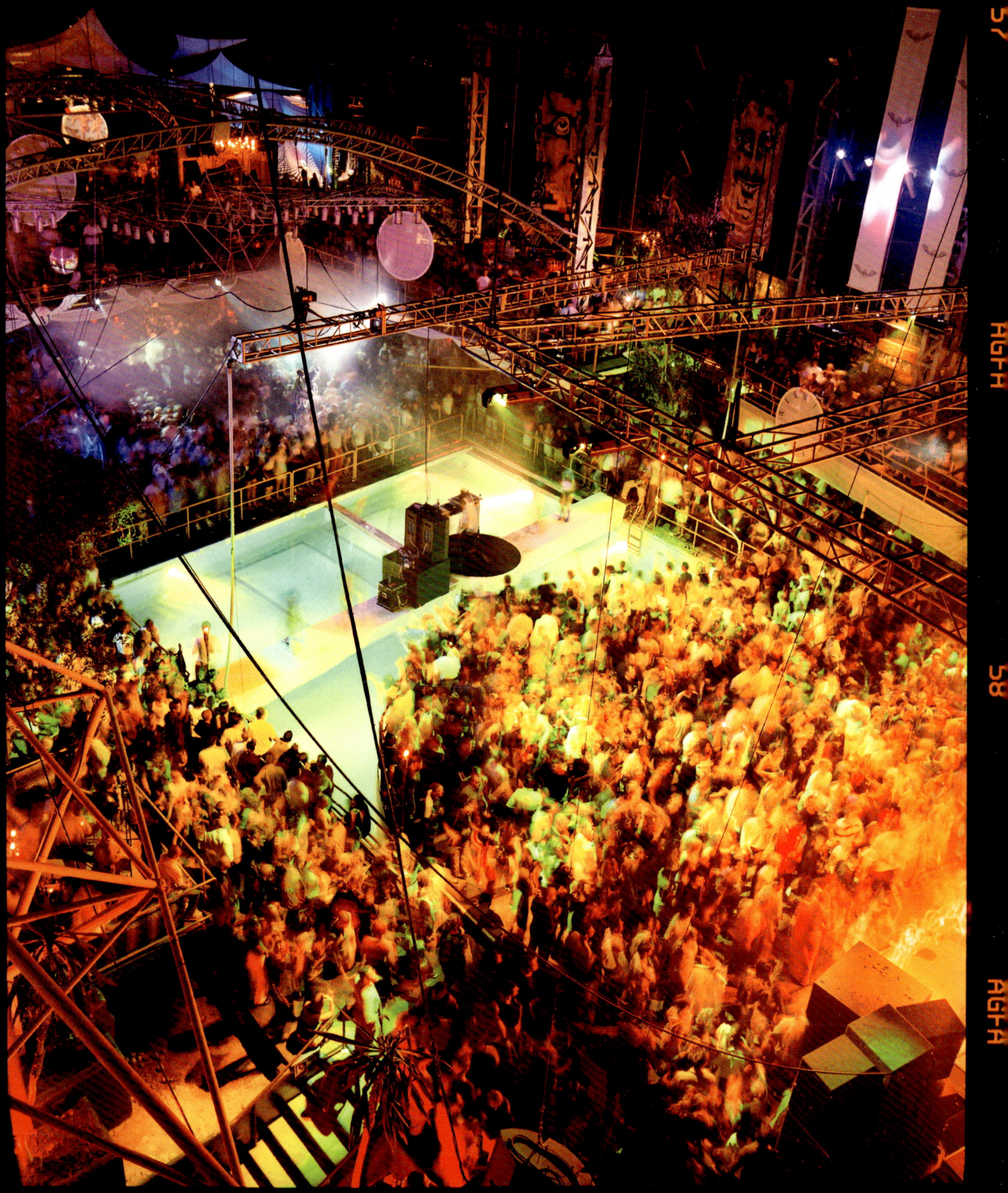

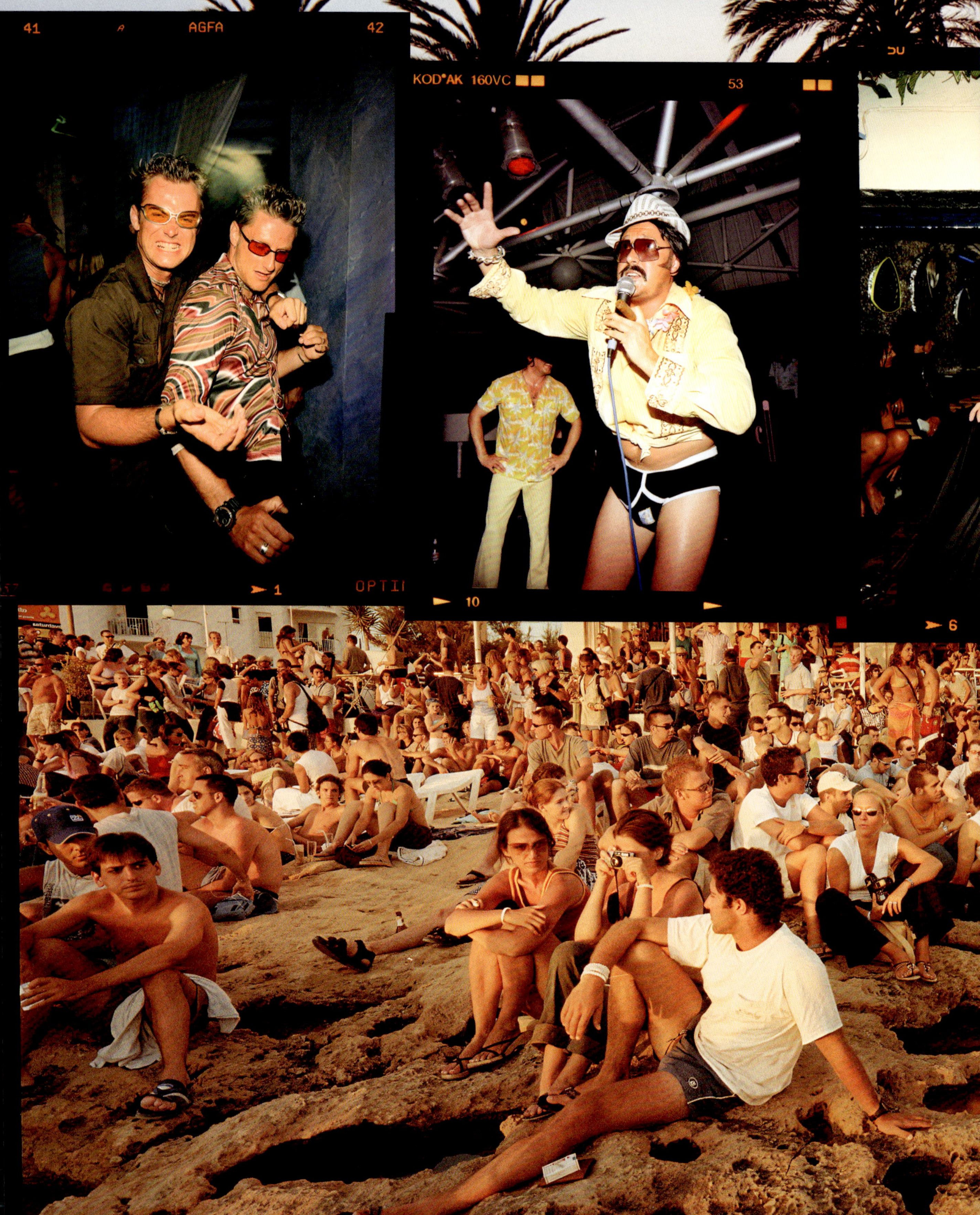

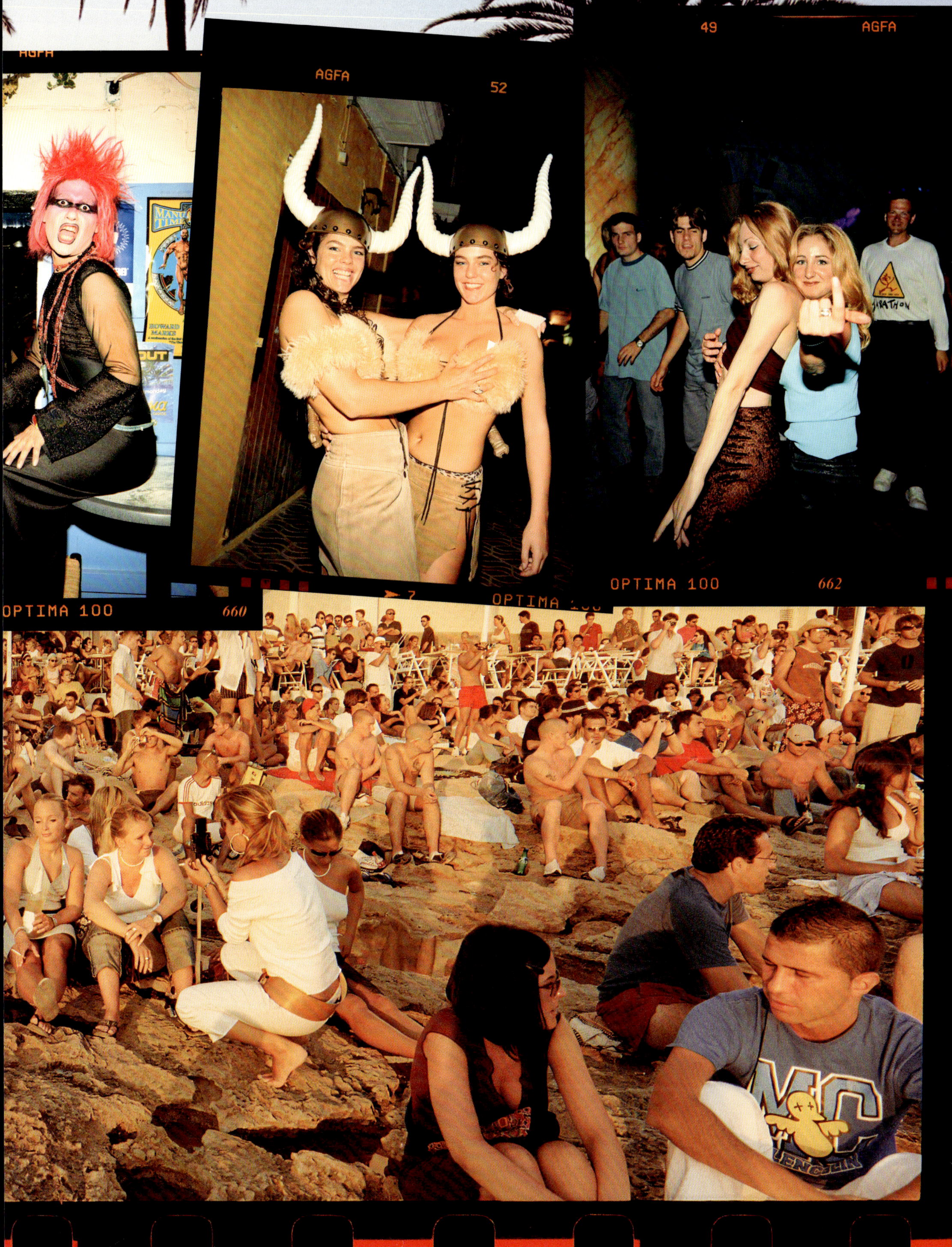
AGFA
AGFA
49
52
OPTIMA 100
OPTIMA 100
662
660

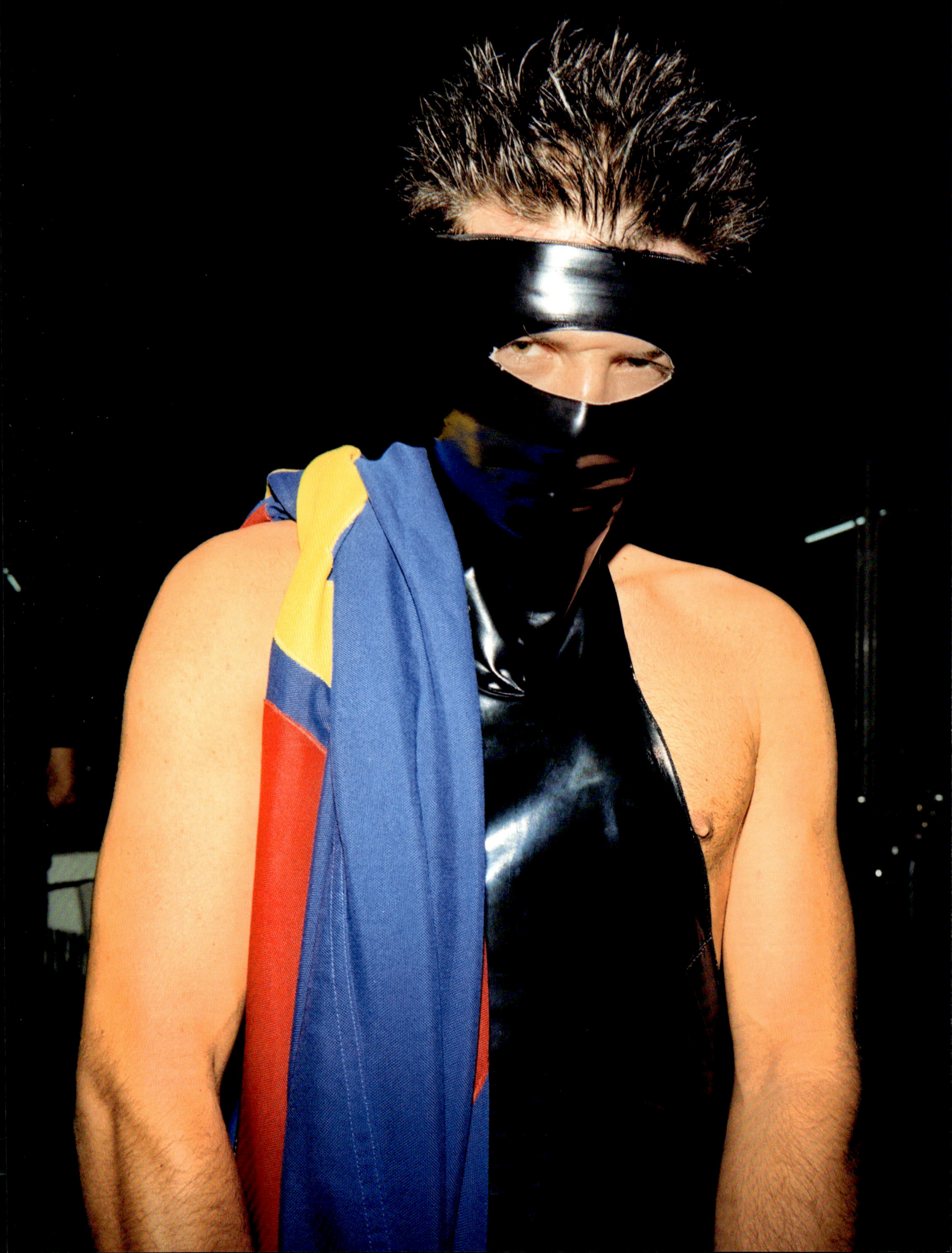

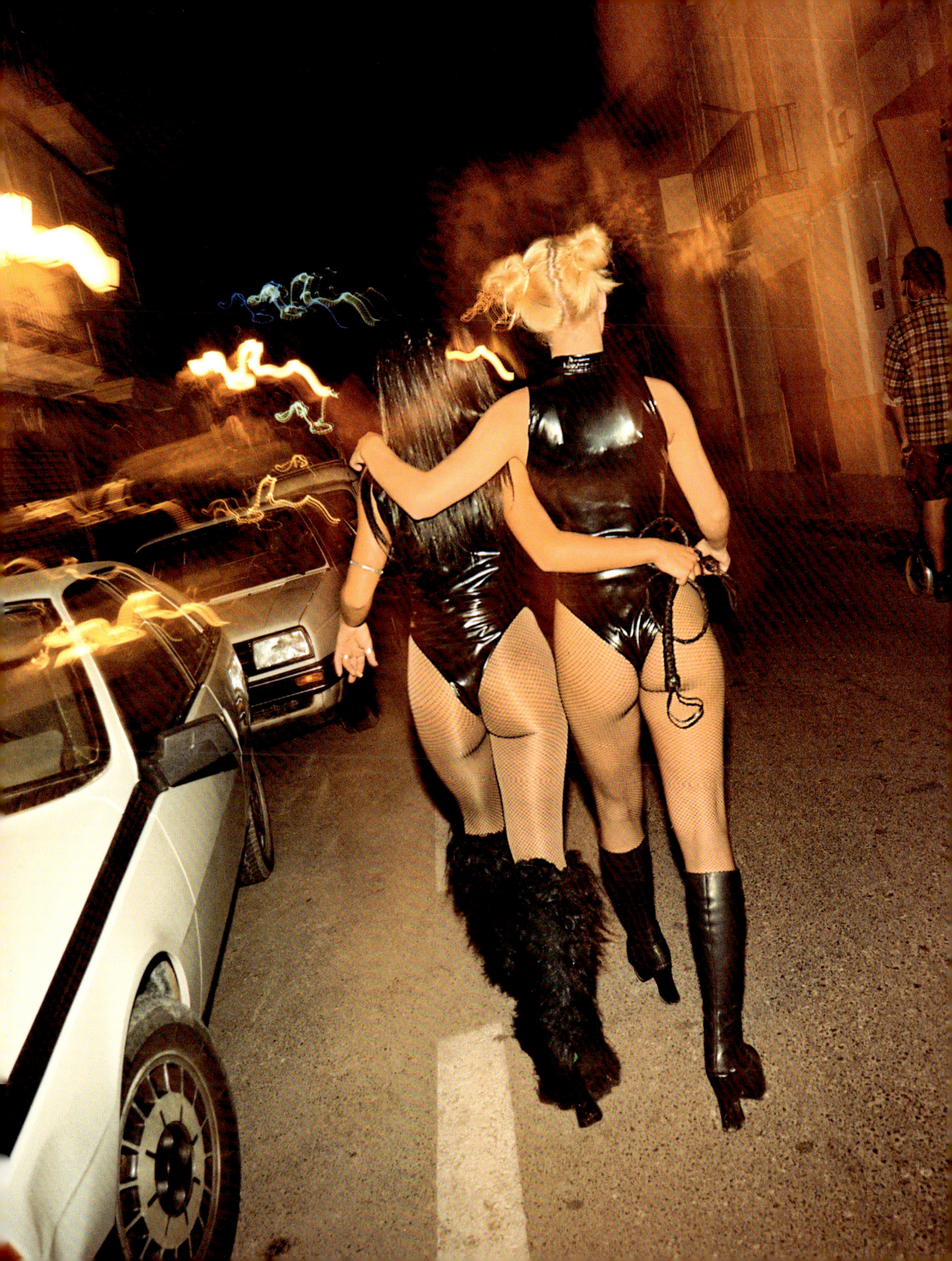

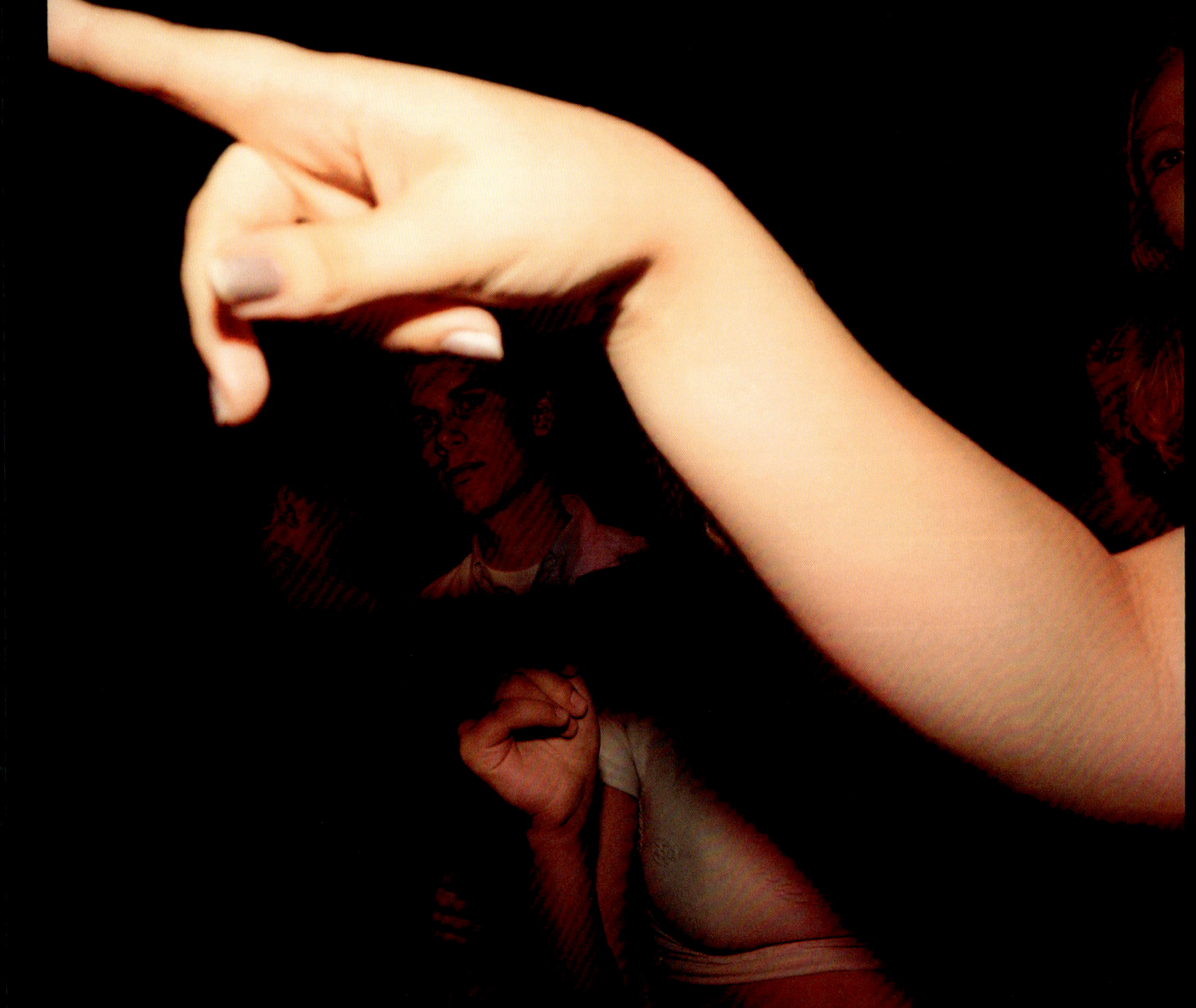

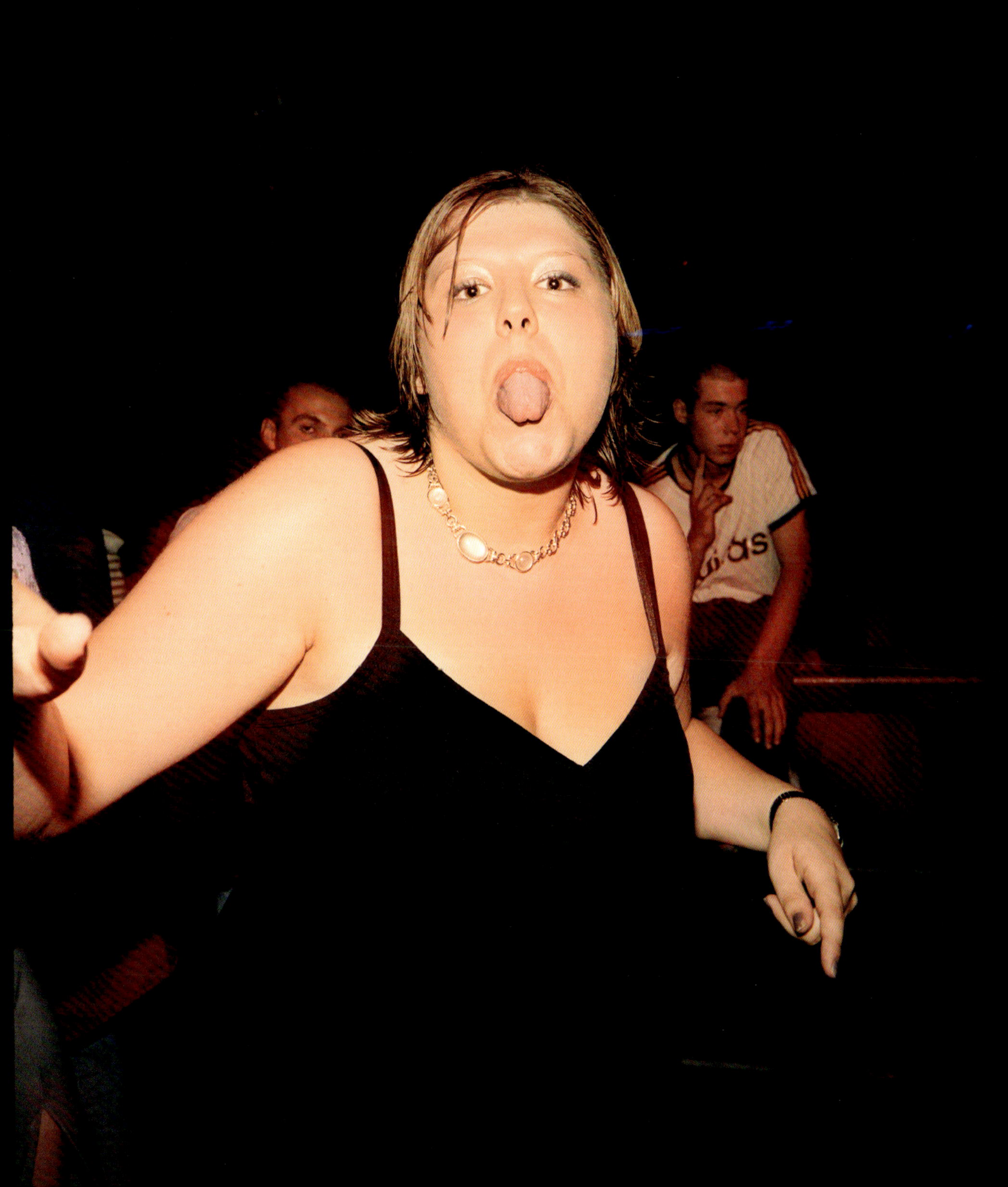

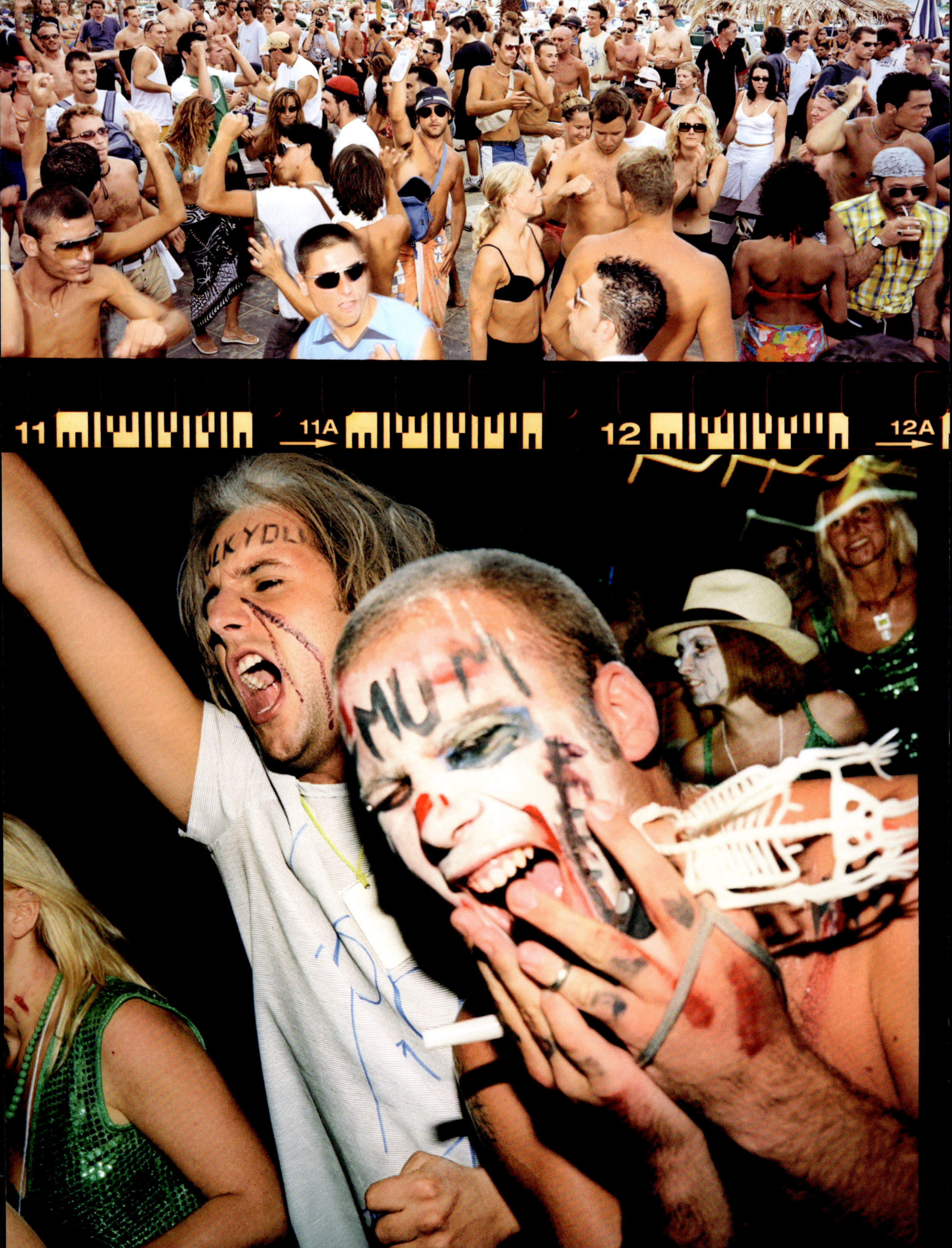
11
11A
12
12A

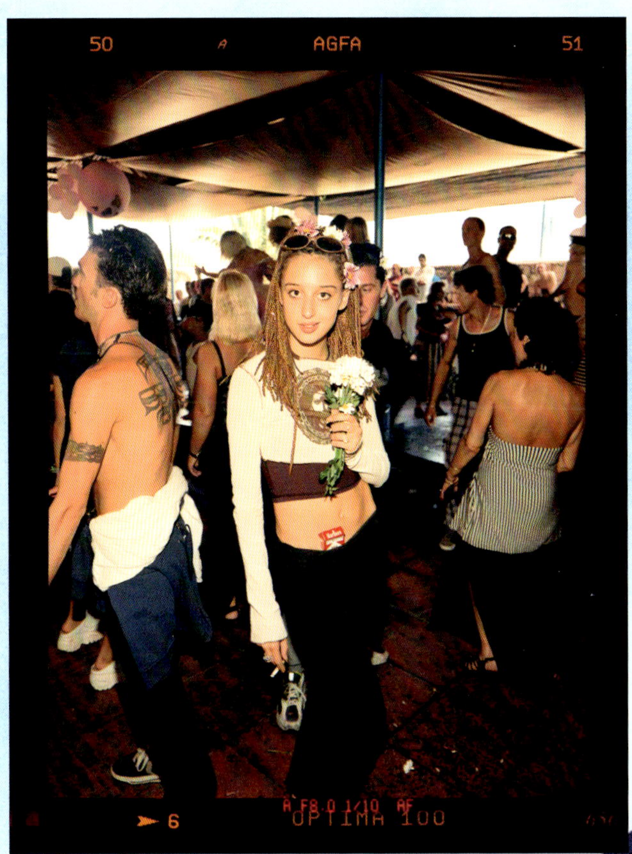
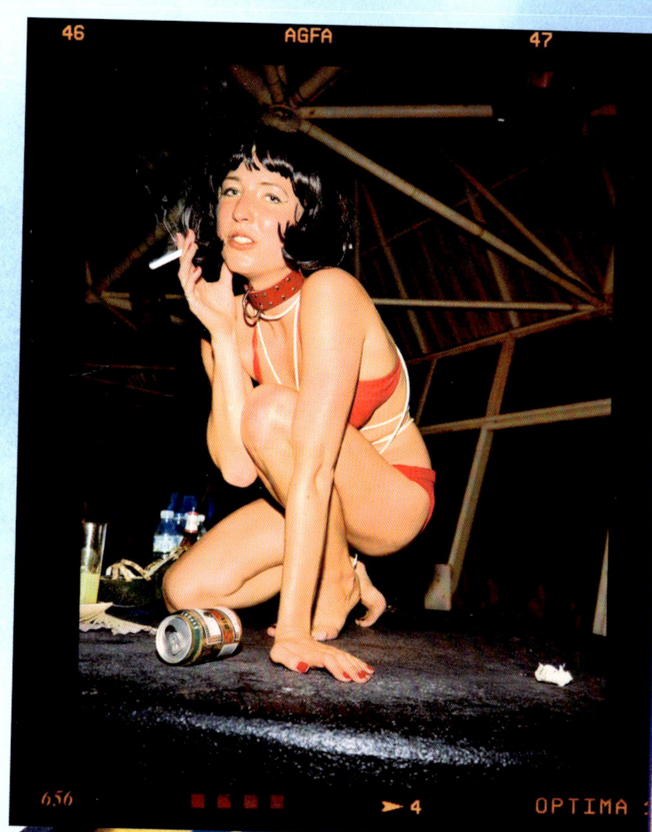
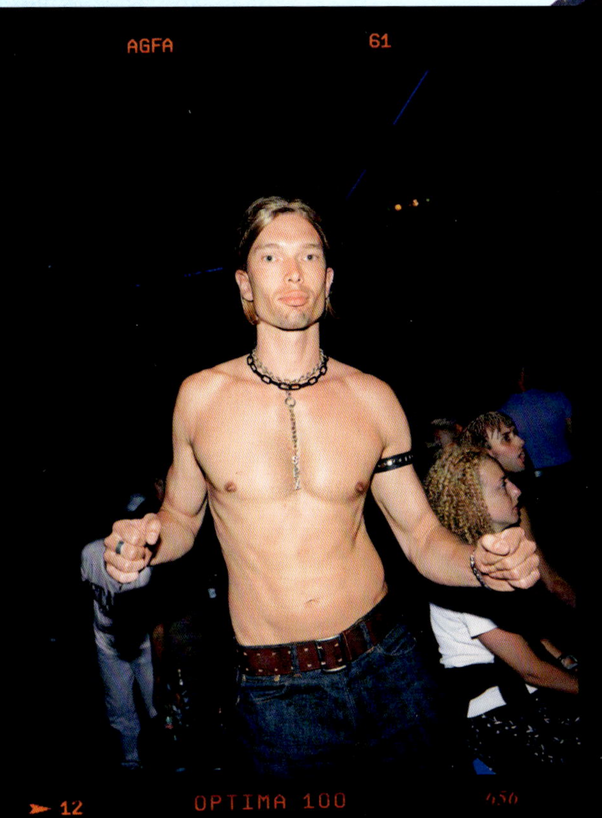
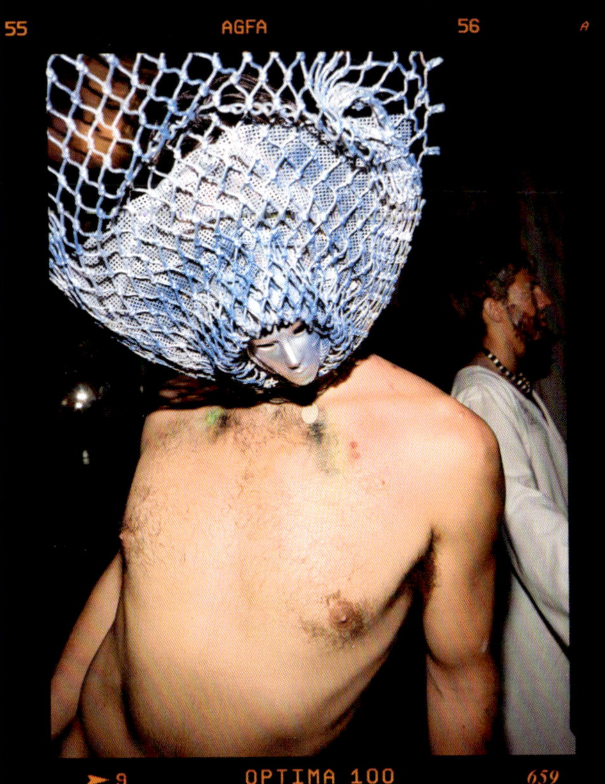

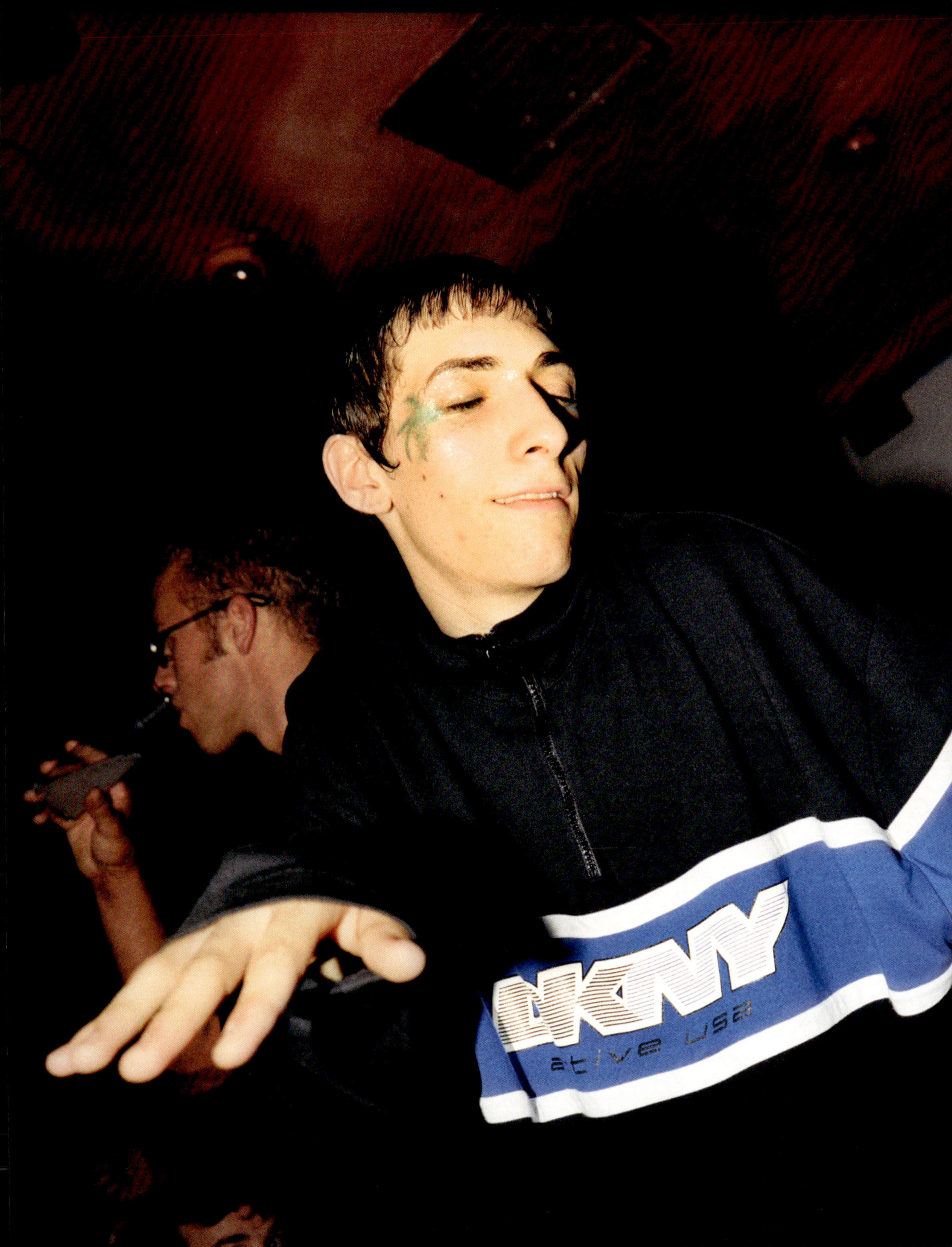
DKNY
at/ve usa

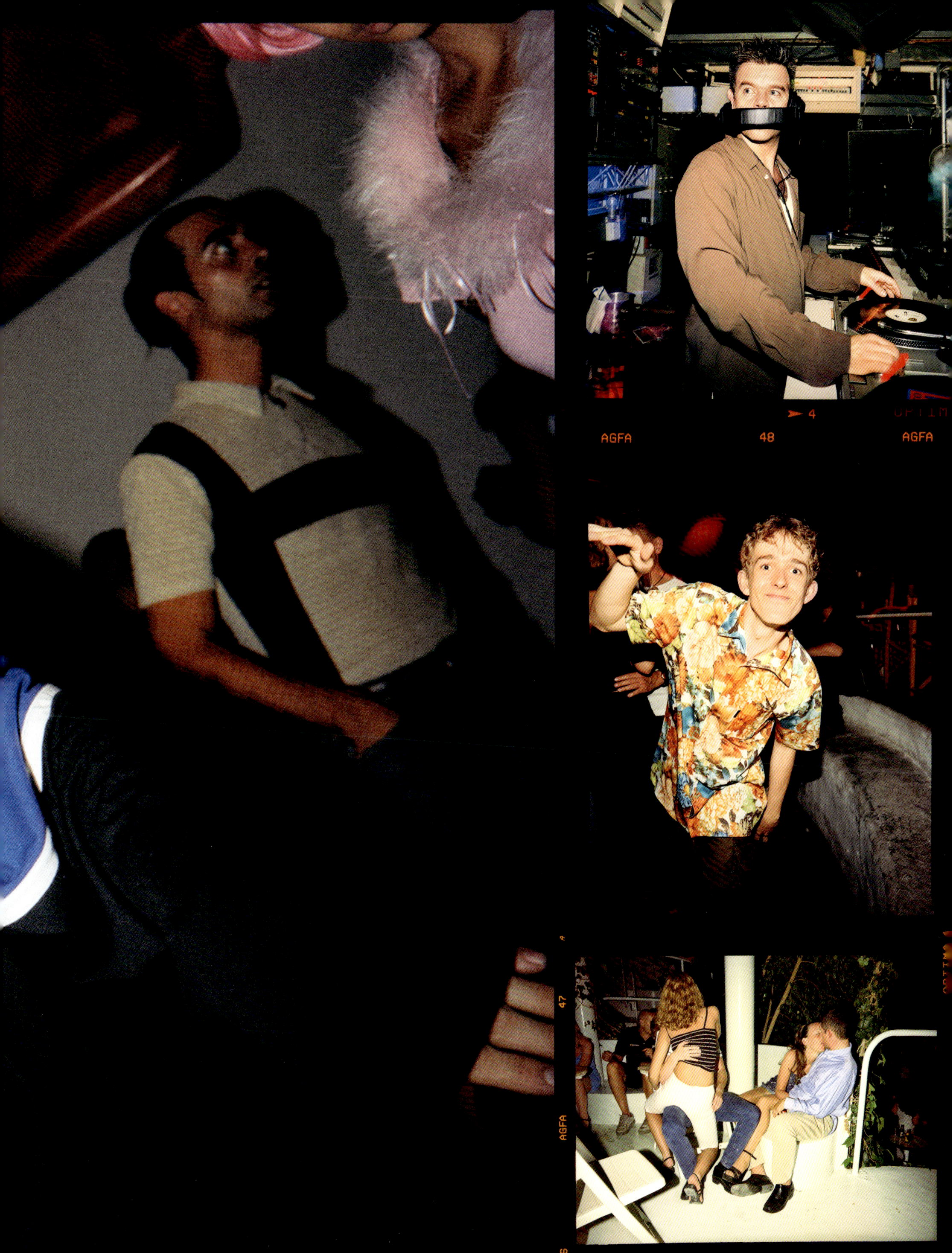

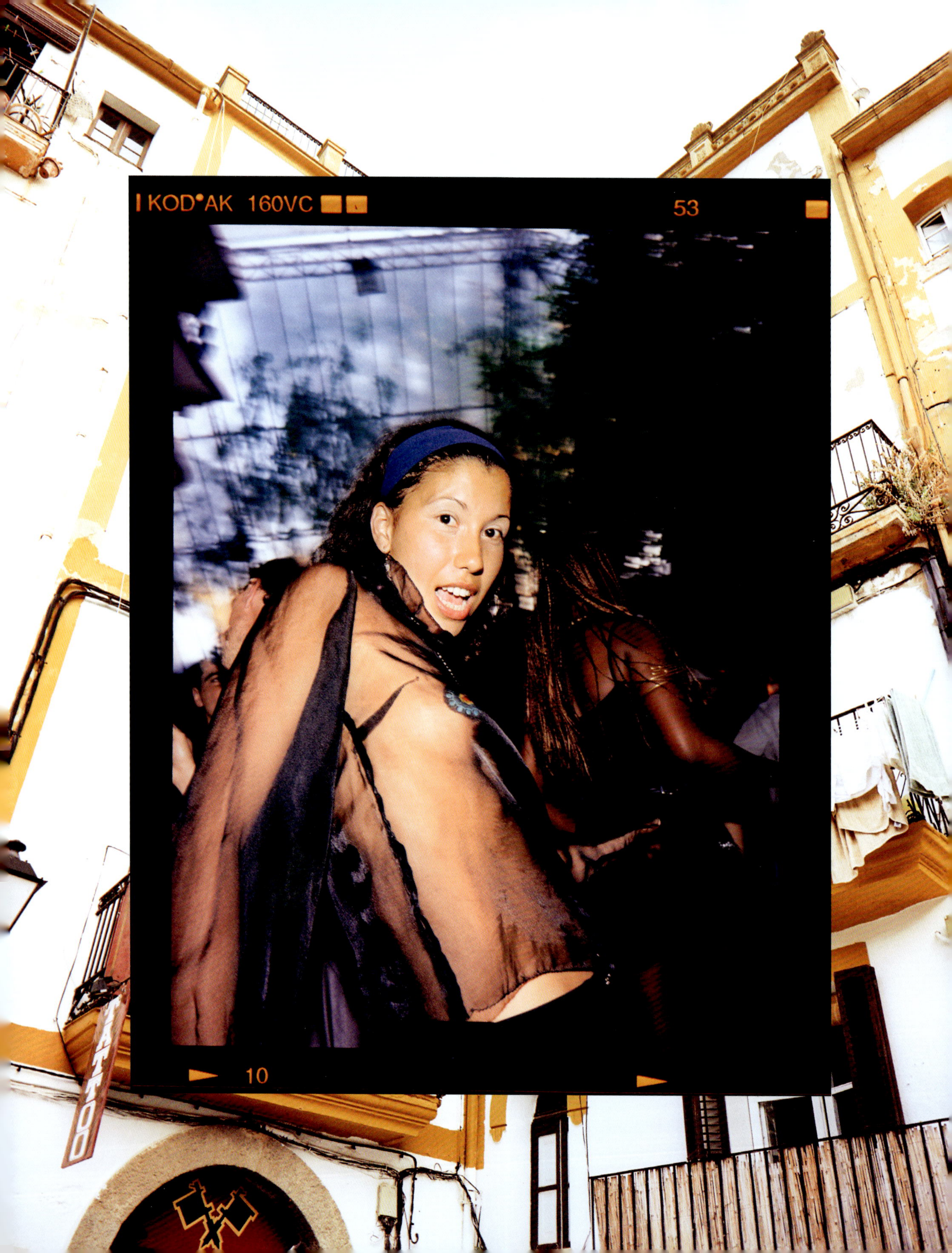
KOD·AK 160VC
53
10

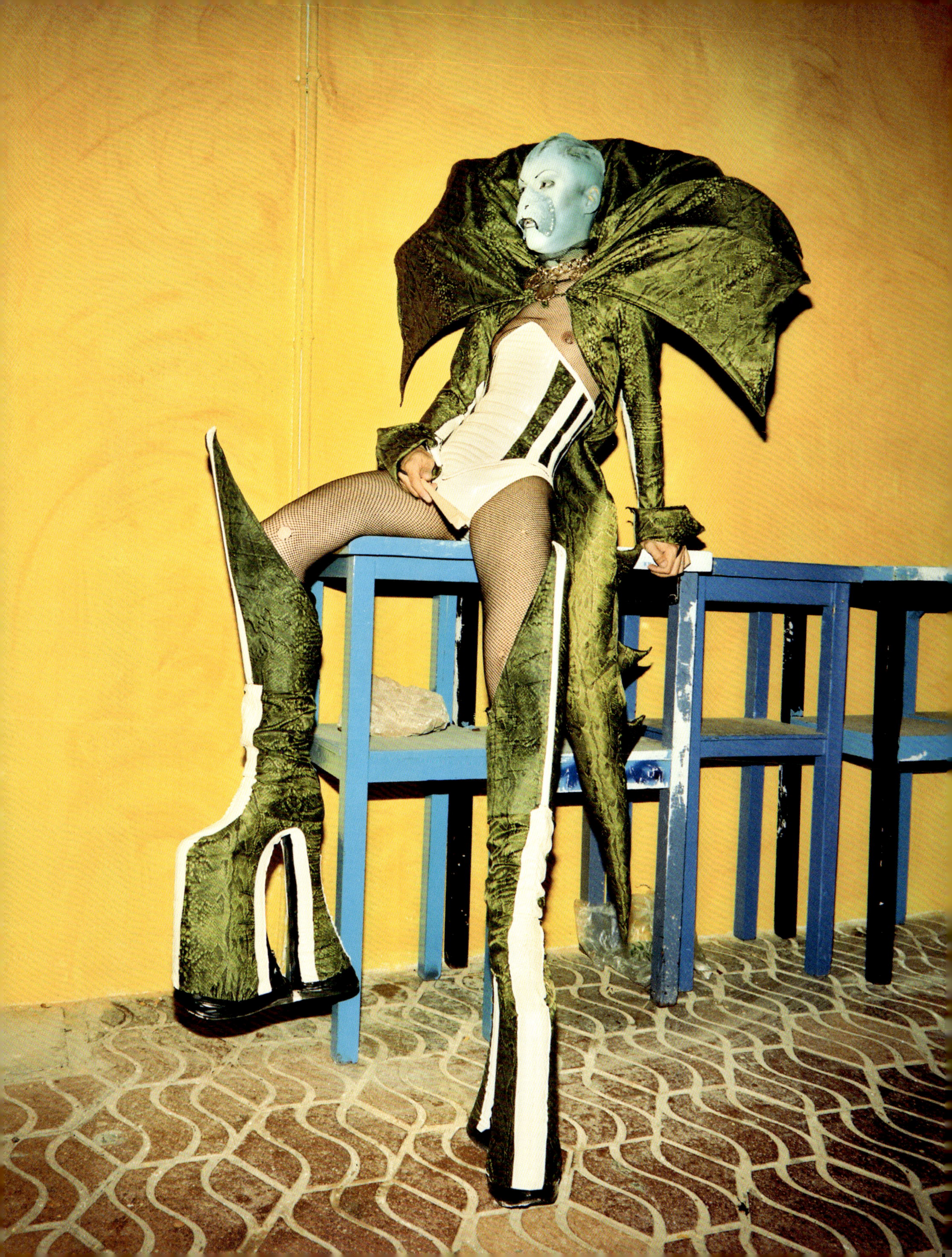

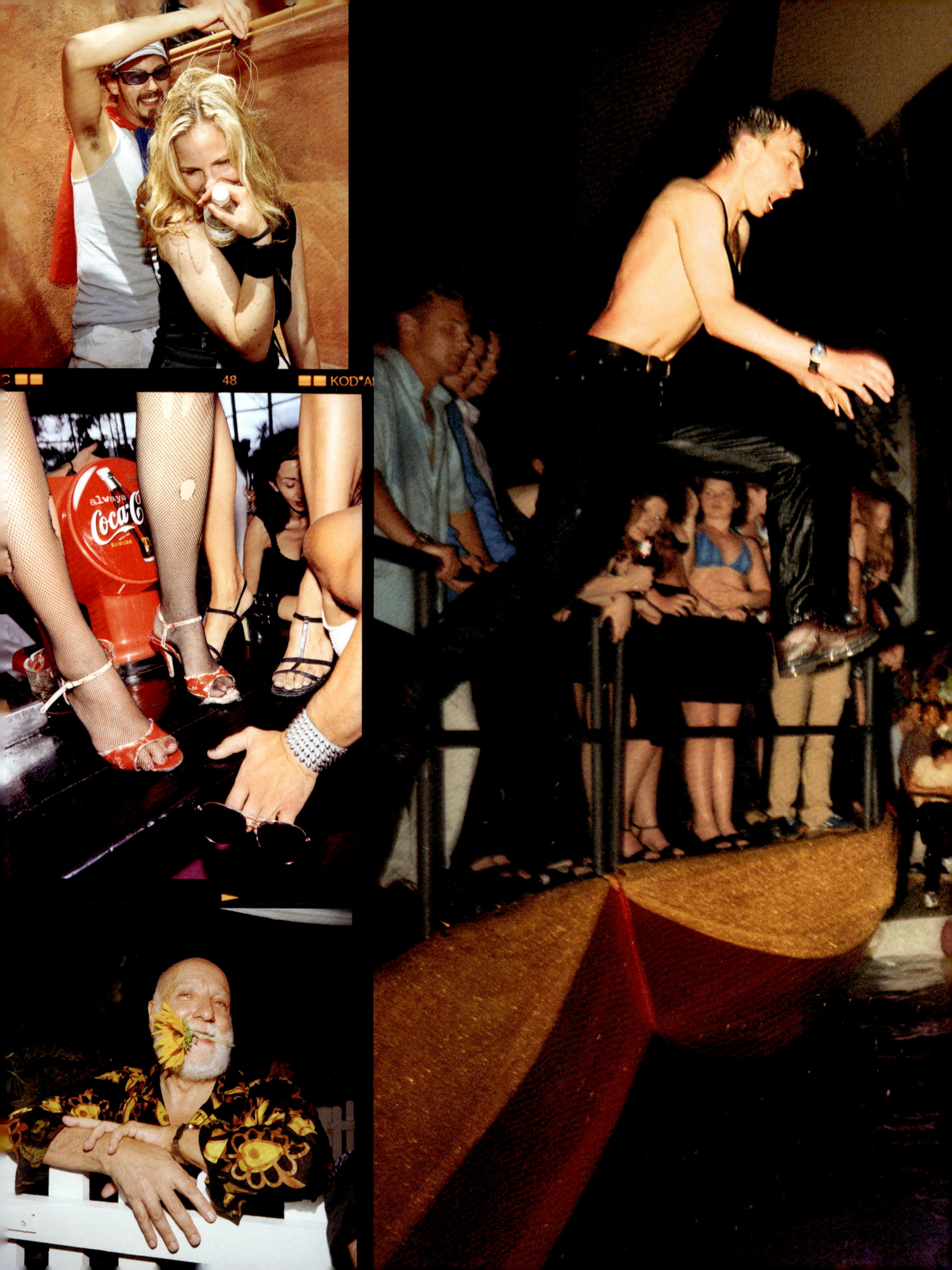

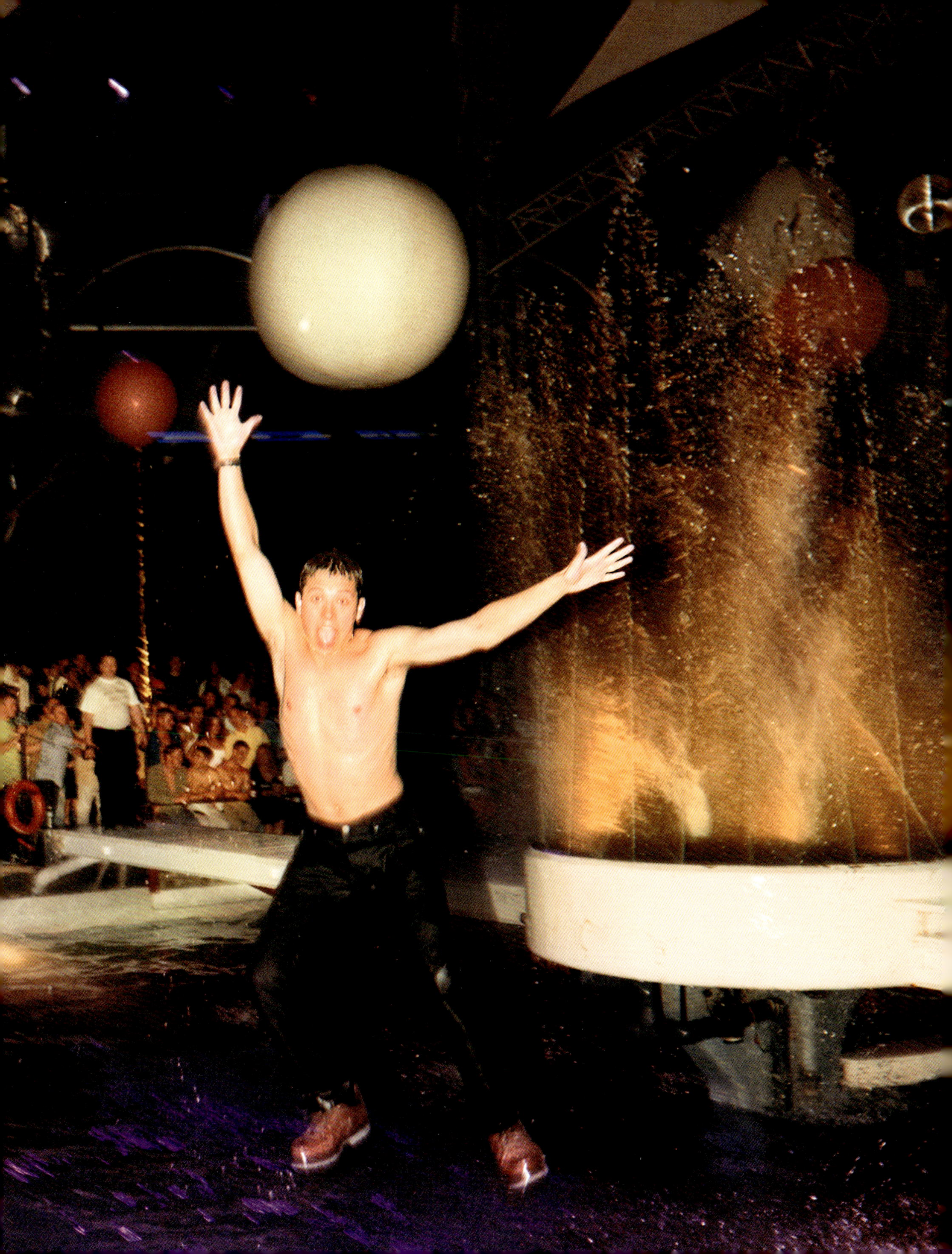

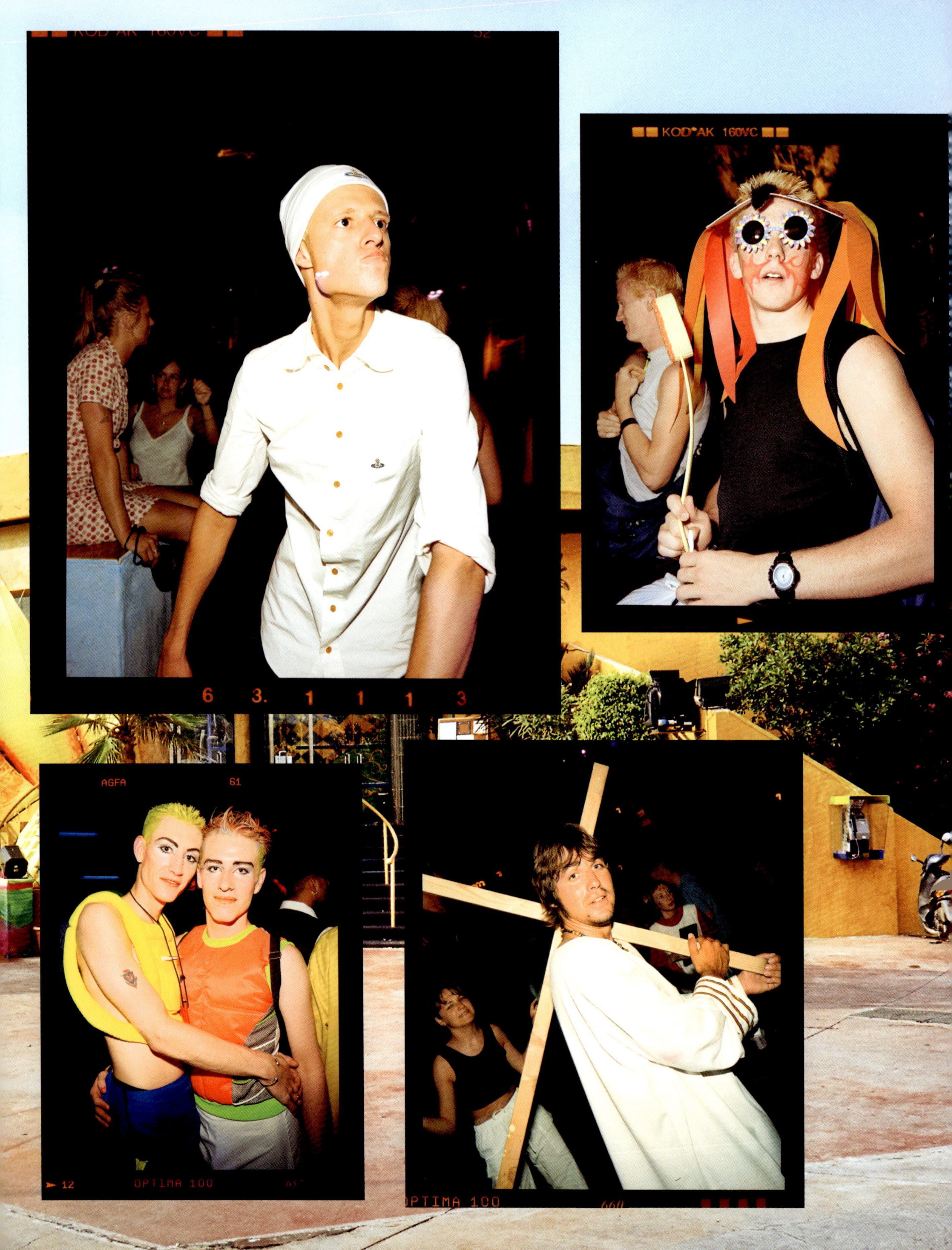

KOD*AK 160VC
KOD*AK 160VC
AGFA
OPTIMA 100
OPTIMA 100

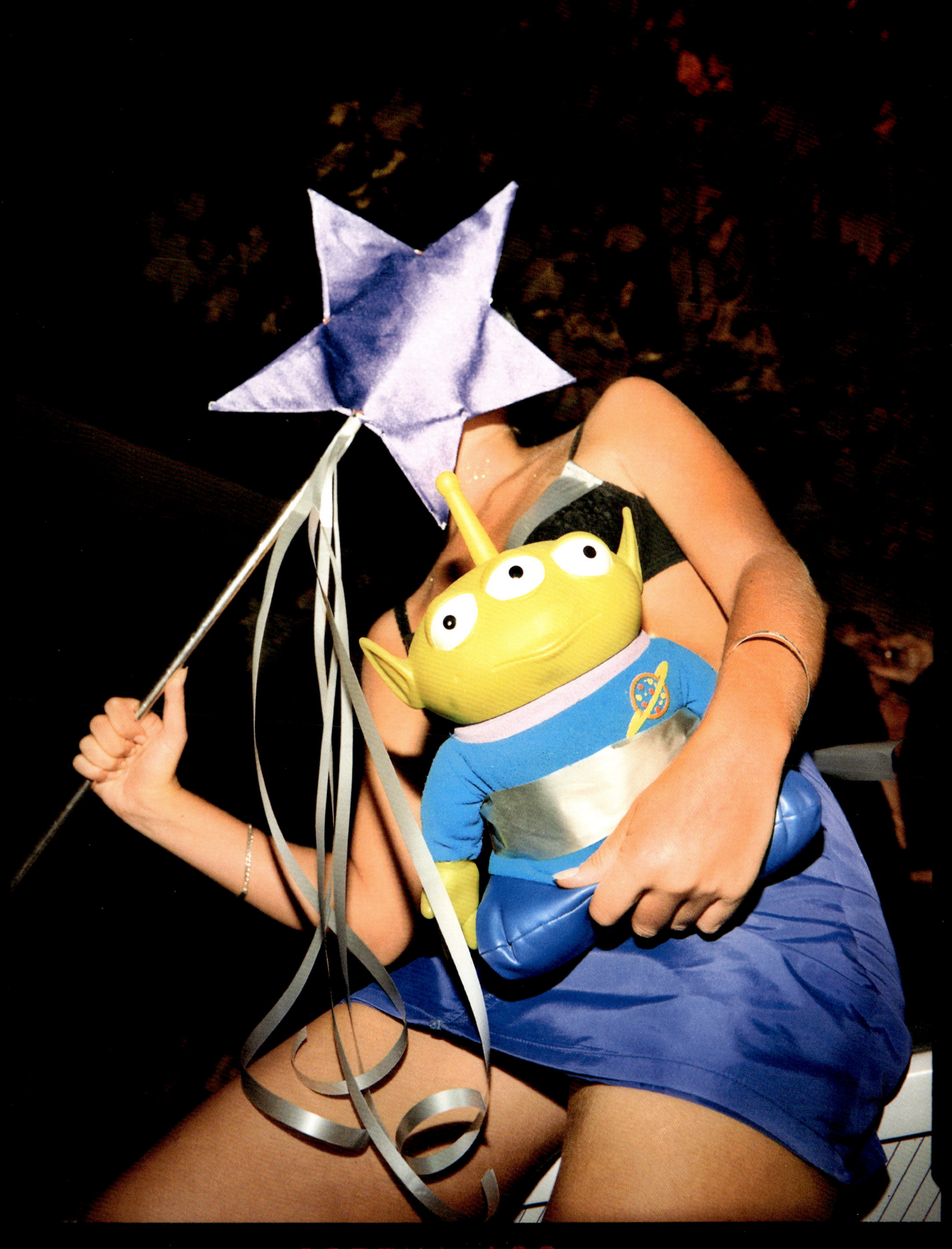

9
OPTIMA 100
657

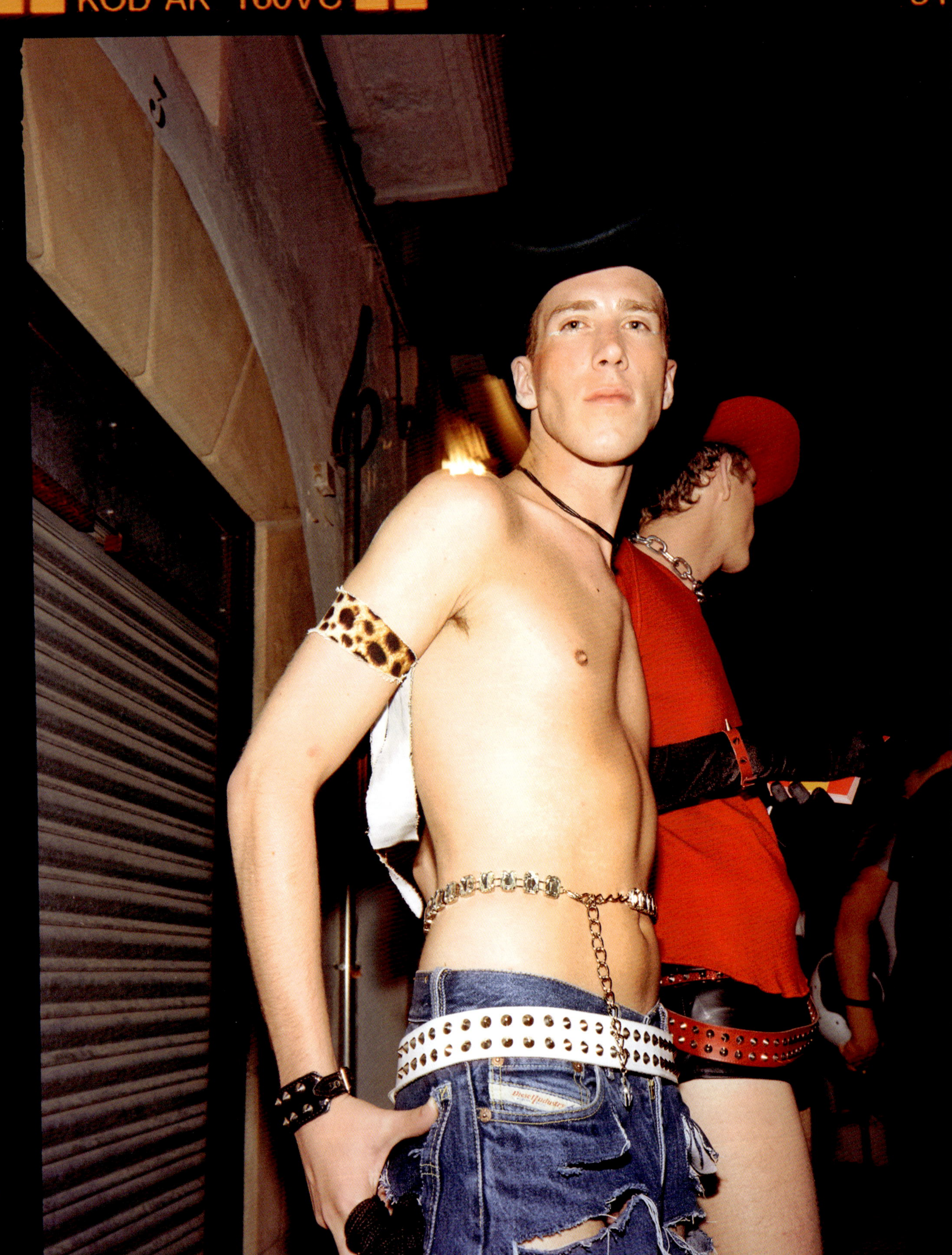
KODAK 160VC
54

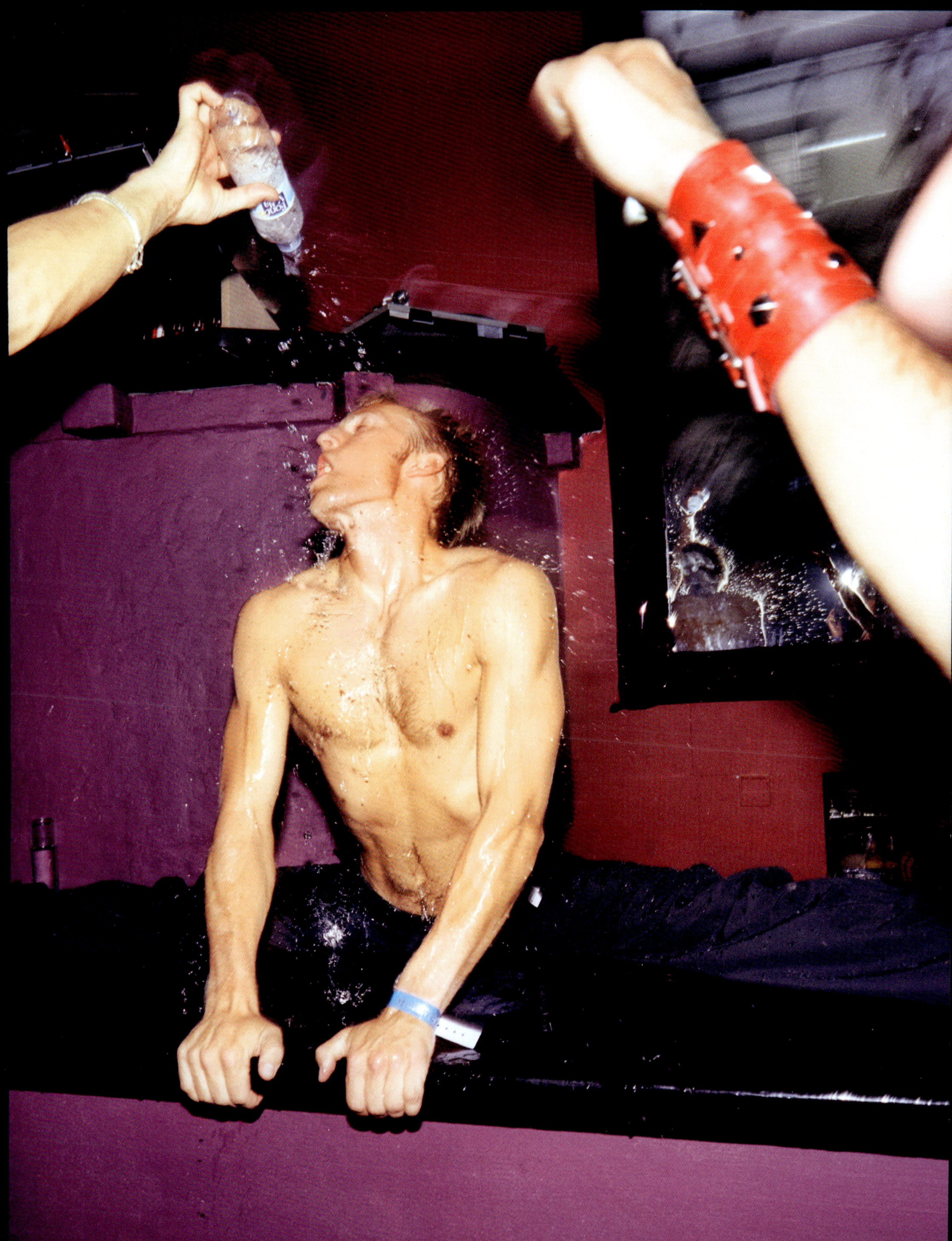

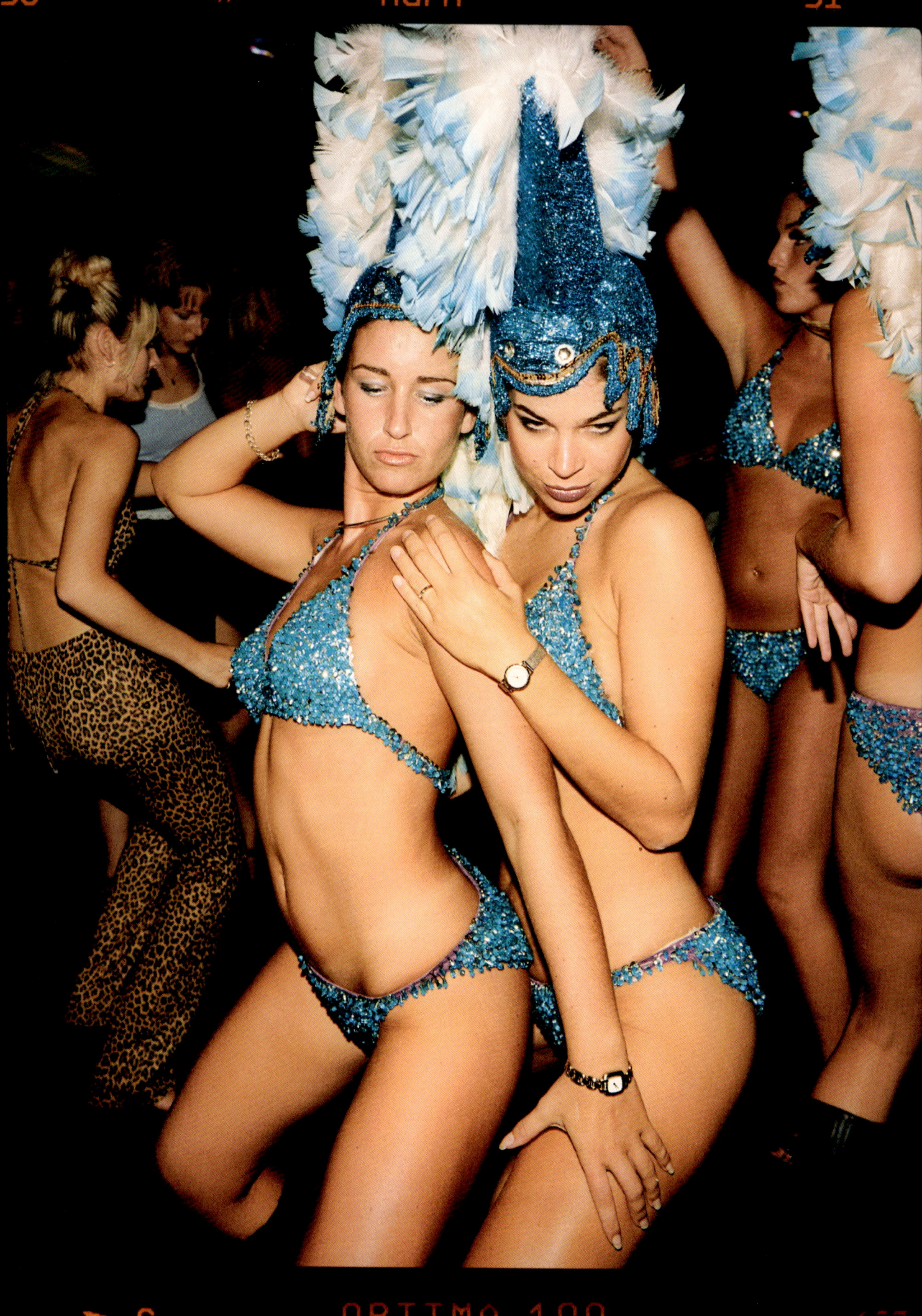
50
A
AGFA
51
6
OPTIMA 100

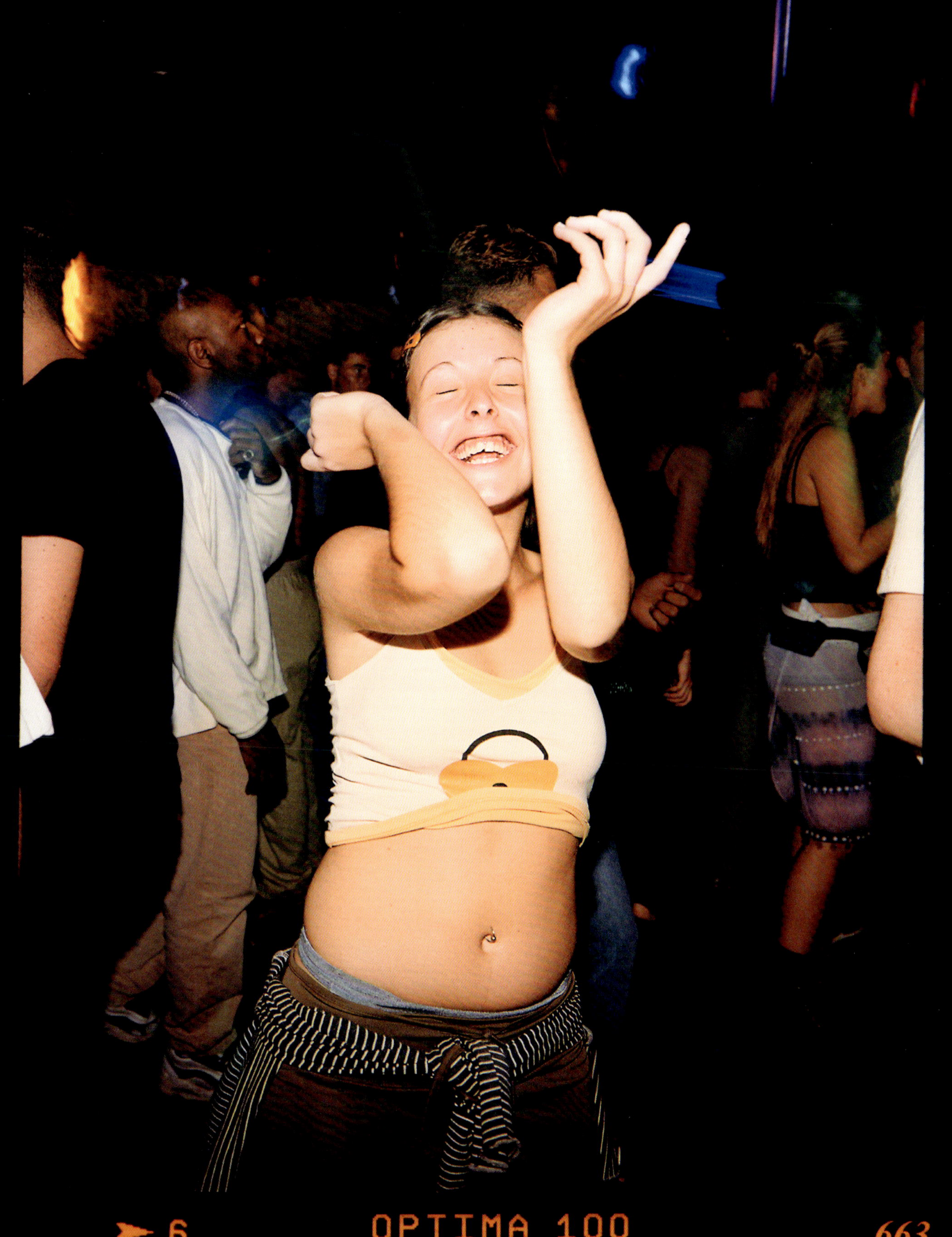

6
OPTIMA 100
663

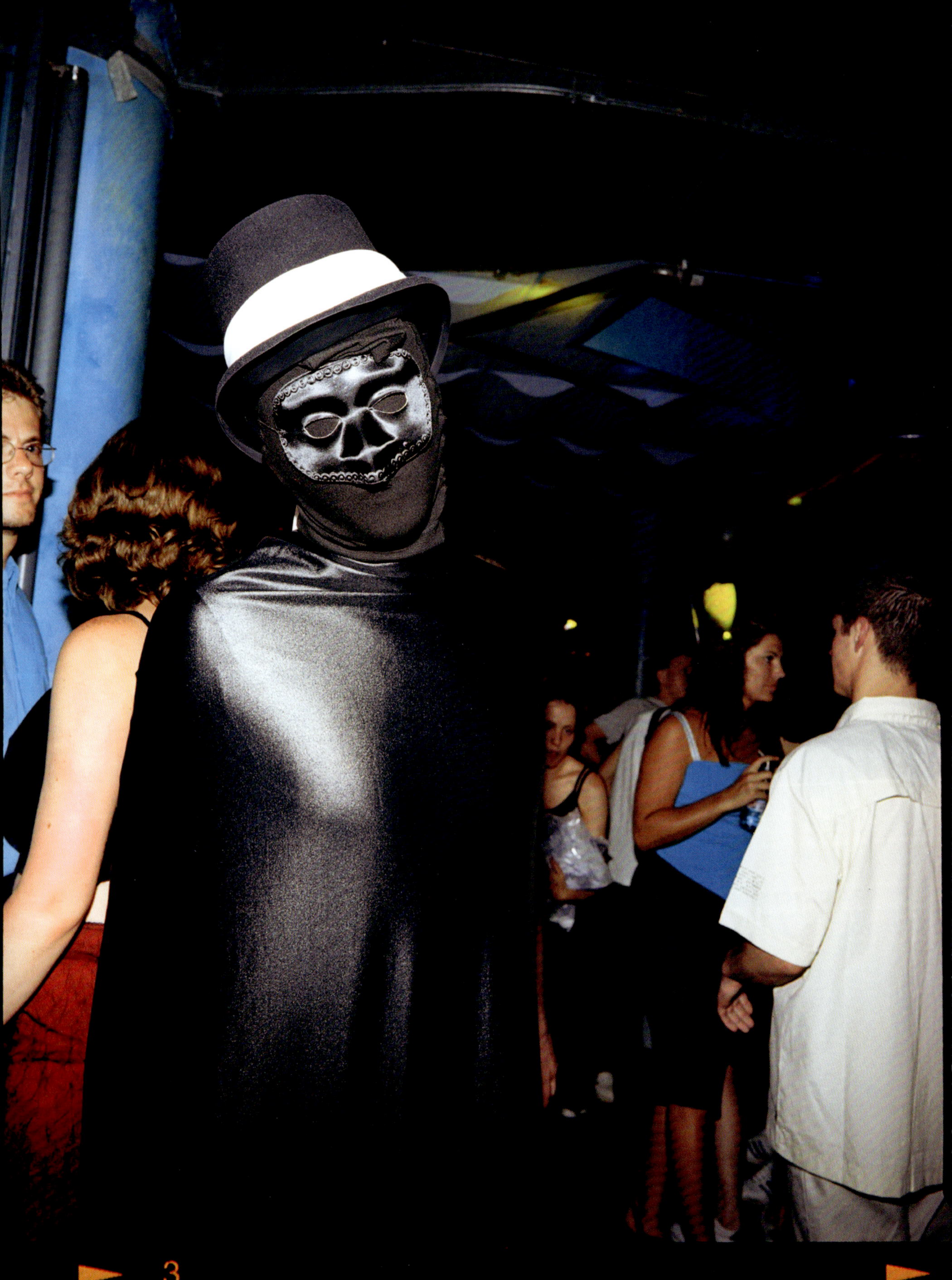

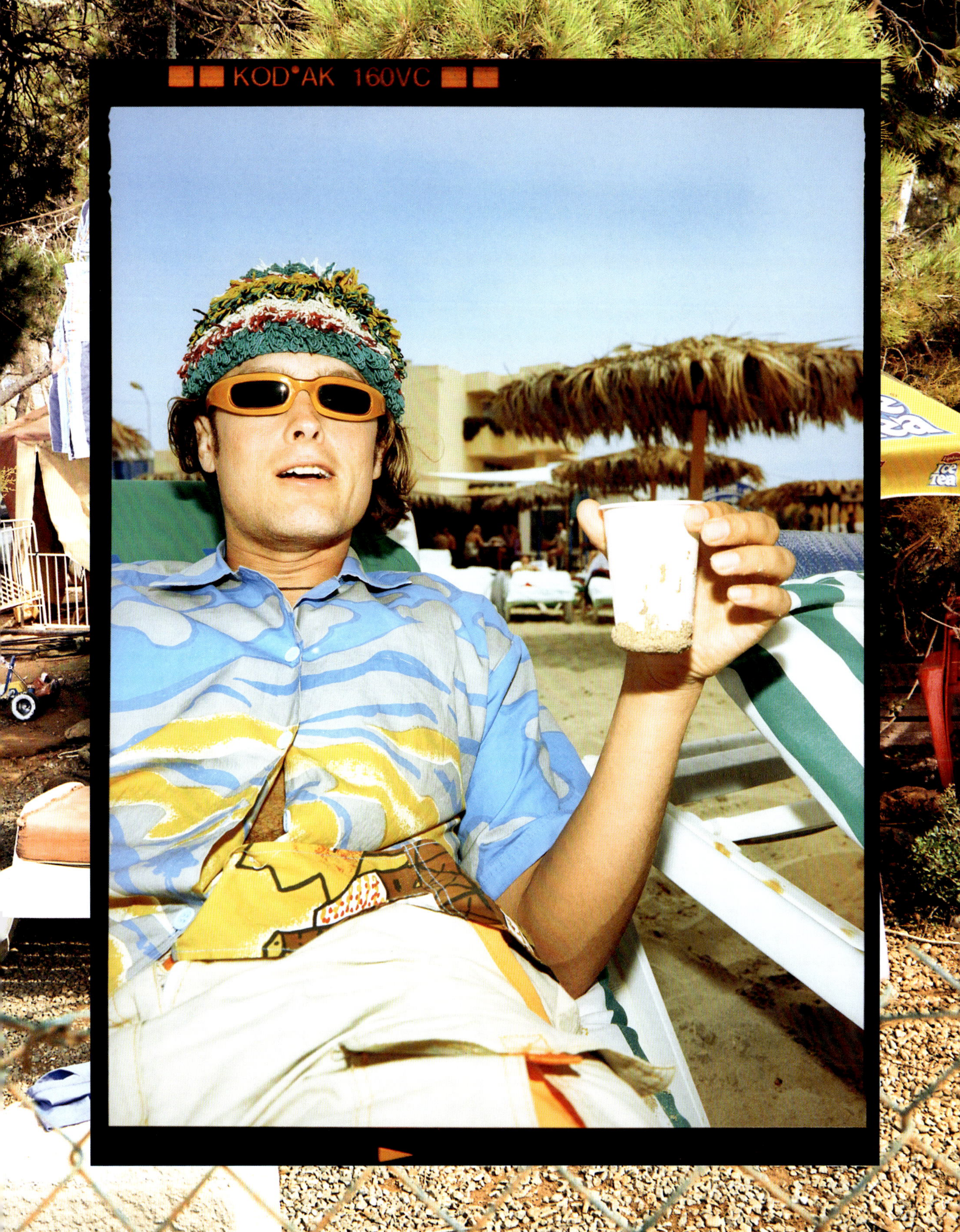
KOD*AK 160VC

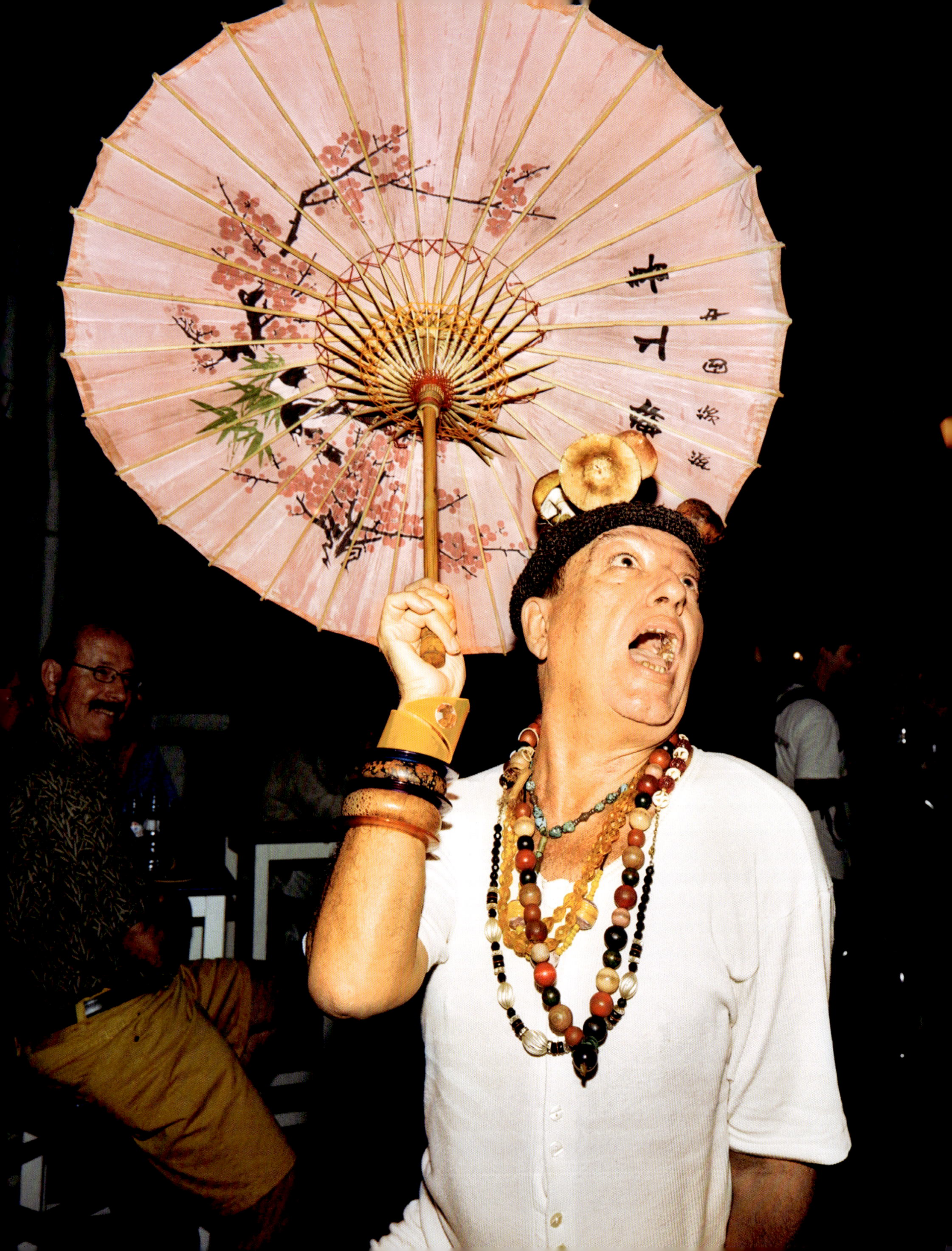

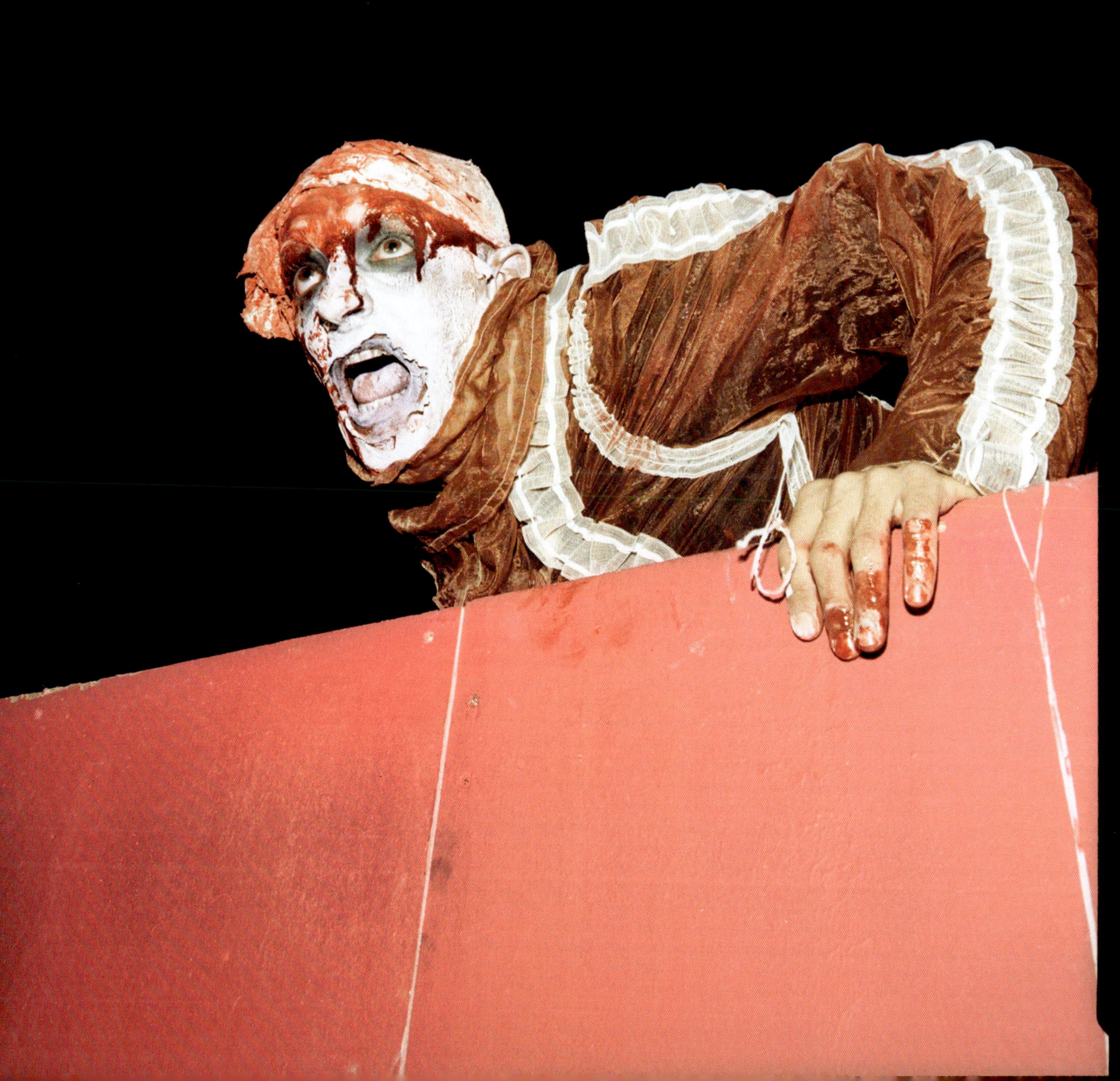

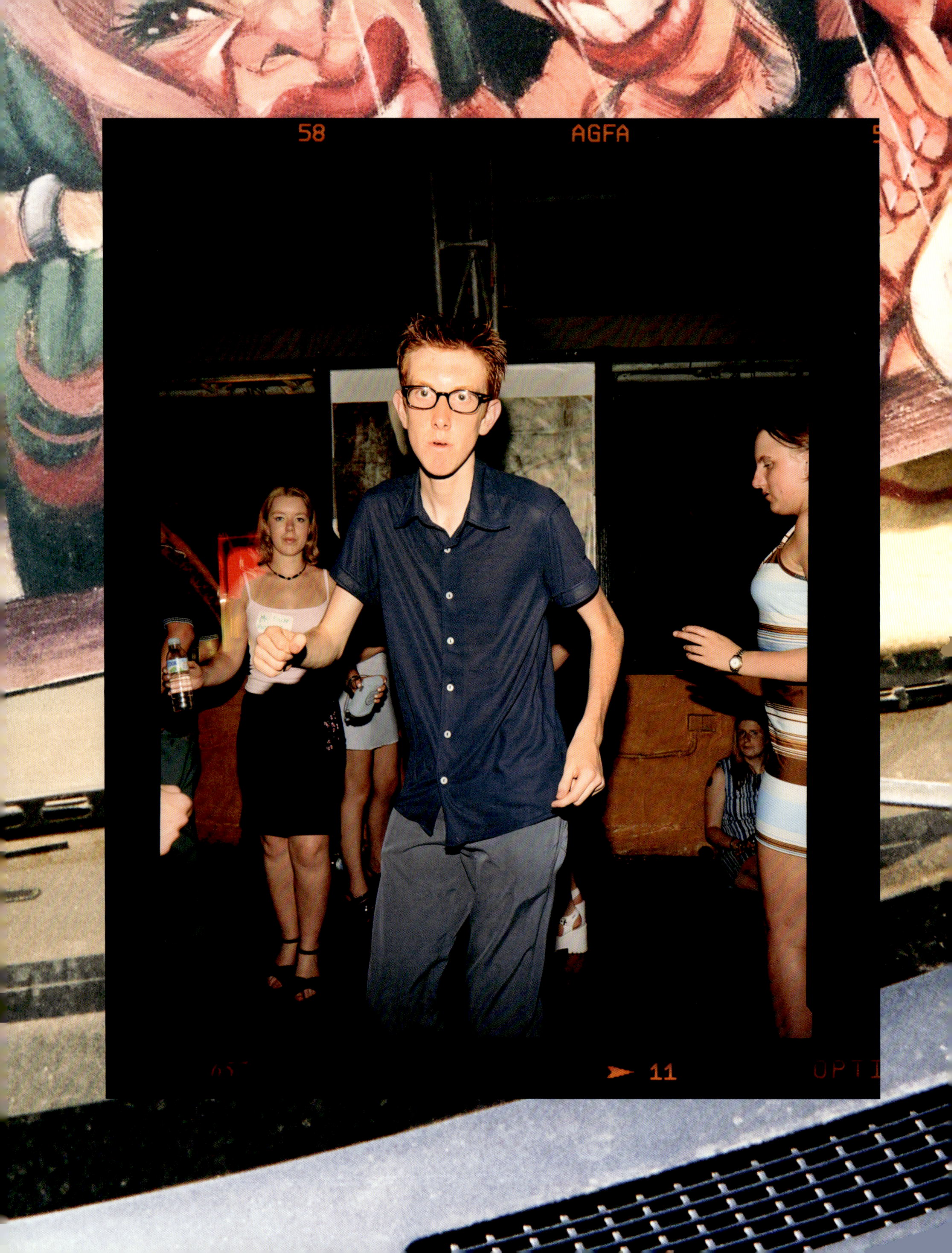

AGFA
56
OPTIMA 100

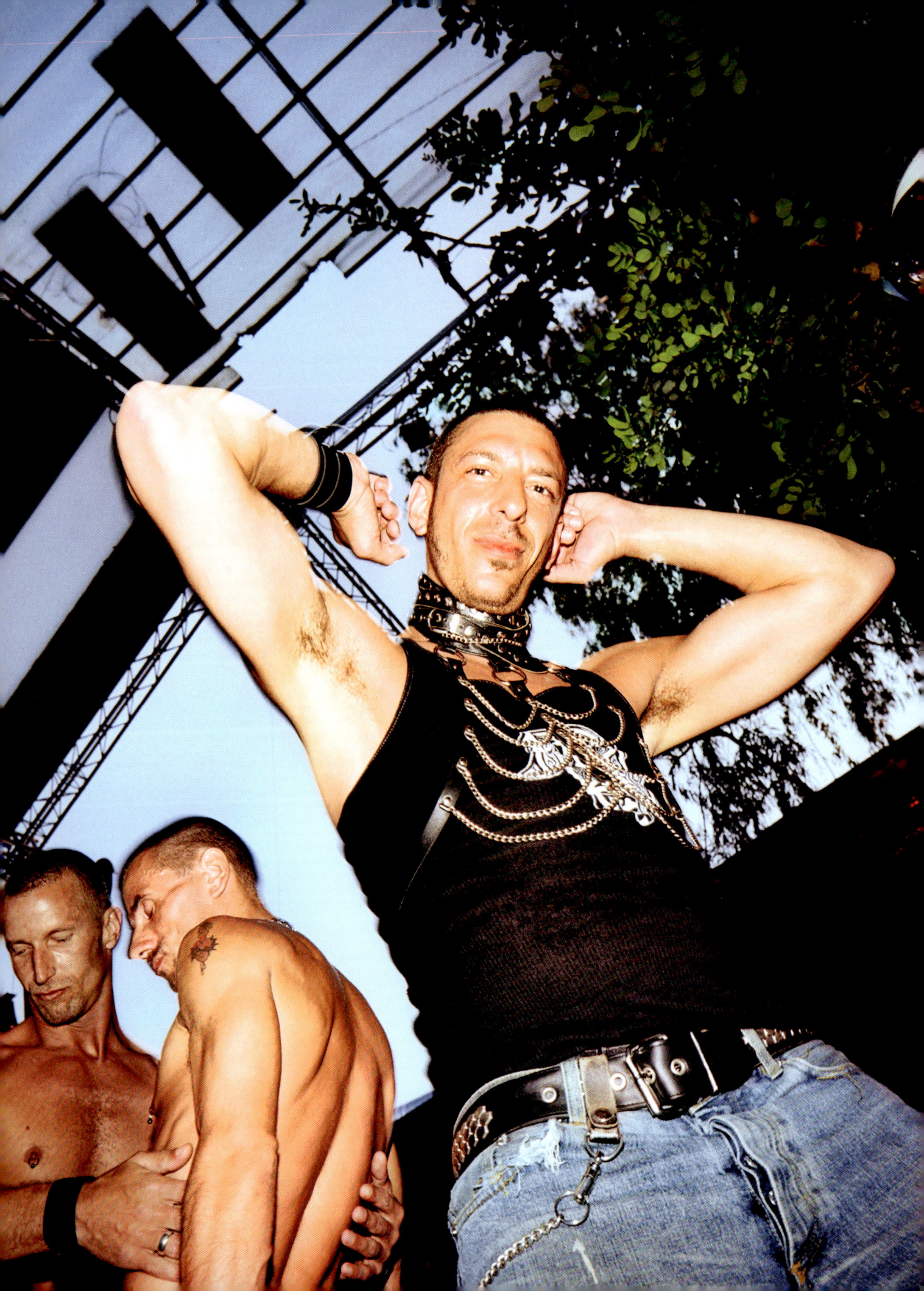

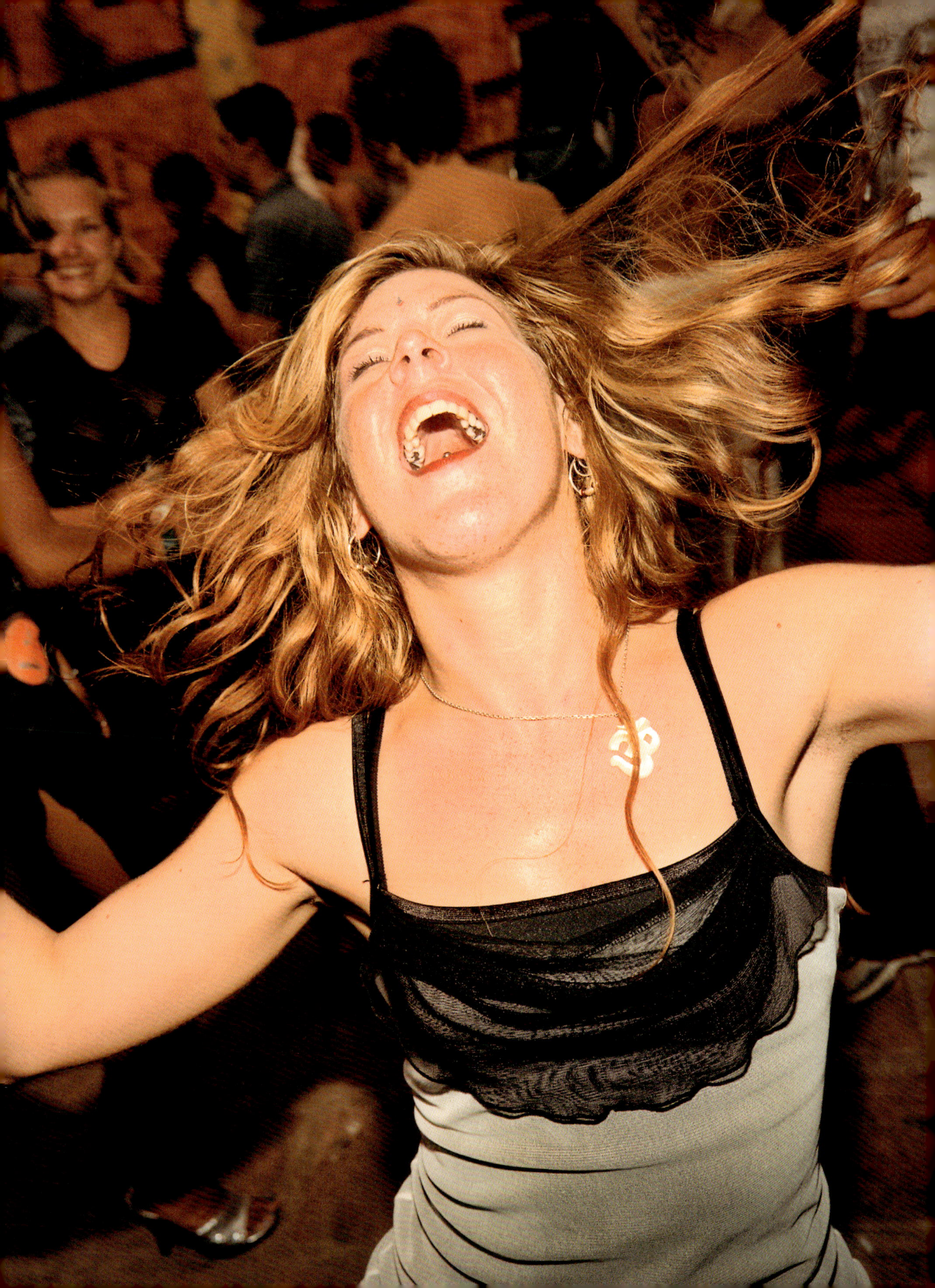

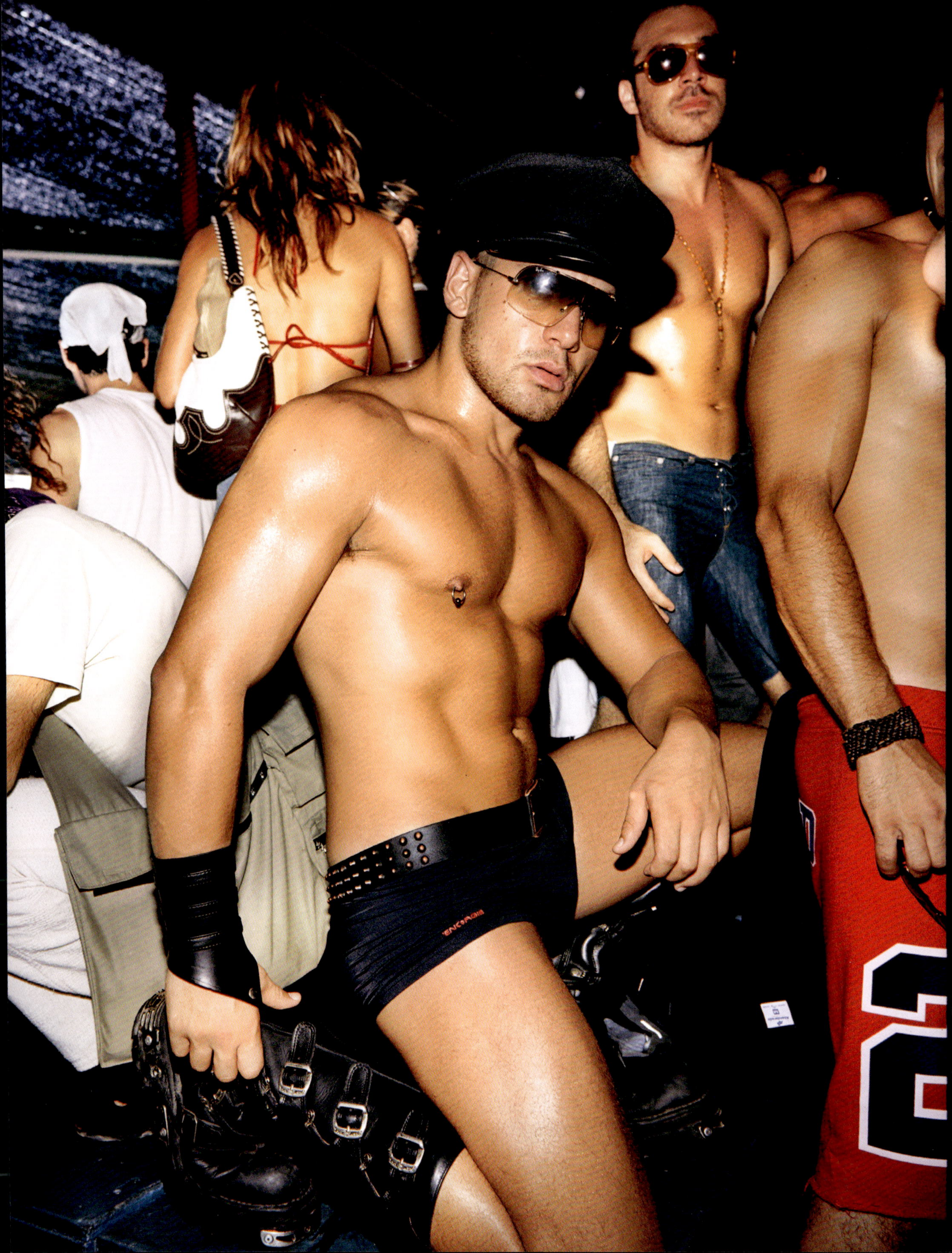

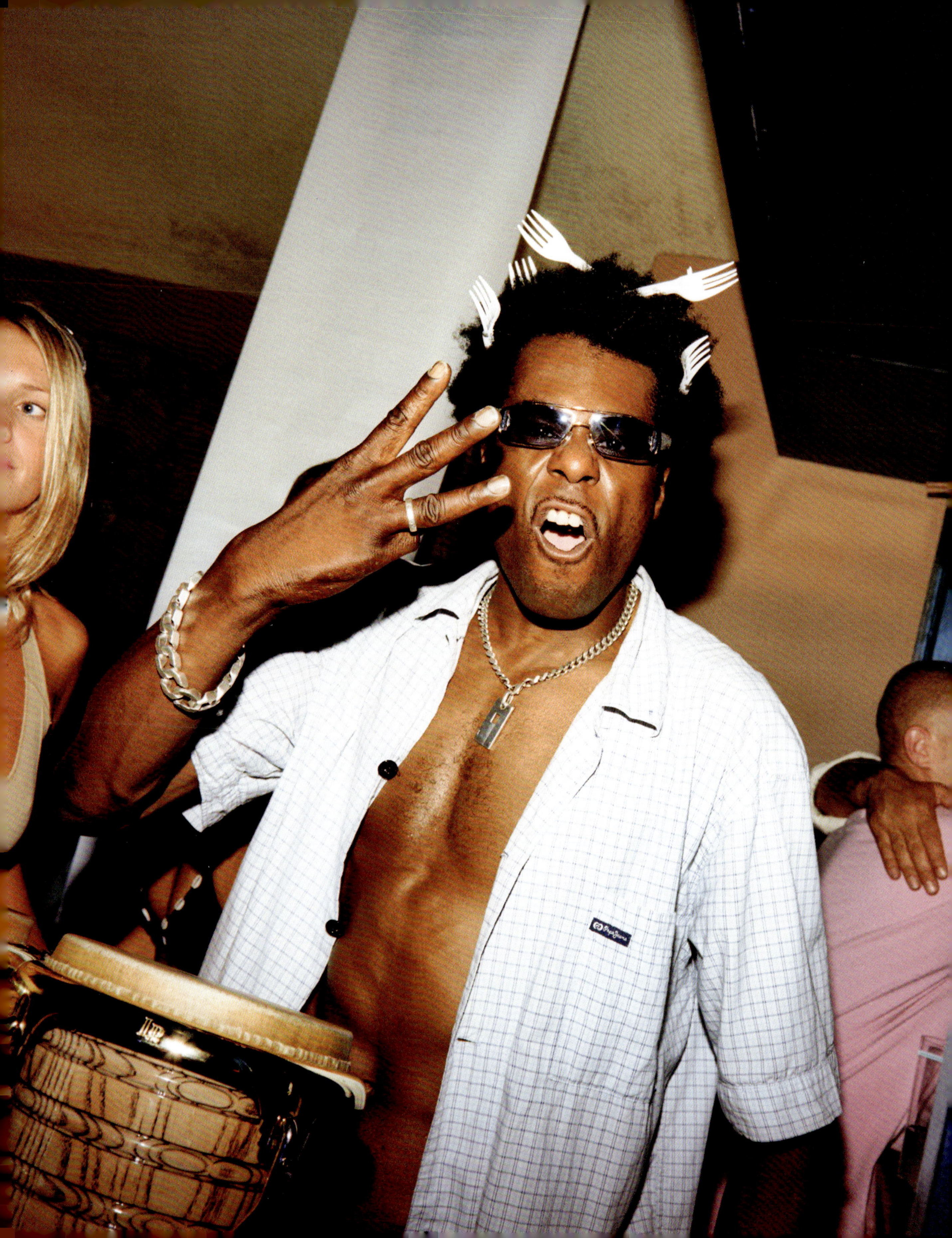

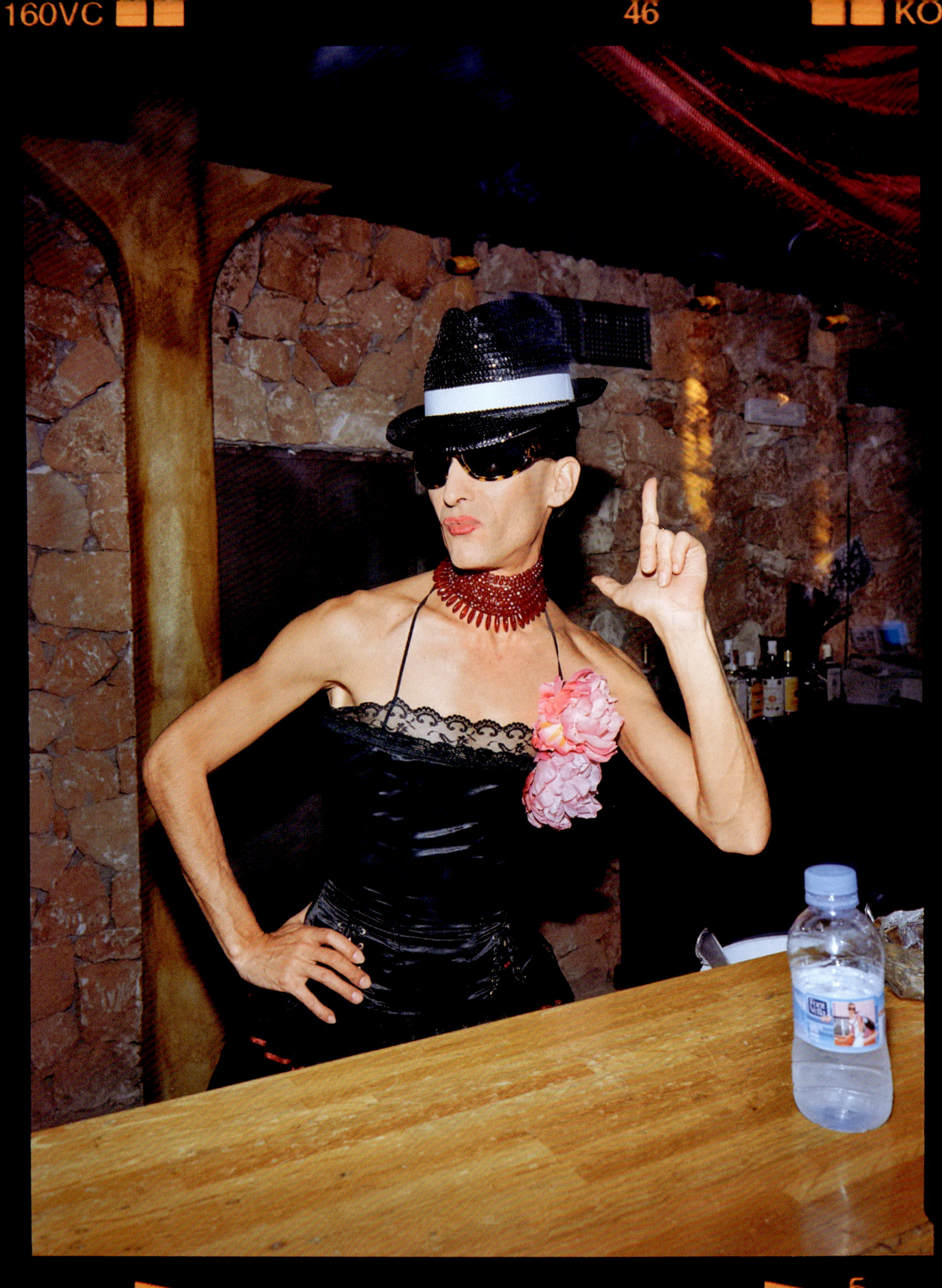

K 160VC
46
KOD

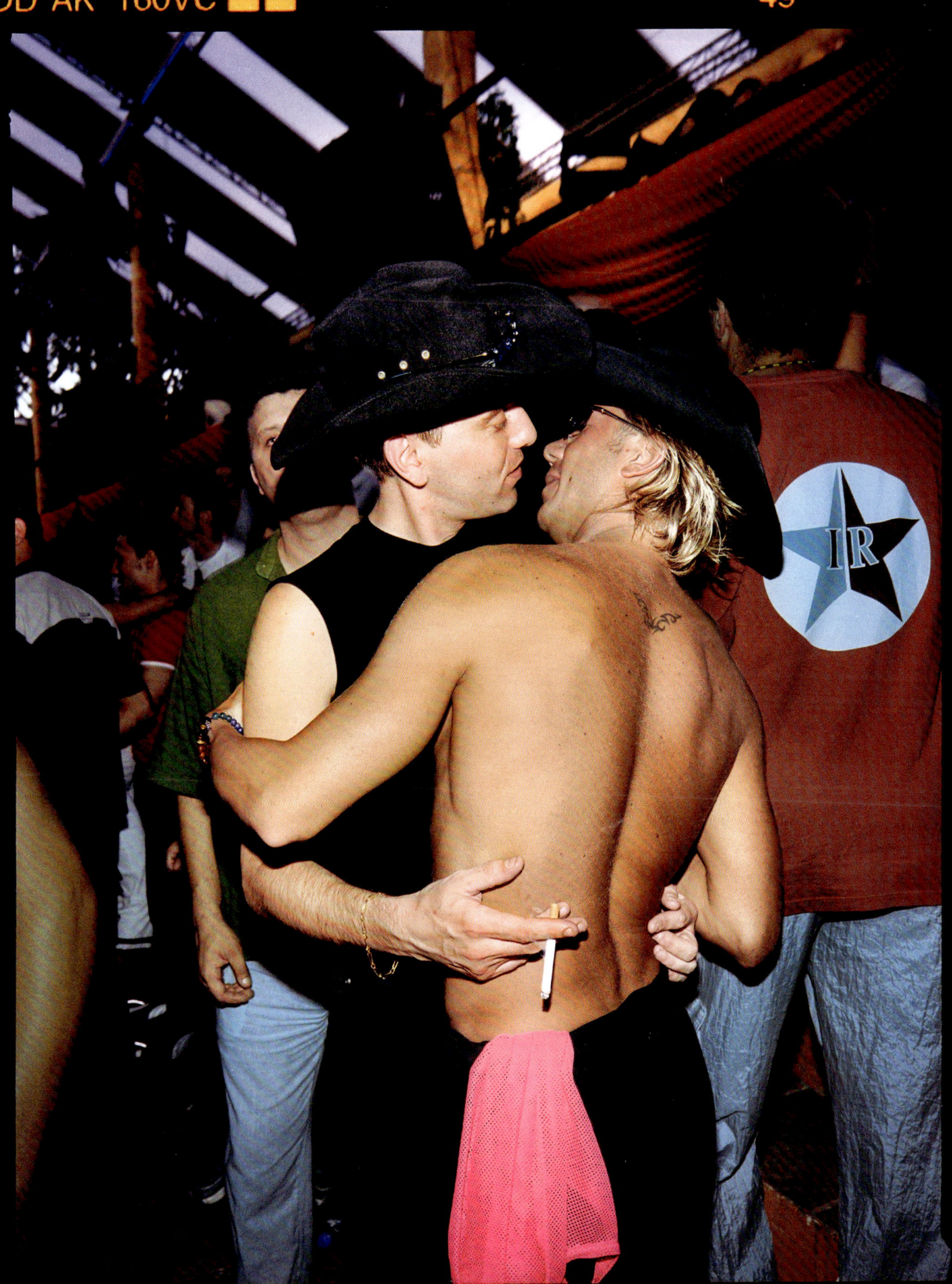

IR

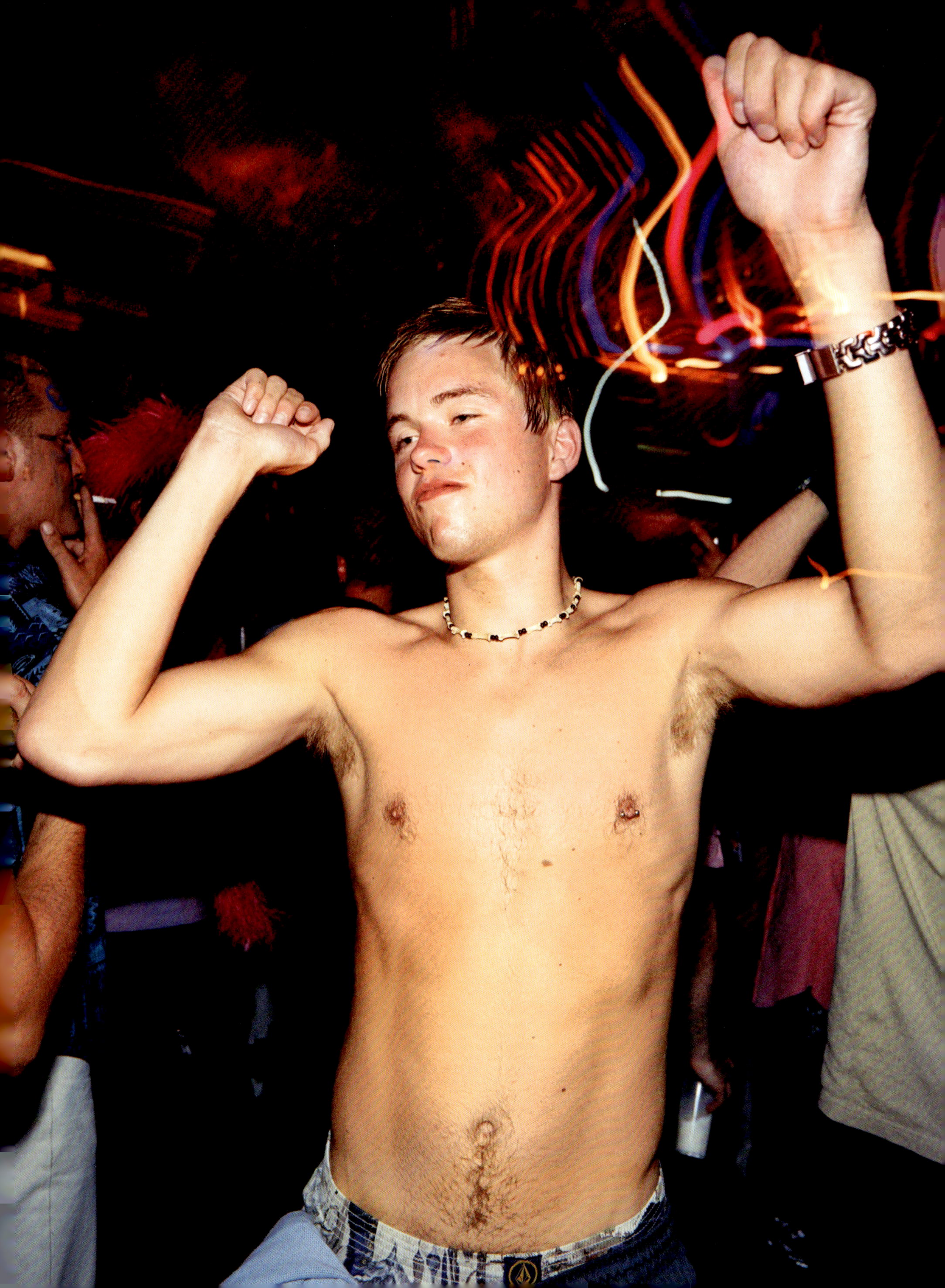

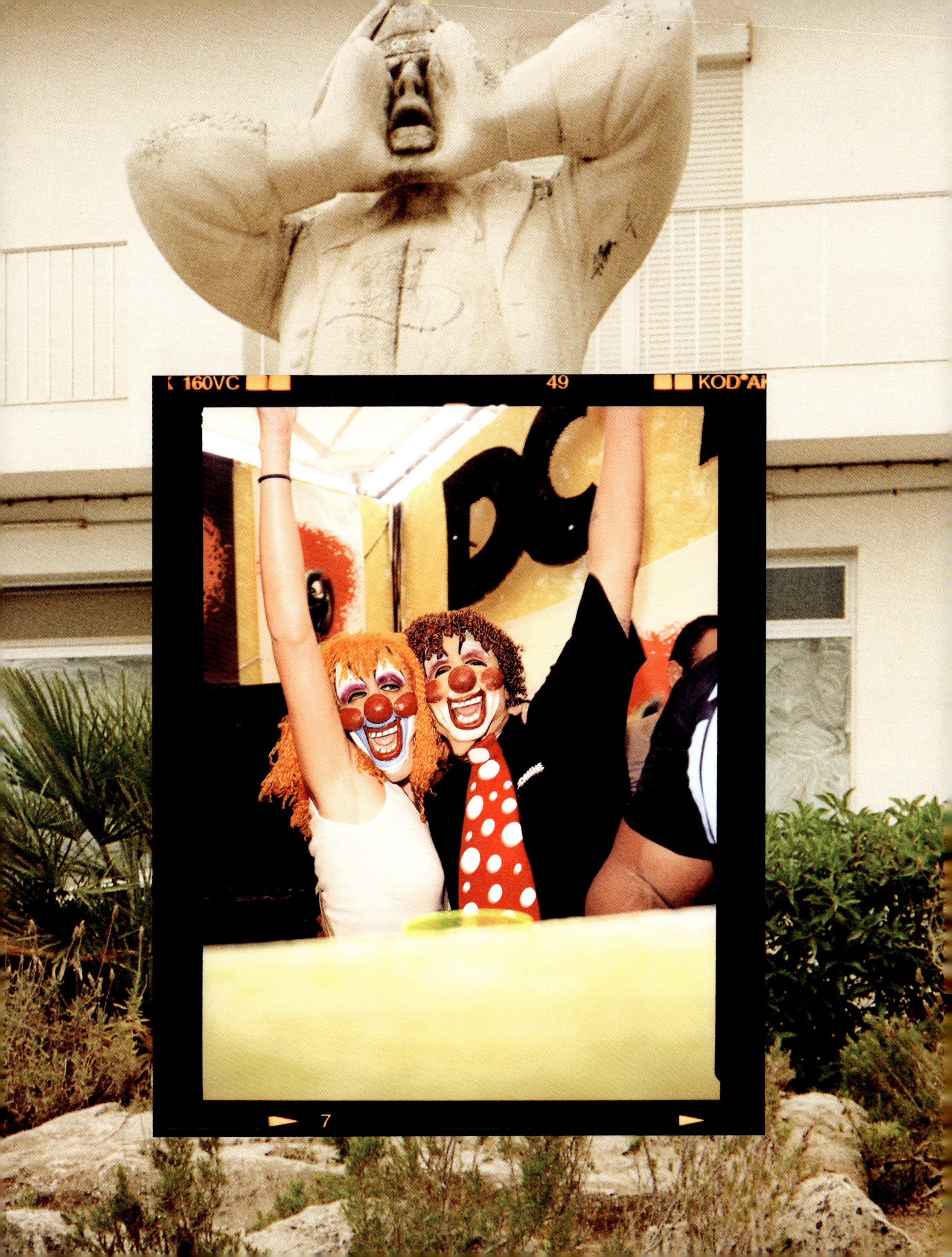

160VC
49
KOD*A
7

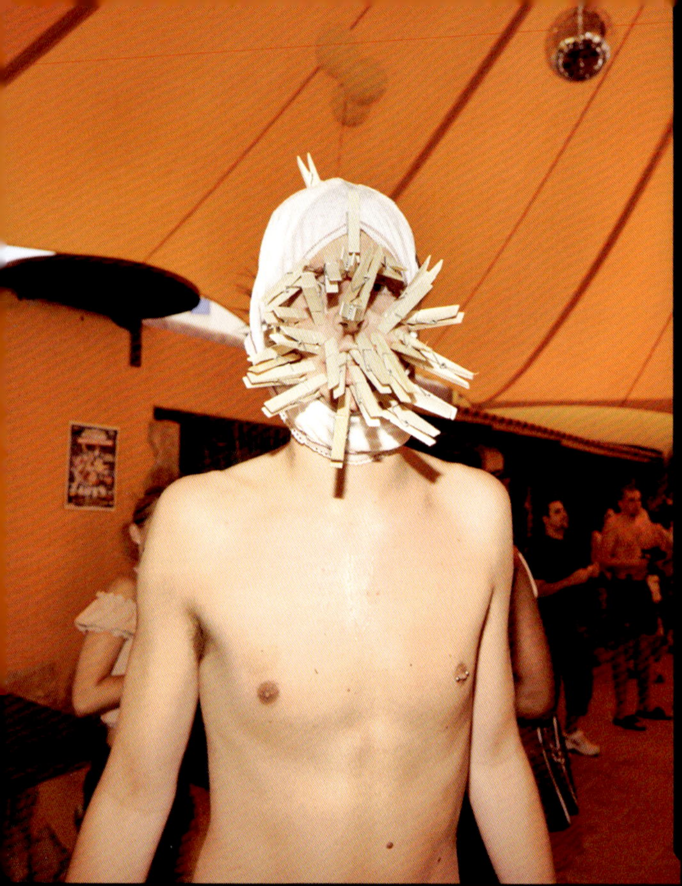

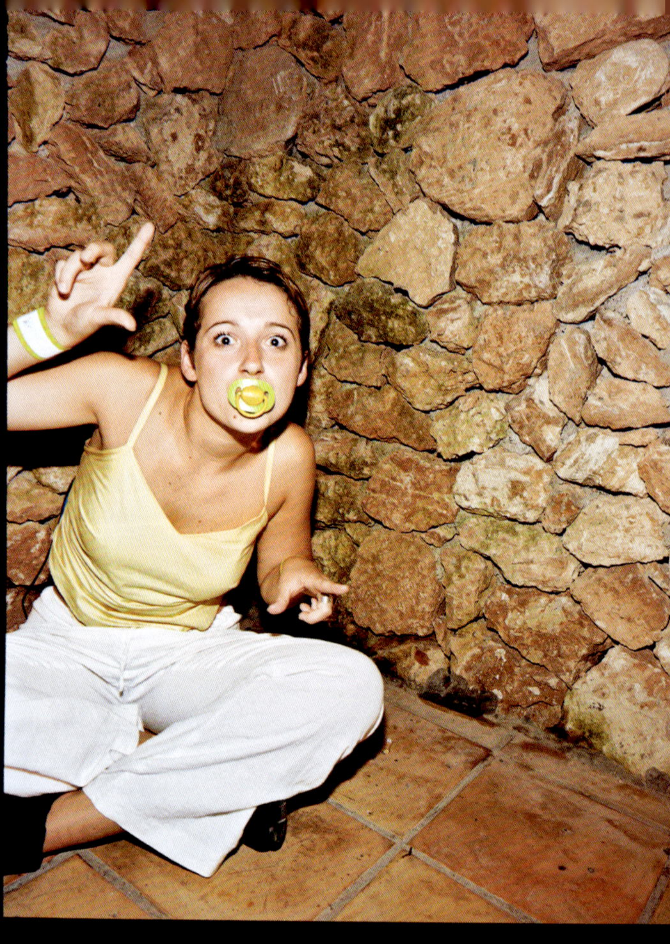

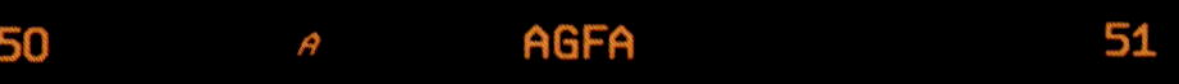
50   A   AGFA   51

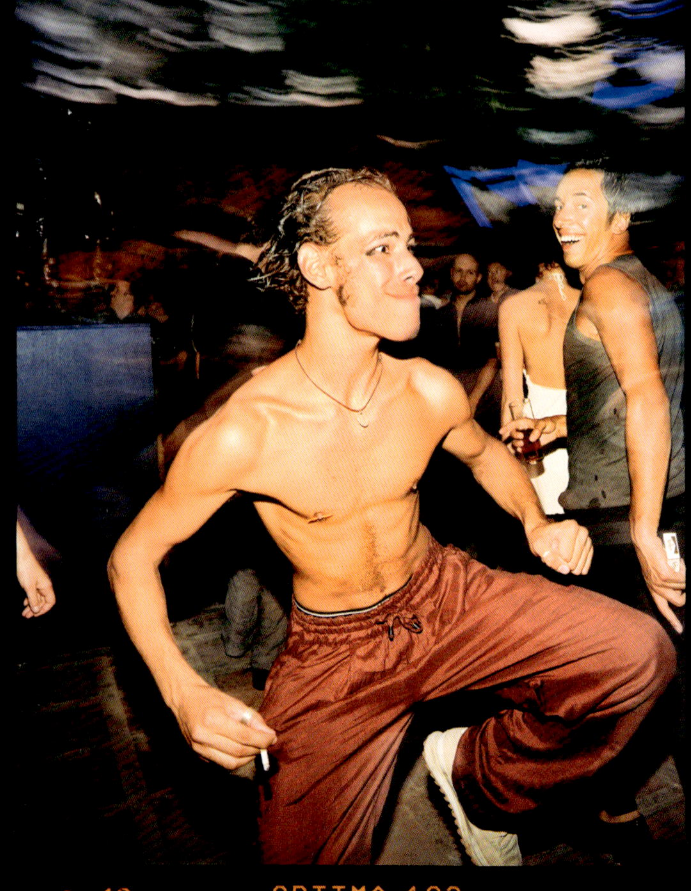

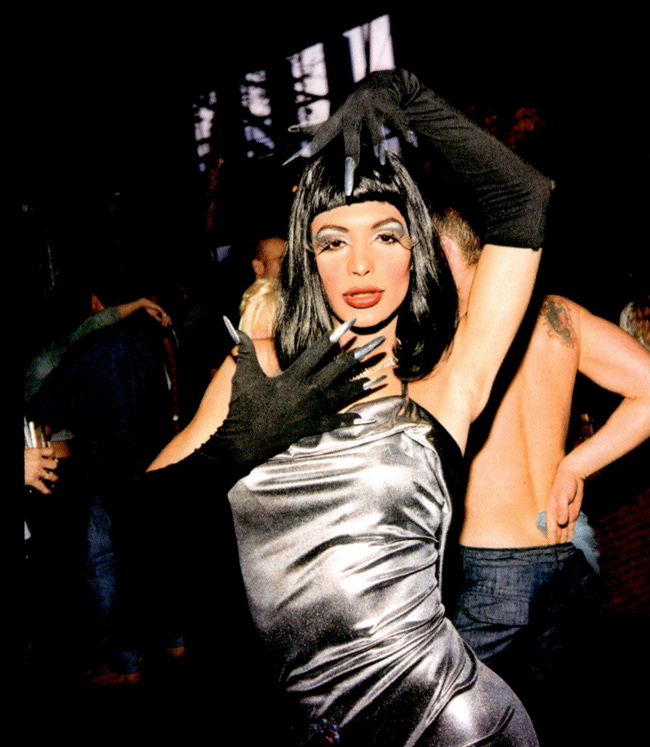

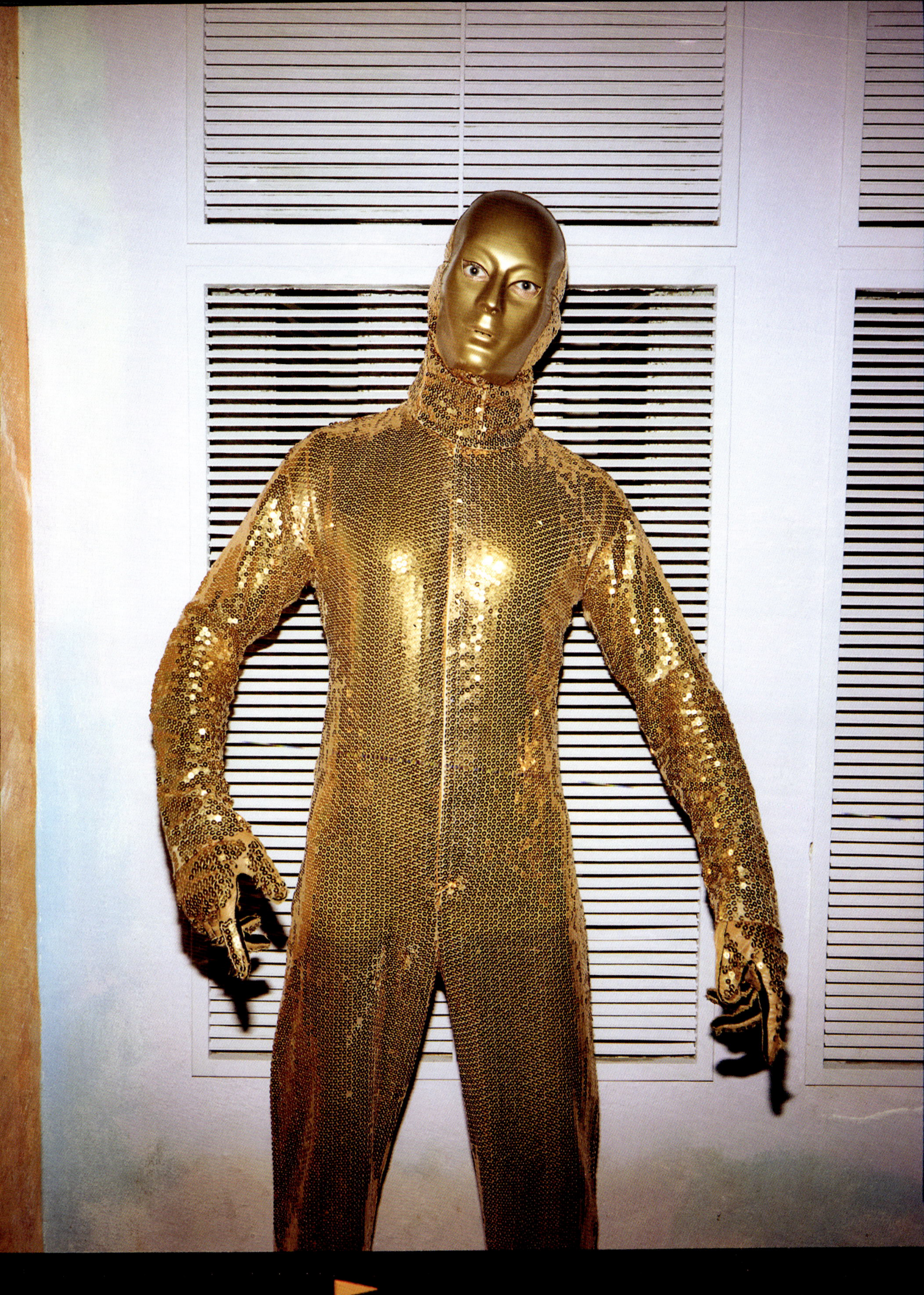

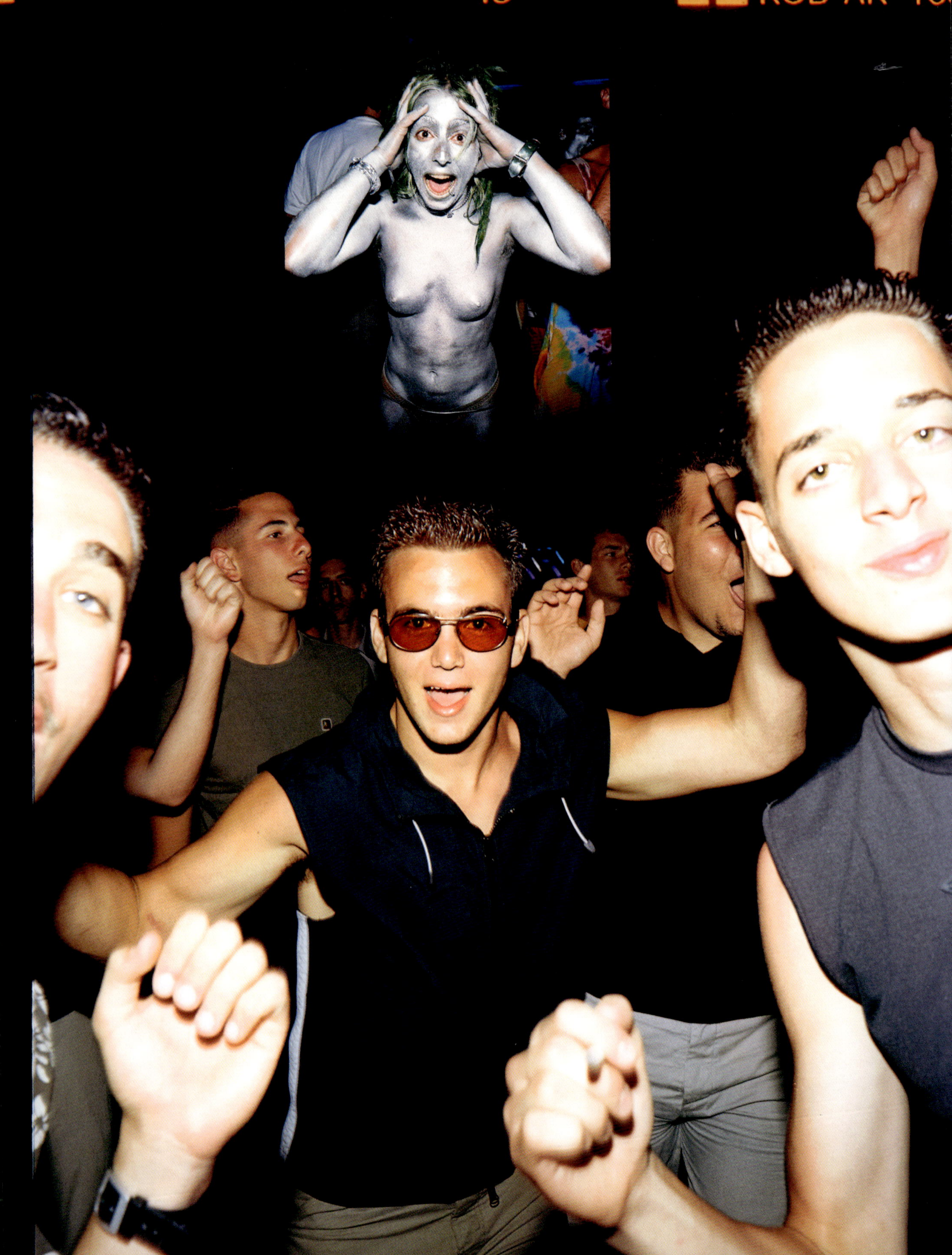

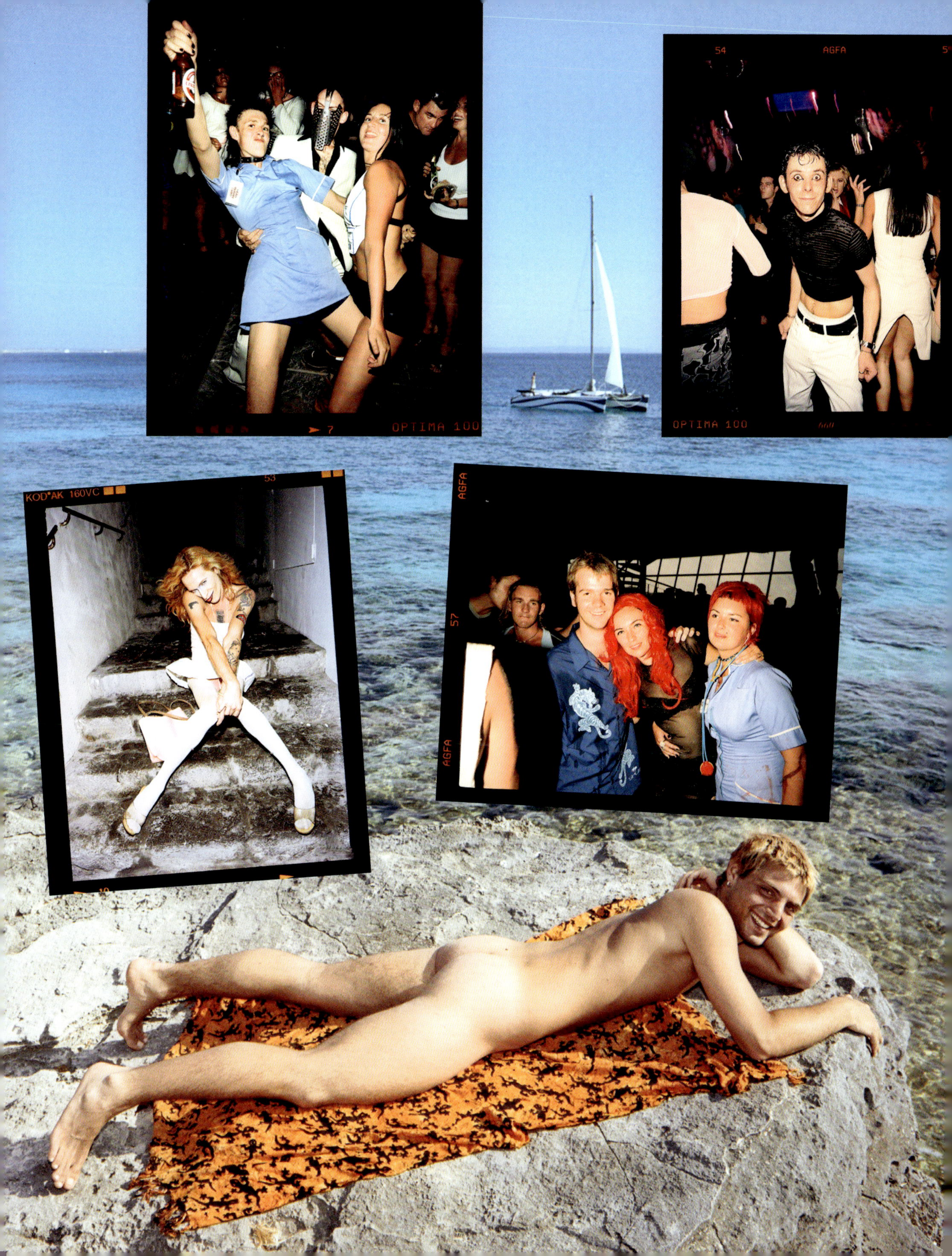

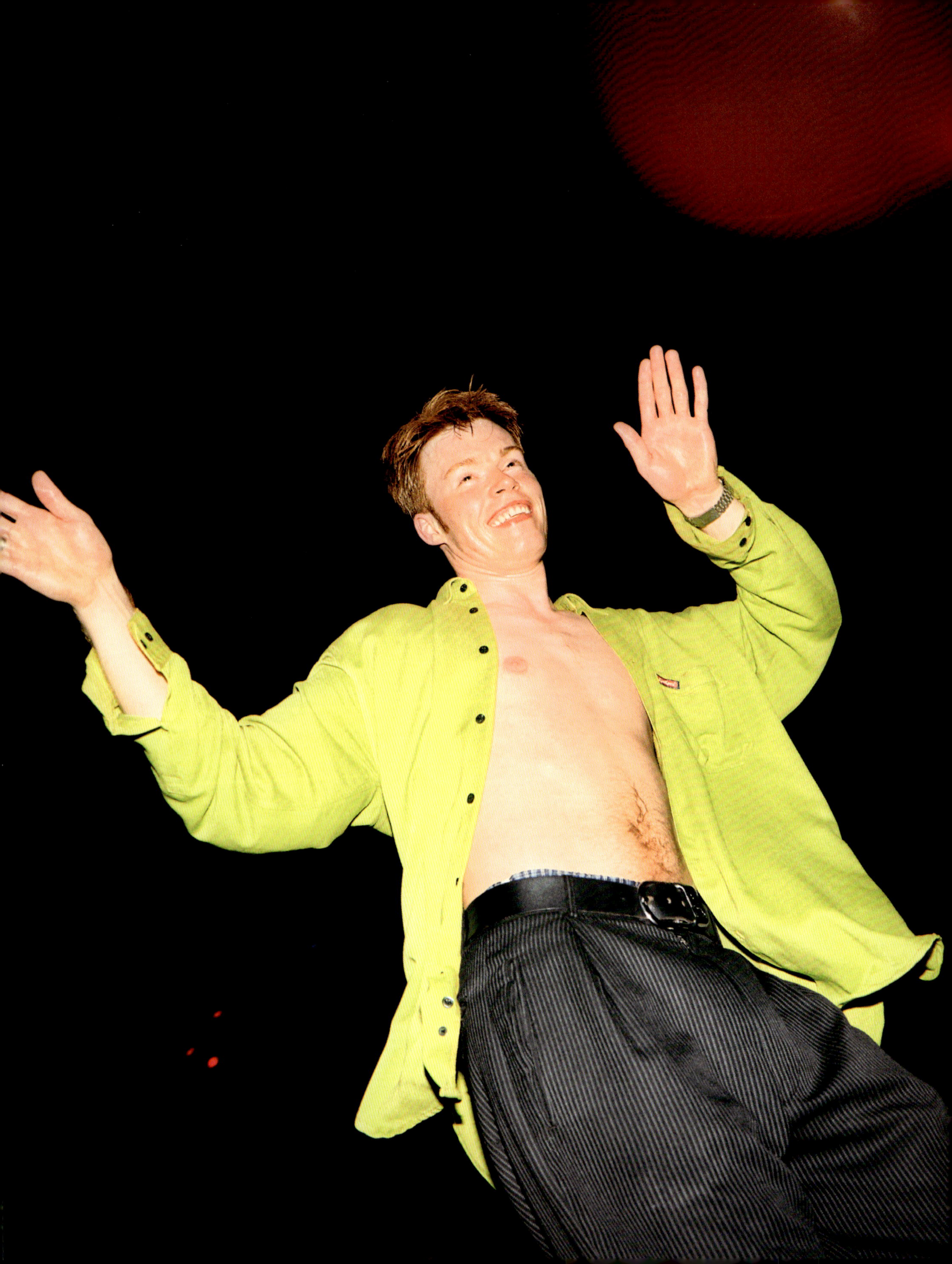

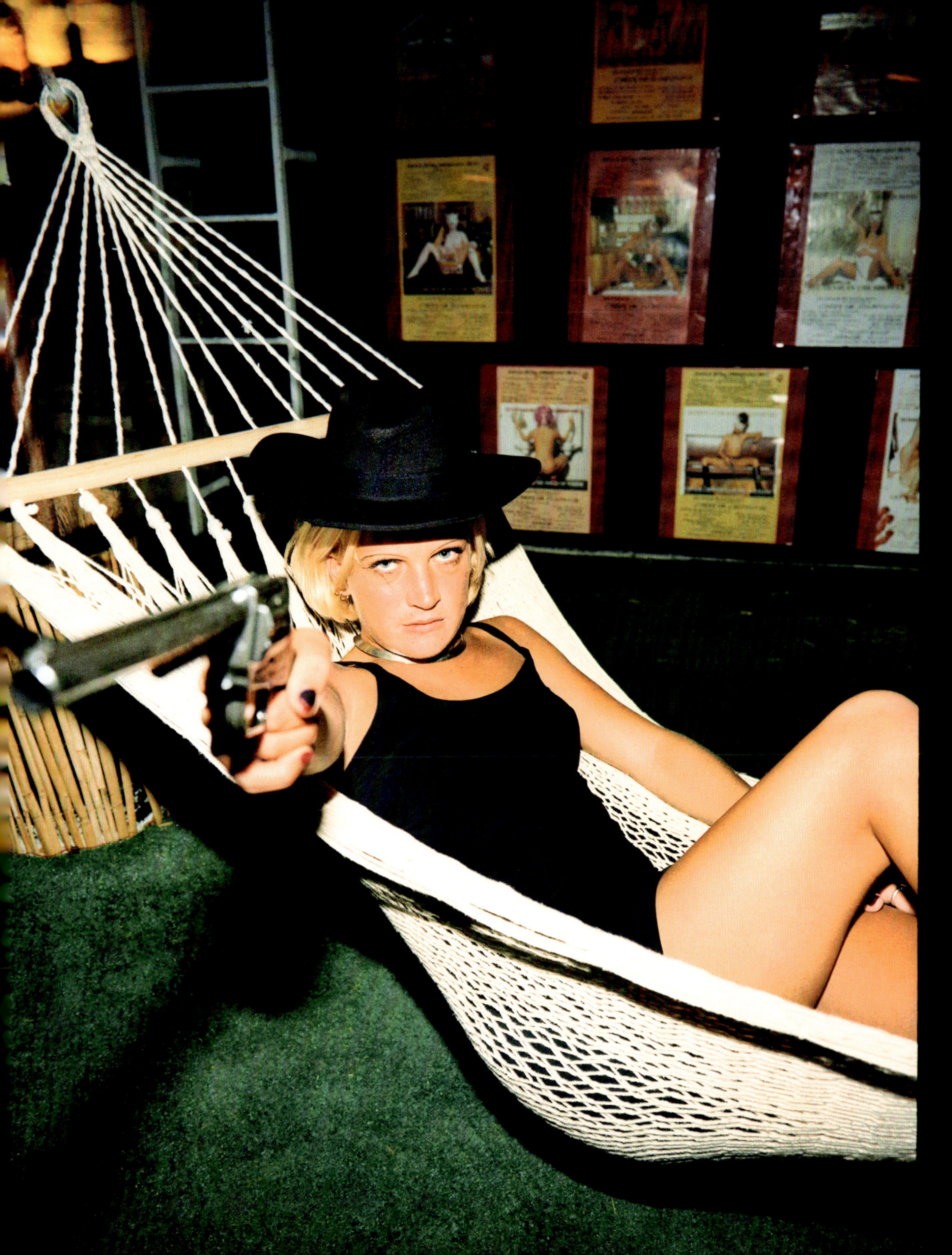

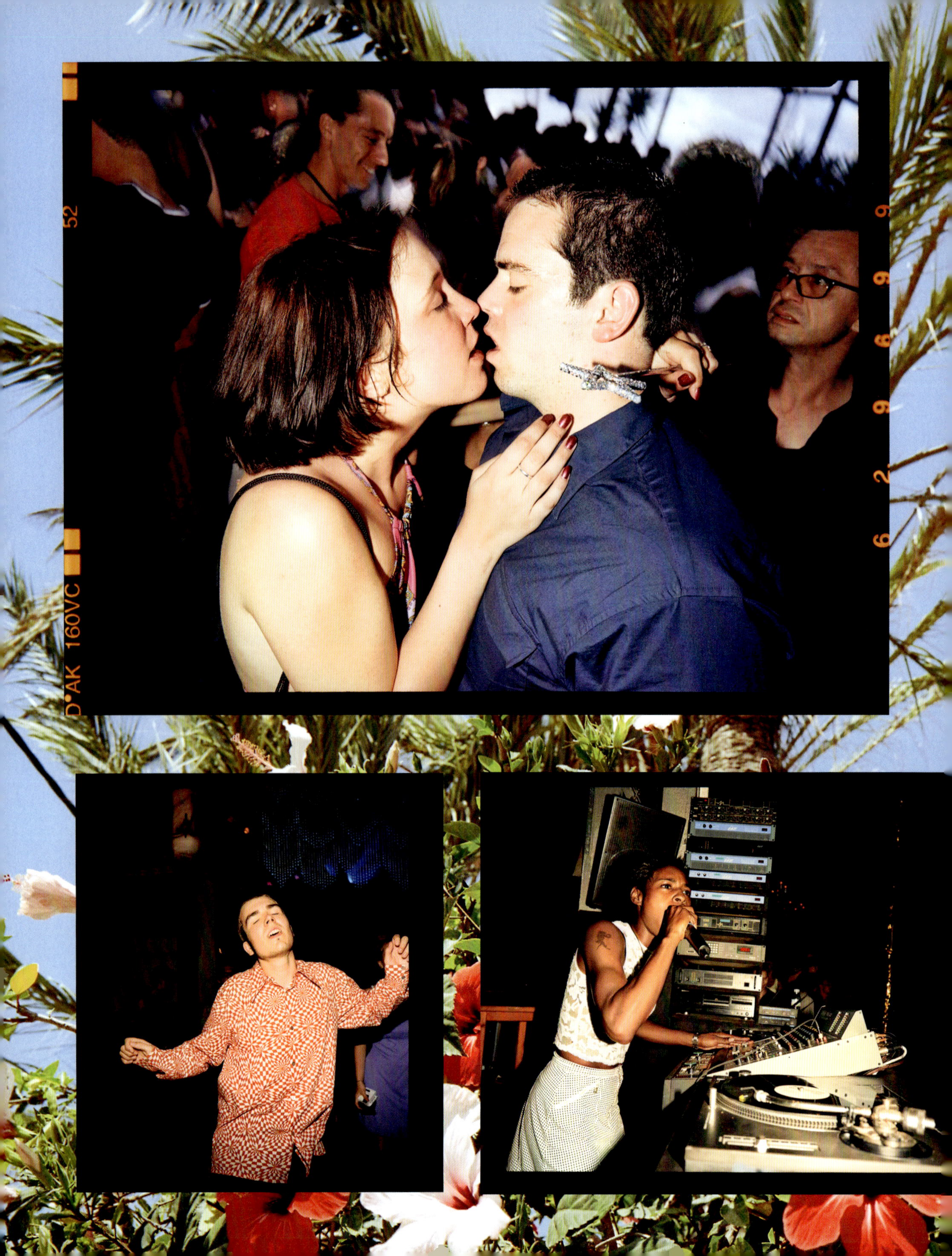

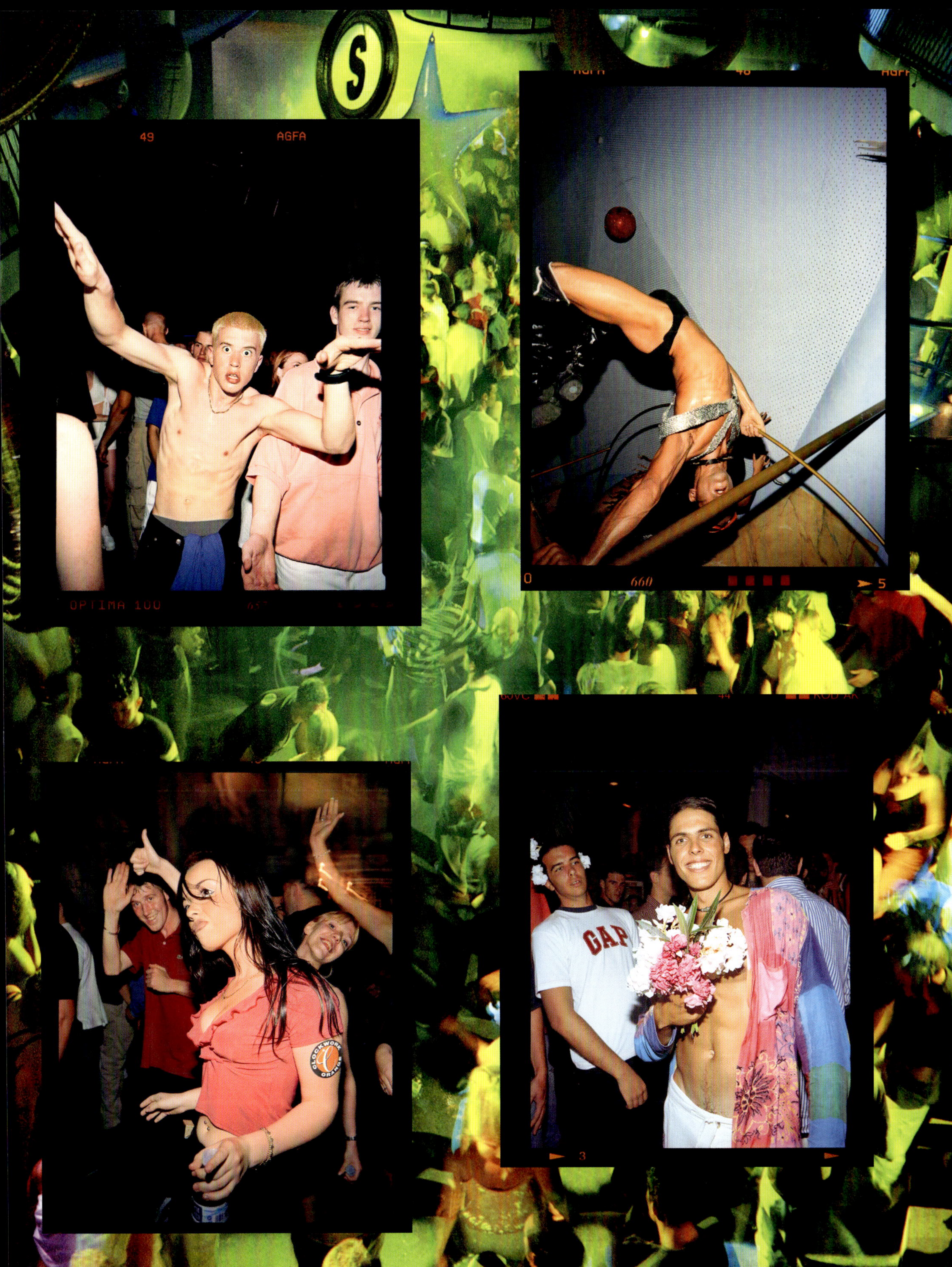

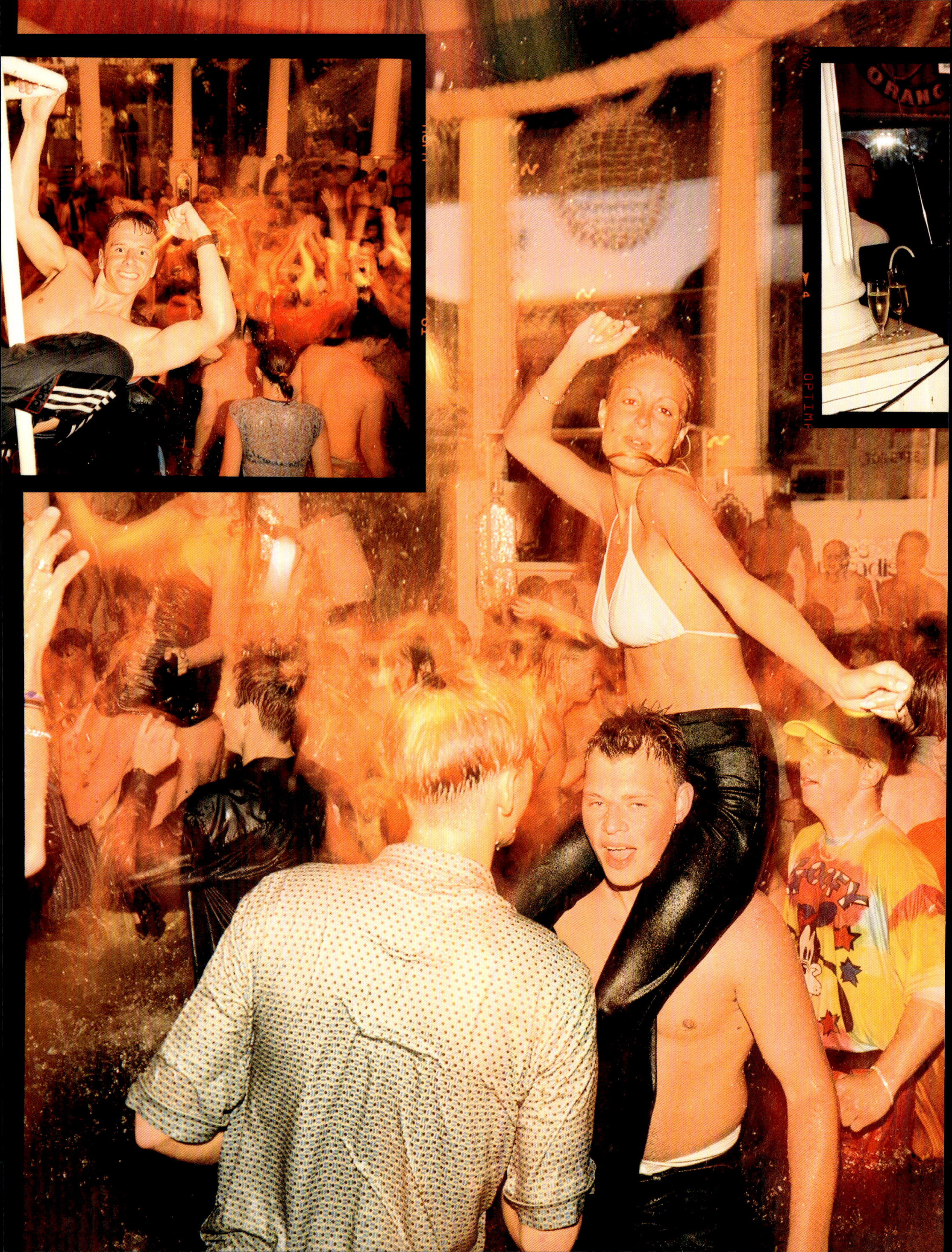

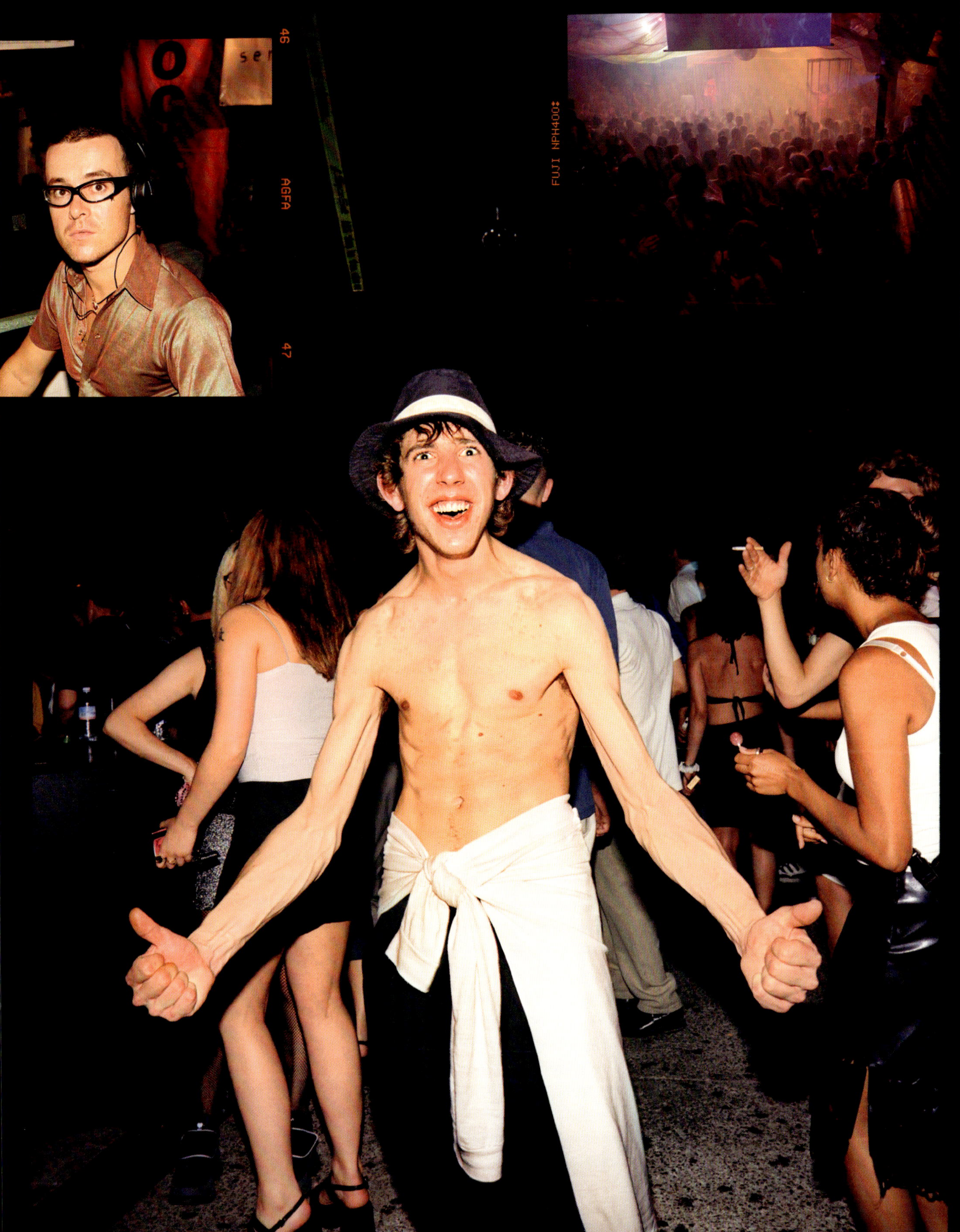

46
AGFA
47
FUJI NPH400

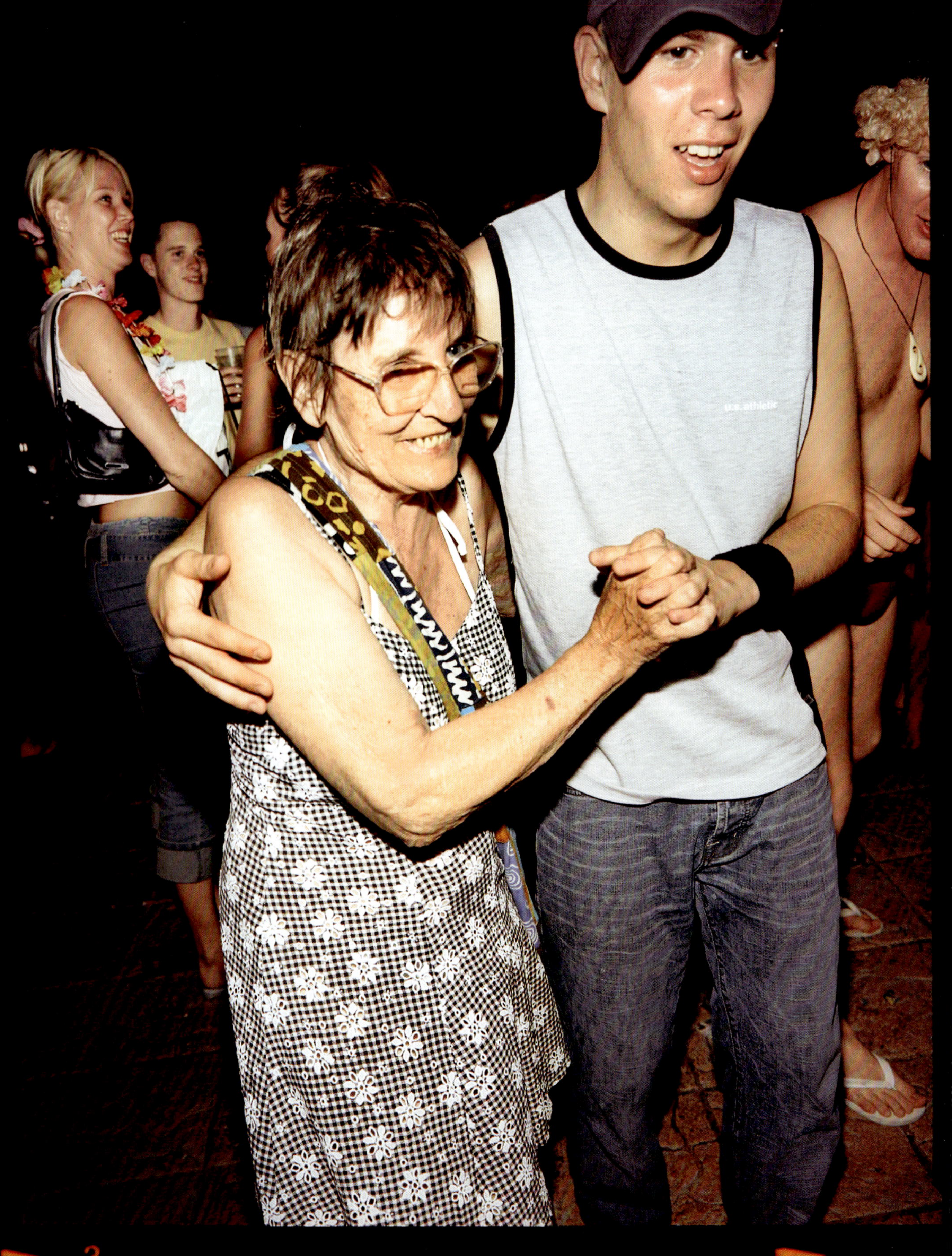

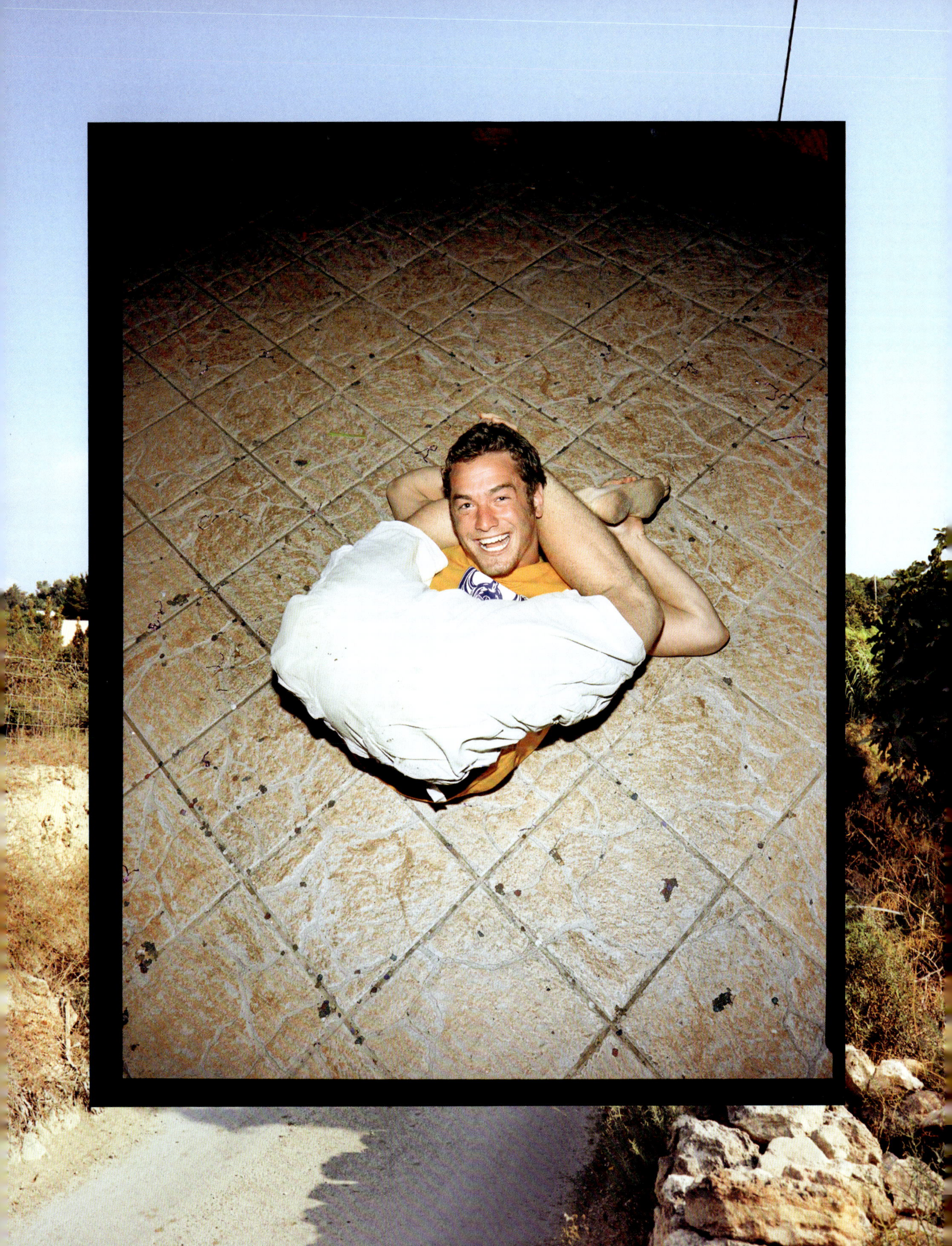

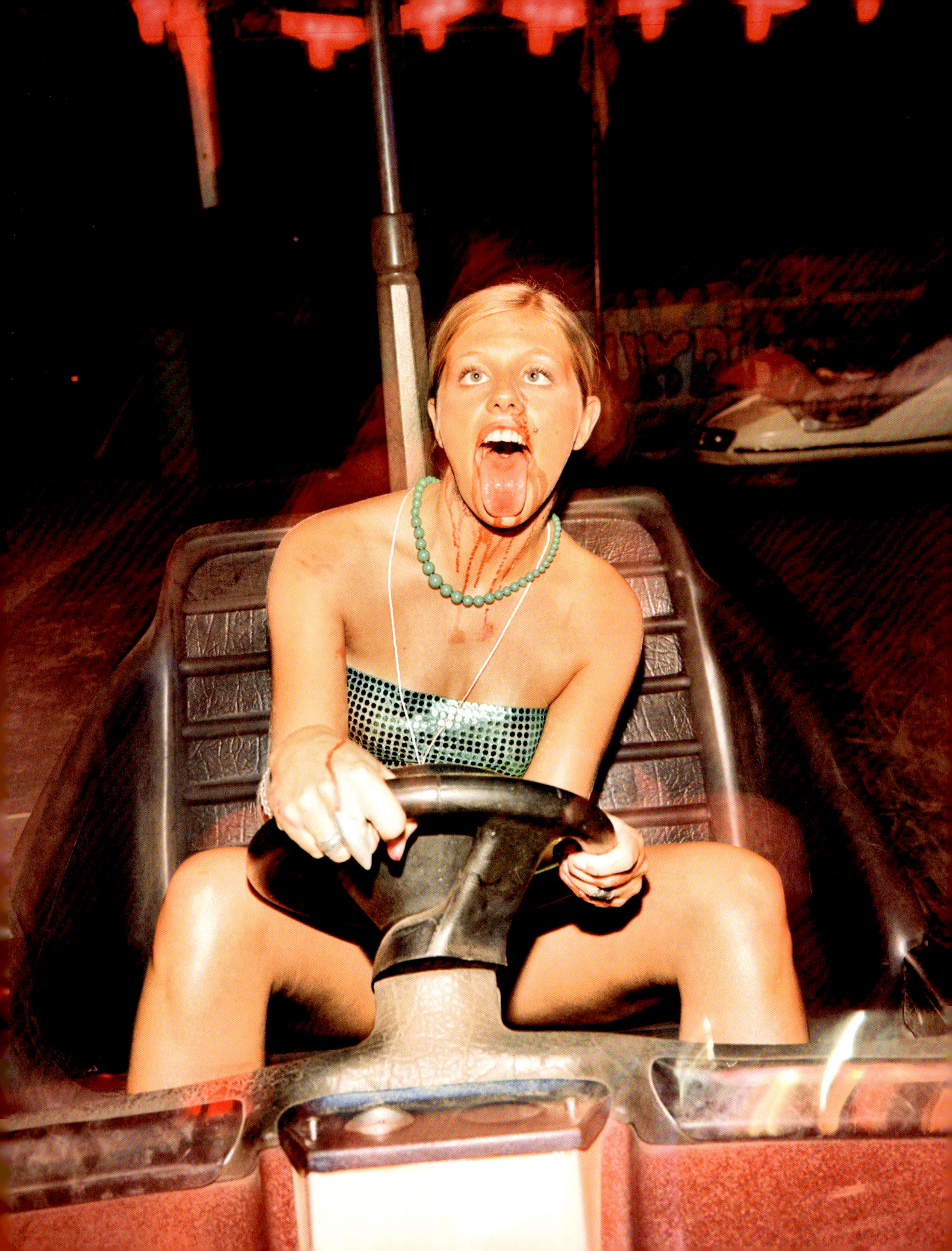

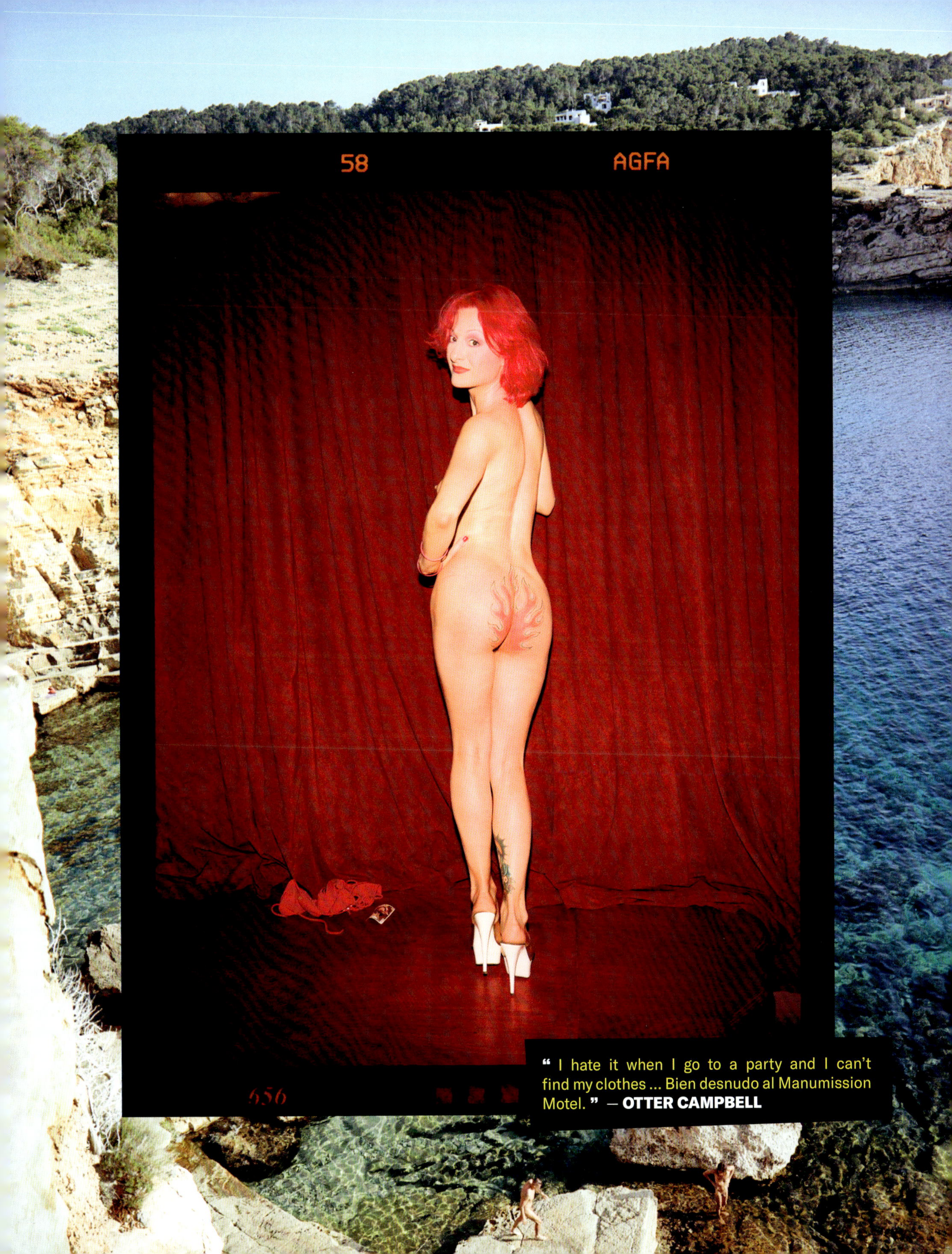
58
AGFA
636

" I hate it when I go to a party and I can't find my clothes ... Bien desnudo al Manumission Motel. " — OTTER CAMPBELL

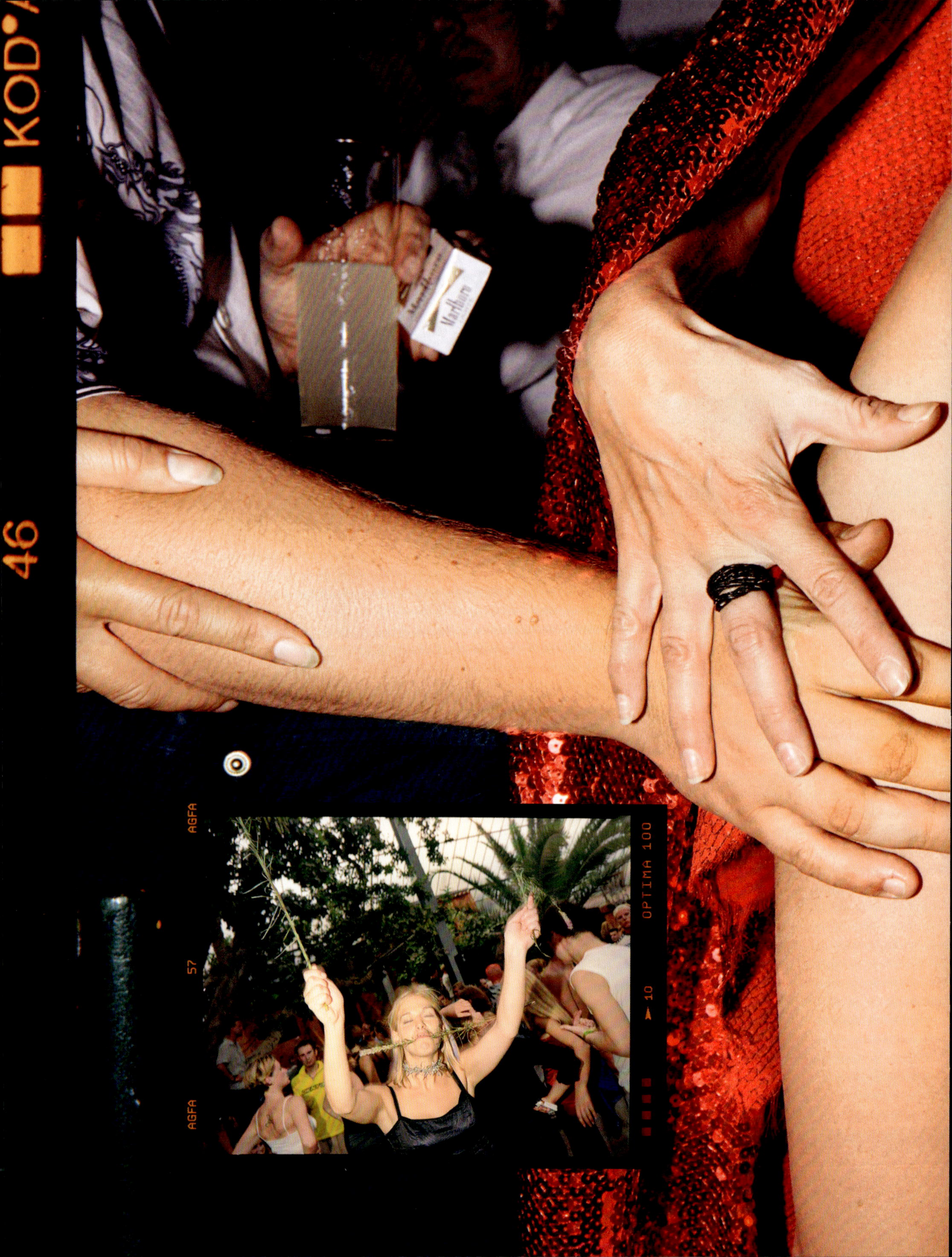

KOD
46
Marlboro
AGFA
57
AGFA
OPTIMA 100
10

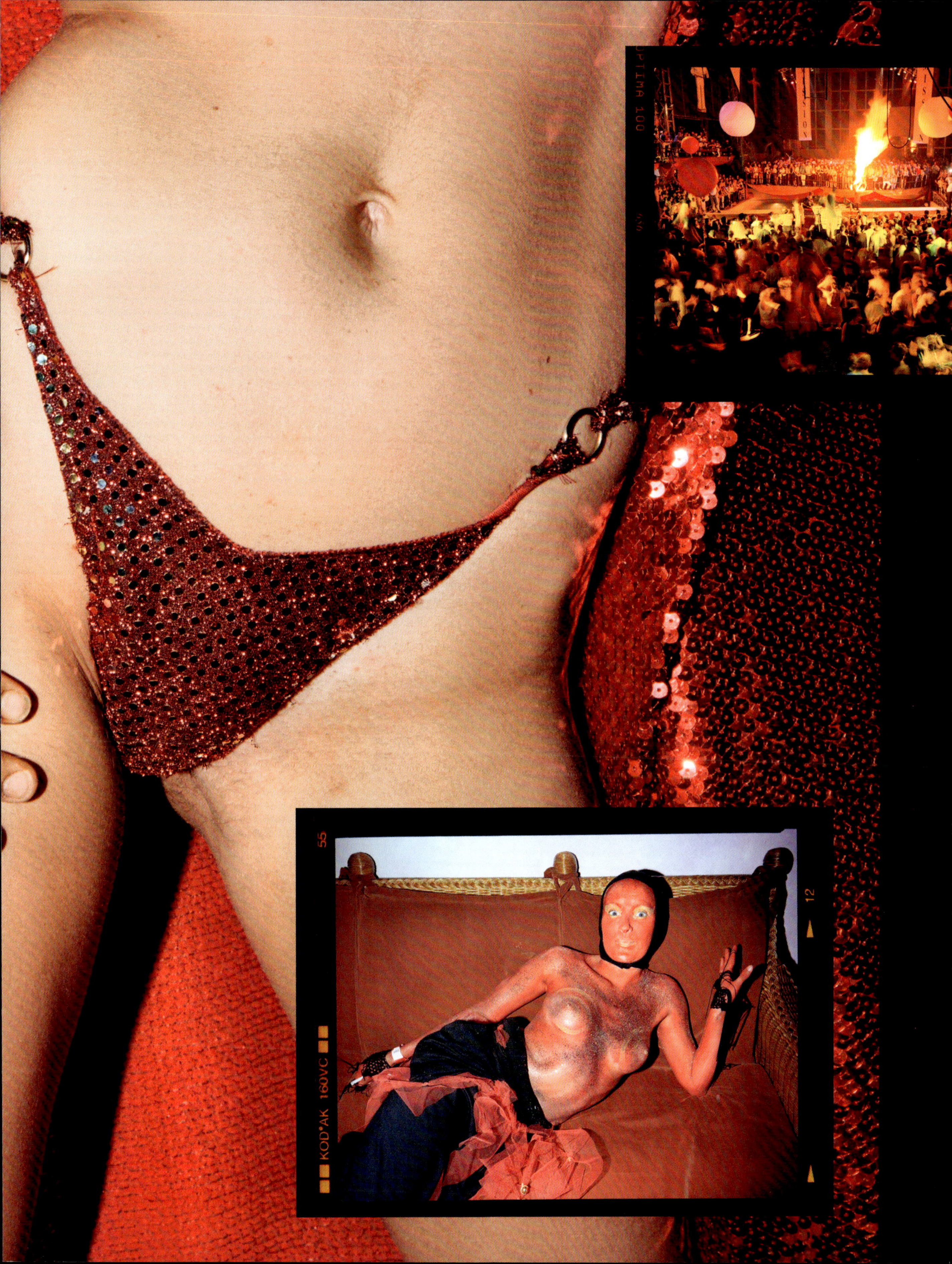

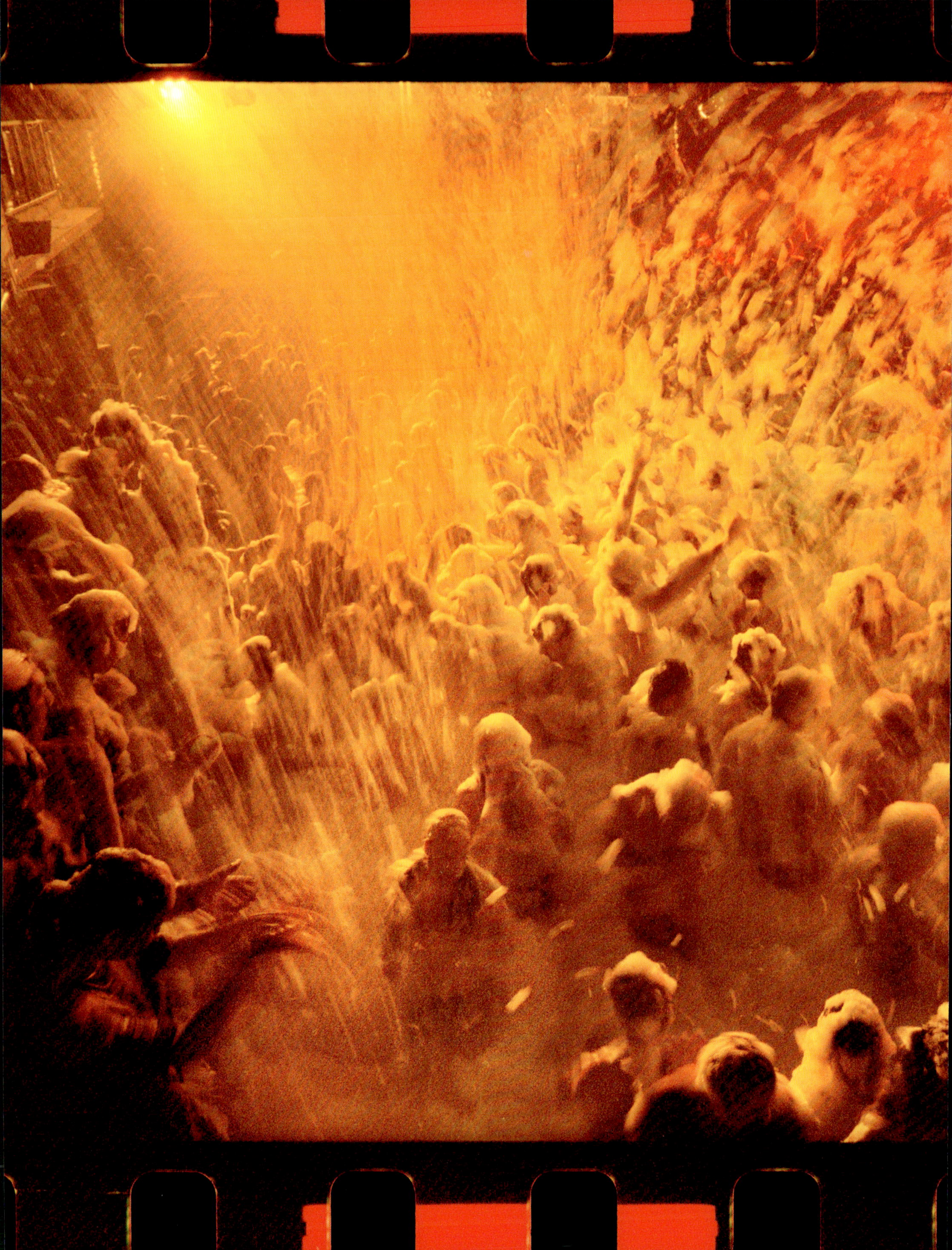

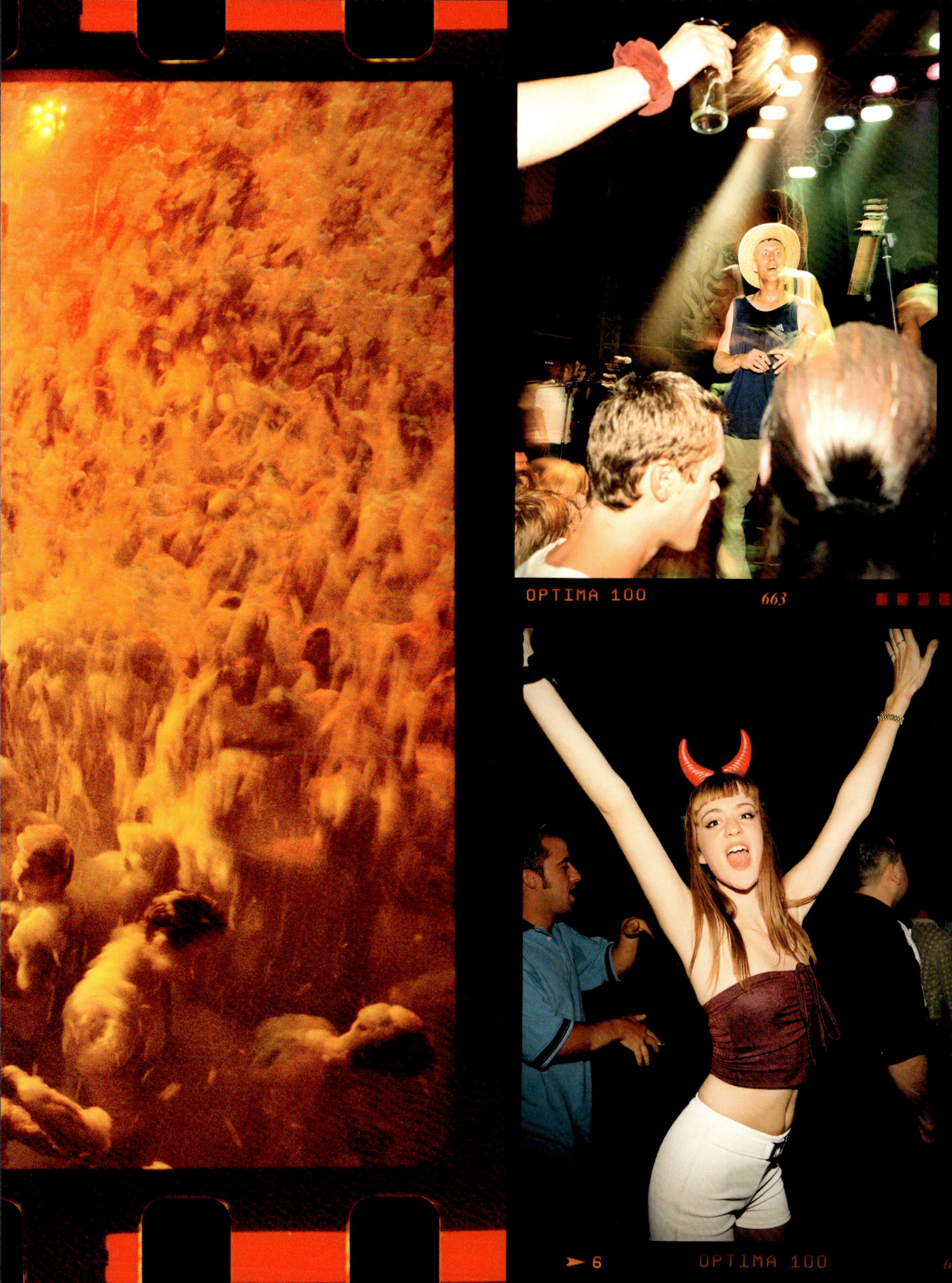
OPTIMA 100
663
6
OPTIMA 100

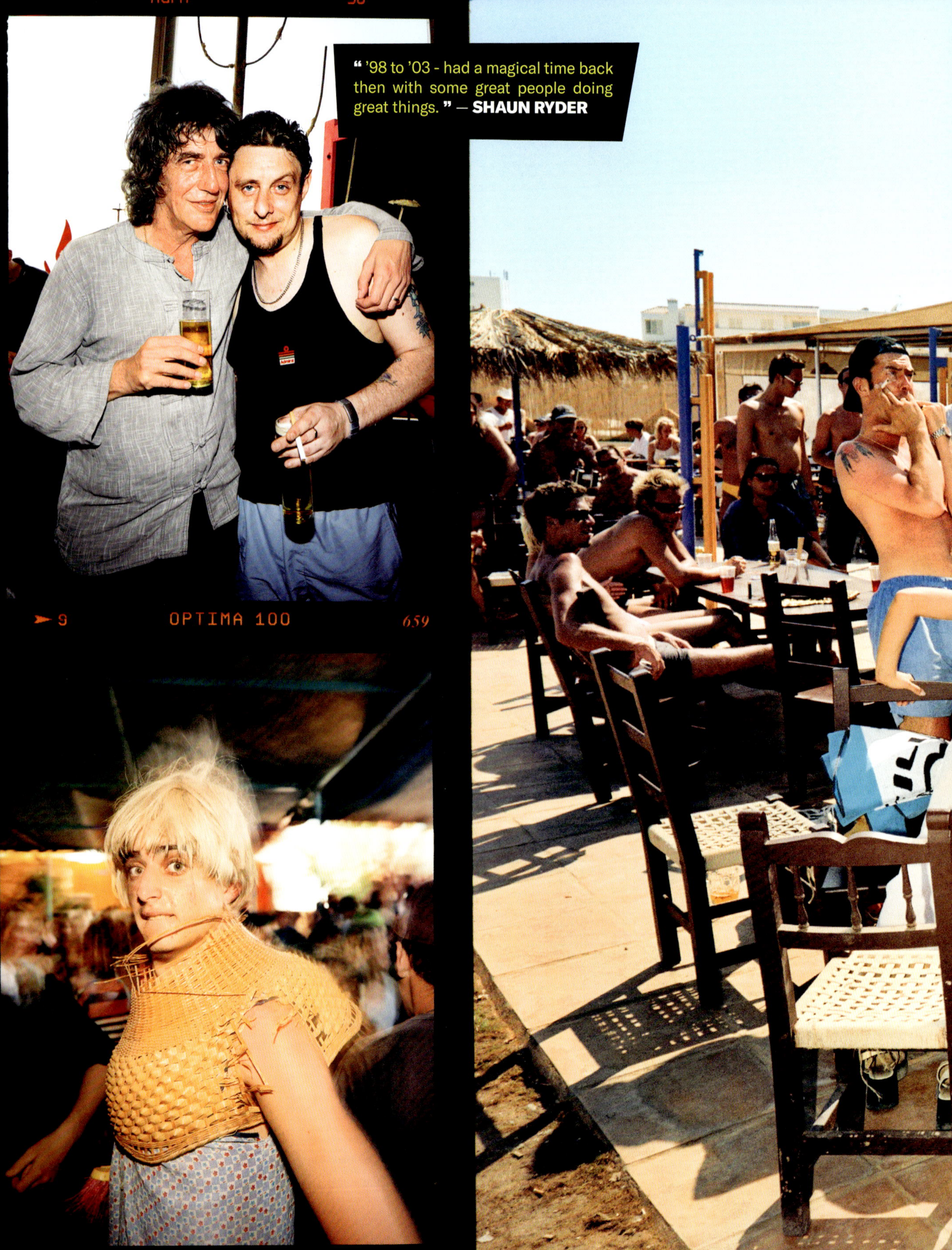
AGFA
56
OPTIMA 100
659
OPTIMA 100
" '98 to '03 - had a magical time back then with some great people doing great things. " — SHAUN RYDER

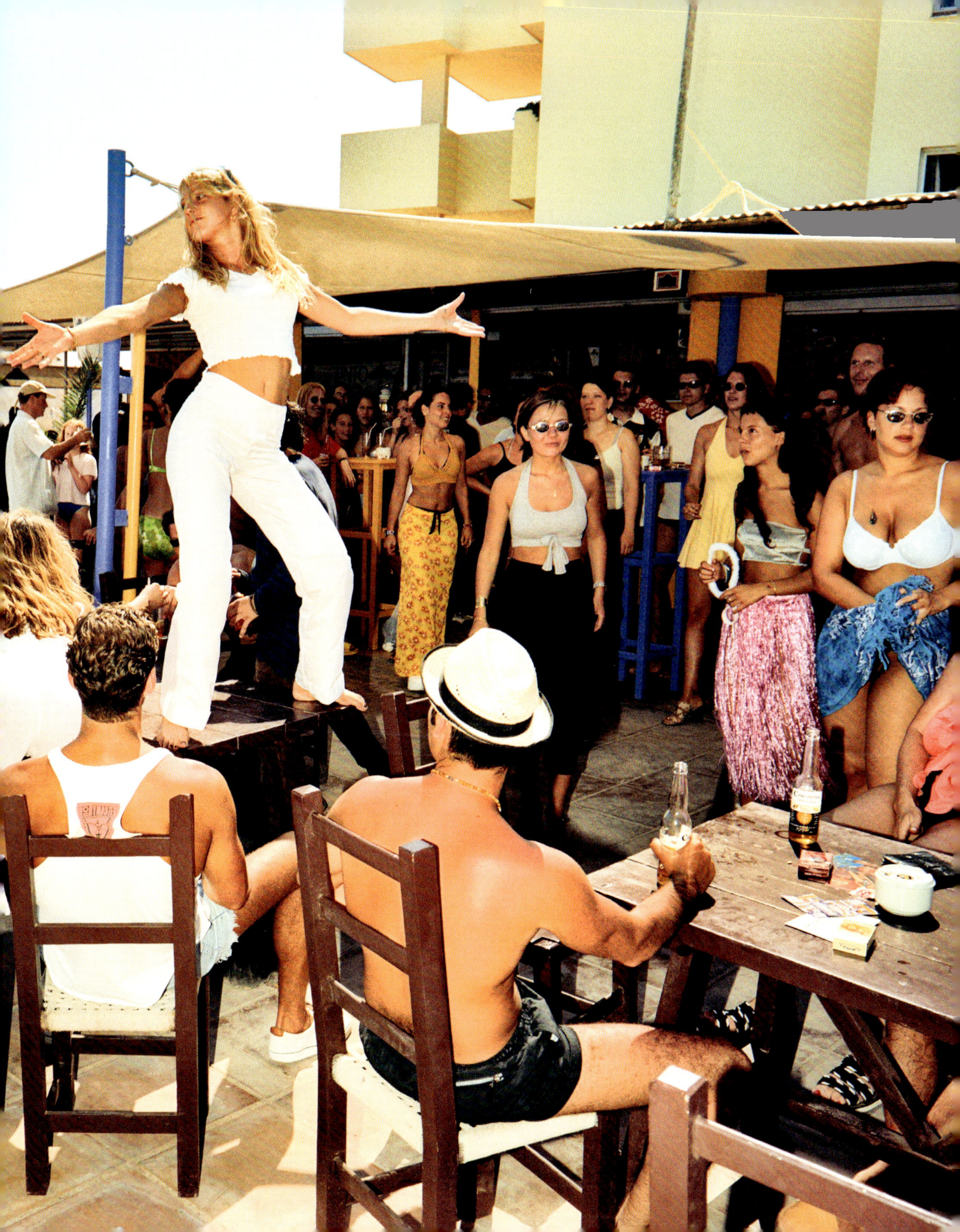

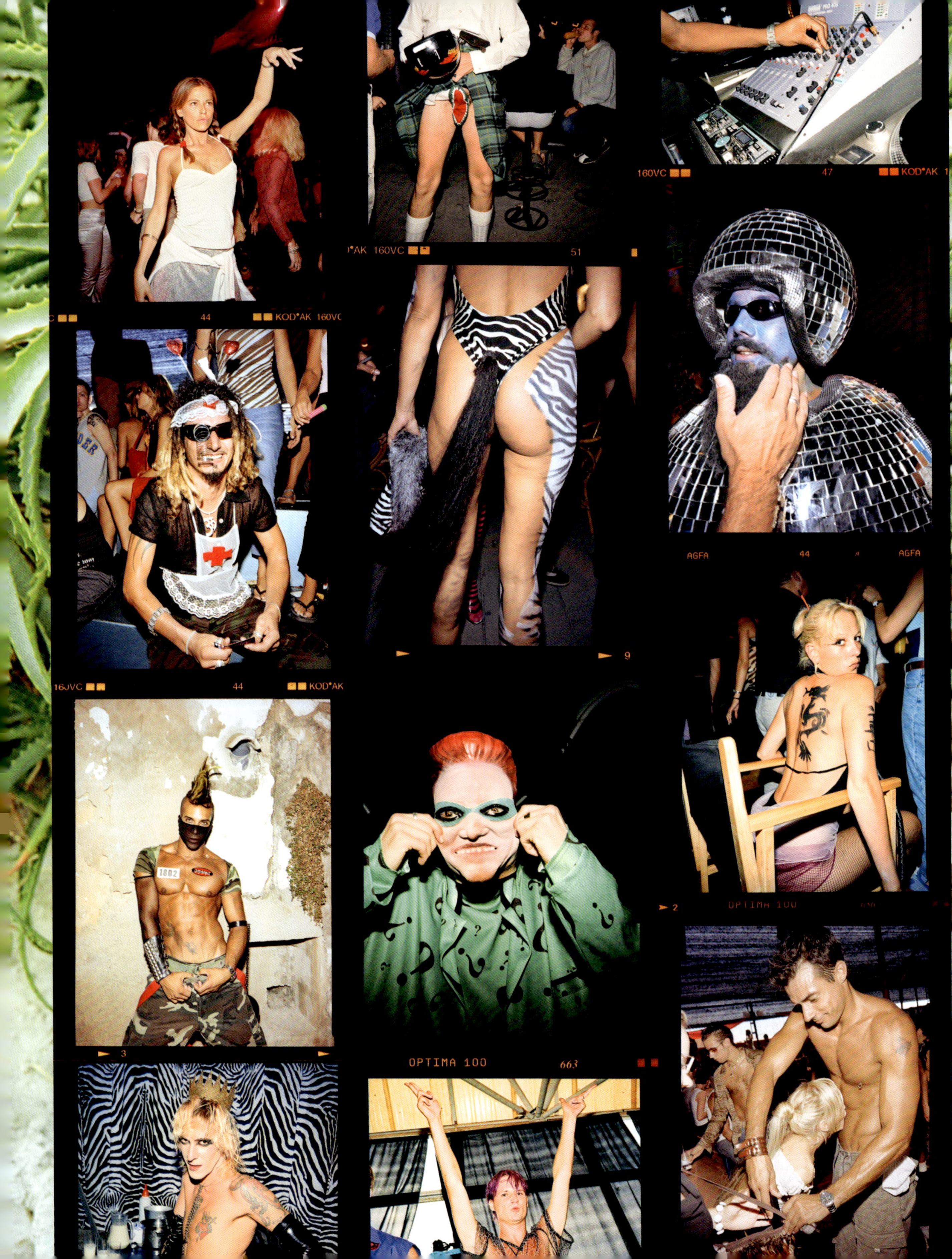
160VC
47
KOD*AK
*AK 160VC
51
160VC
44
KOD*AK 160VC
9
AGFA
44
AGFA
160VC
44
KOD*AK
3
OPTIMA 100
663
2
OPTIMA 100

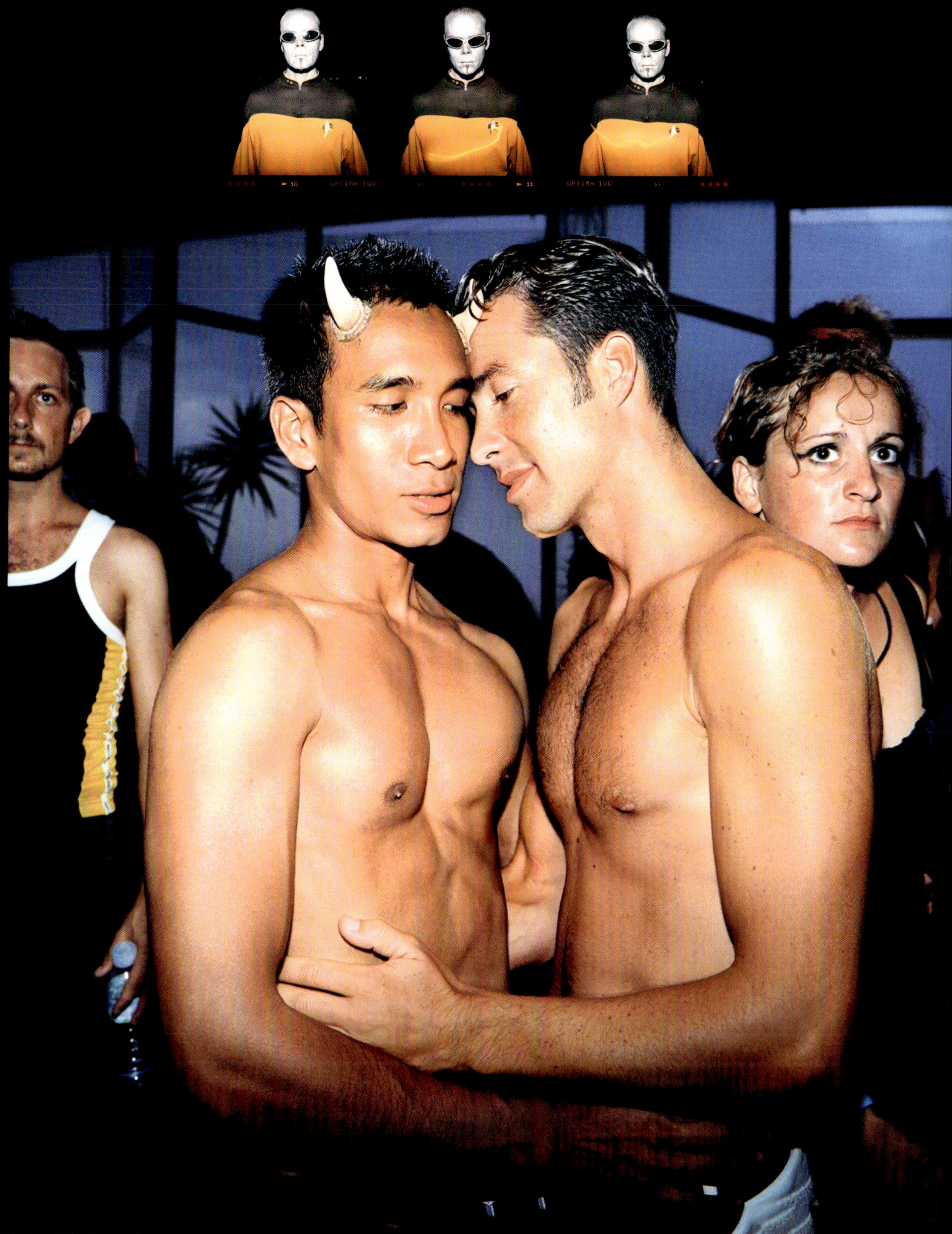
10 OPTIMA 100
11 OPTIMA 100

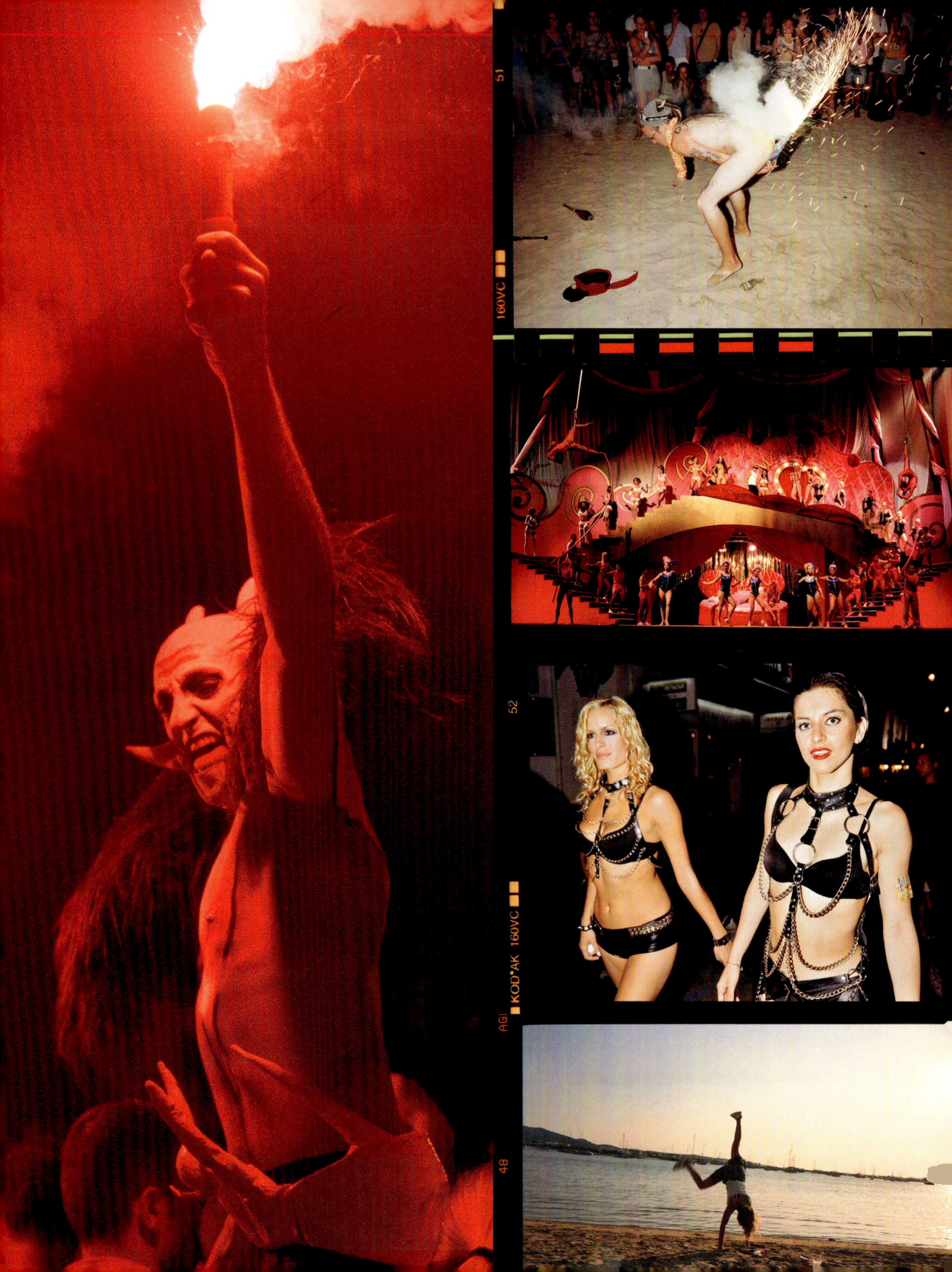

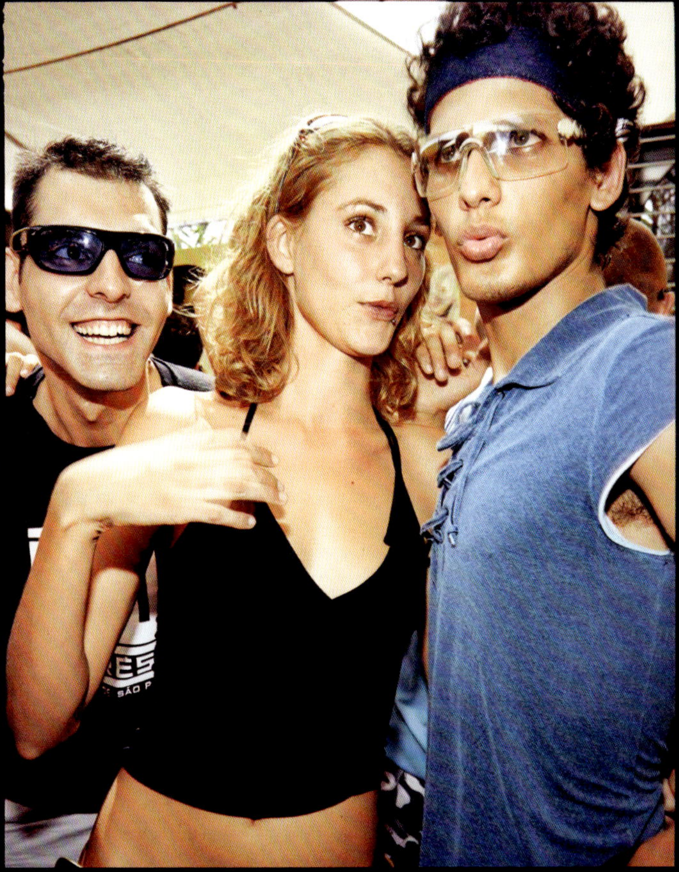

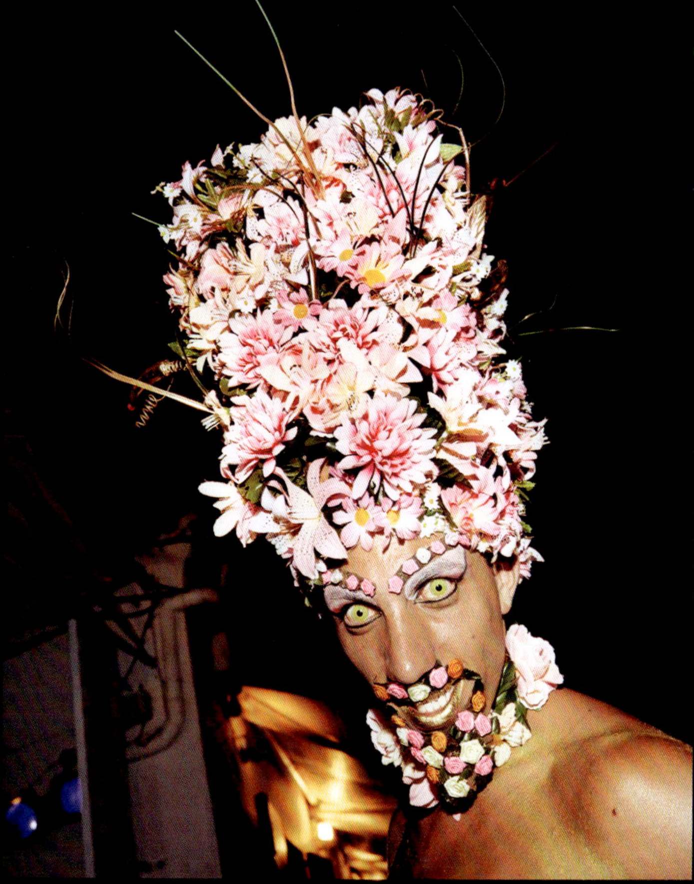

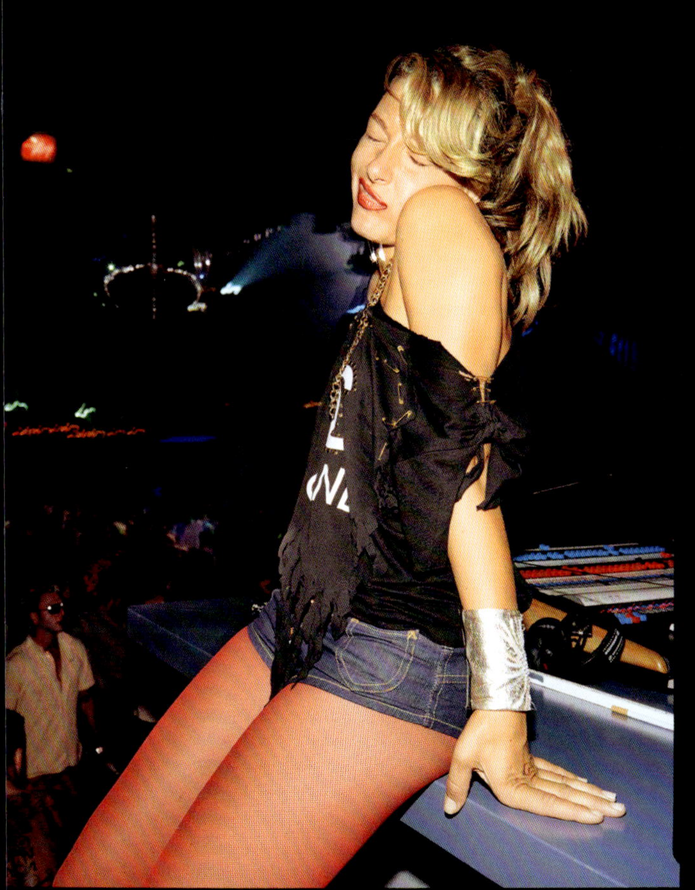
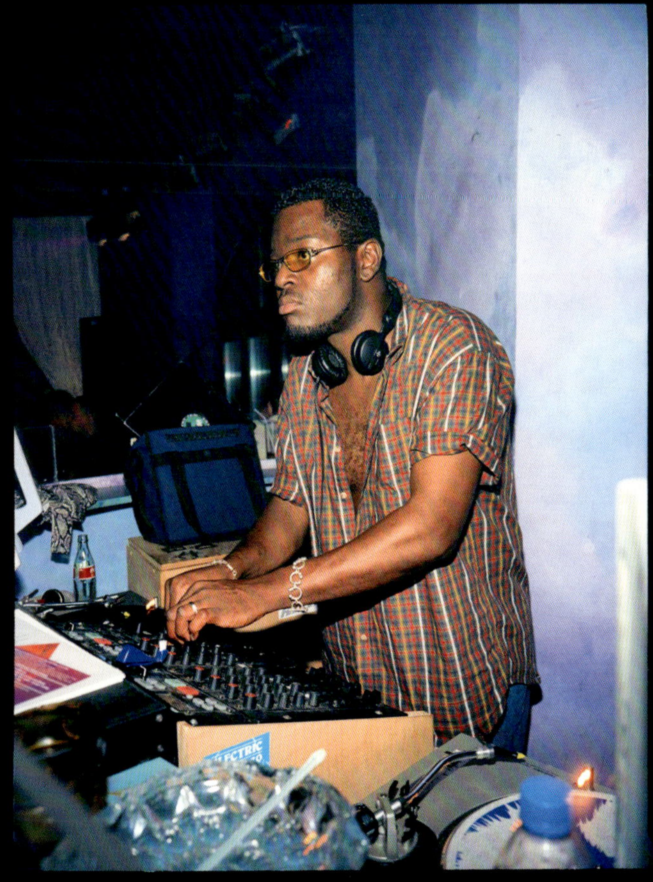

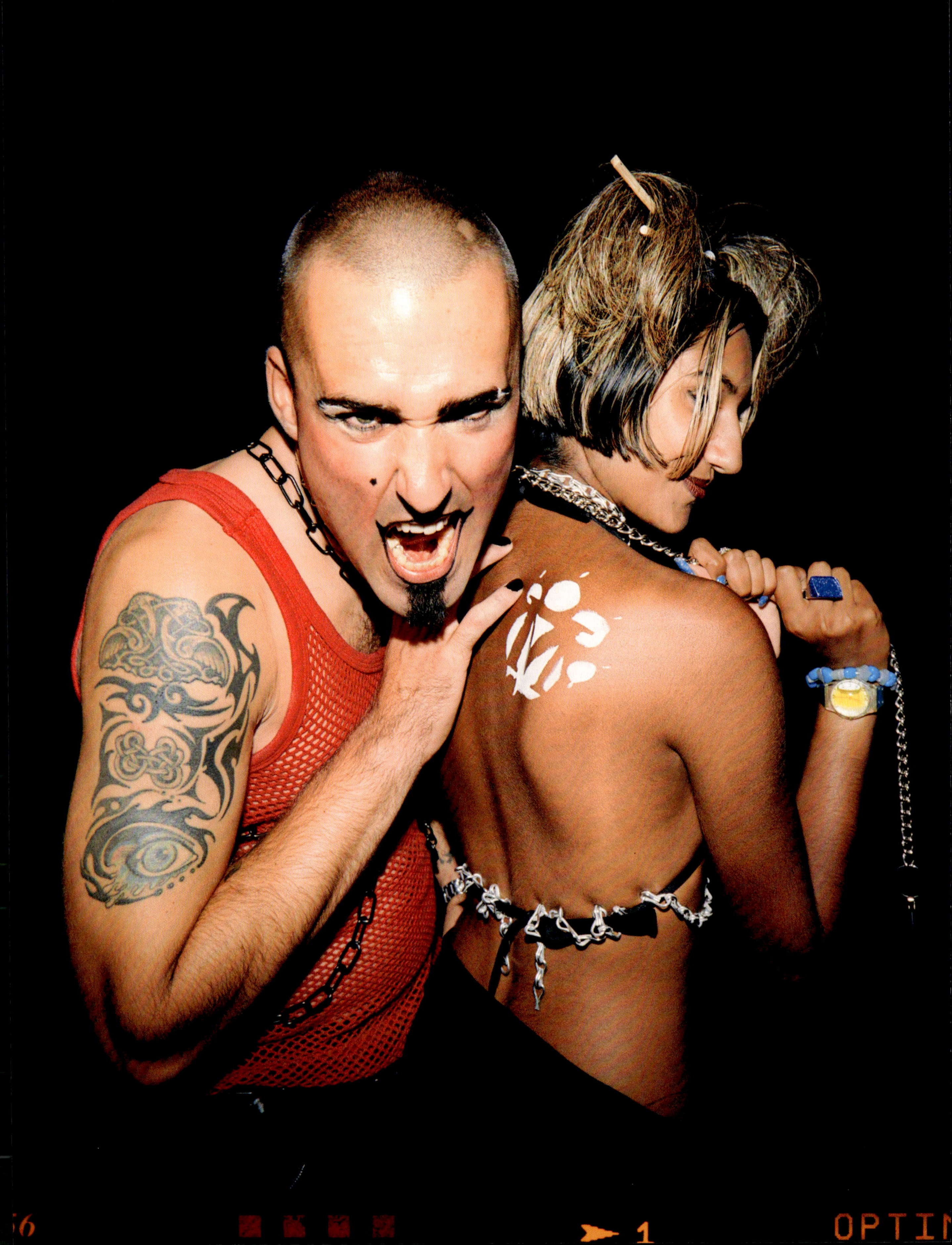

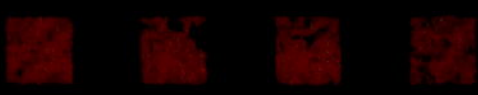

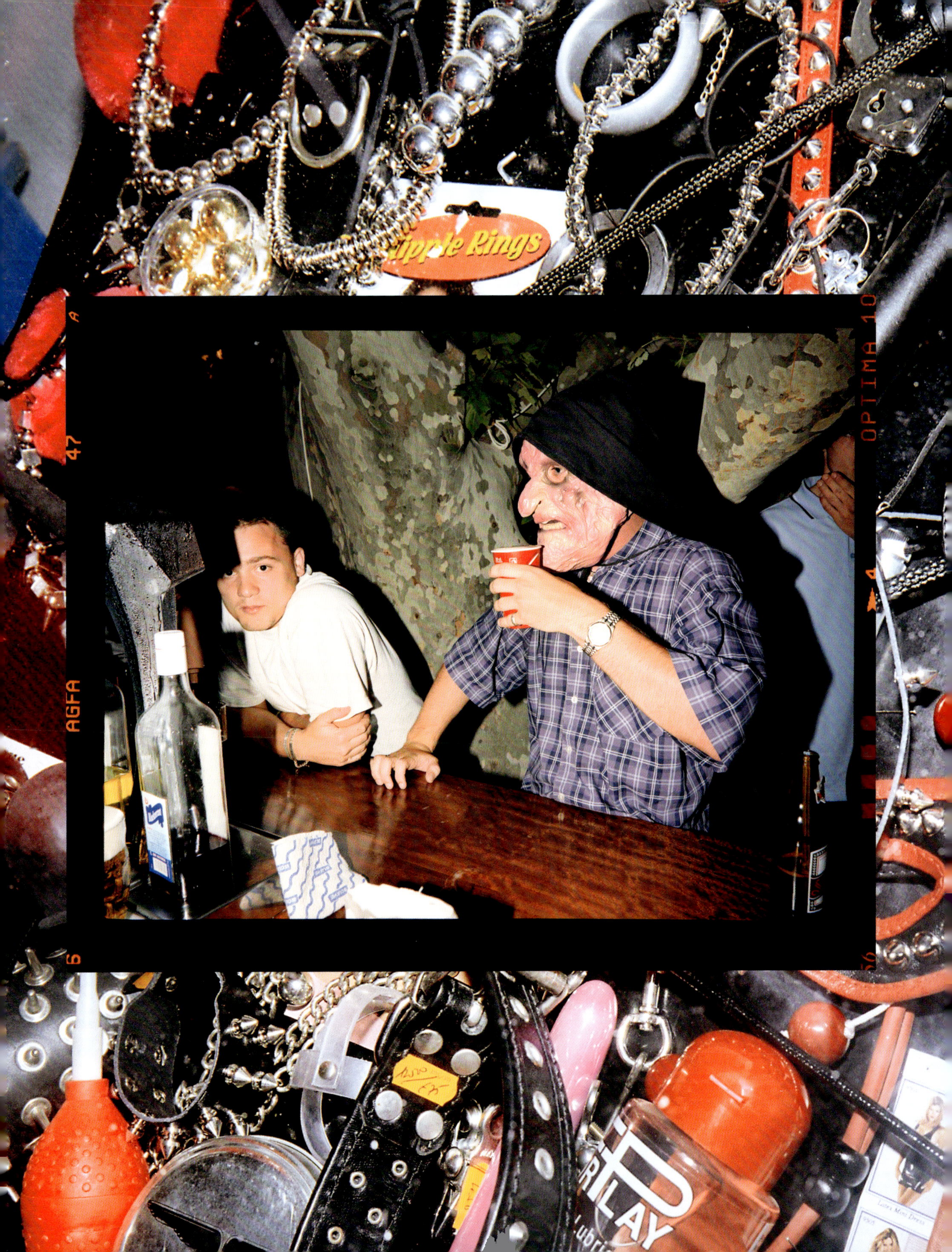
Nipple Rings

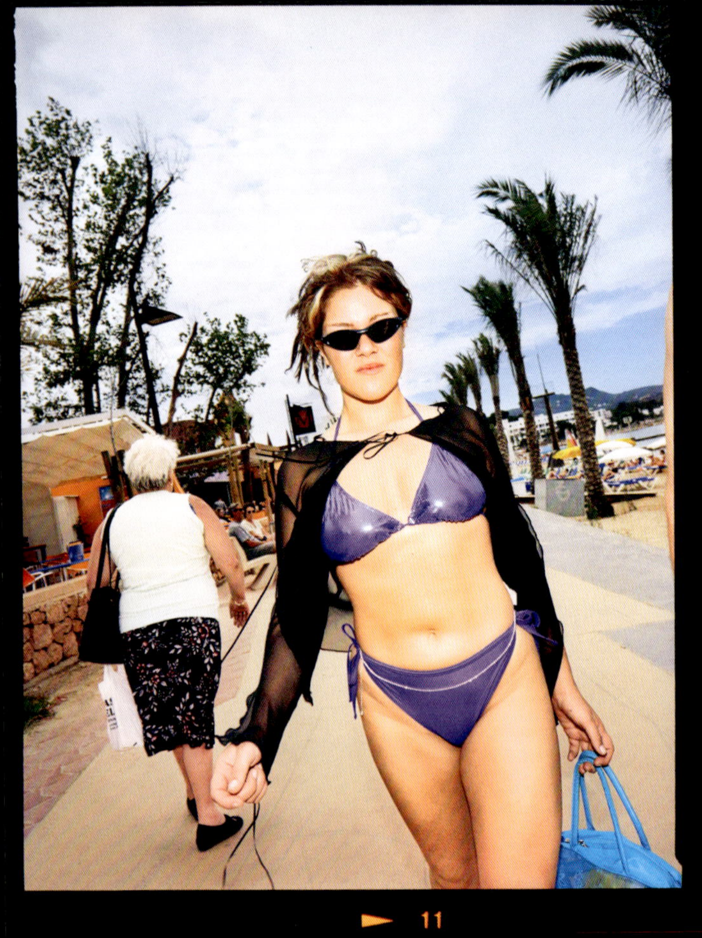
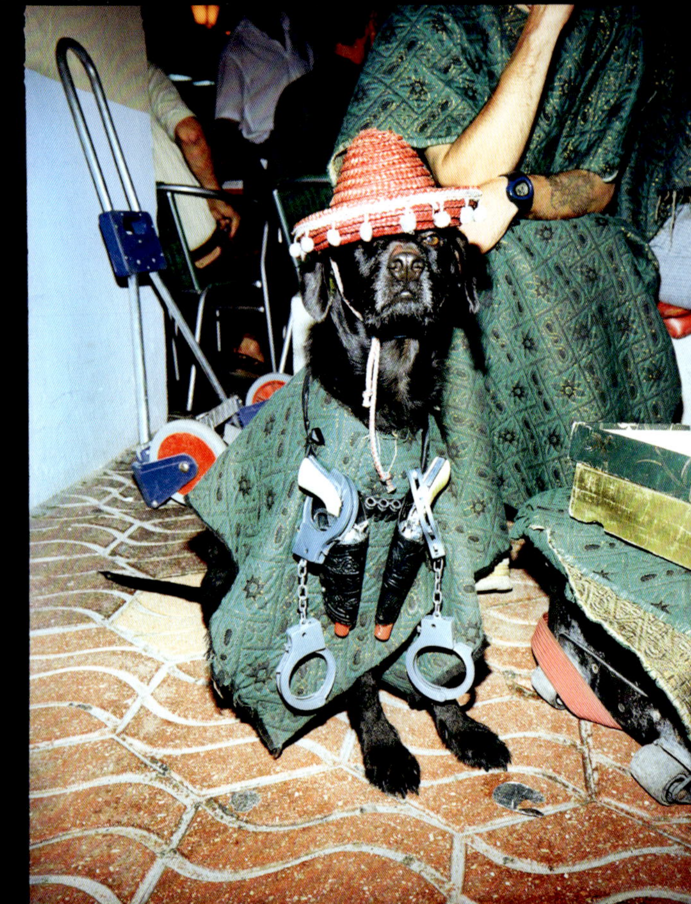

11

160VC
45
KOD

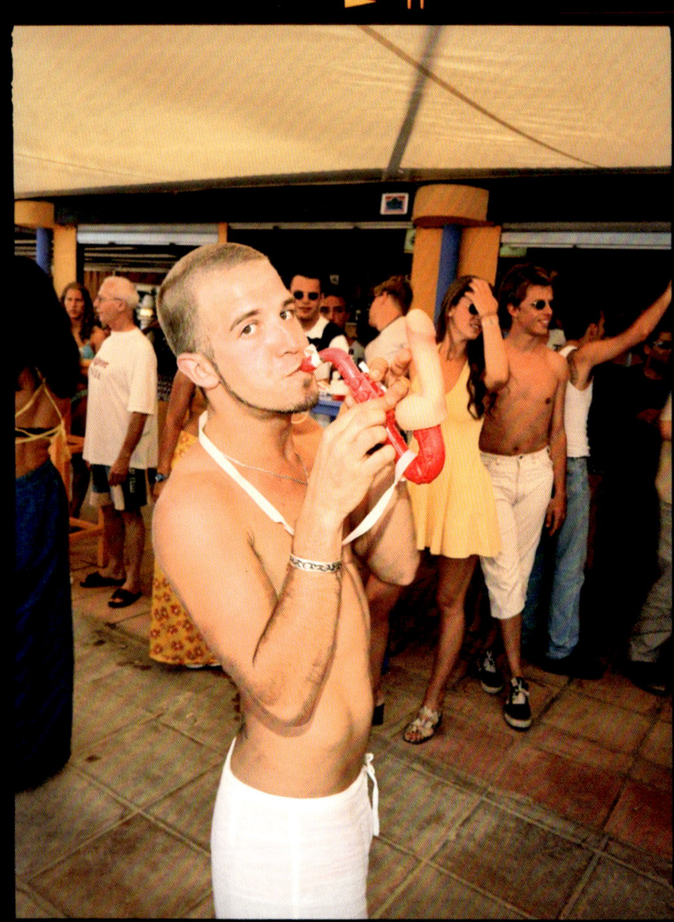
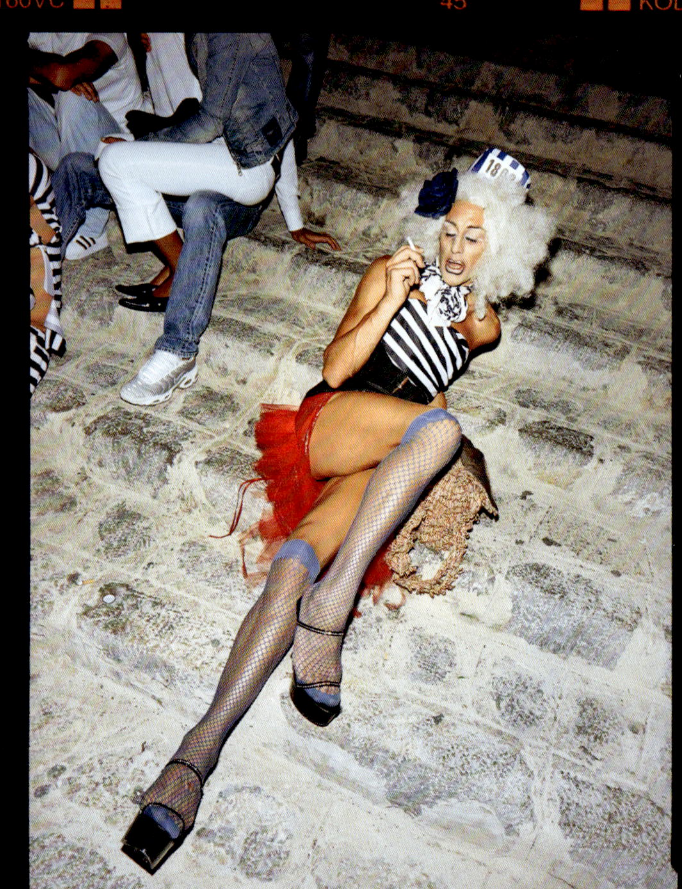

OPTIMA 100
663

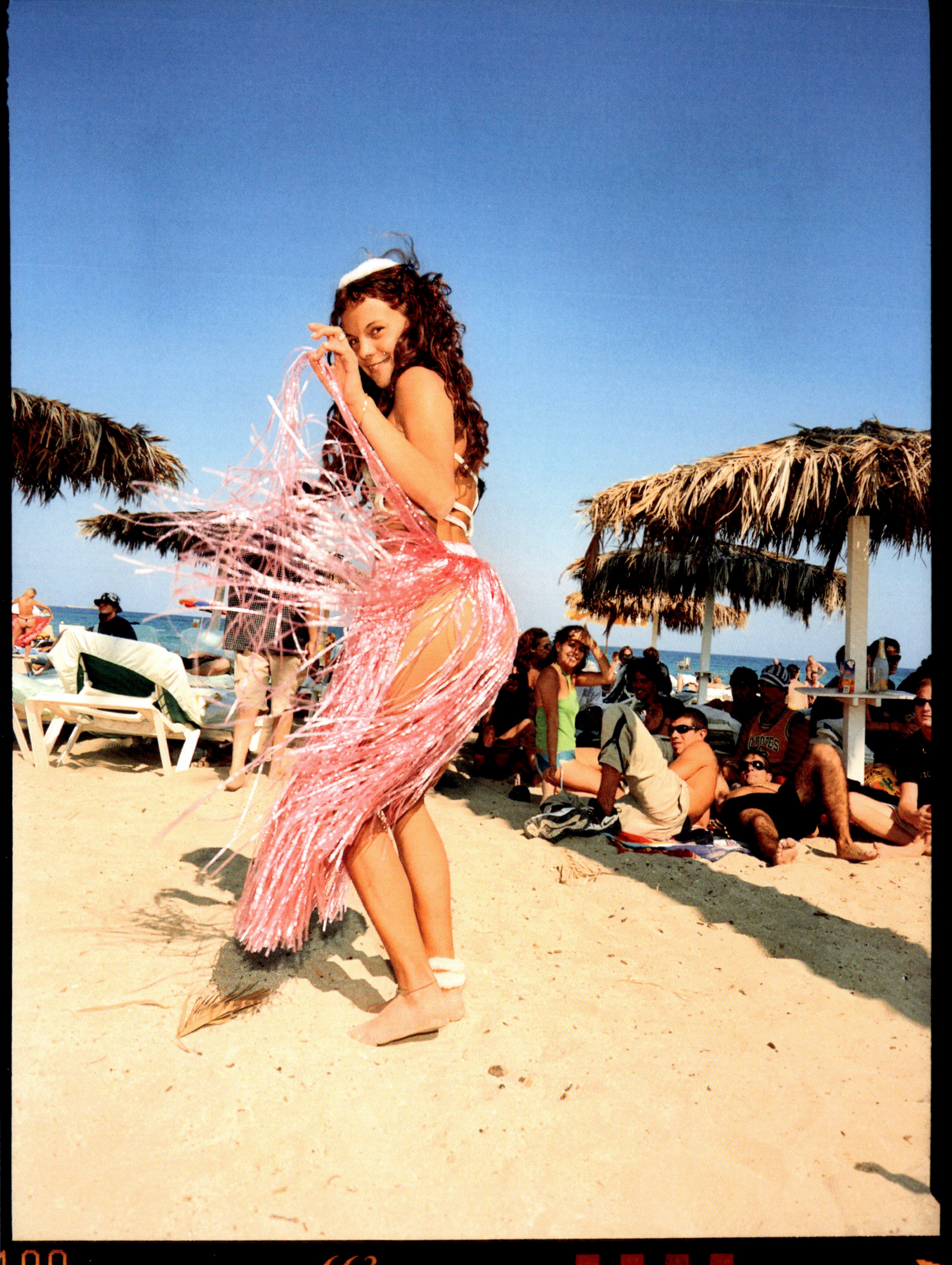

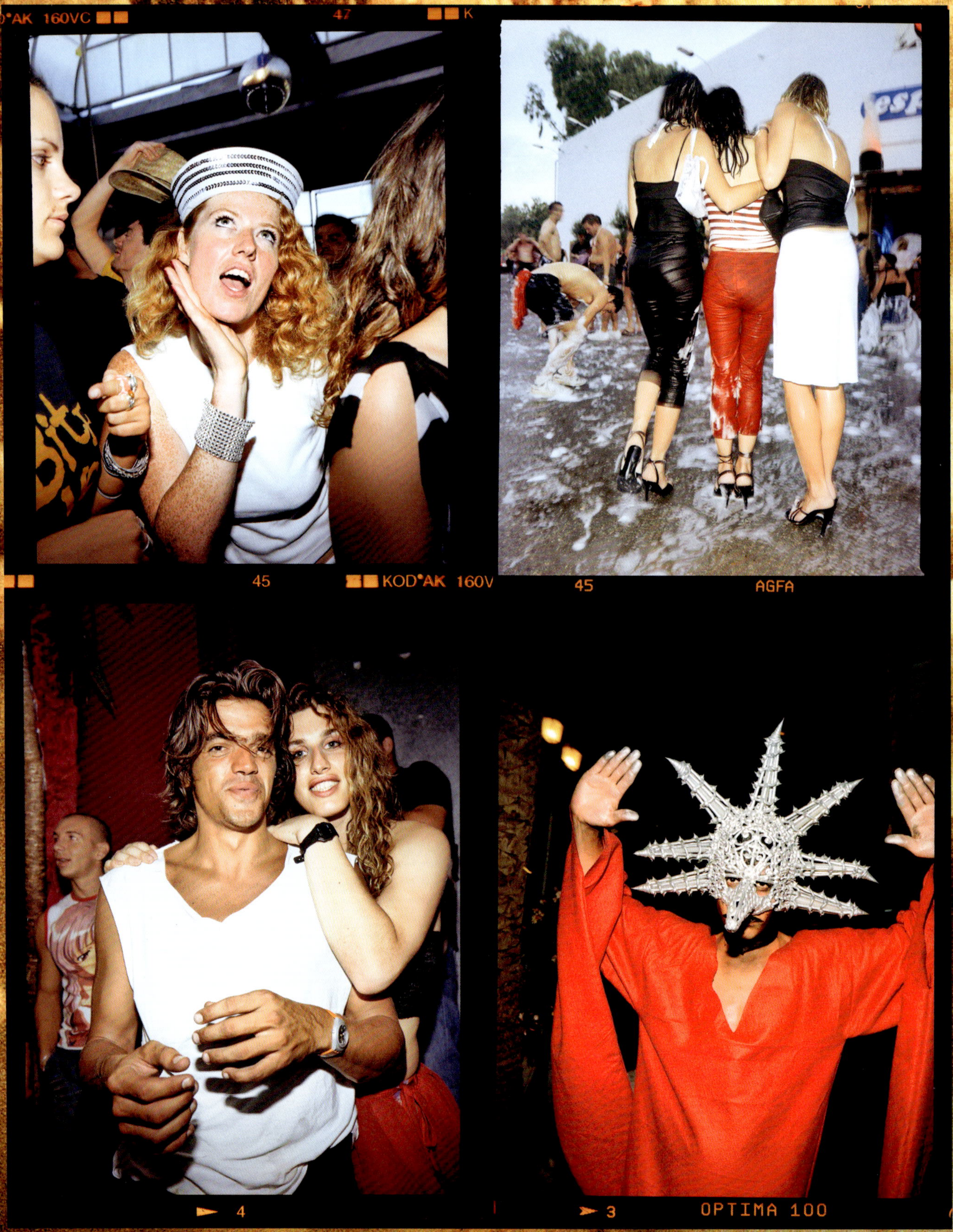

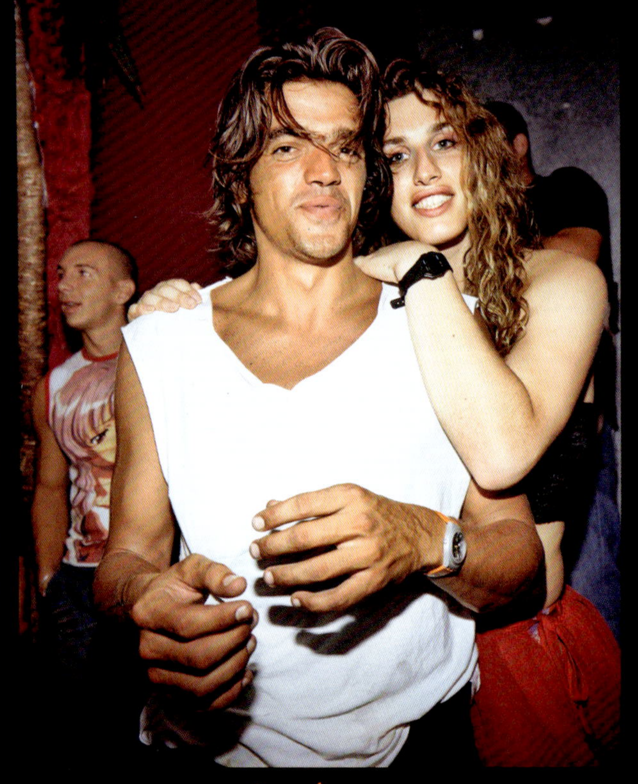
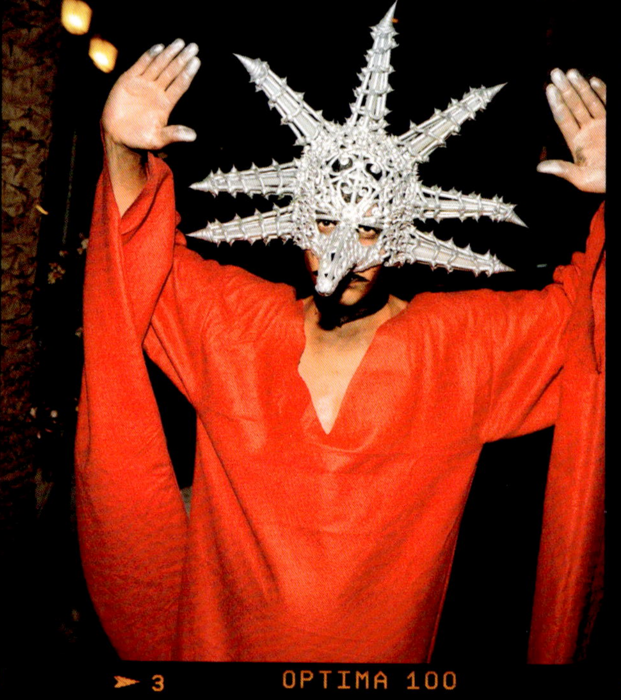

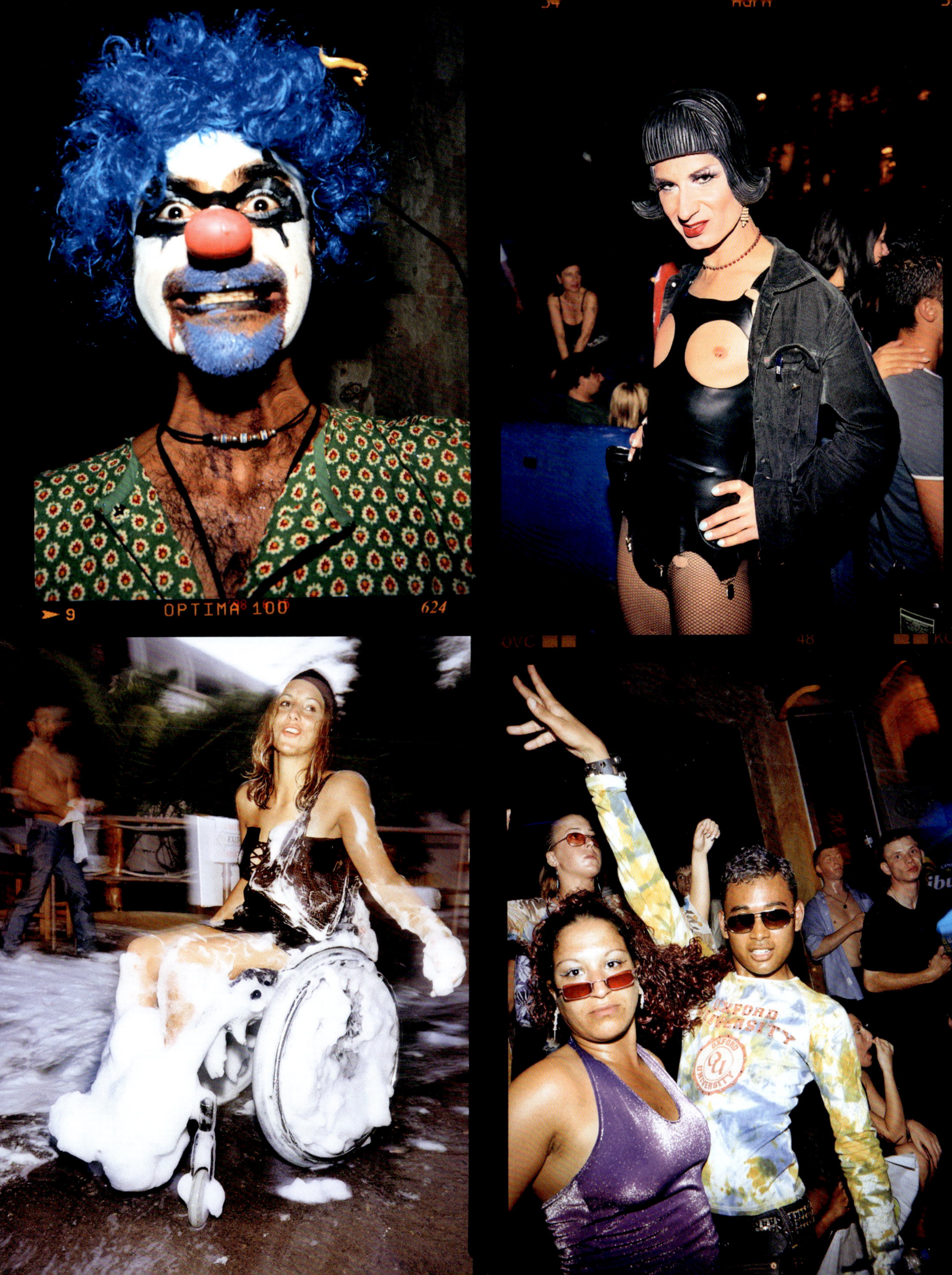

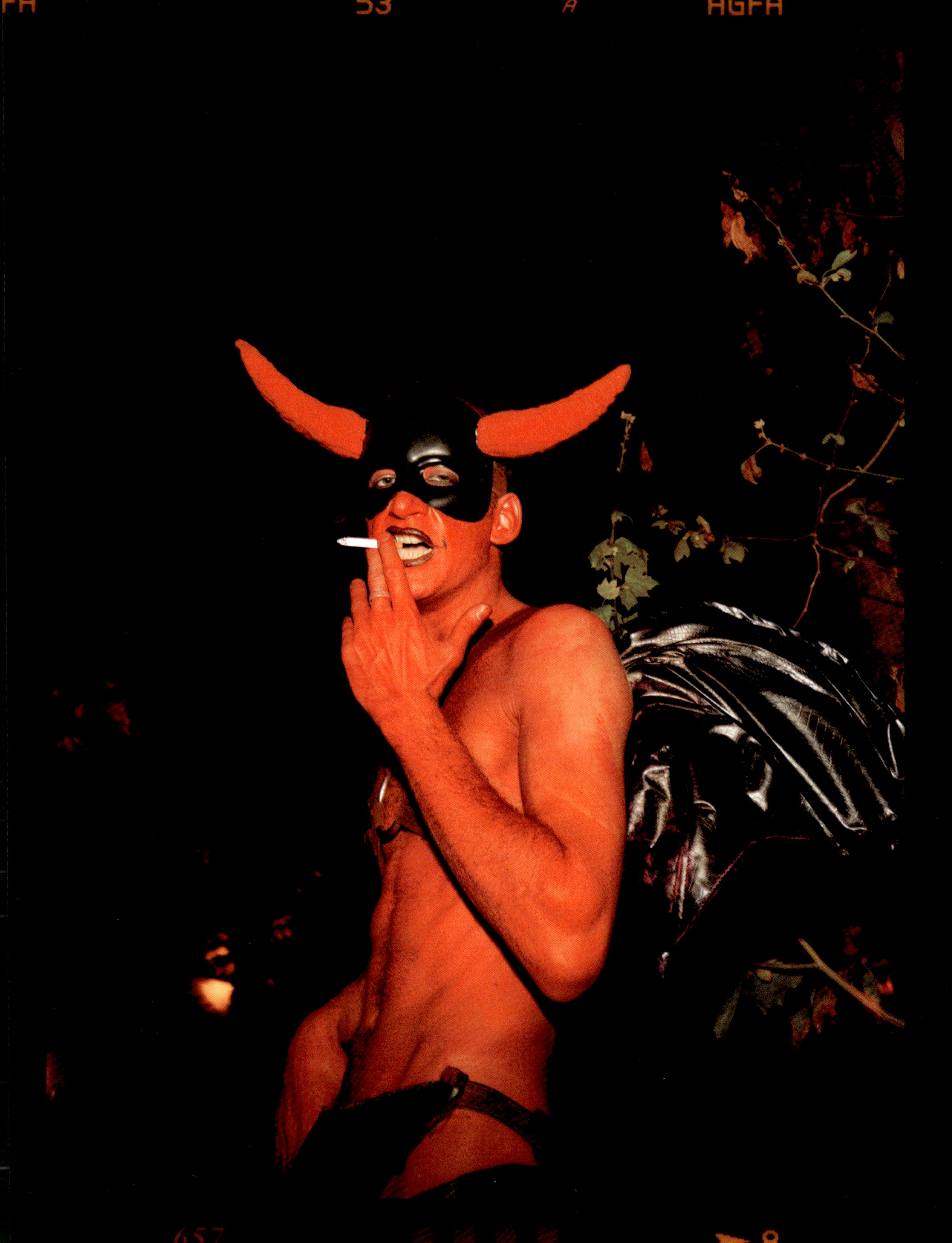

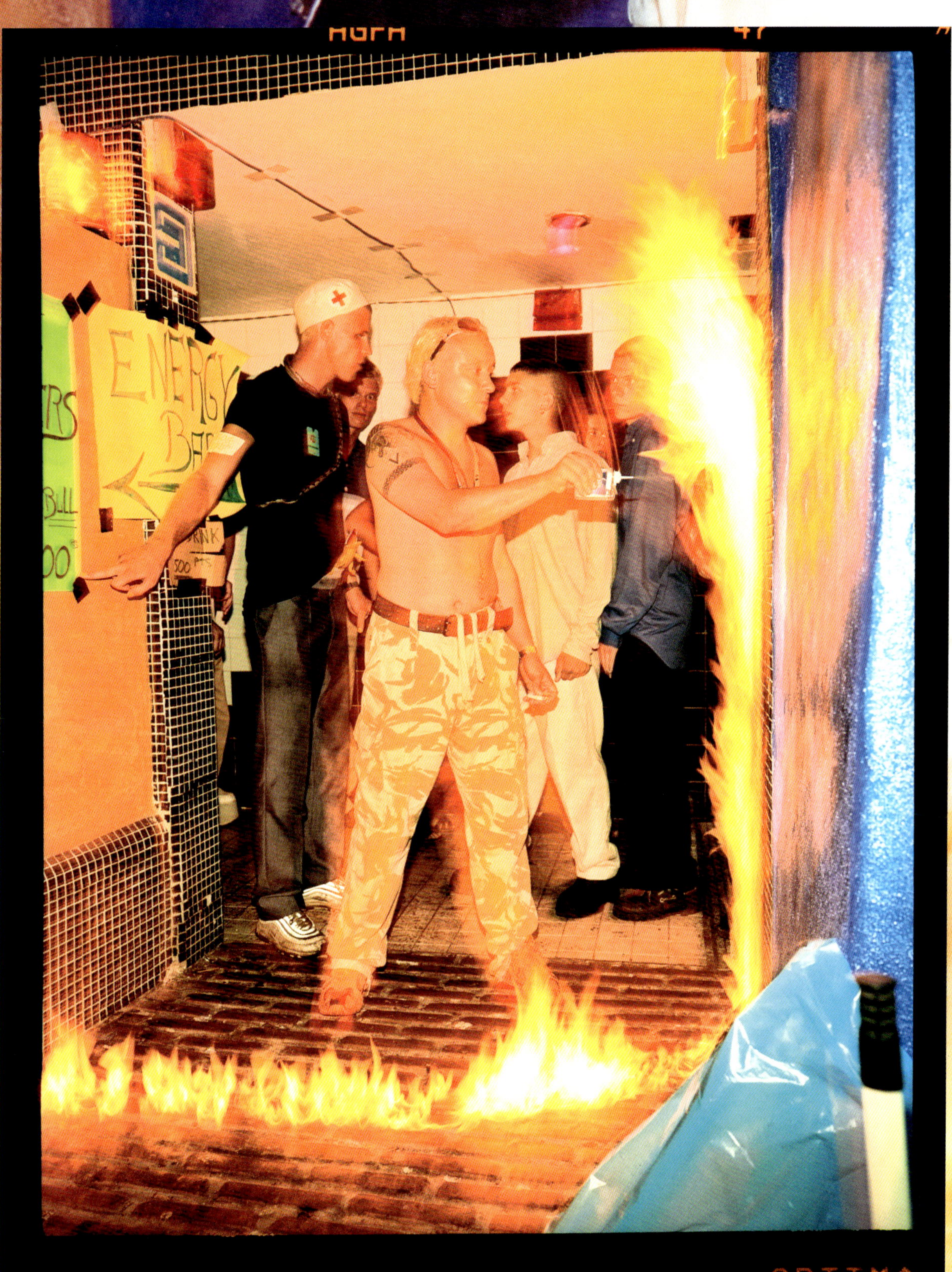
ENERGY
BAR

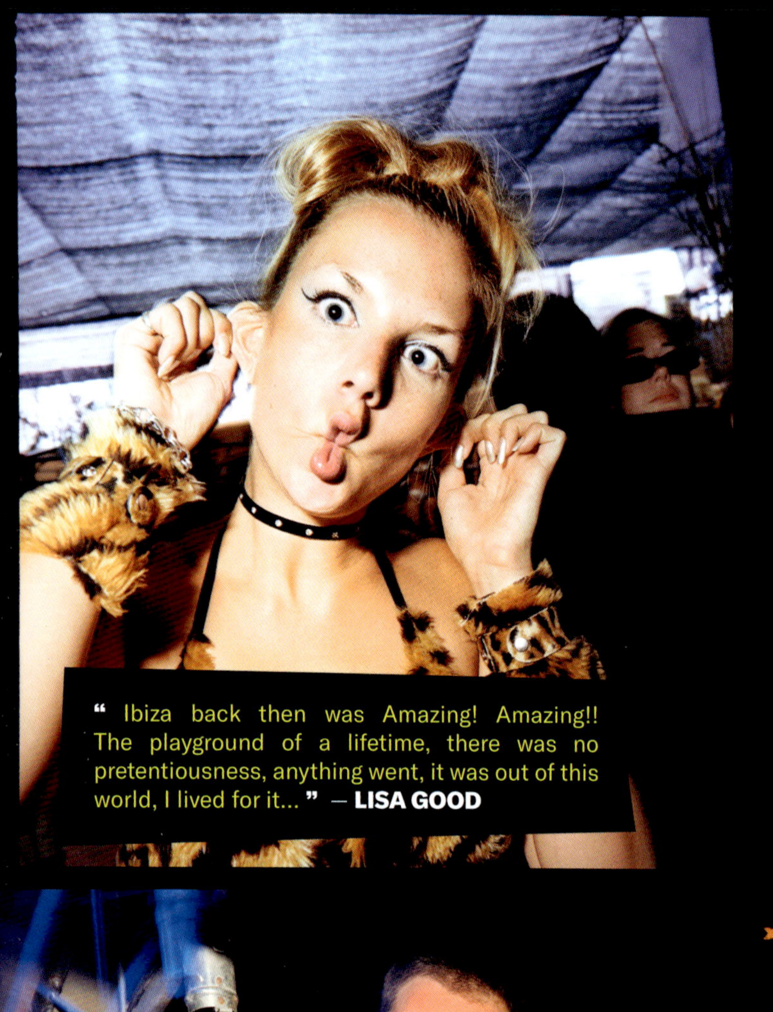

" Ibiza back then was Amazing! Amazing!! The playground of a lifetime, there was no pretentiousness, anything went, it was out of this world, I lived for it… " — LISA GOOD

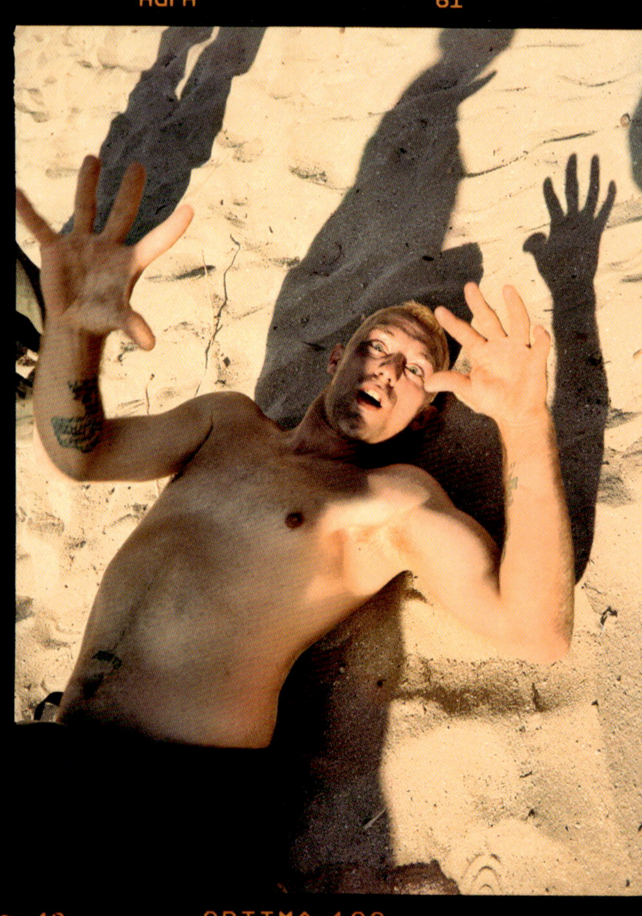

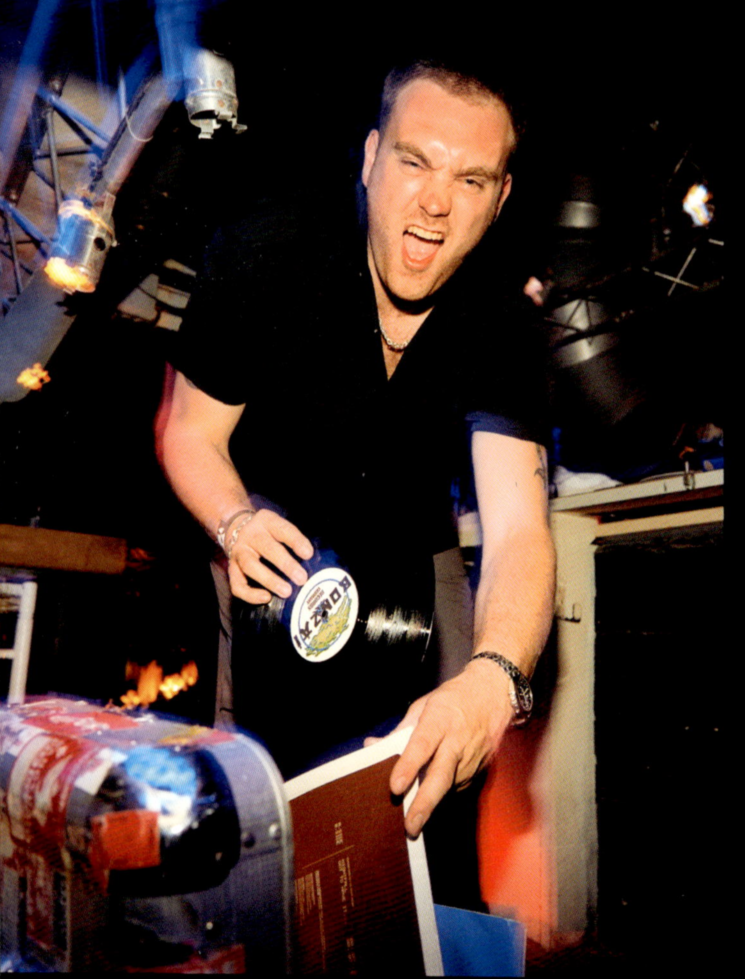

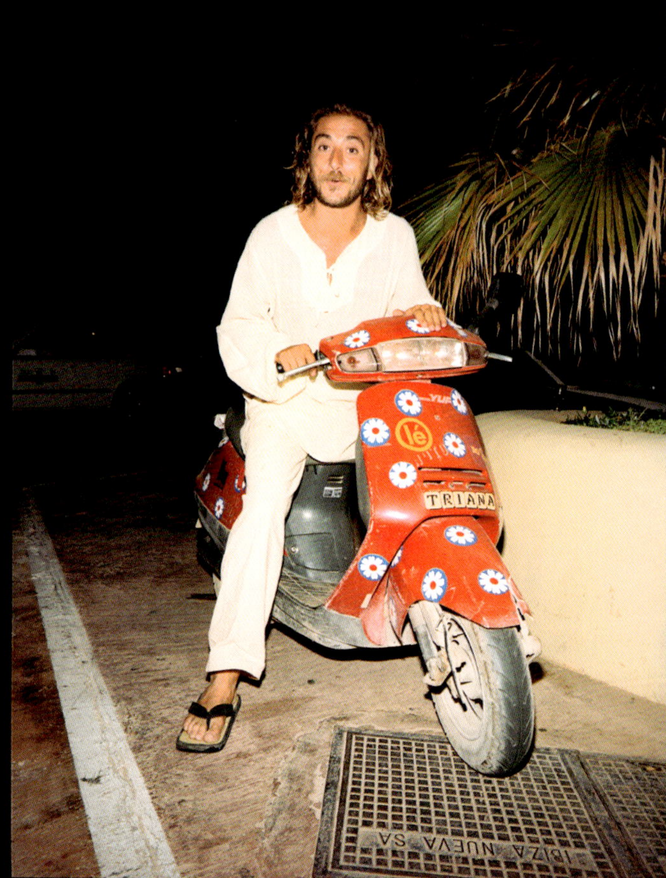

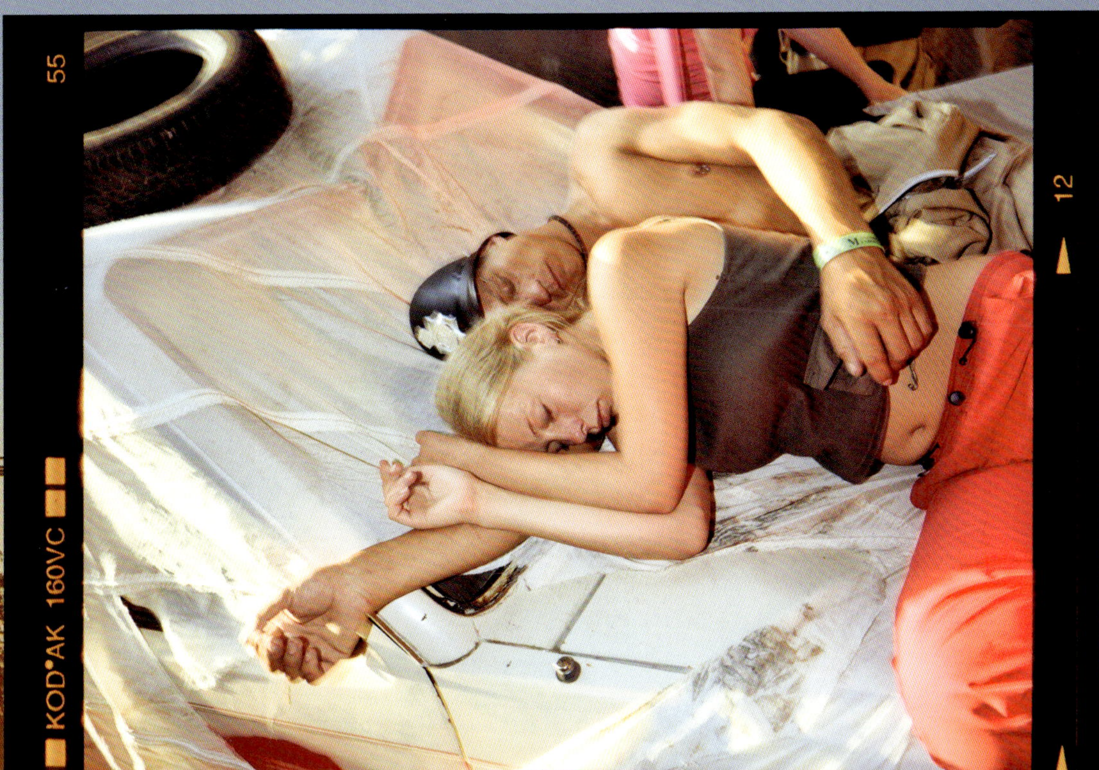

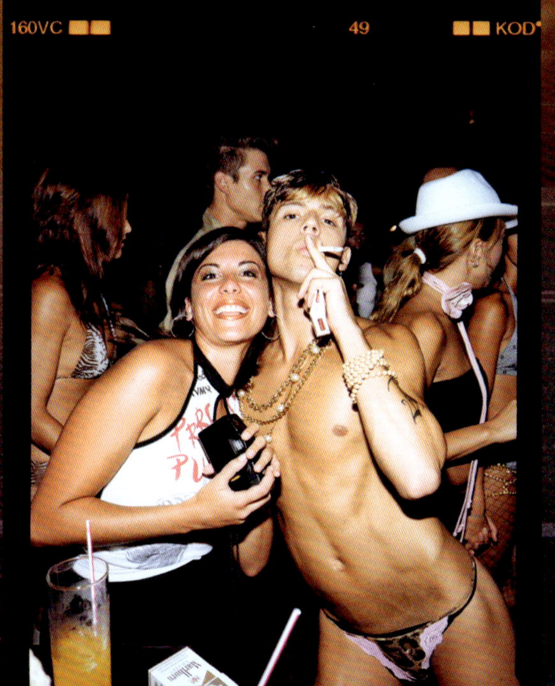

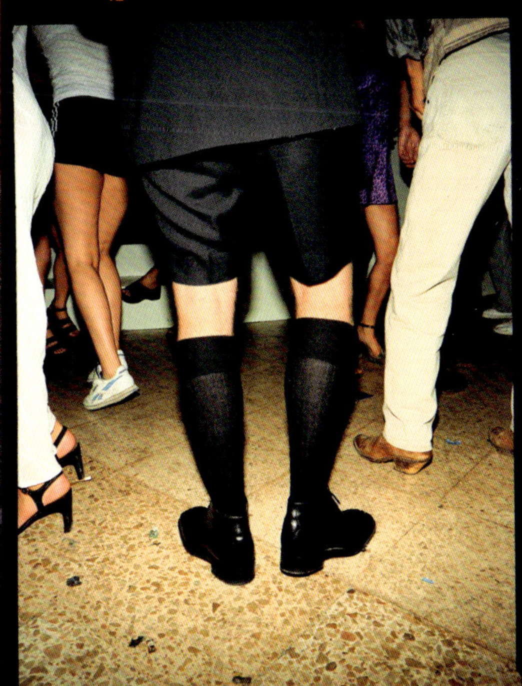

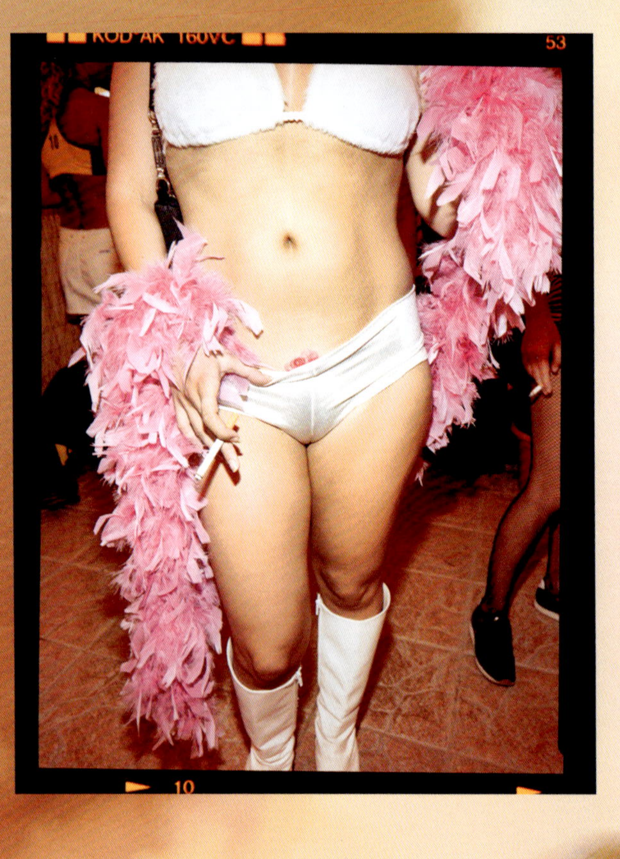
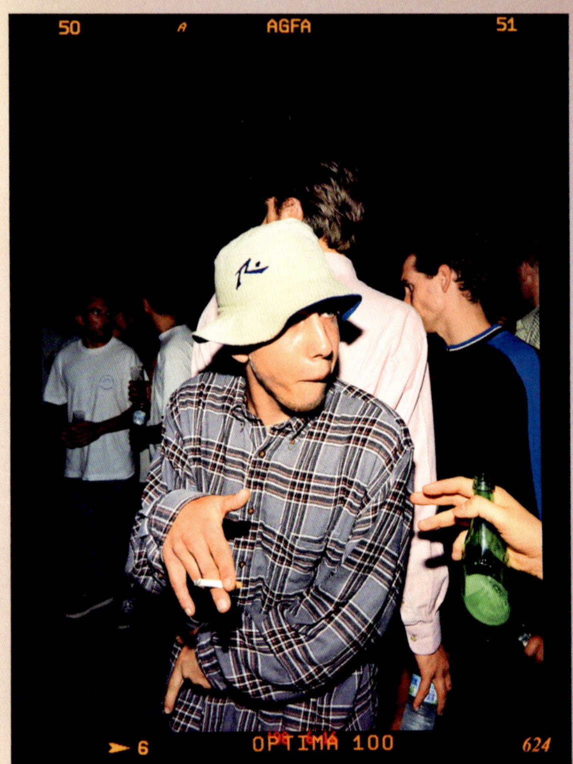

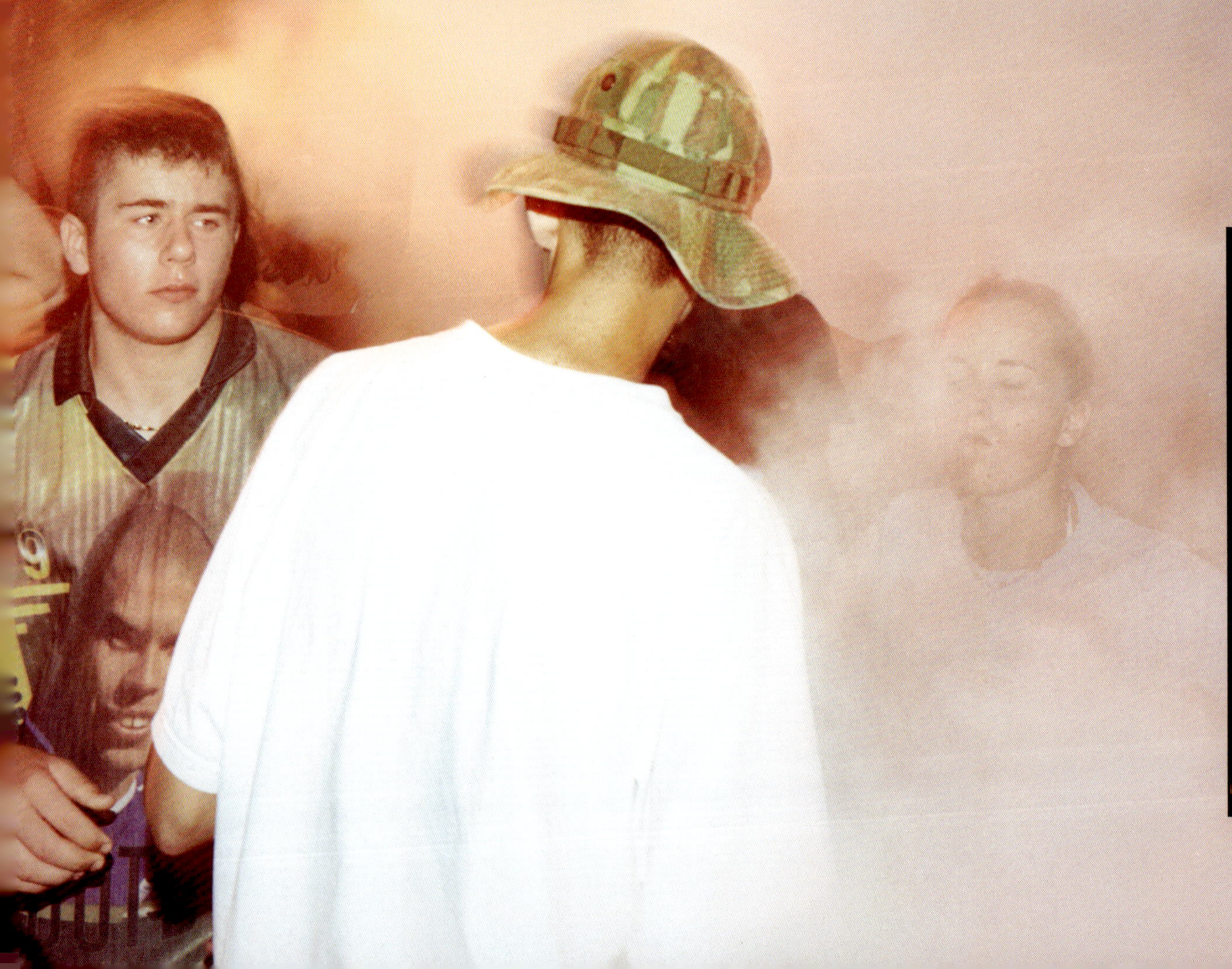

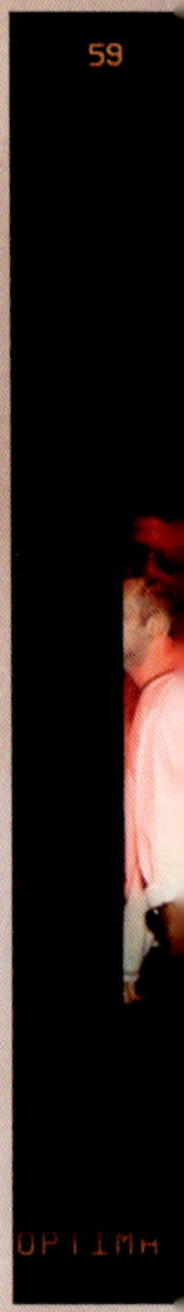

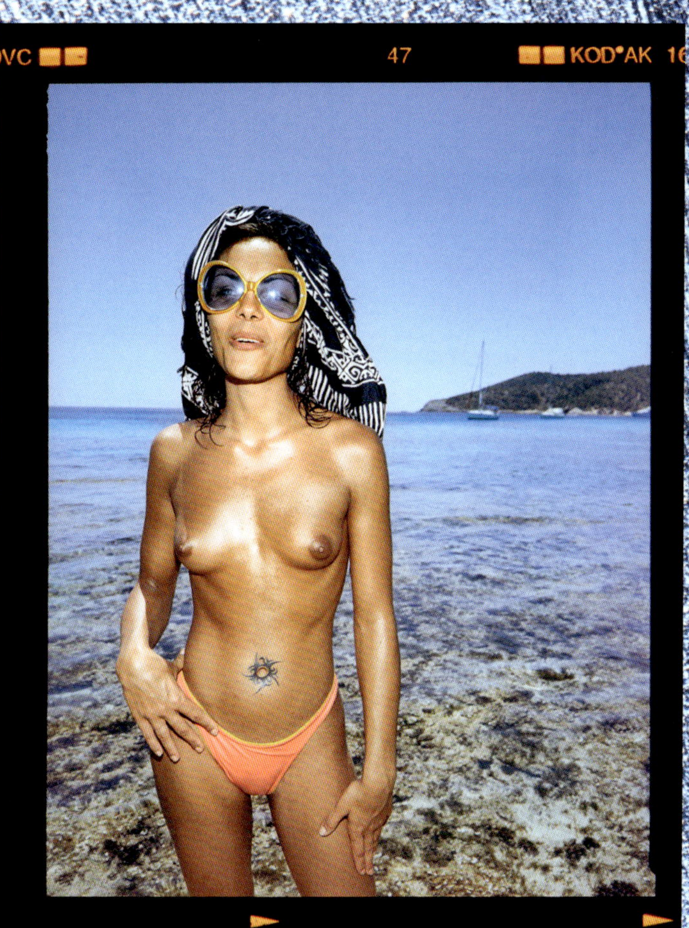
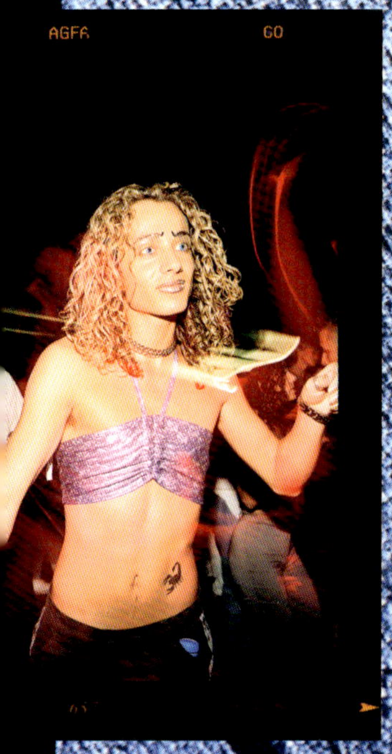
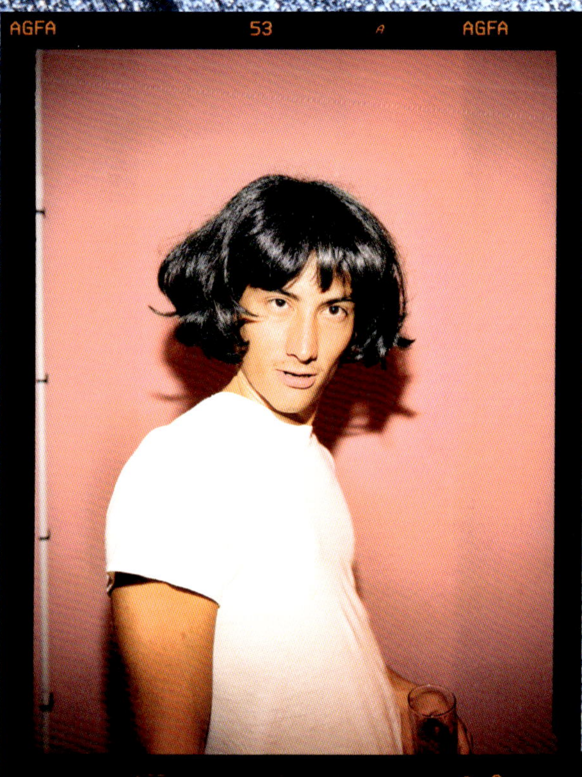
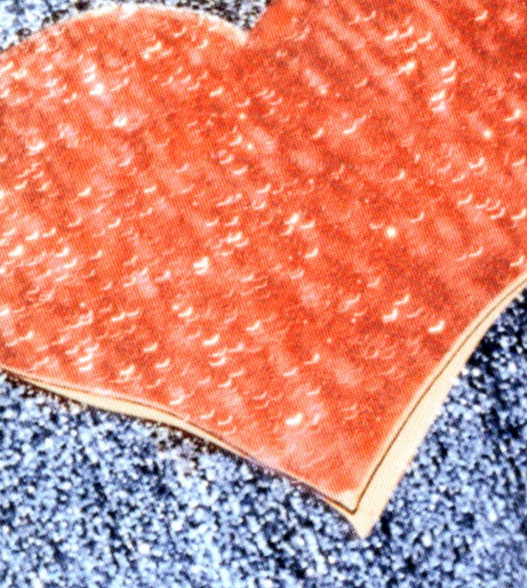

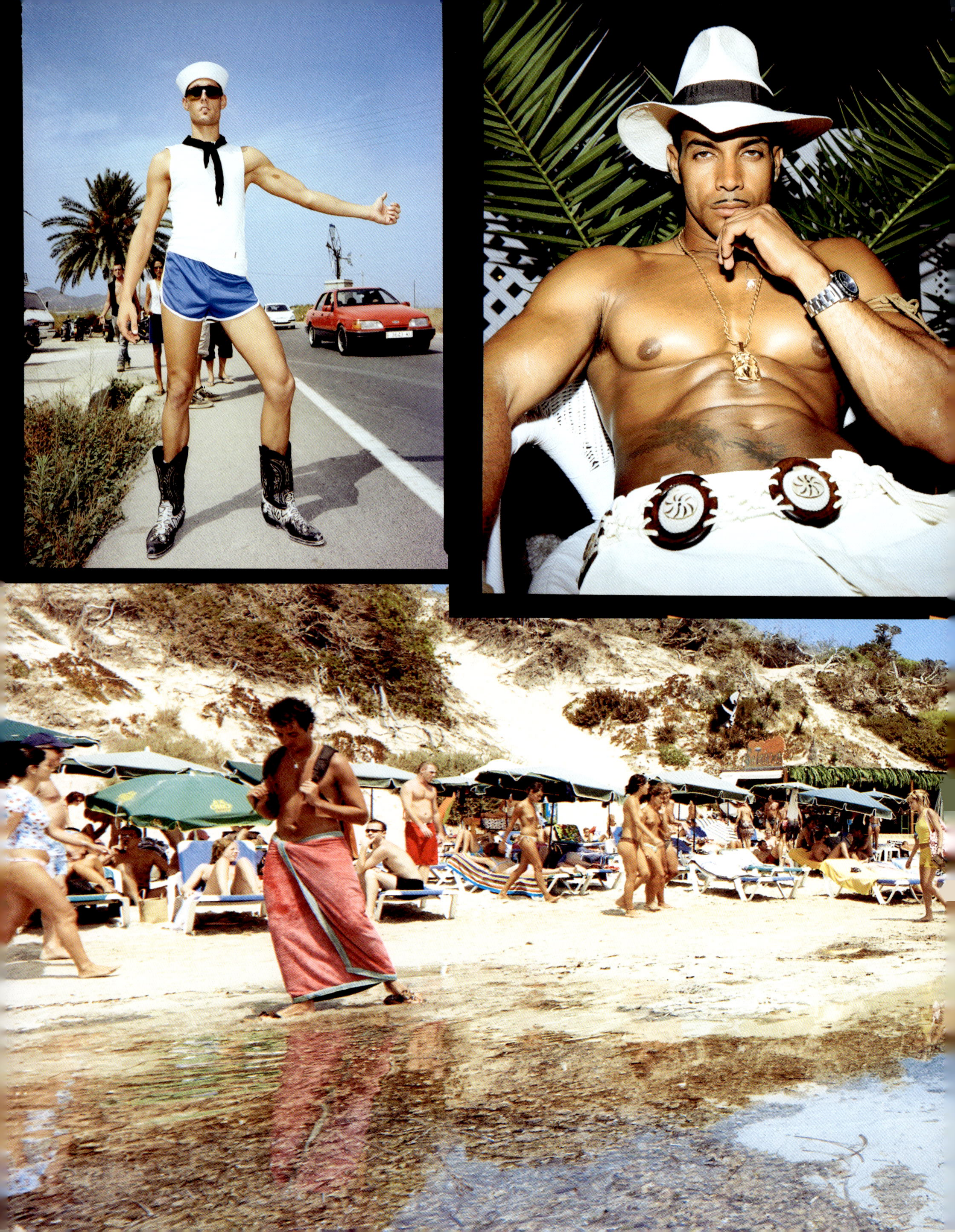

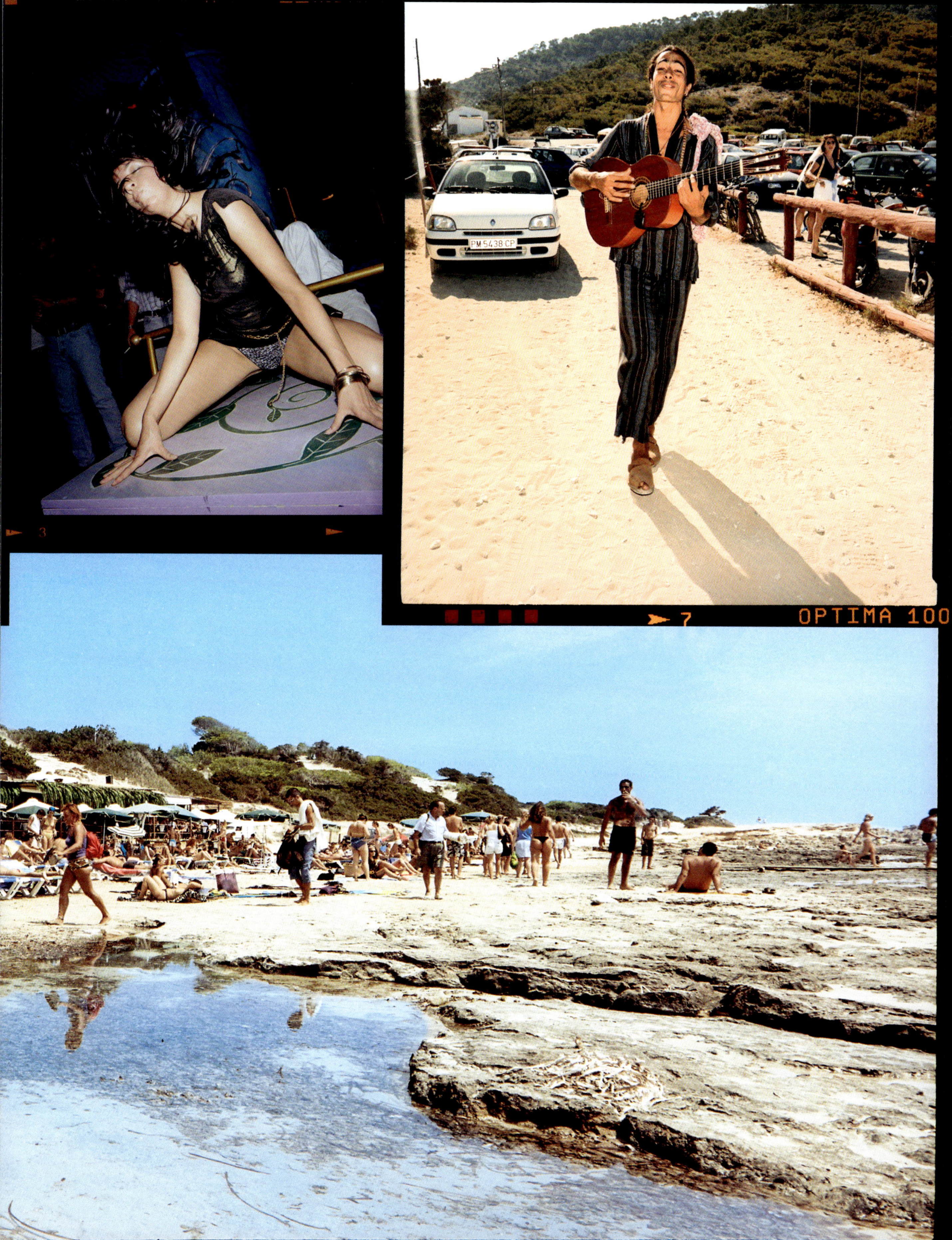
PM 5438 CP
7
OPTIMA 100

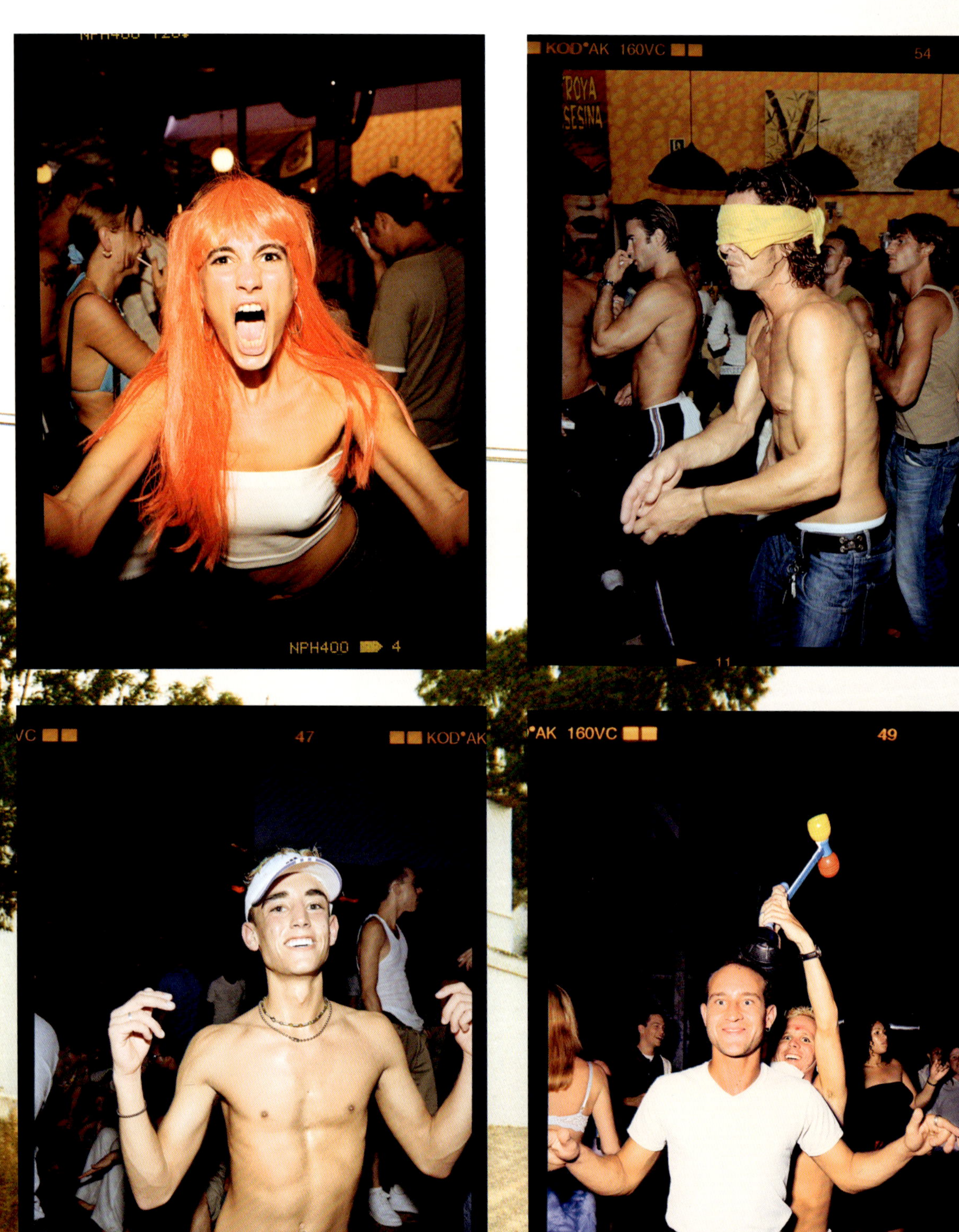

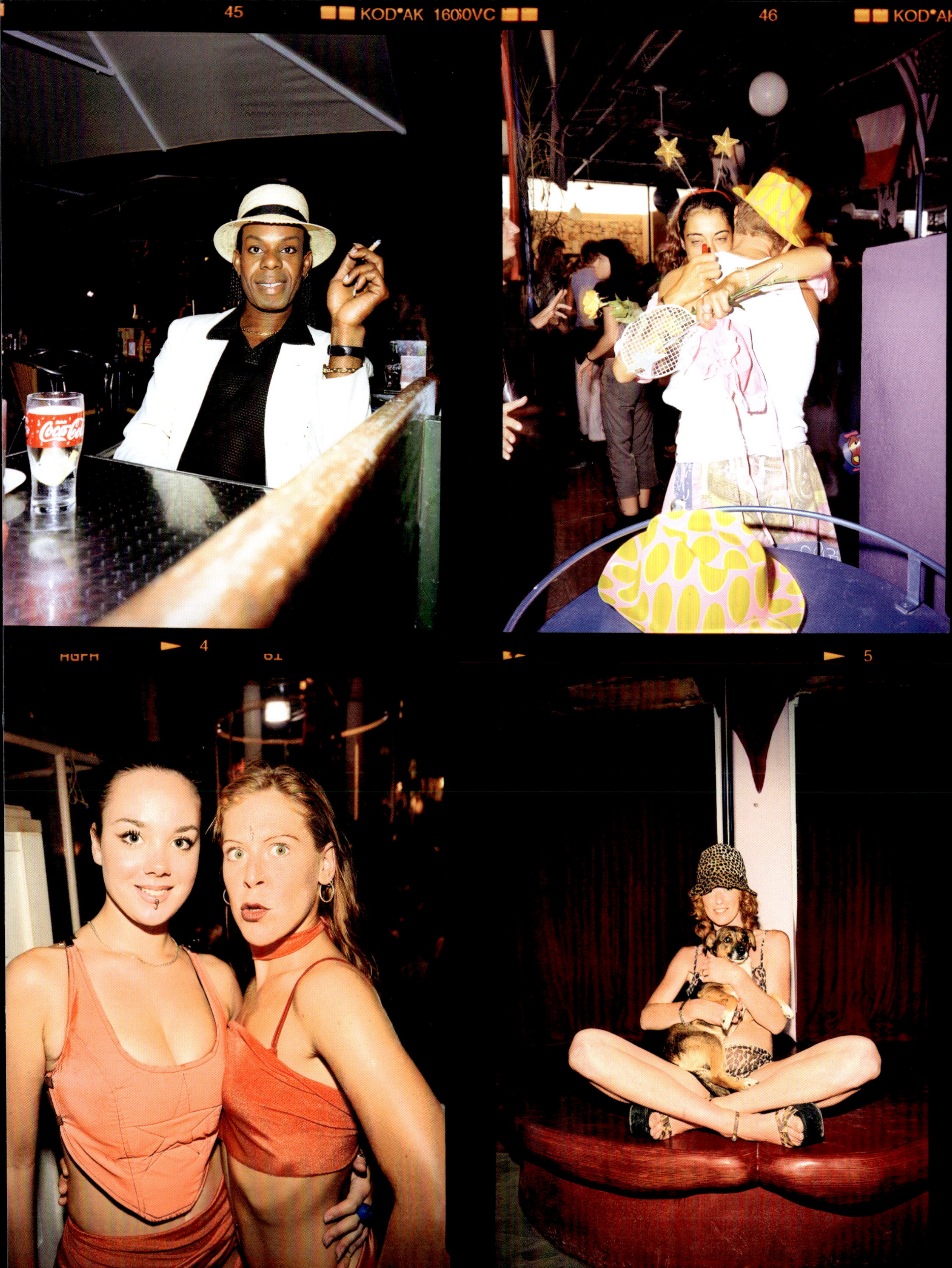

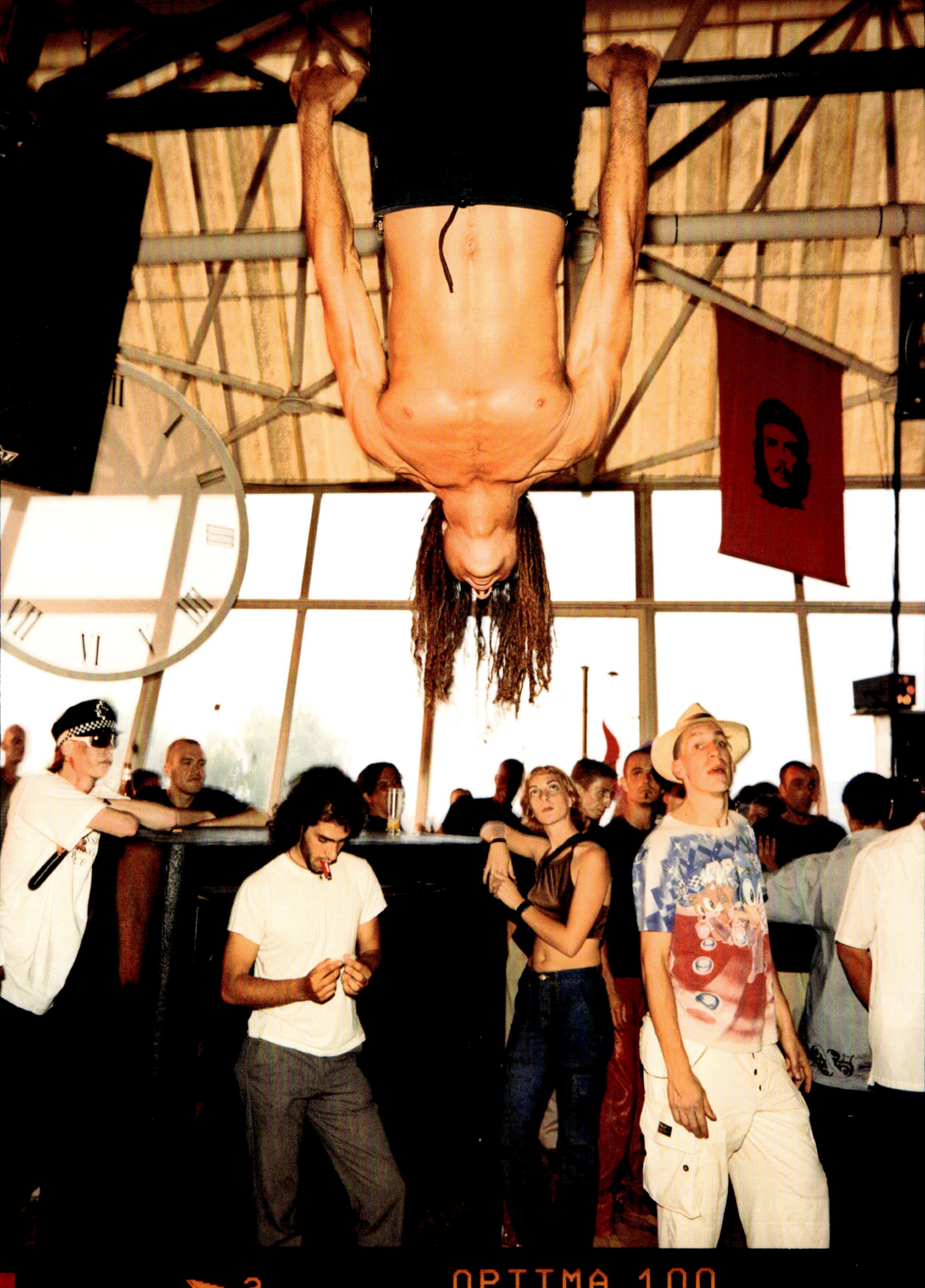
3
OPTIMA 100

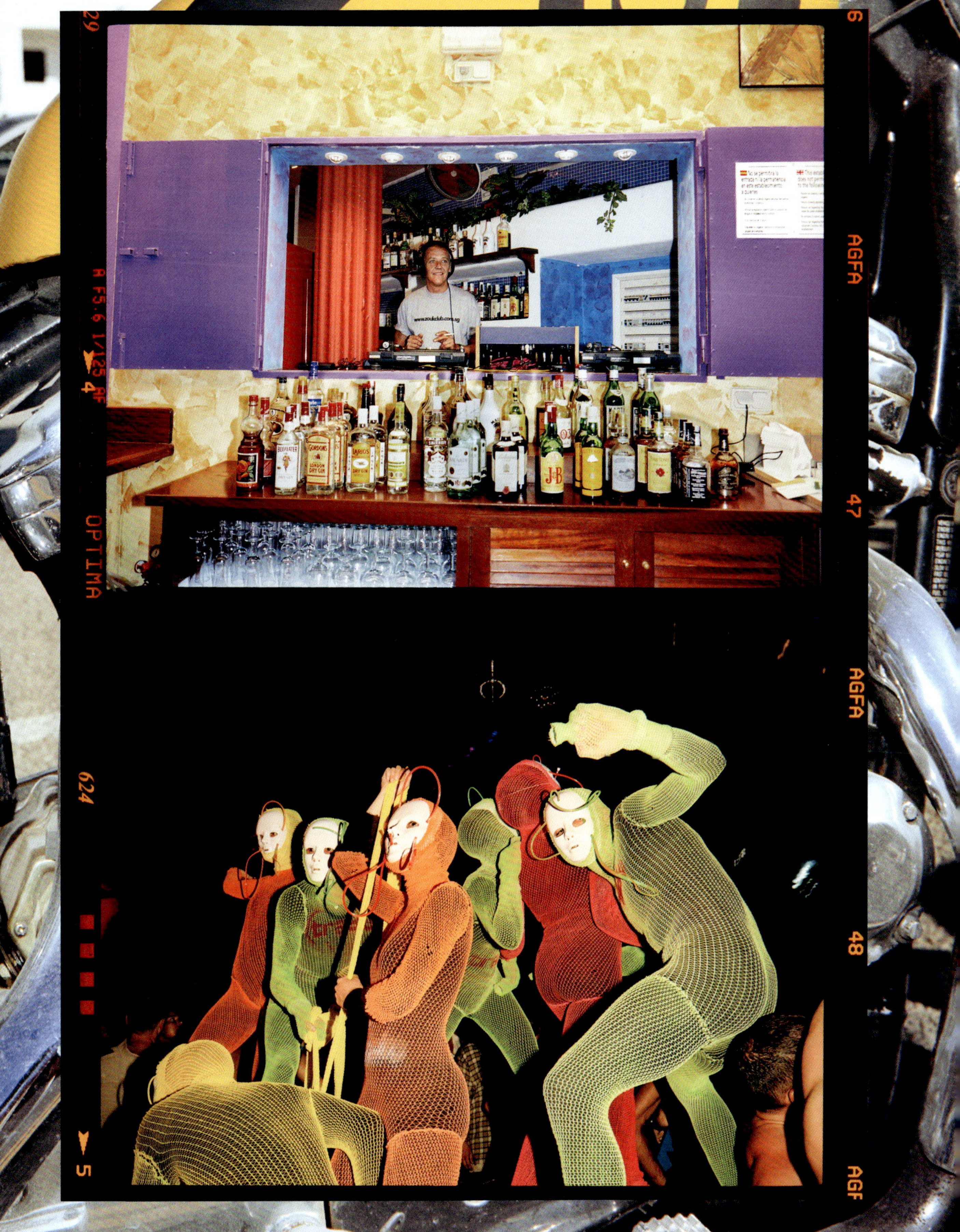

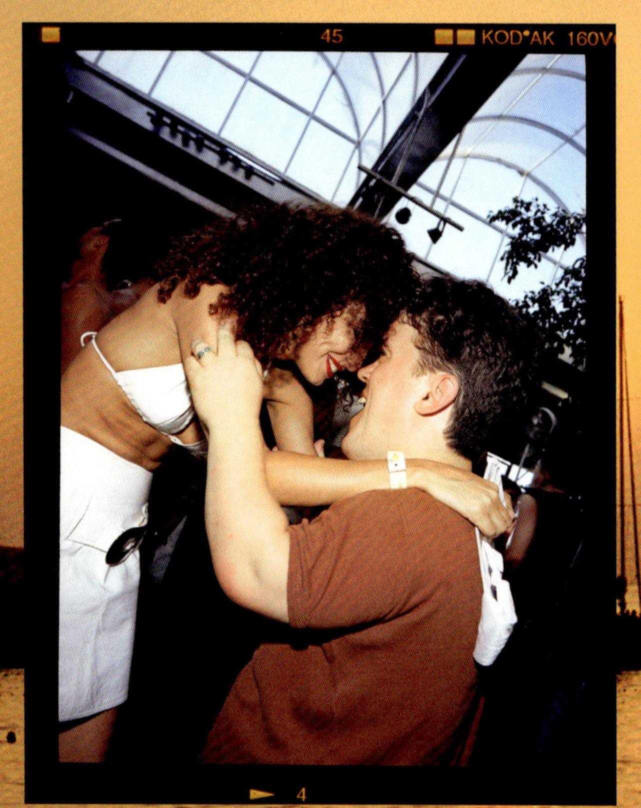
45
KOD•AK 160V
4

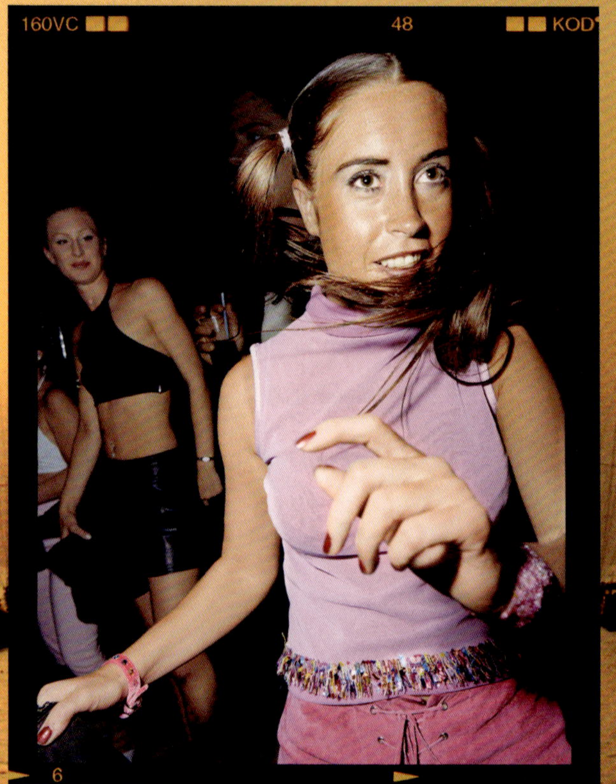
160VC
48
KOD
6

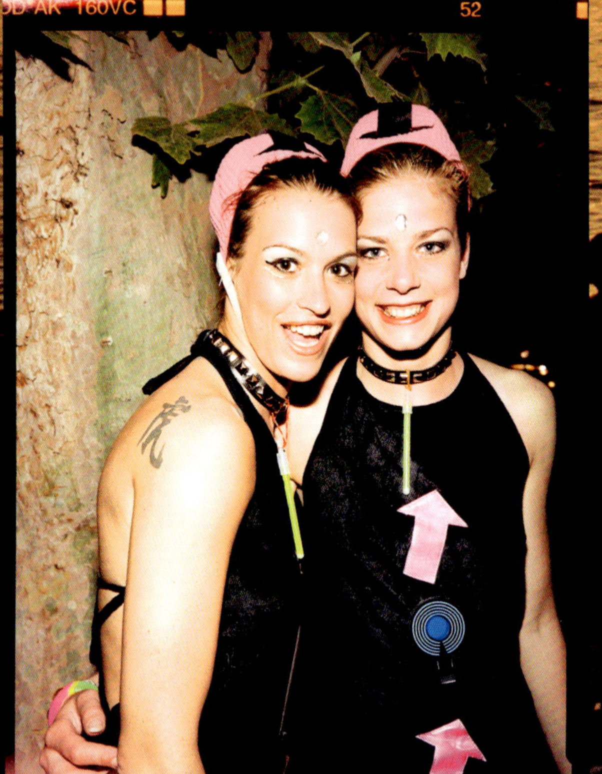
D•AK 160VC
52

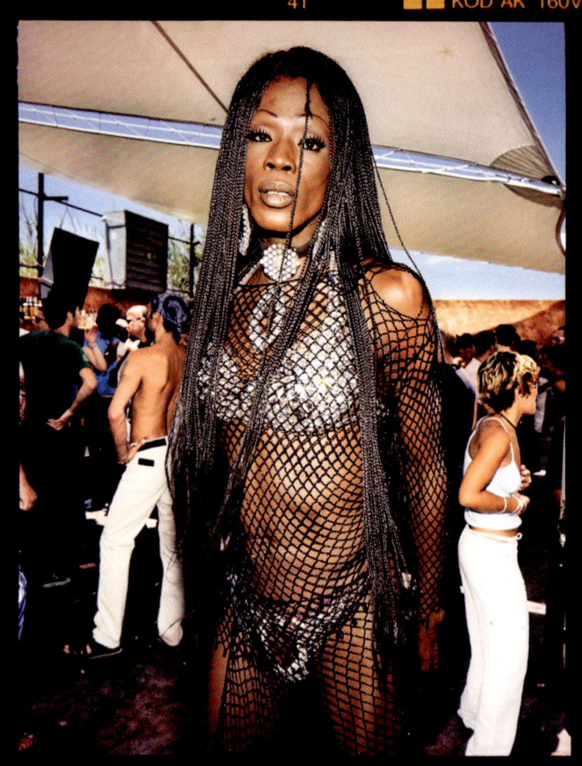
41
KOD•AK 160VC
1

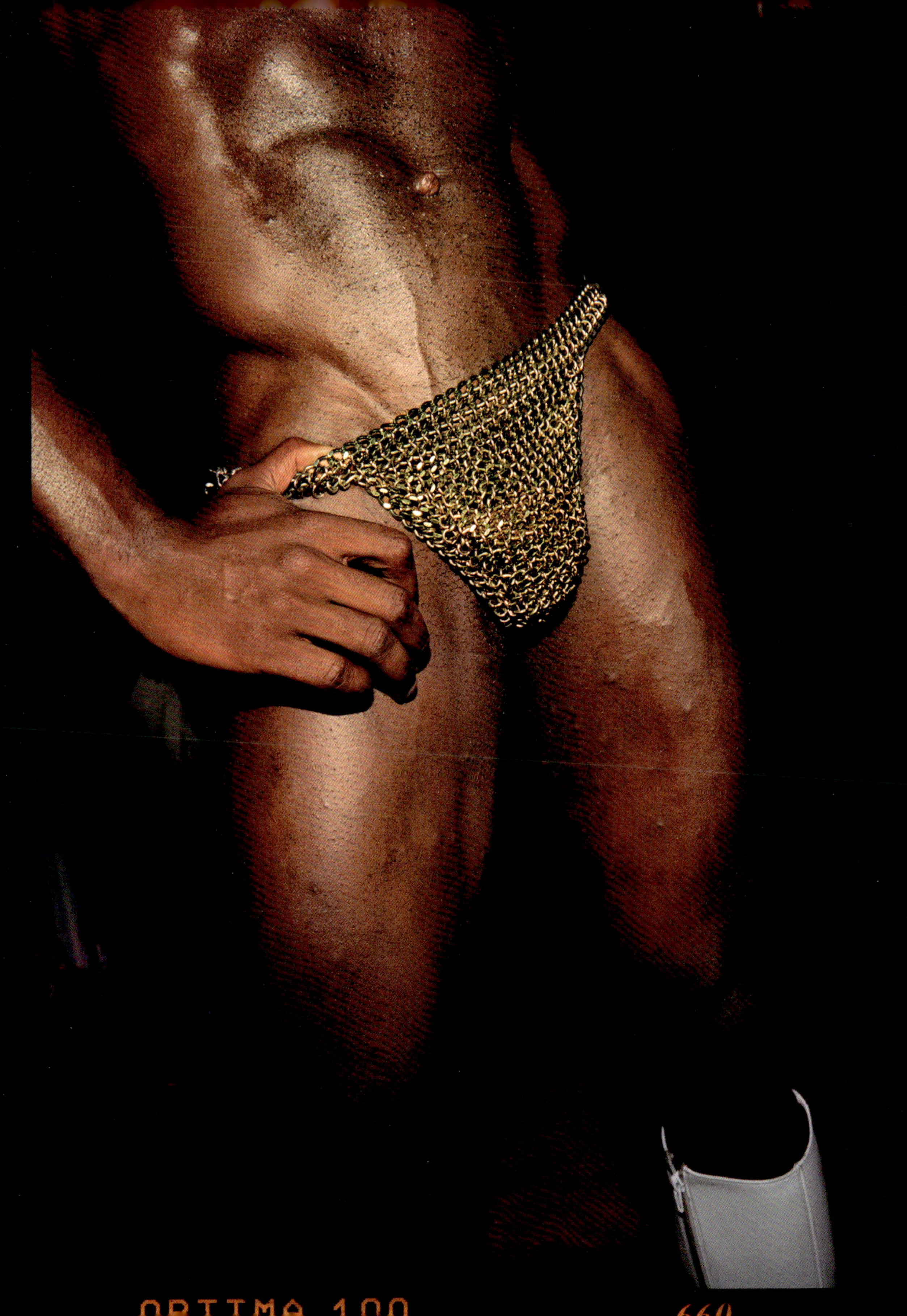
OPTIMA 100
660

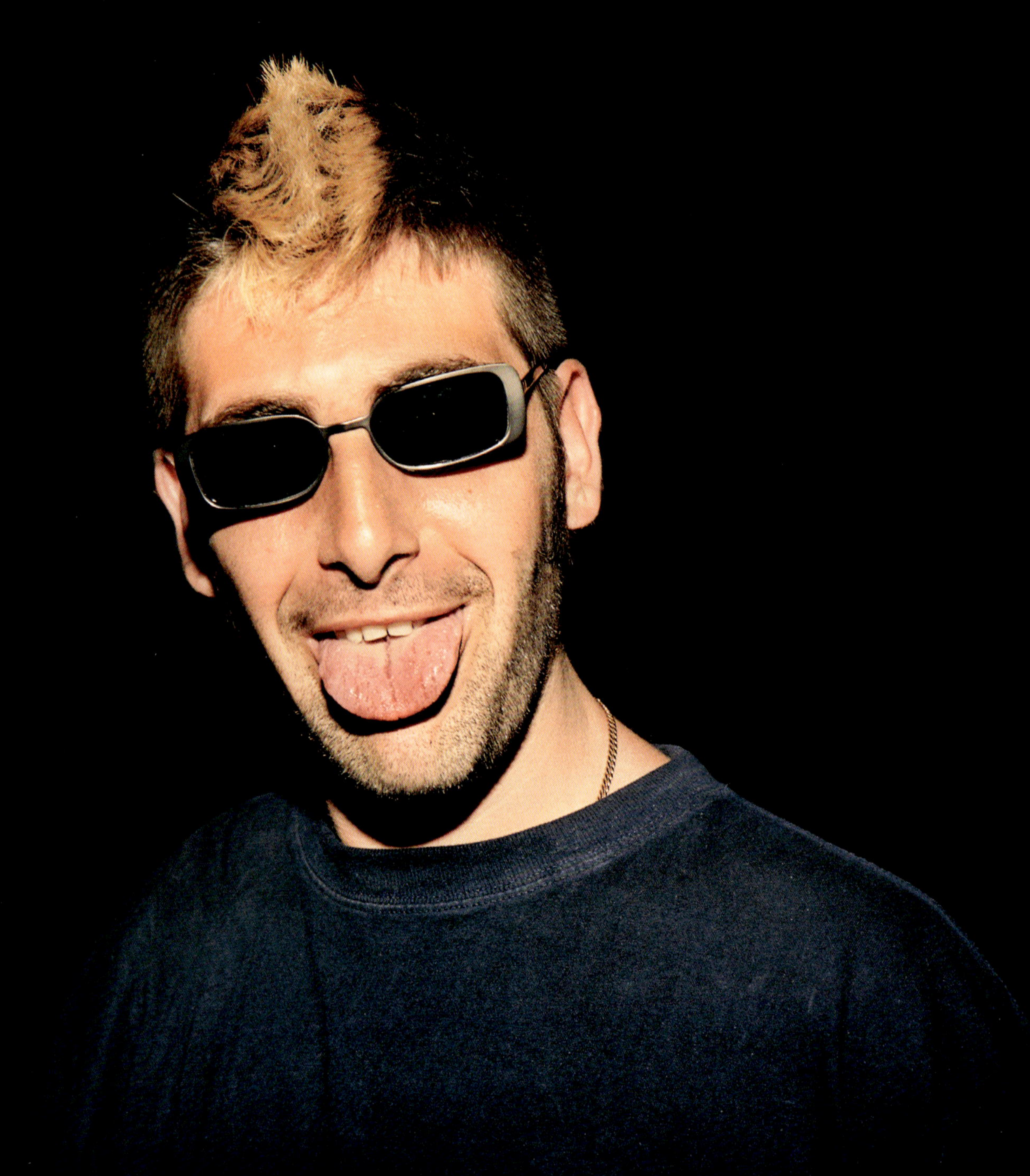

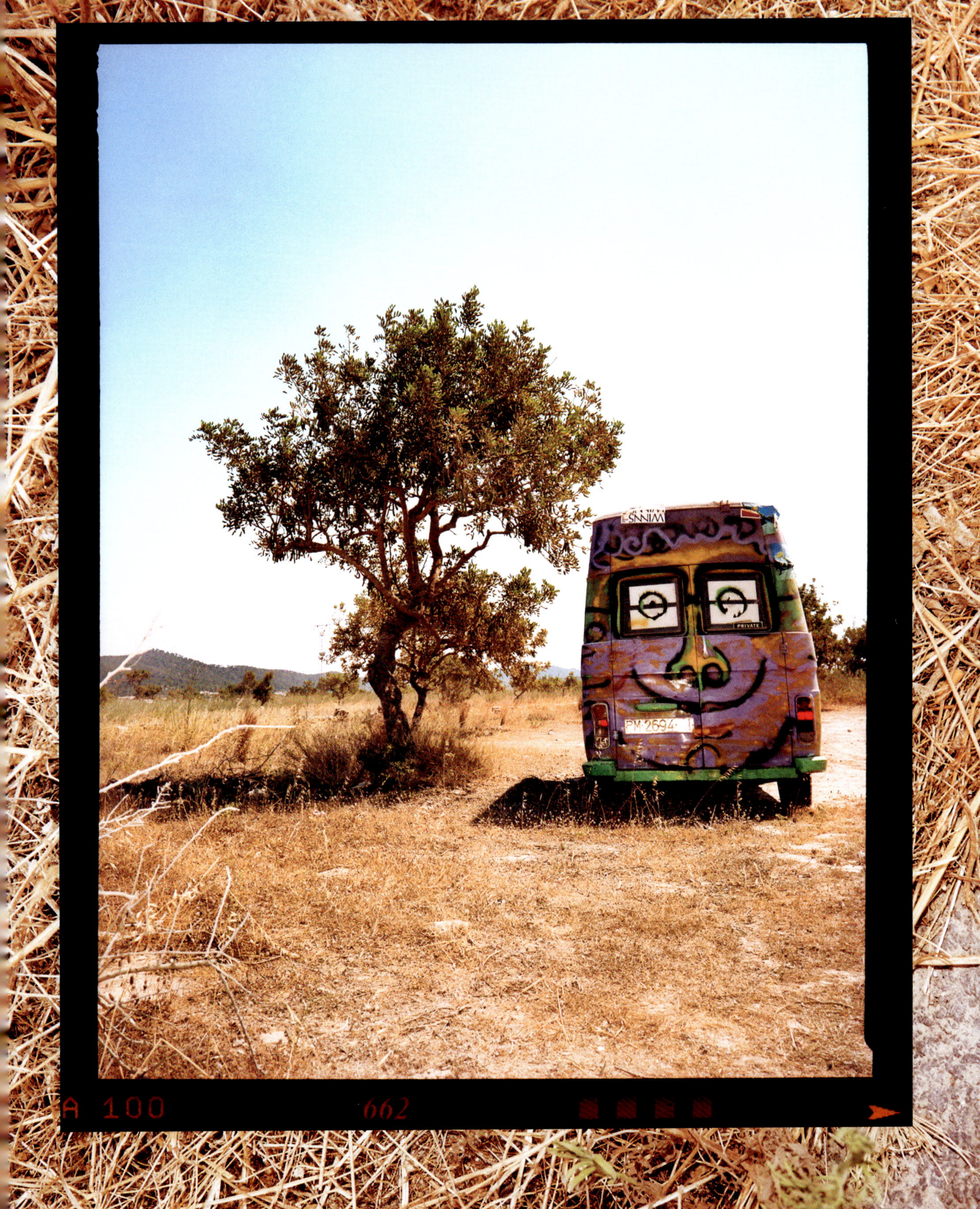
PRIVATE
PM·2694
A 100
662

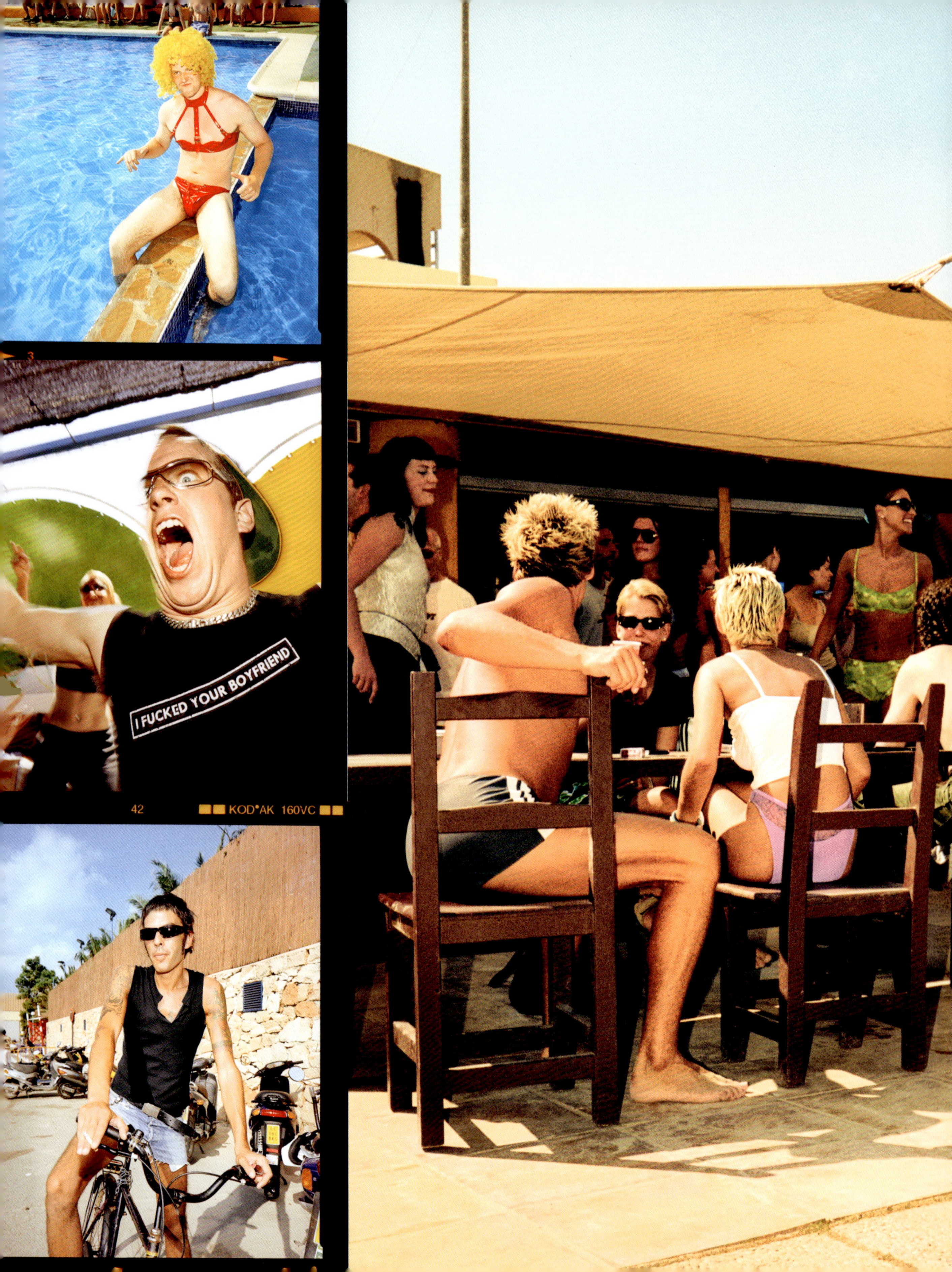
I FUCKED YOUR BOYFRIEND
42   KOD•AK 160VC

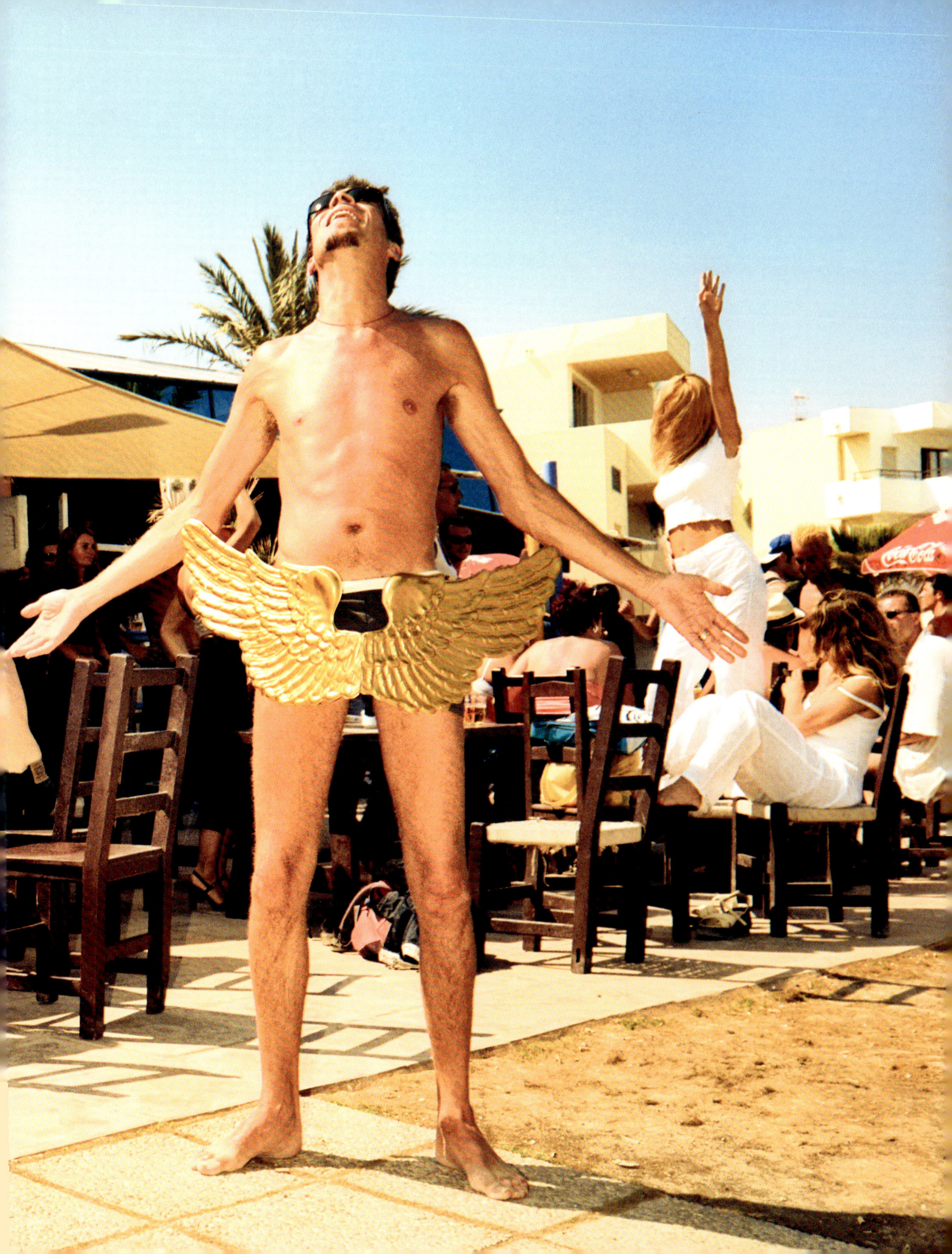

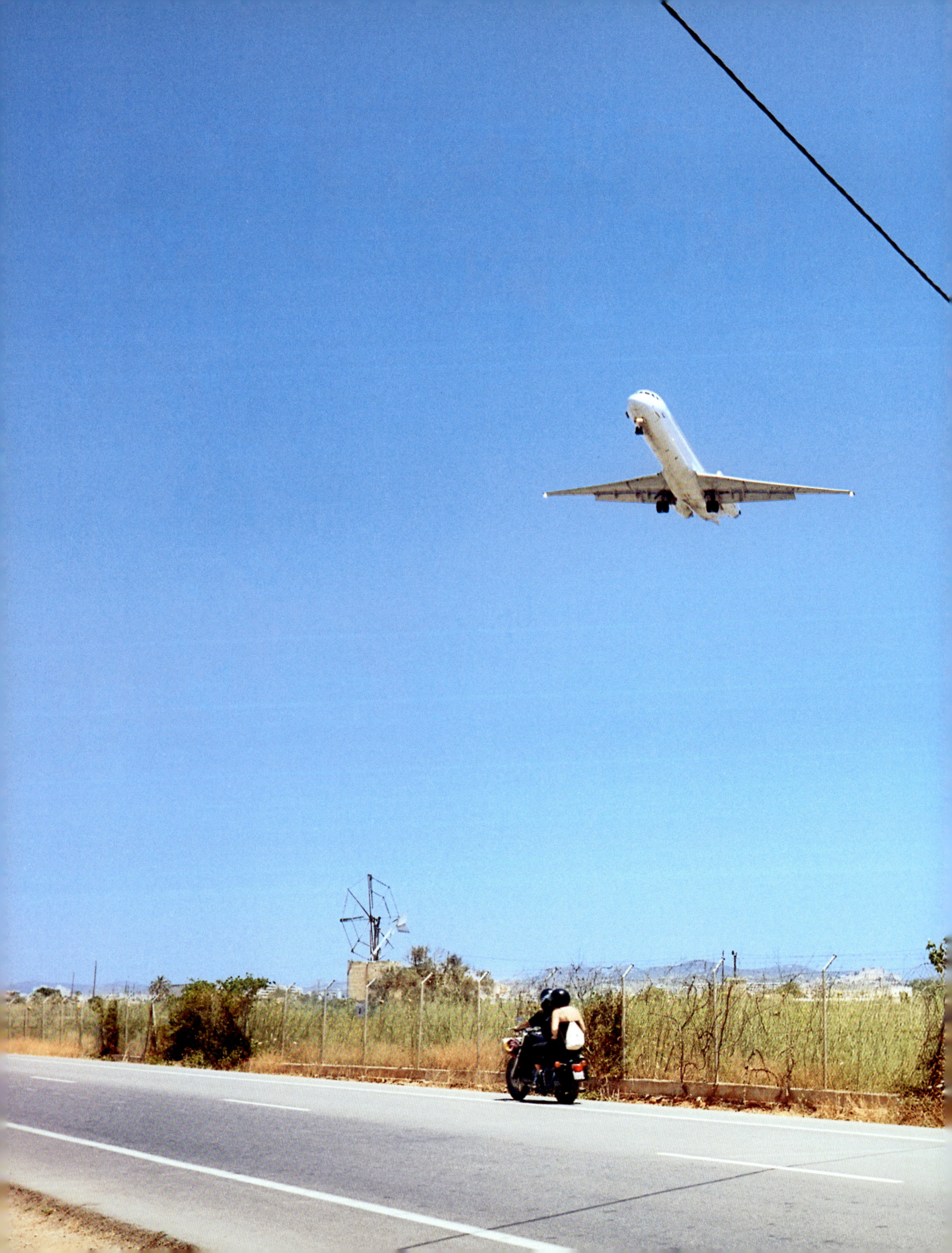

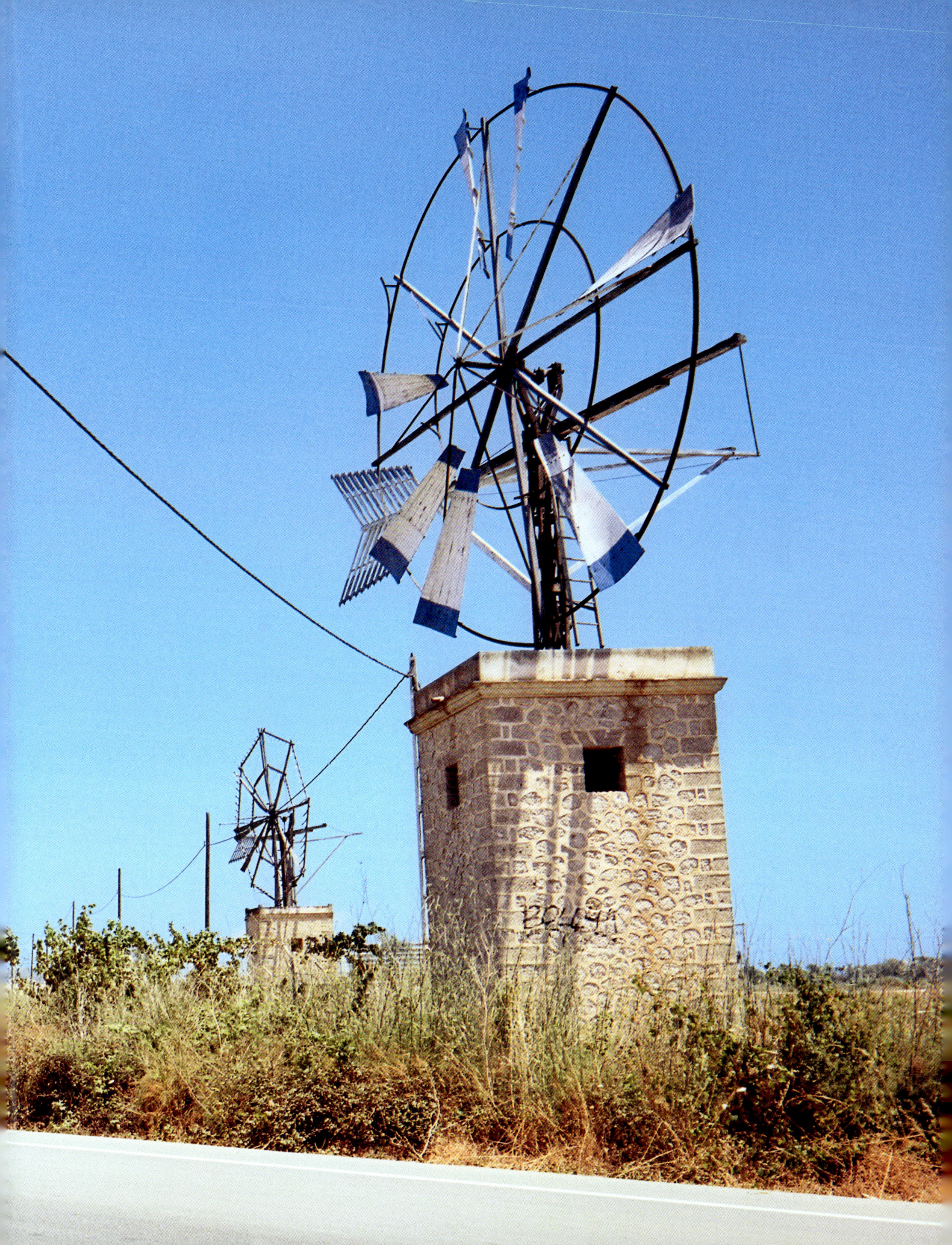

ACKNOWLEDGEMENTS

This book is dedicated to all who rise above the pressures of the world through music and culture.

I never set out to create a sedate narrative, chronologically ordered and neatly compartmentalised for tranquil consumption. Instead, I wanted to plug right into the heart of the action and to reflect the chaos and wonder that prevailed in that incredible period.

With great thanks to:

Everyone who appears in this book. Without you these remarkable moments of humanity and joy would not exist. Even though the click of the camera shutter is only a fraction of a second, your magnificence is eternal... Thank you for being in the pictures.

Paola Cimmino for her unfaltering belief in this body of work. Paola's boundless enthusiasm ignited this project and her skills as a picture editor and producer shaped the result of this book.

Ciaran O'Shea for his amazing design skill, rationale and patience of a saint. This project, like many we have collaborated on through time, grew organically and dynamically, with Ciaran's guidance in the process becoming part of its DNA.

Both Paola and Ciaran have been absolutely crucial in bringing this book to life. Without them, it would never have happened.

Neil Stevenson for writing the foreword to the book and channelling his own brilliant sensibility and also for having faith in me and my work all those years ago when he was Editor-in Chief at *Mixmag*.

Duncan JA Dick for contributing such valuable opinion, information, knowledge and illuminations about Ibiza and the deity Bes.

It was an absolute honour to welcome written contributions from; Bez, Brandon Block, Colleen 'Cosmo' Murphy, Dawn Hindle, DJ Paulette, Howard 'Helvis' Boyle, Lisa Good, Mike and Claire Manumission, Otter Campbell, Shaun Ryder and Vaughan 'Afri' Afrika.

The highest respect to the following for their help; ACC Art Books, Adam Dewhurst, Andy McKay, Anita 'Neetsy' Heryet, David McCullough, Dawn Hindle, Dean Marsh, Isa Hess, James Parker, Jayne Houghton, Jon Swinstead at Museum of Youth Culture, Neil Barker, Nick Stevenson, Will Nicol... and everyone else connected to making this book.

Salutations to the beautiful Island of Ibiza, with its special atmosphere and spirit.

Finally my eternal gratitude is sent to my partner Amanda and my Mum and Dad for their love.

Photography: Dean Chalkley
Design and illustration: Ciaran O'Shea (Discordo)
Picture Editor and Production: Paola Cimmino
Legal: Dean Marsh at Creative Law
Publisher: ACC Art Books
Picture Representation: Camera Press

backinibiza.com
deanchalkley.com

EU GPSR Authorised Representative:
Easy Access System Europe Oü
Company Registration ID: 16879218
Address: Mustamäe tee 50, 10621 Tallinn, Estonia
Email: gpsr@easproject.com
Tel: +358 40 500 3575

Printed by Artron in China for ACC Art Books Ltd, Woodbridge, Suffolk, UK

www.accartbooks.com

Amnesia

Roughly halfway between San Antonio and Ibiza Town, Amnesia lays claim to being the oldest nightclub on the island, and birthplace of Alfredo's legendary 'Balearic' DJ sets in the '80s, which evangelised a generation of European musicians, artists, DJs and clubbers – and perhaps makes it the single most influential club in European history. By 1998, as well as the regular Espuma foam parties, it was home to nights like Cream and La Troya and it's still among the leading clubs on the island today, with nights like Elrow and Paradise.

Bar M

Manumission's warm-up bar was a place where young DJs earned their spurs, expat workers would meet and hang out and marathon nights/days would begin – led on to the disco bus, Pied-Piper-style, by dancers, stilt walkers and performers – and the island's most elegantly wasted flotsam and jetsam would eventually wash up. Later, it became Ibiza Rocks Bar – an important live music venue for a new generation of Brit indie acts, until new outdoor music laws moved the action to a hotel in San Antonio.

Bora Bora

This beach bar and post-party spot in Playa d'en Bossa was a magnet for Ibiza's strangest and, frankly, most over-refreshed characters and one of those places where seemingly everyone visiting the island would end up eventually, from Happy Mondays' Bez to the scores of tourists who'd decided to watch their plane home fly overhead instead of getting on it. Legislation killed the vibe; the bar was demolished in 2023.

DC10

Parked practically under the airport runway outside Playa d'en Bossa in a former aeroplane hangar, DC10 started Circoloco parties in July 1999. By 2002, it had gained global attention for a more underground take on Ibiza club culture. It remains on every credible DJ's bucket list.

Eden

Opening in '99 opposite Es Paradis on the site of the old Kaos club, Eden soon started to attract big Brit promotions like Godskitchen and Judgement Sundays. After various refurbs and relaunches, it's still open today.

Eivissa Harbour

By '98, this strip of bars (Base Bar, Rock Bar, etc) lining the portside waterfront of Ibiza Town had become a bit of a music industry hangout and ground zero for watching the organisers of the 'club parades' get their act together and move through the town.

El Divino

Positioned among the yachting set on the Ibiza Town marinas with promotions like Miss Moneypenny's, this was the most 'glam' spot on the island in '98, certainly for aspirational British tourists. In 2009, it was taken over by Pacha and reopened as the even glitzier restaurant/club, Lio.

Es Paradis

Known for its unique architecture (a huge glass pyramid with a retractable roof) and its famous foam and water parties, Es Paradis' opening in 1975 helped transform San Antonio from sleepy fishing port to tourist hotspot. In the late '90s, it was home to Clockwork Orange, which added credible music to the mix.

Manumission Motel

Opened by Mike and Claire Manumission in 1998 in a converted former brothel on the outskirts of Ibiza Town, Manumission Motel ran separate to the well-established Manumission parties at Privilege. The Motel became infamous as the most debauched spot on the island, a hangout for a revolving cast of performers, sexual adventurers, celebrities, artists and oddballs.

Pacha

Opened in 1973, resembling a traditional farmhouse, Pacha once sat in splendid isolation across the bay from Ibiza Town. First visitors were locals, hippies and occasional counterculture celebrities. By the 1980s, it was a glamorous, star-studded haven. By the late '90s it had expanded to become a 'superclub' – home to promotions including Ministry of Sound, Subliminal Sessions and Renaissance among others.

Pikes

Back in '98, Pikes was owned by the eponymous Tony. It was like the Chateau Marmont of Ibiza, accommodating DJs and celebrities, a little-known playground of the glitterati, where Wham had filmed music videos and Freddie Mercury famously had his birthday party and where stories of great excess were born. Today, it continues to be a charismatic invite-only party spot and hotel.

Privilege

The world's biggest club with a capacity of 10,000 people, the former Ku Club began as a restaurant in the early '70s, became the centre of polysexual clubbing on the island in the '80s and assumed its final form as Privilege in 1995. Equipped with a swimming pool, a giant golf ball-shaped room and the notorious Coco Loco Bar. By 1998, Manumission was the club's flagship night. Privilege closed in 2019.

Space

Originally a rundown conference centre with a waterpark attached, Space Ibiza seemed to grow and evolve every year, with the Space Terrace eventually becoming the ultimate al fresco clubbing destination. Located near the airport in Playa d'en Bossa, the roar of the planes overhead made it possible for the club to open during the day for years without covering the terrace. In 2016, Space was knocked down to become Hï Ibiza.

The Sunset Strip

This rocky coastline in San Antonio has long been one of the best spots on the island to watch the sunset. When DJs like Jose Padilla started to soundtrack the spectacle from behind the decks in the once unassuming beach bar Cafe Del Mar in the mid '80s, a legend began. By '98, Padilla's mixtapes, once sold in the Ibiza hippy markets, had become a million-selling compilation series on Ministry Of Sound. Cafe Mambo, opened next door in '94, and the nearby Kanya (home to Garlands) and Coastline bars challenged CDM's pre-eminence. The Sunset Strip became one of the most crowded spots on the island by dusk each summer night – where people would consistently cheer and clap the sun going down. Today, a wooden promenade extends around the coastline, it's still packed every summer evening, and the people still clap.

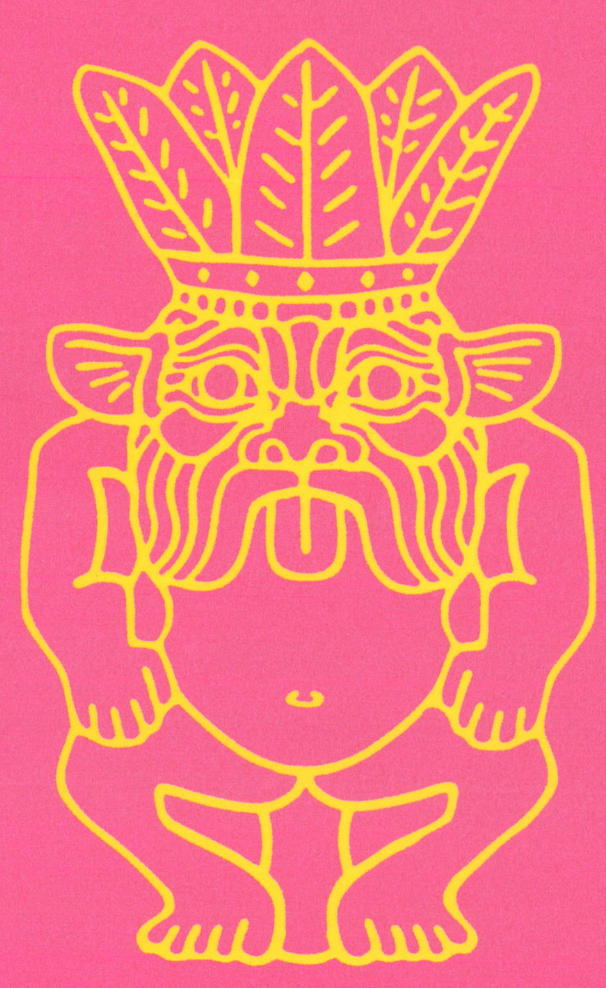